By Donald McLachlan

ROOM 39   *1968*

ATLANTIC ALLIANCE   *1951*

DEFENSE IN THE COLD WAR   *1949*

ROOM 39

a study in Naval Intelligence

Donald McLachlan

ROOM 39

a study in
Naval Intelligence

Atheneum   *New York*   *1968*

My Lord! I do study these men here most
diligently who have this vast and appalling
War-job. There are most uncommon creatures
among them – men about whom our great-grandchildren
will read in their school histories; but of them
all, the most extraordinary is this naval officer
– of whom, probably, they'll never hear.

WALTER H. PAGE
Letter to President Wilson, 1916

Contents

CONTENTS

Foreword

By Admiral of the Fleet
The Earl Mountbatten of Burma, KG

This book tells an absorbing story for any reader. It is also an important story to have on the record for future generations of Commanders of all three Services. I hope it will be a much used book in all Staff College Libraries.

I have a special interest in the Epilogue because in those days my father was Assistant Director of Naval Intelligence (1899–1901) and later Director of Naval Intelligence (1902–4). In fact I was born and bred in an atmosphere of Naval Intelligence for my father continued to talk of the fascination and importance of Intelligence even after he had moved on.

I have a great interest in the body of this book because in 1927, when I was the Assistant Fleet Wireless Officer, Mediterranean, I was instructed to create the 'Y' Service (Naval Wireless interception organization) on the station. In 1942 as Chief of Combined Operations and in 1943 as Supreme Allied Commander, South-East Asia, I realized I could not expect to achieve any successes without really good Intelligence and a knowledge of how to use it.

One of the chief lessons this book brings out is the enormous benefit which the British gained from realizing that Intelligence must be a joint Service activity. The other main impression the book has made on me is the outstanding success of civilians, in and out of uniform, in some of the most vital Intelligence jobs. But I disagree with the author in his advocacy of a largely civilian-staffed Intelligence organization in peace time. I believe there must be a large element of active Service officers in jobs of this kind, not only to supply the necessary technical specialist knowledge but also to spread a proper understanding of Intelligence throughout the Services when they go back to normal duties.

What interests me most of all in the Epilogue is the story, told I believe for the first time, of the integration of Naval, Military and Air Intelligence into a single department of Service Intelligence in the unified Ministry of Defence. I am convinced that this has resulted in a better job being done by fewer people. This integration will be seen as the final stage of a process whose origin can be traced in this book. I have always been heart and soul in favour of this integration.

Preface

Simply defined, intelligence is no more than information about events or people. Give the word a capital letter and it stands for a vast area of state activity, both in peace and in war. Take the capital letter away again and it still stands for something more than bare fact. It should consist of details tested as to source and balanced against other facts, reviewed in the light of the experience and memory of a man or a department, weighed and presented in the form of appreciation, defended and amended under criticism, finally distributed or promulgated – as the Navy calls it – to be acted on. It is remarkably like the process of the law, beginning with the clue that leads to arrest, passing to the charge, the trial, the jury's decision and the conviction. As such it connotes the most painstaking and judicious brainwork.

If Intelligence has come to be associated above all with espionage, violence and skulduggery that is the fault chiefly of fiction writers; but they have been given their opportunity to romance because the word has been used to cover paramilitary operations – like sabotage and subversion, and the counter-measures taken against them – which are generally conducted secretly, manned by civilians and paid surreptitiously. The disguise is adopted as much to protect them against questions in Parliament and inquiries by newspapers as to foil the curiosity of enemies. If it was the intention of those who founded our secret agencies in Edwardian England to surround their work with deceptive and confusing myth – which is unlikely – then they have succeeded beyond any conceivable

hopes. Anyone who sets out to write seriously about Intelligence
has to accept in advance certain limitations. Because it has
been surrounded with secrecy, which has generated myth, the
subject is ill defined. The very word provokes in different
people completely different expectations. Because it has to do
with methods and tricks which may be needed again, some
think it wise to remind enemies as little as possible of past
triumphs and failures. Because so much of the work goes
unrecorded on paper, lost forever in scrambled talk and burnt
teleprinter flimsies, any account must be incomplete. One
runs, therefore, the risk of arousing the historian's interest
without fully satisfying his curiosity. I accept that shortcoming
because the British, as should be apparent from this narrative,
are good at Intelligence and the advantage that this gives
them in a world of hostile nation-states should not be discarded.
It is one of the qualities which make us 'alliance-worthy'.

These limitations having been accepted, is it worth going on?
In the view of a number of senior members of the wartime
Naval Intelligence Division much more can be said than has
hitherto been admitted – and for a special reason. In the final
operations of the war the complete archives of the German
Navy were captured so making it possible, with the friendly
assistance of senior German naval officers in the post-war years,
to find out just how much the enemy discovered about our
secrets and our knowledge of his secrets. We know, for example,
precisely how successful he was in penetrating our naval
communications in the early years and how long it took us to
restore their security. Knowing that we knew, Admiral
Doenitz was able in his memoirs to pay tribute within ten
years of the end of the war to the service given by his cipher
breakers; nearly forty years passed before Admiral Sir William
James was allowed, after difficulties with the Admiralty, to pay
a similar tribute to the British cryptanalysts of 1914–18. This is
only one facet of the subject which has been opened up by
access to the archives, as the narrative will show.

Foremost in the minds of those who helped to get this book
started was the conviction that so long as nothing is written

about this aspect of the war against Germany, Italy and Japan, the historical record would be seriously incomplete and unbalanced. The respective parts played by brains and force, cunning and courage, scholarship and leadership would remain misunderstood. Official historians, working on a brief drawn up soon after 1945, are mostly silent about Intelligence. In most volumes of the official history, the word does not appear in the index. Only in the four volumes of *The War at Sea* can it be said that an effort is made to give credit and apportion blame to Intelligence; perhaps because the author, Captain Stephen Roskill, had been a Deputy Director of Naval Intelligence and knew his way about an explosive field of activity.

I hope that this study – it is neither full enough nor sufficiently documented to claim the word history – may open a new vein for historians' mining. It should throw light on a much neglected aspect of government in war and peace; on the political and personal pressures which influence decisions, and on the role of Intelligence in correcting or resisting them. It should also show that the work demands special kinds of skills and courage, that it merits more respect as an intellectual and administrative activity than Service opinion has generally given it, and that the picture of it created by fiction writers is for the most part a great nonsense. When one studies the history of modern British Intelligence and sees the tiny, frail, cheap beginnings of it in peacetime, one can only marvel that the Empire survived as long as it did.

The sources available have been limited by the fifty years rule which, at the time of writing, is only just giving way to the thirty year rule about access to official documents. They consist in the first place of the personal memories of a large number of people. Historians are trained to be suspicious of such sources and to demand documentation. I can only say that adequate documentation does not and cannot exist for an episode such as the decision to scatter convoy PQ17 in the summer of 1942 and for countless other significant Intelligence occasions of which I had personal experience. However, it is relevant that most of the persons consulted were specially trained to be objective, accurate and attentive to detail. Where their memories faltered it has not been difficult to check with others senior or junior to them.

Some had kept diaries or written up after the war accounts of episodes that interested them. Some had been asked to contribute to memoranda in which the Admiralty tried to record the lessons learnt during 1939–45 in the Naval Intelligence Division; and those have been used by the Naval Historical Division of the Ministry of Defence to check more personal statements. I have had access to fragments of a history of the NID written during the war by the late Charles Morgan and to German, American and Norwegian sources. Above all, it has been possible to consult both wartime directors, Admiral John Godfrey (1939–42) and Vice-Admiral Edmund Rushbrooke (1942–6). The former in particular allowed me to make generous use of his unpublished memoirs and some of the products of his post-war research. I am further indebted to members of his personal staff, former colleagues in all sections of the Division, in particular Lord Justice Winn and Vice-Admiral Sir Norman Denning, the last Director of Naval Intelligence before Service intelligence departments were integrated in the present Ministry of Defence. Intelligence having become, as the war wore on, increasingly an inter-service activity, I have also consulted with much profit Major-General Sir Kenneth Strong, the first Director General of Intelligence at the Ministry of Defence and General Eisenhower's chief intelligence adviser in the North African and Normandy campaigns, and Mr Victor Cavendish-Bentinck who was Foreign Office chairman of the Joint Intelligence Committee throughout the war. To at least two hundred NID friends I am most grateful.

Sources being so personal, uneven and diverse this study may appear as unbalanced as it is incomplete. Much more space is given to the first four years of the war than to the last two, for that was the time of experiment, growth and recovery from inter-war weakness. The régime of Godfrey therefore receives

more attention than that of Rushbrooke, who would be the
first to admit that he took over a fully worked up and trained
department; but if Godfrey created it, it was Rushbrooke
who took it into the final supreme action of 'Neptune' and
'Overlord', and to victory. Then again, the naval war in the
Pacific and the Indian Ocean is dealt with rather cursorily
because the main intelligence operation in the Far East was
American and the Admiralty could not be the operational
headquarters that it was for the Battle of the Atlantic. Likewise,
only items of special interest have been picked out of the
Mediterranean campaigns because methods and for the most
part sources were the same there as in London; indeed,
Malta and Alexandria, and later Algiers and Caserta, were in
the Intelligence role branches of the Admiralty's Operational
Intelligence Centre.

It has not been possible to make of this a step by step narrative linked to the chronology of the war with which so many are
familiar, for the various branches of Intelligence grew at very
different speeds; some that were prominent in 1944 barely
existed in 1941. I have concentrated on the most interesting
and creative episodes, richest in lessons not to be forgotten. The
reader will therefore be asked from time to time to retrace his
steps to Chapter I and the year 1939, as if he were examining
one by one the tentacles of an octopus of which Room 39 was
the brain.

For the attempt to distil in the last chapter some lessons from
the NID experience I take sole responsibility. Some of the ideas
will be recognized as those of leading personalities in the
Division; others have been formed from discussion with experienced staff officers; a few are, so far as I know, my own. I
have described the chapter as a 'prolegomenon', so, in a way is
the whole book – a preliminary discussion of a great theme.

Like all writers and students of naval affairs, I am very
grateful for the indispensable help given by Commander
Peter Kemp, head of the Naval Historical Branch of the
Ministry of Defence and his colleagues Admiral Buckley and
Mr Lawson.

ROOM 39

a study in Naval Intelligence

1 The room and the man

To pay a call on the Director of Naval Intelligence in 1939, you entered the Admiralty by the door in the Mall behind Captain Cook's statue, were announced by telephone, escorted a good sixty yards along a bleak, echoing corridor in the style of a Midland town hall, and guided into a short transept. There you were handed in to uniformed messengers in a lair of booking-office proportions opposite Room 39, full of papers in transit, boxes and trays, kettles and milk bottles and the paraphernalia of tea-making. If you were one of the officers of the Division with the entrée to this personal staff room, you kept straight on, turned the handle of 39 and walked in. Time and again, as one entered, the eye was caught by the historic scene from the three tall westerly windows facing the door: the garden of No. 10 Downing Street straight opposite, the Foreign Office – St James's Park lake – Guards War Memorial composition to the right of it; and to the left the elegance of the Horse Guards, the Treasury and the old Admiralty, terribly frail buildings, one thought, to house the brains of a great war machine. In the middle of the picture was the parade ground used by the Guards for Trooping the Colour, now littered with the impedimenta of the balloon barrage.

More than ever in peacetime, this was the traffic junction of the High Command: Prime Minister, Foreign Secretary, Chiefs of Staff, Cabinet offices, Planners and Intelligence Heads, the regular civil servants and the irregular wartime bosses moved to and fro within this complex of buildings. Just below Room 39 was a private exit from the Admiralty to the Horse Guards Parade, which the First Sea Lord would use on his way to obey some summons from Churchill or the Chiefs. To have a key to this short cut was one of DNI's privileges. Above was the First Lord's vast room, where the political head of the Admiralty wielded what little power was left to him by the Cabinet and Their Lordships. One felt the atmosphere of a great headquarters in a historic setting: a Pentagon in five parts.

However, the occupants of Room 39 looked and sounded like the staff of any other office: a dozen or fifteen people telephoning, arguing, dictating, shuffling papers, writing minutes into that combination of thin cardboard, string and paper called a 'docket'. 'Remember', the Director's former Private Secretary wrote to the author of Ian Fleming's biography, 'we were all of us pen-pushers'. Indeed, the room – large, uncomfortable, with cream painted walls – was best compared, for what was coming into it and what was going out of it, to the news room of a great daily newspaper. At times it became like a club smoking room. When it was known that the Director was away and there was no one in his room next door, (Room 38) to sound the bell or thrust a formidable brow around the baize partition in the corner, a small group would form in front of the big marble fireplace and its iron coal scuttles to gossip about the horrors and anxieties and perplexities that had crossed their desks in the day's signals. No one dominated the group; the room had no head; the RN officers in the section had early given up, if they had ever seriously pressed, the attempt to impose some kind of routine or discipline in what was known among the 'secret ladies' and typists as 'the Zoo'. Nor were they exclusive, save on certain highly secret topics which only a few were entitled to discuss; for most senior members of the department were conscious of being personally selected by the Director; and if some of them happened to be in Section 17 of the NID, and in Room 39 itself – well, there were disadvantages. Yet Room 39 was efficient, even if there was no mess life to knock off corners and give a common purpose beyond daily toil.

For the man behind the baize door in the first three years of war, Rear-Admiral John Godfrey, was exacting, inquisitive, energetic and at times a ruthless and impatient master.* Like the driver of a sports car in a traffic queue, he saw no danger or discourtesy in acceleration; with his own quick and penetrating mind he expected other minds to keep up. Not for nothing had he been a successful ship-handler in the *Kent* and the *Repulse*. Once he had set up a section, designed a policy, mapped out a course of action, he expected others to see to the details in his own meticulous manner and not bother him with them. Last week's top priority on his desk might be this week's lowest. So if errors or delays occurred in his Division, the initial explosion was liable to take place without warning in Room 39. True, Ian Fleming (Personal Assistant) sitting at the desk closest to the baize door, or Ted Merrett (Private Secretary)* would take the first blast; that was what they were there for; but not without the wave and the chill being felt all through the room next door.

Paper poured in and out of this room. Had enemy saboteurs staged a hold-up at the height of the war – and there were no armed men there to stop it – they would have made a haul of most secret signals, staff papers, reports and maps which, had they reached Germany, would have helped its naval staff considerably to win the war they only just lost. Secrecy was a necessary part of the room's character but not its essence; that was rather curiosity, enterprise and a ruthless scepticism about claims, hunches and 'lines' passed off as facts. Ideas, too, poured in and out, not always on paper. Some of them just stimulating or nonsensical; others with the germ of achievement in them. For example, Fleming's idea that the feats of Skorzeny and his paratroopers in Crete, where they made a dash for British papers and ciphers which might help their code-breakers, should be emulated by ourselves when the time came to go over to the offensive, led eventually three years later to the seizure by a special team of the whole archives of the German Naval Staff – tons and tons of documents – invaluable to the education of the Admiralty and its future efficiency. Or the plan of May 1941 to capture the German naval weather-reporting ships, *Muenchen* and *Lauenburg*, in the hope of seizing intact their cipher machine, code books and other papers; an operation which succeeded with crucial benefits to the Navy. Or the great administrative plan to ensure that British troops landing on hostile shores should not again lack terrain intelligence as they had in Norway in 1940: that was hatched, reared and sustained in the room overlooking the Horse Guards Parade.

3

To identify the whole Naval Intelligence Division of some two thousand people (at its full growth in 1943–4) with one room will seem absurd, unless it is understood how strongly had survived, from the first world war, the memory of Room 40 in the Admiralty. There, the team of code and cipher-breakers under Ewing had built up a tremendous reputation for cunning and skill, which was all the greater because so few people ever knew the full facts. The prestige of Jellicoe's DNI still stood high. In 1939 Admiral Sir Reginald Hall was still about the place, advising and helping. Never had a British Intelligence chief enjoyed such power as 'Blinker' Hall had. Now that the Navy was back at war, the tradition came alive in Rear-Admiral John Godfrey and his staff. So legend and performance both played a part in giving Room 39 its reputation.

NID 17, the section of a dozen men and women working in and to this room, has been called a power station, a clearing-house, a brains trust.* Between them, it is true, this personal staff generated much power, representing as they did the Admiralty's interest on some of the most important committees of the British and Allied war machine. Brains, too, were present but no more conspicuously than in the other twenty geographical and technical sections of the Division where the proportion of civilians was higher. Keeping the machine working; receiving ideas and facts, and seeing that they reached the right departments and were not then ignored; forming a body of day-to-day opinion which could be quoted as the NID view – this was also part of the function. To embrace them all, the best phrase is Godfrey's own 'co-ordinating section'. It supplied ideas but it also created order.

Not least of its duties was to see copies of all signals and telegrams – the volume was vast – and to ensure that anything of importance at once reached the Director or his deputies. As well as Admiralty signals, copies of the majority of signals to and from the Chiefs of Staff came through the section. Many were marked in the highest grade of secrecy and had to be signed for when taken from special locked boxes. Someone, therefore, had always to be ready to take the necessary co-ordinating action; and every member of NID 17 had to be ready to do his colleague's work. Each day some officer from

4

the room would be seen setting off to one joint service committee or another. Drake (17 D: Commander RN) to the Joint
Planners or Joint Intelligence Committee to discuss current
intelligence needs and views with the soldiers, airmen and
Foreign Office; Fleming (17 F: Lt-Cdr RNVR) to the secret
organizations like the Special Operations Executive (SOE) for
sabotage and subversive activities in enemy countries, the
Political Warfare Executive (PWE) for propaganda, rumours
and information policy for enemy countries), and C himself,
head of the Secret Intelligence Service; Montagu (17 M:
Lt-Cdr RNVR) to those esoteric groups which conspired in
such deception mysteries as 'Operation Mincemeat'; Lewes
(Commander, RN) to the Inter-Service Security Board, where
he sat with MI 5 and MI 6 – as they were then known – and
with service colleagues and the Chief Security Adviser to consider the choice of operational code-words, the control of all
deception plans and the safeguarding of the secrets of all
combined operations. Lastly, there was the barrister, Pen
Slade – later Christopher Shawcross – (Lt-Cdr RNVR) going
off to NID 5 and 6 at Oxford to supervise the production of
geographical handbooks and the collection of every kind of
terrain intelligence required for future operations.*

Two other important functions remain to be mentioned; it
was the job of NID 14, the personal secretariat also sitting in
Room 39, to see to it that the most secret intelligence reached
only those who needed to see it; that it was circulated in the
right kind of folder or box marked BY HAND OF OFFICER, or
EYES ONLY, on specially coloured paper, and that references to
it in any NID paper were couched in suitably cautious terms.*
A delicate duty, if only because of the natural curiosity and
inquisitiveness of the senior officers and civil servants who were
not on the circulation list, sometimes for reasons which could
not be explained to them. The DNI, responsible for security in
the Navy, had to set an example in such matters. The other
outstanding exercise in staff duties was to draft for the Director
or his deputy papers on the problems put to them by the Prime
Minister or members of the Board or other departments. Whatever the shape in which these papers reached their last destination, they left Room 39 written in the simple and vigorous
language of Section 17, which was the offspring of good naval

staff training blended with the news-agency gusto of the former Reuter man, Ian Fleming.

Sometimes the job had to be done verbally; as Captain Drake has described it in a letter to the author:

We all learnt to face up to the necessity of having to beard any of the Sea Lords in their rooms and beds at any time of the day or night. This required some courage, particularly when it became necessary to shake Admiral Tom Phillips (then VCNS) out of a sleep into which he had recently fallen. He was a little man in stature but had a remarkably sharp bite and, in my experience, he got out of bed more suddenly than any one I know. I once found myself groping near his bed. I was alarmed when a telephone rang close to my head and it became immediately apparent he was being told by another the very message I had for him. He immediately barked down the telephone, I think, 'Send the DNI to me at once'. I had then to reveal myself and explain that I was acting for the Director and to follow this up by answering, in the darkness, a series of detailed questions about which I knew only that the answers were available on the slip of paper I had in my hand. This little man could be very alarming when upset; I once saw him even frighten Churchill, shaking his fist in the PM's face.

The impression has sometimes been given that great plots were hatched in this room, that Godfrey and Rushbrooke – like Hall in his day – sat at the centre of a web of activity which had little to do with naval intelligence and more to do with politics and skulduggery.* If that was so at the beginning of the war, it did not go on for long.

Before the Special Operations Executive was formed in 1940, the initiative for proposing 'irregular' projects lay with the Directors of Naval and Military Intelligence and the Secret Intelligence Service, which was responsible for carrying them out. But it was difficult to obtain official approval at a high level for such operations; senior officers, as a Somerset Maugham character says in *Ashenden*, 'were willing to take advantage of an accomplished fact but wanted to shift onto someone else the responsibility of bringing it about'. Not surprisingly, in view of his division's previous record, Godfrey with Fleming at his elbow took it upon himself to initiate a number of clandestine operations aimed at cutting off Germany's supply of Swedish iron ore, blocking the Danube, crippling the Rumanian oil refineries or briefing double agents. Some of these projects were not strictly naval and these were the days before Churchill had issued his directive to 'set Europe on fire'. As First Lord, Godfrey recalls, Churchill made only marginal incursions into clandestine activities. His caution might be attributed either to the restraining hand of the Foreign Office or to the lack of money or to both.

Room 39 was not sorry when the whole paraphernalia of clandestinity was turned over to the new SOE, because the reluctance at the top of the Naval Staff to take responsibility for such things – nothing could be done without permission of the Chief of Naval Staff or his deputy – made all attempts laborious. True, this overt section 17 had many covert connections; but Godfrey's chief interest was in organizing the supply to the Fleet of hard intelligence. Commodore Rushbrooke, who found little new to create when he took over in January 1943, shared this preference. None the less Godfrey would interest himself eagerly in such projects as Sefton Delmer's plan for a great 'grey' radio operation against the enemy's armed forces, complete with music and entertainment, which was first discussed in this room and received Admiralty support against its critics in Whitehall and the BBC; it was in Room 39 that the Australian Sidney Cotton's plans for free-lance photographic reconnaissance of the German Fleet were supported against fierce RAF hostility; there was even a brief flirtation with astrology.

For a description of the role of the man who became by far the most celebrated of this personal staff the historian cannot do better than quote Ian Fleming's own account of the job of Personal Assistant, written in 1948:

In wartime much use is made by DNI of civilian contacts outside Whitehall and a large proportion of his contacts in his own Division are with civilians in naval uniform. In the last war the DNI found it convenient to canalize the majority of these through a senior RNVR officer who acted as his Personal Assistant. This officer had command of three languages and widespread interests and contacts. As a result, 'bright' suggestions by the many brilliant civilians in uniform working with a junior rank in NID often received more encouragement than if they had gone through the normal head of section – DDNI channel to DNI. In fact the

7

Director found his PA of use in most matters not directly concerned with the Naval Service.

This officer was also a convenient channel for confidential matters connected with subversive organisations, and for undertaking confidential missions abroad, either alone or with DNI.

The DNI also found it convenient to have an officer not concerned with ordinary section duties to represent him in inter-service and inter-departmental committees.

It is recommended that such an appointment should be created in any future war. The officer holding it should be chosen with considerable care and, if possible, retain his appointment throughout the war and thus ensure continuity in the handling of particularly confidential matters.

If not the wisest of the staff in Room 39 who operated day by day on behalf of the Director, Ian Fleming was the most vivid and became the best-known personality. His gift was much less for the analysis and weighing of intelligence than for running things and for drafting. He was a skilled fixer and a vigorous showman, and he seemed to transmit the energy and wide-ranging curiosity of his first chief by whom so much was delegated. Never, as a colleague put it, did Fleming 'sleep with a problem'. He would throw out the hint of a solution or initiate immediate action, trusting to the staff machine to grind down the difficulties and filter out the errors. His judgements could be vehement and might give offence; a paper specially addressed to the Director would be intercepted by him and come back with the remark 'Absolutely of no consequence 17 F'.

Opposite him at the same desk sat for three years a retired RN Commander, Charles Drake. Here was the judicial weigher of intelligence, who as a Captain represented DNI at the Yalta and Quebec conferences. Short and fair, slow-moving and deliberate in speech, quiet in temper, a good navigator and a better stockbroker than Fleming would ever have been, he offered a striking contrast to the thirty-two-year-old RNVR officer, tall and dark, elegant in his uniform and elastic-sided sea boots, with the worried down-the-nose look, and the leaning loping gait.

Drake tells how he would start work on a paper to be written for the Joint Intelligence Staff and ask across the desk for help. Lighting one of his gold-banded cigarettes and adopting a bantering, impatient manner, Fleming would say 'Now what is it, Quacker, what's the trouble?' as if preparing to help a worried child with his homework. Drake would suggest a quiet talk in the waiting room to get away from the din of Room 39, but Fleming would say, 'No, let's get Miss Cameron in and start drafting. The great thing is to get something down, get it started'. With fluency and confidence he would then dictate the draft paper, which would be typed and returned within the hour. It would then be shown straight to Drake who would exclaim after reading two or three paragraphs, 'But my dear Ian, you've got hold of completely the wrong end of the stick; this is all the wrong way round.' 'All right,' the reply came, 'take out the first paragraph altogether and then change the rest as you want it' – and a good paper would emerge.

Fleming suffered not at all from Very Senior Officer Veneration. He was ready – indeed, more ready than Godfrey himself – to stand up for a case against a sceptical Vice-Chief of Naval Staff or Director of Plans. This easy confidence made him very effective in defence of the DNI's sideshows, some of which were to expand famously and create all kinds of unfamiliar problems for the Admiralty's civil servants, while others just died quietly.

The author had for a time the job of ensuring that the Government's propaganda machine of open and covert agencies, ranging from the 'white' BBC to Sefton Delmer's commando-like 'black' establishment in Bedfordshire should give the maximum attention to the Navy's needs. One could be sure that a complaint about difficulties created by a Brigadier or a high BBC official or a Foreign Office Assistant Under-Secretary would provoke an instant telephone call by Fleming to some luminary like General Dallas Brooks or Sir Ivone Kirkpatrick. Using freely the name of the DNI, whether Godfrey or Rushbrooke, he would explain the problem and ask that the subordinate should be instructed to think again. 'Admiral Godfrey feels very strongly about this,' he would say, 'he has to report to the First Sea Lord about it': and a few days later one would find oneself in the presence of very senior officers offering explanations, joined to inquiries after the health of Ian Fleming, a giant among name-droppers.

9

Godfrey said in later years: 'Ian was a war-winner', and Rushbrooke, his second Director, thought very highly of him. He seemed to take the shortest possible distance between two points. The effect on others was that they felt impelled to live up to his standard of alertness, however boring and fruitless the work in hand. His real achievement, in the author's view, was to set a standard of independent, critical and forceful behaviour by RNVR officers which was of crucial importance in a Division where civilians had such big parts to play.

Much more important than Room 39 in the day-to-day struggle was the Operational Intelligence Centre fighting the war at sea* in the Citadel round the corner. So, too, was the naval section of the great communications centre outside London, which I have called in this book Station X. There the vast mass of intercepted enemy signals, collected from all over the world, came in for analysis by technicians, cryptanalysts and specialists on the three enemy navies. So was the branch of the Secret Intelligence Service which was operating in company with allied intelligence staffs to get information the Navy needed, through networks in occupied Europe and the Middle East, of which the Norwegian one was outstanding.

But it was in Room 39 that staff was fought for, promotions arranged, expenditure justified, conduct defended. It was the bridge of the NID ship. What was done there can, of course, be romanticized. For here came some of the first hints – as early as 1939 – of the rockets and guided weapons that were being experimented with at Peenemünde, sent in by the Naval Attaché, Stockholm. Here the smuggling of precious ball-bearings from Sweden was mooted. From here the Chief of Naval Staff was briefed for his tussles with the Prime Minister over bombing policy and the use of aircraft. Here the foundations of the rejuvenated American intelligence system were laid. And so on. But no one who worked there would claim that the normal day's work was of this order.

Nor would any member of NID 17 claim that no errors were made, no complaints heard from other parts of the Admiralty or Whitehall. The Division had its critics and enemies; the reasons for this will appear in later chapters. It was also under exceptional pressure. Again I quote Captain Drake:

I think the speed with which we had to deal with the swarms of dockets which flooded into Room 39 meant that often matters of not immediate importance were passed right out of the Naval Intelligence Division without being sufficiently promulgated by us within the division. We couldn't help it, but it was a bad thing all the same. Nearly everything was tallied 'Most Immediate', 'Most Secret', 'Pass by hand of Officer Only', or in some similar phrase, sometimes quite inappropriately, and one just had to pass over those which, at first glance, appeared not to add anything to our existing records. Then, later on, we would see something else which confirmed what had gone before, and realize our error. There was no easy remedy, as copies were not allowed to be made.

The fact was that the war, from mid-1941 onwards, was too big. The flow of paper of all sorts and in all directions became a torrent; it would have required a modern computer to sort it and relate it all.

We did our level best, but I am well aware of our many short-comings and we often had them brought vociferously to our notice by the heads of the various NID sections and others from the Operations and Plans Divisions. Some of the telegrams we had to read were so harrowing that at times (in my case certainly, and I'm sure for others) we felt physically sick.

It was on such occasions one pressed hard to be allowed to go off to sea again to take an active part in the fighting, particularly those of our team who had many years' service in the Navy. As the DNI carefully explained, he wanted to do the same himself, but appreciated that a term of at least six months had to elapse in the case of all of us, during which we would have to be divorced from any secret matters, before we could be exposed to the risk of becoming prisoners of war.

Anyway, he disliked changes in his team and at times showed his anger at being approached with such requests. Did we not think we were doing a worthwhile job with him? And so on. Very frustrating, but there it was and so we stayed on.

The man

What kind of man had been picked by the Admiralty for the exacting job of Director of Naval Intelligence, with its world-wide responsibilities to the Fleet? Whoever made the choice in 1938 – it was probably Admiral Sir Roger Backhouse, then First Sea Lord, on the recommendation of the Naval Secretary – must have calculated that war was inevitable soon. In that event the new man must be very senior in the Naval Staff, must have a wide range of experience beyond the normal limits of an executive officer, and some standing and proven ability in the handling of words. It would not do to select a senior naval officer on the way out of the service, who would regard this as his last job and the rank that went with it as his last promotion. Too often in the past had such selections been made. The job must go to a man with a future, and it would be best of all if he had also had contact with or practice in Intelligence in the previous German war.

Captain John H. Godfrey, CB, aged fifty, due shortly to pay off the battle-cruiser *Repulse*, had all these qualifications and the backing of his Commander-in-Chief in the Mediterranean Fleet, then Vice-Admiral Sir Dudley Pound. To tell the story of his appointment is to throw interesting light on what was thought of Intelligence at the time and on the state of mind of the Admiralty and the Navy just a year before the outbreak of war.

For John Godfrey it was the chance of a lifetime. To be invited to take over as the DNI in January 1939 was to be offered an opportunity of combining organization with ideas, administrative responsibility with intellectual creation, which staff work rarely brings to the serving naval officer. War was coming sooner or later; there was no question in his mind about that. There would be money to spend, specialist staff to engage, powers to assume which in peacetime both Treasury and Admiralty stubbornly denied. Above all, there would be intense interest: their Lordships would be urgent for the best information on a world-wide scale, as their predecessors had learnt to expect it twenty-five years earlier, when 'Blinker' Hall was in charge.

There would be expansion and experiment in what had been, during Godfrey's last period at the Admiralty, a run-down department. There was almost nothing its Director could not do in war – so ran the tradition – and as senior member of the Naval Staff (directly responsible to the First Sea Lord) he would have status and opportunities beyond those of his opposite numbers, the Director of Military Intelligence and the Chief of Air Staff (Intelligence). For the Admiralty was an operational headquarters; it controlled the Fleet at sea. The

War Office and Air Ministry were not in the same degree operational. DNI would be at the heart of the struggle against Admirals Raeder, Doenitz and Canaris and very close to the supreme direction of the war.

For the fifty-year-old captain, sitting on 1 August 1938 in the day cabin of the battle-cruiser *Repulse*, then in Malta, with a momentous letter from the Admiralty in front of him, it was the last thought that was decisive. He had been no back-room sailor, in spite of four years instructing at the Greenwich Staff College and a spell in Plans Division at the Admiralty between 1934 and 1936. He had escaped Home Fleet duties and enjoyed an unusual amount of travel. He had served with distinction in a number of hot spots:* on the China Station patrolling the Yangtse River; in the Dardanelles campaign as a navigator and staff officer; as assistant in 1917 to Commodore Burmester, Chief of Staff to the Commander-in-Chief of the newly created Mediterranean Command, with its local intelligence centres and first experiments in the convoy system. His Admiral described the Lieutenant-Commander at the age of thirty as having exceptional ability: 'he has what may be called a staff mind and possesses a remarkable aptitude for working out and expressing in orders the details of operations involving the co-ordination of large forces.' Most important to Godfrey himself, who had the normal naval officer's intense dislike of being considered a shore man rather than a sea-going commander, was the fact that he had recently, for two years, been working up the modernized battle-cruiser *Repulse* to a high state of efficiency in company with the *Hood*. Pound, his Commander-in-Chief in the Mediterranean Fleet, was known to think well of him: 'one Captain who knows how to behave like an Admiral'. Andrew Cunningham, in his autobiography, described him as 'widely read and most able'.

All that was said in the confidential letter in front of him which came from the Naval Secretary to the First Lord, was this:

I expect you will be requested to come to the Admiralty early next year to relieve Troup as DNI. I hope this will suit you. This is for your own personal information.

So the decision had been taken and Godfrey was free to express a preference if he wished. In fact he had none. He was

13

impressed, delighted and flattered by the tip from the First Lord's office. In some ways he had been preparing by his reading, his friendships, his experience between wars for this kind of opportunity. One point, however, did worry him, as it would have worried any successful executive officer. Would he, at the end of the usual three years as DNI, get to sea again? Once into the Naval Staff it would not be easy, especially in wartime, to get out again. It would be said that those who had done well on land should continue there, and that no one could be given command at sea who was without wartime operational experience.

Godfrey decided to go ashore and consult his C-in-C, Dudley Pound. It seemed possible that he would be one day First Sea Lord and therefore Godfrey's master at the Admiralty. The C-in-C gave him to understand that there was no reason then known to him why a return to sea later should be out of the question and promised to help him when the time came. He was sympathetic, but he could say no more. This ended the future DNI's lingering doubts; and although this qualified promise had to be broken in 1941,* he never regretted for a moment the decision taken that summer day in the Grand Harbour – just two months before the events at Munich in 1938 caused the Fleet to be mobilized on 28 September, including the *Repulse* which had only just paid off at Plymouth.

The creation of a reinvigorated Division began with the arrival of the new Director in January 1939. The Admiralty had deliberately chosen a man of whom it could not be said disparagingly that he was a staff specialist or even an intellectual. He would understand what the men at sea wanted and needed; he would have the tactical and strategic knowledge to judge what was in the enemy's mind. He might be employing intellectuals – goodness only knew what kind of minds would be applied to the naval war once it began – but he himself was a seaman, a proven trainer of men, and a strong administrative character.

There was another reason for the choice, more apparent then than now. In the higher ranks of the Navy there were only half a dozen men who knew how Intelligence had worked in the first German War. There were legends about Sir Reginald Hall and his cryptographers and the officers who had worked with them. But also someone was needed who understood that success in the days of Jellicoe and Tirpitz had been won as much by hard work and by the skilful handling of all kinds of evidence, as by the reading of the German naval signals presented to the Naval Staff by a small group of mathematicians and naval officers. Godfrey had clear memories of those days. As a young Lieutenant-Commander on the staff of C-in-C Mediterranean he had come to London to see how top secret Intelligence worked. He had been taken to see the famous decoding room at the Admiralty, Room 40, and noticed with surprise his brother, Headmaster of Osborne Naval College, working there during the school holidays. The Godfrey family had been told that he was tracking Zeppelins, whereas he was in fact helping to decipher naval signals.

Later Godfrey had visited SIS and MI 5 to get their help in organizing intelligence for the Mediterranean Fleet.* As a junior officer he had visited British Consuls abroad to keep them in touch with the Fleet's requirements and see that their codes and ciphers were up to date. He had penetrated further into the secret places of Whitehall than most naval officers of his generation, though this fact was not necessarily known to those who chose him as DNI. At the end of the twenties, when preparing his lectures at the Greenwich Staff College, Godfrey had studied the contribution made by intelligence to naval operations. The thread of continuity was slight, but this appointment – and others still to be mentioned – strengthened it. So that when one day, not long before war began, 'Blinker' Hall visited Godfrey in Room 39, it was almost as if naval war with Germany had never stopped.

Indeed, this knitting of past and future became, early in the war, almost novelistic when the DNI moved into the flat at No. 36 Curzon Street, belonging to Hall. It was felt he would be rather safer there from the Blitz that had begun than in his top-floor flat at Buckingham Gate. 'Although,' he wrote, 'I was provided with a two-and-a-half foot wide bunk in the new Citadel, under ten feet of concrete, but found sleep did not come easily in the fuggy atmosphere, smelling of air conditioning.' There was also to recommend Curzon Street the fifteen-minute walk across Green Park to his office, the direct telephone line the admirable Dulcie Wright to cook, serve and housekeep,

for he was no great clubman. All was as shipshape as in the
Repulse. One of the marks of its Captain had been that he did
things in style: kept a good table, cultivated non-service company, came to the difficult points after dessert, and was as
warm and generous and patient a host as he could be a cold
and irritable and exigent commander. This background was
to be useful,* in a post which required, among other social
duties, the wearing of morning coat and silk hat to pay formal
call on diplomatic missions.

Nothing would be more misleading than to suggest that the
new DNI took over with clear-cut ideas of what he would do.
On the contrary, he knew from his time in Plans Division the
difficulties that would face him until war actually began:
Treasury scrutiny of every penny; civil servants' misgivings
about changing or extending accommodation; determination
of the Second Sea Lord to keep the best officers for sea appointments.* Above all, lack of clear and resolute political leadership.
The Admiralty atmosphere was still only a little better than he
had described it as Deputy Director of Plans in 1934:

> I was conscious of a certain lack of design which we did our best
> to mitigate by creating a future of our own devising, but one
> uncorrelated with politics and the temper of the country, or with
> the personality of cabinets and prime ministers . . . Thus the
> planners found themselves working in a strange atmosphere in
> which past, present and future, facts inferences and wishful thinking,
> became intermingled and all sense of resolute purpose was blurred.
> Again, our prime ministers were peace-loving – pacifist or passivist
> – and could not bear to think of war or the threat of war.

Yet Godfrey himself has admitted, looking back on the
Lowry-like canvas of those years – packed with people and
events, then so big, now so small – that it was the starting of
new things that fascinated him; seeing a need, working out the
way to meet it, getting it on paper from his eminently literate
helpers and forcing it through the civil servants and the Naval
Staff; picking the heads of a new enterprise – and then leaving
them to get on with it.

To see the prospects of peace for himself before taking command of the *Repulse* in 1936, Godfrey had spent three months
in Germany and Eastern Europe talking to people of all kinds,
most of them anti-Nazis or ostensibly so. He brought away two

main impressions: one of a nation in blinkers, obsessed with itself and its grievances, the other of an Establishment convinced of a common interest with Britain – if the British did what the Nazis wanted. 'Those I met,' he wrote, 'were pathetically anxious to talk about German politics, but were not interested in the points of view of other nations and had no conception of the effects of Nazism abroad.'* And Captain Densch, chief of staff to Admiral Raeder, commanding the German Navy, declared that he was 'convinced that Germany really aspires to have the largest army in Europe and for England to have the largest navy and to rule the world together'.

It was to be shown, in practice, that the Division in this war must be very different from what it had been in the previous one. MI 5 and MI 6, still in their infancy in 1914, were by 1939 experienced and independent organizations, both under civilian control. Cryptography and all that went with it had become the business of an independent organization also under civilian control. The Special Operations Executive had yet to be born; but already in 1939 the idea that clandestine operations should not be controlled by the Services or by any one of them was forming in Whitehall minds. These developments meant that NID's scope for independent executive action was substantially reduced from the days of Hall, who saw nothing wrong in such enterprises as negotiating peace with the Turks or arranging the capture of Sir Roger Casement. Likewise, if one compares the organization of 'Operation Mincemeat'* in 1942 with the deception plan which is said to have set the scene for the Battle of the Falkland Islands in 1915 (recounted in Von Rintelen's *Dark Invader*), the differences are immediately obvious: the latter was conceived, organized and carried out by the Admiralty alone; whereas the former was created and organized by a group representing virtually all the intelligence agencies of Whitehall, even if the initiative came from the Admiralty.

However, none of this was obvious in 1939; and Godfrey was pleased when he took over in February 1939 to be guided in some measure by his famous predecessor. He himself has said:

To no one am I more indebted than Reggie Hall, the DNI during the Kaiser's war. He came to see me on 27 March 1939 and thereafter very unobtrusively offered me full access to his great

17

store of knowledge and judgement on this strange commodity, Intelligence, about which I then knew hardly anything. He realized that I needed contacts and these he produced in large quantities. It was through him that I met Sir Montague Norman, the Governor of Baring's, Olaf Hambro, Chairman of Hambro's Bank and the two Rothschilds, all of whom helped me in a variety of fruitful and helpful ways, particularly in the recruitment of wartime staff.* Above all Hall warned me of some of the political pitfalls that lay in my path in wartime; and experience soon convinced me that I had an awkward commodity to sell, that in 1939 the cupboard was bare and the DNI extremely vulnerable.

2 Sources

'Say from whence you owe this
strange intelligence?'

(Macbeth I. iii)

To the intelligence officer, of whatever rank or importance, his or her particular sources are a cherished and confidential possession. Just as the hypochondriac boasts of 'my doctor' and the litigious man boasts of 'my solicitor', so the naval, military or air specialist may speak proudly and mysteriously of 'my source'. In fact, however, some of his best sources will not be under the control of his own service. Agents between 1939–45 were ultimately under the control of separate Departments responsible to the Foreign Office and Allied Governments, never under the DNIs or DMIs, and for a time photographic reconnaissance for the Navy of ports and bases of occupied Europe was controlled by the Air Ministry. Prisoner-of-war interrogation and control, whether men came from U-boats or from the Luftwaffe, was on an interservice basis, but their guarding, feeding and housing were a War Office responsibility. None the less an NID geographical section responsible for informing the Fleet had for the sources available to it an almost fatherly concern, sometimes flavoured with jealousy. Its officers liked to believe, until proved wrong, that in one way or another their particular kind of information had the edge over someone else's.

From this feeling sprang the kind of sharp and salutary competitive spirit that scholars so often reveal in reviewing one another's books. On this spirit the man at the top – in the case of NID, it would mean the chosen man in Section 17 or the Director's deputy – could count when making up his mind whether to pass on the intelligence and, if so, in what form.* He would know that an argument over the credibility of the source and the likelihood of the facts had already been fought and won. Indeed, by 1941 NID was sufficiently worked in as a team to give confidence all down the line. Highly disciplined Marine officers had come to trust their newly-trained and easy-going civilian colleagues; the civilians, in uniform or out of it, had shed whatever 'Very Senior Officer Veneration' (VSOV – a favourite expression of Godfrey's) they might have had at the outset, and there was a continuous and good-tempered rubbing together of minds.

A list of sources, in rough order of reliability and importance, gives a picture of the mosaic into which the intelligence worker had to fit his own particular fragments.

1 Interception, deciphering and reading of high grade enemy signals: top secret and almost always graded A.1.

2 Captured documents and communications material taken from ships and submarines, headquarters or prisoners of war.

3 Fixes of enemy ship positions from bearings taken on signals intercepted by 'Y' stations; also plain language and low-grade cipher material from the same stations.

4 Air photographs taken by the RAF's special reconnaissance units, with the explanations provided by photographic interpretation units. Graded according to weather conditions and other circumstances.

5 Sightings of ships by aircraft crews: either by observers trained in ship recognition and sent to search, or by untrained observers doing something else.

6 Information of all kinds from agents or friendly secret services: variously graded but all top secret.*

7 Prisoner-of-war interrogations and monitored records of talk between prisoners of specialist interest and importance.

8 Deductions from the volume and pattern of enemy's naval wireless traffic.

9 Enemy communiqués; monitored propaganda; reading of enemy and neutral press. Open and ungraded.

10 Hints and facts from letters intercepted by civilian censorship in Britain and outside; also from the cor-

respondence of prisoners-of-war, some of whom used simple codes which they had been taught.

11 Topographical and technical information from open sources (e.g. The Royal Geographical Society or the British Museum Library) or from private contacts with personalities or offices (e.g. engineer with detailed knowledge of lock gates at St Nazaire).

12 Friendly and neutral observers: often diplomatic and consular but also commercial, shipping and fishing.

13 Technical and tactical information from our own and allied ships collected during operations at sea: e.g. enemy bombing tactics, range and behaviour of torpedoes, U-boat methods when shadowing convoys.

14 Sightings by merchant ships and coastal watchers: e.g. SOS from ship attacked by armed merchant raider.

15 Reports from RN and Merchant Service survivors, giving clues to the identity and whereabouts of enemy warships at fixed times.

16 Intelligence from other services likely to throw light on naval movements; sometimes so decisive as to put it in the highest grade of naval information.

17 Directives passed by enemy intelligence to their agents under our control, in other words double agents. Of more general and strategic than naval and operational interest. Always most secret.

That there should be seventeen, identifiable types of source may surprise the layman; but it should be apparent how useful one can be for checking the other. For example, on 3 June 1942, Admiral Nimitz was waiting anxiously at Pearl Harbor for the first sign of the great Japanese fleet which was to make a surprise attack on Midway Island. From Washington's reading of enemy naval signals, he knew in some detail what was intended; but he could not be absolutely sure until ships were actually seen that the Japanese had not staged an elaborate deception operation which the Americans were meant to overhear. That very morning the confirmation he needed was provided by a flying-boat patrol which sighted the enemy on the expected course. It required that simple human verification to confirm a whole mass of top-secret documentary evidence;

yet without the help of that evidence, put together by crypt-analysts, the pilot would not have known where to look.

Before dealing in detail with the various sources it is necessary to explain the method of grading intelligence that was adopted in the Admiralty. Typical of the far-sightedness and initiative that Godfrey brought to his work was the decision to devise and introduce such a system. Without it material of very diverse value would find its way into signals, appreciations and summaries: it would be passed on with such comments as 'from a usually reliable source', 'from someone in a good position to know', or even in the form 'this highly probable report is from a source which is so far untested'. With such casual handling visual information, perhaps laboriously collected at great risk by an agent in a Norwegian fjord or a Biscay port, might be lumped together with gossip from a Naval Attaché's drinks party or with rumour deliberately planted by the enemy through a respectable neutral source.

This anarchy the DNI found intolerable. Could no method be devised of showing briefly and clearly to everyone the value of a report, distinguishing wherever necessary between the rating of the source and the rating of the information? For good intelligence might come from a disreputable source and false information from a good source. It was insufferable that questions should be asked – and answered – at meetings, about the reliability of sources or about methods of securing intelligence; likewise it was unreasonable that a commander at sea like C-in-C Home Fleet, or a staff colleague like the Director of Anti-Submarine Warfare, should be asked to accept operational information without some clue to its weight and authenticity. On a highly graded report a risk might be taken – and the mighty expense in money and fuel of putting a fleet to sea could be accepted. On something less good a different set of calculations would come into play.

It was, in the event, a simple yet subtle system of letters and figures ranging from A1 to D5 that was decided on and gratefully copied, at DNI's suggestion, by other service ministries. The initial letter gave the reliability of the source, and the number after it the probability of the information as being correct. I owe the following explanation of the system to an officer who helped to devise it:

A good source in a hospital at Brest might be graded A as to the number killed and wounded in an air attack, but might be a C source on the extent of mechanical damage caused to a ship in the dockyard. An equally good source in the Port Chaplain's office who had seen the ship's defect list, might be A on damage caused, but C on the number killed and wounded. A very junior engine-room rating taken prisoner and speaking in good faith may be an A or B source on the particulars of the engine of which he is in charge, but will be C, D or E on the intended area of operations of the U-boat in which he served.

The final grading by the Admiralty was the grading given by NID. The authority responsible for grading – on whose discrimination, honesty and integrity the whole system depends – was under an obligation not to suppress evidence merely because he did not understand it or because it looked improbable, unless he had a good reason for disbelieving it. Low grade information (e.g. C3) may prove to be of the highest importance; for example, the first reports of V1s and V2s were received in this form.

There are some subjects on which it will be well nigh impossible to obtain high grade and precise reports, e.g. on future operational and weapon developments. The line of development may not have been decided by the enemy; there may be differences of opinion amongst the high command; it may not be certain that the gear will pass its trials; an operation may have been planned but then cancelled. For these reasons the first reports of new weapons will be graded low, but this does not mean that they may not be of the highest importance, and all evidence in support of these pointers must be carefully followed. Some of the most novel developments in the war were originally indicated by low grade reports of which little notice was taken at first.

A special problem of grading might arise from language used. A very accurate report might be made about a weapon, e.g. a flying bomb – giving correct dimensions, method of propulsion, range and so on – but the source might call it a 'torpedo with wings'. When the report was circulated, Director of Torpedoes and Mining in the Admiralty might say that to talk of a torpedo with wings and a range of 140 km was nonsense. The report might then be discredited, despite the fact that everything except the name and purpose was absolutely correct.* (This report was actually received and passed to

DTM.) Again, the enemy is sometimes himself deceived. A source may, as a result, pass false information in good faith, but he must not therefore be discredited. Our own cover and deception plans sometimes came home to roost in this way through an agent or foreign Naval Attaché or prisoner of war and might not always be recognized.

In grading reports on prisoners of war, special difficulties presented themselves. The interrogators would assess the integrity of the source, his competence on the subject and the likelihood of the evidence being correct. The head of the prisoner-of-war organization had then to take into account such factors as the qualities of the interrogator, the circumstances in which the interrogation took place and the evidence from other prisoner-of-war sources. He would then superimpose *his* grading of the source and of the information.

Evidence from photographic reconnaissance was not always A1, for one cannot ask a photograph a question. Grading may be A2, B1 or lower. There are several reasons for this, such as the human error of the interpreter or the possibility of mistaking one ship for another of the same class. Photographs of defences may report guns which are in fact dummies, or may correctly report the existence of guns, but will be incapable of reporting the vital information that there are neither men to man them nor ammunition for them to fire.

Having listed so many sources of naval intelligence, it is tempting to start casting them into a hierarchy; but the attempt breaks down because the main test of intelligence, at any rate of service intelligence, must always be whether it brings the enemy successfully to battle. Thus, a brief and accurate signal from a warship or aircraft giving its position and so leading to contact and victory, may be as important in the long run as the agent's reports or the intercepted intelligence which contribute some element of success in a much bigger operation. Although the staff officer is naturally inclined to rate very high the various mysterious sources from which he draws his intelligence on land, notably that obtained by the study and interpretation of wireless traffic, he has to recognize that the good air photograph or the accurate sighting at sea, or even the report of one eye-witness, may be every bit as valuable as these other sources from which he stocks his file.

There is another reason for not taking the notion of hierarchy too seriously. It is that no piece of information is normally of great value on its own. When first received it is like a sentence without its context. Signal intelligence, for example, in its raw state is seldom intelligible on its own to anyone but the expert who extracts it or deciphers it: a few figures, a position or two, an order, all in the local jargon of a foreign tongue. It cannot be read and understood, even when translated, in isolation. A report from an agent or even an air photograph will not have much significance outside the context – what I have called elsewhere the mosaic – of other intelligence bearing on the situation that has led to the taking of the photograph or the reading of the signal. That is why the passing of tit-bits of information to commanders, because they may be 'interested', is a dangerous practice among obsequious staff officers.

What are the special weaknesses and advantages of these sources and how are they used?

Interception

Interception of the signal or message which is intended to be private or secret will always rank high in the hierarchy of sources. It played a decisive part in the German campaign of 1941 against the Red Army. It would normally earn the grading A1 on the grounds that the source is, so to speak, the horse's mouth and that what comes out of it is the plain truth. But the intelligence officer has always to guard against the possibility of deception. The enemy may know that his cipher is being broken or his telephone line tapped; instead of immediately taking steps to stop the intrusion, he may first plant on the listener or cryptanalyst false information which will be highly regarded. The classic case of such deception was the British 'Operation Mincemeat', which provided the Germans in 1943 with what they believed to be private correspondence 'at the highest level'. The Germans secured from a Spanish source, which they trusted completely, photographs of documents found on the body of a British Marine Major washed ashore near Huelva. Everything about the corpse and the briefcase chained to it seemed above suspicion. The papers were of the most crucial interest and appeared to provide A1 information. For they included a personal letter from the Deputy Chief of the Imperial General Staff in London to General Eisenhower in North Africa which made unmistakable references to Allied intentions of invading Greece and Sardinia, rather than the real target in Sicily.

Here the source was indeed the 'horse's mouth'; what could be better than a hand-borne letter, marked Top Secret, from the Deputy Chief of the Imperial General Staff to the Allied Supreme Commander, signed 'Archie' and accompanied by other documents of a secret and personal nature? German Intelligence, we now know, treated the information as A1 and circulated it as top secret and for urgent action. On the face of it they were right. The source was sure, the intelligence of Allied intentions was circumstantial and highly probable. Even though Sicily seemed to be the obvious next step for Eisenhower and his armies, the island was known to be strongly defended. None the less, the information was incorrect, the document was a plant, and its unique quality lay entirely in the fact that the British Chiefs of Staff had allowed themselves to be persuaded, for the first time in their history, to take part personally in a deception exercise.

By breaking the low-grade cipher, by listening in to telephone conversations, reading top secret or even confidential correspondence, copying operational orders or intelligence appreciations, it is possible to enter into the mind of the enemy – just as the car-borne criminal listens in to the radio messages of the police chasing him. Not only are facts made known which the enemy believes to be secret, but his way of judging events and facts also lies open to study. If, for example, Hitler's conversation with his commanders and advisers had been recorded and passed to London during the last war, some of the strategic appreciations made by the Joint Intelligence Staff (see page 240) would have been fundamentally different from what they in fact were. They would not have assumed, as they had to, that the Fuehrer reasoned from available facts or that he took advice from a professional staff as objective and politically independent as was the JIS itself.*

The means and techniques of interception are diverse. A traitor in a headquarters of one power may steal and lend to the agent of another power a high-grade cipher which is then photographed and used to read a whole series of messages and reports. Cicero, as the valet of the British Ambassador in Ankara was known to the Germans, did this with diplomatic summaries and reports which showed the whole pattern of future Allied strategy. Or a ship may be sunk in action or by mine, so that there is an opportunity to salvage her code book and use it to read a whole range of operational signals – and perhaps enable the cryptographers to break into other series as well. This happened with a Japanese submarine sunk off Port Darwin, Australia, early in the war and with the British cruiser *York* sunk off Crete in 1942. Rarely, very rarely, a ship is captured with its secret documents intact; the captors can then sit down to an intelligence officer's feast – and, of course, a cryptographer's – for just so long as the enemy does not know or suspect what has happened.* It then becomes the task of the security side of Intelligence to limit the knowledge of the capture to the fewest possible people. Ingenious brains have, if possible, to devise a 'cover' story to explain certain events which many people cannot be prevented from seeing: for example, the towing into port of a foreign submarine, the arrival in an office of a large bunch of enemy documents, the sudden communication to those interrogating prisoners of war of an up-to-date list of technical terms and slang expressions.

But the most interesting – because it is the most difficult and expensive – form of interception is that achieved by the crypt-analyst.* It is also the most secret because the fruits of years of work and knowledge can be lost overnight by an indiscretion leading to a change of cipher that has been broken or of a machine that has been mastered. There is a passage in the memoirs of Doenitz describing his dismay when the British changed their low-grade naval cipher after the German crypt-analysts had given him a sequence of most damaging successes against Atlantic convoys. Suddenly, after months of operating his U-boats with the British daily summary of U-boat dis-positions in front of him – seeing not only into British intentions but into the Admiralty's day-to-day judgement of German tactics and plans – the staff of the U-boat Command found themselves dependent on such ordinary sources of intelligence as U-boat sightings, direction and intensity of wireless traffic, agents' reports from America (nothing worthwhile ever came

27

from Britain). Instead of a clear and full picture, presented to them sharp and intact and instant, they had now to work from a mosaic, or fragments of a mosaic patiently put together by themselves in a hard day's thinking. Once again they were at the mercy of their own commanders' exaggerations, of the mis-judgements of pilots, of the amateurisms of agents and of the ruses of the British.

Little wonder that intelligence staffs took – and still take – almost fanatical pains to conceal and disguise their successes in this A1 branch of their work. To read the enemy's operational signals is the triumph of aggressive brain and organization over defensive brain and organization, the equivalent of the decisive fleet action; to allow one's own signals to be read and used, unobserved, by the enemy is the equivalent of a critical campaign lost.

On the other hand, experience on both sides in two wars and in peacetime has shown that an intelligence organization which lived on cryptographical expectations alone became spoiled. It lost the skill and application that make the fullest use of other sources, such as air photography, prisoner-of-war statements, neutral observers, and even press and radio in-discretions. One might say that easy knowledge corrupts and entire knowledge corrupts absolutely. The decline of British Naval Intelligence between 1920 and 1938 may have been partly due to the overconfidence generated by the code-breaking activities of Admiral Hall's Room 40 during 1915–18. It was implicitly believed that the British in case of war could quickly do the same again: and it was forgotten, except by half a dozen experienced individuals, that the crypt-analysts need a wide and steady flow of technical and opera-tional information; their job is not just a matter of mathematics and guessing. They also need a working capital of factual background and practice in problems arising from enemy movements which peacetime does not offer in any quantity. Above all they need the luck which brought the cruiser *Magdeburg's* secret books to the Admiralty in 1915.

The best known episode in the history of secret signal intelli-gence is the brilliantly successful surprise attack of the American aircraft carriers on a much stronger Japanese fleet at Midway Island in 1942, already referred to above. The Japanese, confident in the security of their own top-grade ciphers and maintaining strict wireless silence during their southward journey across the Pacific, believed they could surprise and capture Midway Island, lying across the line of communication between the USA and Australia. They calculated that this blow, coming a few months after the disaster of the US fleet at Pearl Harbor, would be intolerable to Admiral Nimitz. He would be ordered at once to relieve and recapture Midway, so exposing his carriers to their superior bombers and fighters. (Thanks to their own exaggerated claims at Pearl Harbor, unchecked by cold intelligence or by American admissions, the Japanese believed he had only two, whereas in fact he had three carriers remaining. The *Yorktown* had been repaired and got to sea by superhuman efforts in days instead of months.)

Nimitz was fully informed by Washington's cryptanalysts of Japanese intentions and timing. He was therefore able to achieve decisive surprise with weaker forces. Good luck also played a part, as it always does, but the facts remain that the decisive naval battle of the Pacific War could not have been fought and won by the Americans at that date without the assurance of superior intelligence, the foundations of which had been laid years before.

The Pearl Harbor disaster may have helped to make this later victory possible. For it brought home in the cruellest fashion to those who were recording and processing AI intelligence that such material is useless unless passed on suitably presented and interpreted as quickly as possible to those in charge of operations.* When Congress, through its Joint Committee, inquired into the Pearl Harbor attack, it was learned that neither Admiral Kimmel, C-in-C, Pacific Fleet, nor any of his senior officers knew what the Secretary of the Navy, the Chief of Naval Operations and the Director of Naval Intelligence knew; that there was unmistakable AI evidence of the Japanese intention to launch a pre-emptive attack somewhere. The messages to Tokyo from Yoshikawi, the Japanese Navy's trained agent in the consulate at Honolulu, were being read in Washington; but as similar detailed messages were also being received from other consulates, the significance of the Honolulu traffic did not stand out sharply enough. The Americans were in fact deceived by the cover plan with which the few Japanese

29

officers planning the attack were concealing from their own staffs in Tokyo the fact that Pearl Harbor was the target. Had the few men in Washington who knew the secret found a way of recommending or ordering regular air reconnaissance and other precautions from Pearl Harbor, the Japanese success might have been limited.

Be that as it may be, the episode illustrates two points about signal intelligence. First, that it can be used to achieve decisive surprise, for which commanders are afterwards inclined to take the credit themselves. Second, that it can be so closely guarded as to make it useless to operational commanders. One of the lessons taught by the First World War which had fortunately not been forgotten in London, though it was forgotten in Washington, was that naval – or indeed, air and military – intelligence about the enemy is incomplete and ineffective without full knowledge of one's own naval operations and plans. *What the enemy is doing is significant only in relation to what one's own forces are doing or planning to do. Intelligence must be supplied to a total situation* – in a whole war or a whole battle-field – and that is possible only if the fighting men and planners will reveal to the intelligence men what they are doing or intend to do, and if the intelligence men confide to the fighting men all that they know without necessarily revealing how they know it.

More will be said in Chapter 4 about the cryptographers and their allies the 'Y' operators. All that needs to be established here is that most sources of intelligence have to be assessed in the light of this one, for none gives such certainty so quickly. It may not show the whole truth; it can even provide material that is false or misleading; but it is the enemy speaking. And it may cover diplomatic, economic and political traffic as well as military. That is why, in every Intelligence Service it is known by some special noun or adjective; known only to very few in the fighting services and to even fewer in politics. It is the equivalent in strategy and operations of the tapped telephone in police work and of the 'bugged' room in industrial espionage; deceitful, disreputable perhaps, but a great saver of lives – for the side that is listening.

Documents

The captured document is often, in its special way, an AI source. For example, papers and maps taken from a German raider or supply ship would provide information about swept channels, routes to be followed by ships that had taken prizes, orders for wireless contact and rendezvous with other German ships at sea; a code book (if the Captain had not had time to destroy it), information about other ships. With the aid of such documents, the Operational Intelligence Centre of NID, which had built up a whole technique of tracking raiders and supply ships that kept complete wireless silence for weeks at a time, could greatly enlarge its knowledge of the enemy both in tactics and strategy.

Sometimes captured documents were chiefly of retrospective value; for example, the bringing back to England in 1945 of the whole German Naval archives dating from 1871 gave invaluable information about many aspects of naval war which had puzzled the authors of staff studies and official histories, and must have added considerably to the awareness and carefulness of Naval staffs of the future. Documentary material was also of the greatest value for technical reasons. Anything dealing with torpedoes, management of engines, radar, listening apparatus, speeds and diving capacity of U-boats – all would be of immediate use to the technical departments of the Admiralty and even more use to those who were trying to build up an up-to-date vocabulary of the enemy's language for future use, whether in interrogating prisoners or deciphering signals.

HF/DF

As the telegraphist in his warship sits tapping out the messages that have been enciphered by his officers, able only to guess at their meaning, dealing all the time with outgoing and incoming symbols and figures, it is hard for him to visualize the vigilant interest of which he is a centre. Say he is the operator on board a German armed merchant raider, returning to home waters after fifteen months at sea. She has maintained wireless silence for all that time; the British are looking for her because they have heard of her victims sunk in the South Atlantic and the Indian Ocean; the Germans are expecting her back,

31

wondering by what route she will come, whether U-boats will by chance meet her. So the 'Y' services of both countries are waiting for her and the vast world-wide high frequency direction-finding (HF/DF) network of the Allies, ready to plot any signal she makes, however short, will pass on the location to the Admiralty, which will in turn alert warships and warn long-range reconnaissance aircraft.

By far the most successful open intelligence activity of the naval war was the finding and fixing of enemy ship and U-boat positions by 'Y' stations. These intercepted a signal, passed the frequency immediately to D/F stations which then got bearings from different positions on the enemy transmitter. When these bearings were plotted on a chart, the point at which they crossed marked an approximate position of the signalling ship. This was often of astonishing accuracy, just how accurate would depend on weather and wireless conditions. Fixes in the Arctic regions, for example, were especially hard to get; but more often than not the fix was sufficient to provide a narrow and precise area of search (say, three hundred square miles) for aircraft and groups of ships which had been put on the trail by a signal from the Operational headquarters. As the German naval records testify, the combination of clues provided by HF/DF and long-range air reconnaissance with radar was deadly. Indeed Britain's access to the overseas bases on which such a network could be set up gave her a decisive defensive advantage in the Atlantic and the Indian Ocean.*

A subsidiary but important source in this category was the ability to study the characteristic touch of an enemy wireless operator, especially in U-boats. Long practice with an invention called TINA, introduced by the first secretary of the Joint Services 'Y' Committee, made it possible to identify and study the methods of a particular telegraphist. His signal would be recorded on an undulation tape, and measurement of the symbols would show characteristics which were as revealing and reliable as fingerprints to the specialist looking for them. This method of radio finger-printing had a special value in the hunting of U-boats. For it was normal for a boat to carry along with its young telegraphists one experienced operator who could make the important operational transmissions. If his touch could be identified during his boat's patrol, its move-

32

ments could be plotted and tracked on the great chart in the submarine tracking room* so revealing valuable information about intentions, tactics and even the number of the U-boat when added to the other information in each boat's biographical dossier.

Yet another safeguard against U-boat attack, affording tactical intelligence which was invaluable at sea, was provided by giving convoy escorts MF/DF for navigation. During 1940 captured enemy documents had revealed to OIC that a pack of U-boats making attacks with closely concerted movements would use a medium frequency homing procedure, the details of which were known to us. In January 1941, listening watch for these transmissions was begun in order to devise a warning system, and by September 1942 no Atlantic convoy was sailing without a number of such 'Guards'. But the real U-boat killer was the high-frequency direction-finding receiver (HF/DF) which took an individual bearing of a U-boat signal.

The very extensive effort generated to meet this end, in terms of operators in action and in training at positions widely dispersed, brought special problems. For example, it caused heavy pressure on the channels through which 'Y' stations sent material back to headquarters in Britain for plotting, sifting and deciphering where possible. Urgent and valuable 'Y' material was having to compete with a vast naval traffic on the available networks. Indeed, it was not until the spring of 1943 that the service's own network was available, making this source effective at maximum speed and on the heaviest scale.

One very useful source of tactical intelligence was created as the result of combined work by the signals departments of all three Services in the late spring of 1940. The RAF 'Y' Service, intercepting and monitoring enemy signals in France, reported that the Germans were using plain language on VHF for messages between tanks and aircraft. This traffic across Channel could be read in Kent. So, when the invasion threat was at its height later that summer, Section 9 of NID opened at a few hours' notice a small station at North Foreland with Civilian Wireless Service operators and a few linguists borrowed from the Army. From hints in captured documents and from other clues NID 9 deduced that the German E-boats (fast and

33

heavily armed torpedo boats and gunboats) when operating in the Channel and the North Sea would talk among themselves on VHF.

In the light of the North Foreland experience, stations for listening in to plain language and simple code were built on the south and east coasts and enabled the OIC to give early warning of attack to convoy escorts. This was a great life- and ship-saving operation at a time when the German air and sea attack on the east coast convoys was seriously threatening the fuel and food supplies of London and the South. Later, German-speaking ratings were put into our destroyers with listening apparatus and gathered their operational intelligence from the enemy traffic at sea.

Air Photography

Probably next in importance for the Navy came the air photograph. Ships sooner or later have to go into ports and good, regular air photography will show something of their condition, any damage they have sustained, their readiness to leave for sea and so on. A major unit does not travel alone when it leaves port in a war area; it has a satellite community of minesweepers, barrage-breakers, patrol vessels, oilers and other craft, the movements of which can be observed by regular photography and which hold clues to the movements of the main unit, whether it is a pocket battleship or an armed raider. In the early part of the war the Admiralty called in vain for regular high-quality photographic reconnaissance of German fleet bases in the Baltic. It was not until 1942 that a regular flow of excellent pictures was coming into OIC and into the RAF headquarters at Medmenham, where a school of skilled interpreters built up a technique of measurement and interpretation which was able eventually to answer any questions that the Admiralty might want to ask. The good air photograph, allowing for camouflage and deception, was in some cases as near an A piece of evidence as one could wish for, and it played a decisive part in Cunningham's Mediterranean operations.

Above all, a constant repetition of photography revealed changes in readiness in a way that no other form of intelligence

34

could. This method made it possible to calculate with the help of agents' reports, just when the *Scharnhorst* and *Gneisenau*, for example, would be ready to leave Brest; and throughout the war after 1942 a very close eye was kept on the German fleet in the Baltic, on U-boat building and also on Italian naval bases in the Mediterranean. Conversely, it was the inability of the Germans to make regular photographic reconnaissance of the British ports and coastline that enabled the Allied invasion of Normandy to be, in June 1944, the complete surprise that it was. Once the Germans had lost air superiority over France and over the Channel their PR was crippled. To show the absence of a ship – that is to say its departure or non-arrival – in a certain place, a search by Coastal Command offered incomparable speed and certainty, if weather conditions and the local defences allowed a good picture to be taken.

The camera, it is often said, cannot lie. None the less, the enthusiast for the camera may claim that it can do far more than it can actually achieve in normal conditions of light and weather. Clever camouflage can defeat it, as study of the defences of foreign ports has shown; the fact that a picture does not reveal a battery or other defences does not prove agents' reports to the contrary are false.* The battery may be mobile. A photograph may give the slope and size of a beach but it cannot judge the quality of its sand, which is what the drivers of vehicles and the skippers of landing craft want to know. Oil tanks and gasometers have been confused from 25,000 feet. It is only when all considerations are brought together by an impartial analyst that the truth begins to emerge.

Sightings

If I put next in order sightings at sea and sightings from the air – whether by Fleet Air Arm pilots from carriers with the Fleet or by land-based Coastal Command aircraft – it is with the reminder that German warship silhouettes were deliberately deceptive and made it difficult for any but the highly-trained to distinguish between a pocket-battleship, a heavy cruiser and a large destroyer. The Germans had similar difficulties with their observation of the British Mediterranean and Home Fleet, but this was due more to the refusal of the Luftwaffe to let

35

the German Navy have its own reconnaissance than to failures by pilots. Sighting reports were seldom completely accurate unless accompanied by pictures, but they would at least give accurate locations (although errors could be made even in this respect) and, what was more valuable, the direction of the enemy and her estimated speed and condition.*

It was a Catalina aircraft sighting that led directly to the sinking of the *Bismarck*. When Cunningham in 1941 was pursuing the Italian battleship *Vittorio Veneto* and planning the night attack which followed the Battle of Matapan, he had his own special observer catapulted from the *Warspite* late in the afternoon of 29 March to make expert reports of her progress, speed and direction. Lieutenant-Commander Bolt, RN, was able to judge accurately and expertly what an ordinary pilot or observer could have only guessed at, and this intelligence proved first class.

On the other hand it is now known that one reason for the German hesitation to attack the notorious PQ17 convoy with the *Tirpitz* and other main units in July 1942 was the report from a Luftwaffe pilot which incorrectly described a floatplane belonging to one of the British cruiser escort as a carrier aircraft. (Hitler had given strict orders that an attack would be allowed only if no British aircraft carrier was within striking range of the German units.) So it can be said that accurate sightings by trained pilots give very good intelligence, but that some sightings by the unskilled could be dangerously misleading.

A classic – and tragic – case of a sighting report which carried a note of doubt and helped the battleship *Scharnhorst* to disaster occurred on Boxing Day, 1943, off Norway's North Cape. While setting out on a second attempt to attack one of the Allied convoys to Russia, she was informed of a signal from a reconnaissance aircraft stating that it had sighted five warships north-west of the north coast of Norway which she had left sixteen hours earlier. At headquarters in Kiel, Admiral Schniewind, commanding the fleet, could understandably assume that it referred to his own battle-cruiser's destroyer escort, returning to base because in the heavy seas they could not keep up with the *Scharnhorst*. A few hours earlier, he had ordered Rear Admiral Bey, commanding at sea, 'to consider the possibility of cruiser action by the *Scharnhorst* alone', after

36

receiving from him a signal saying 'action by destroyers severely restricted by weather'.

What was not known in Kiel was that the Luftwaffe intelligence officer, on receiving from his reconnaissance aircraft the signal 'five warships, *one apparently a big ship*, NW of North Cape', had struck out the words in italic on the ground that only definite information and not conjectures should be passed on to the Navy (a sound principle of intelligence if observed with discretion). To Schniewind those missing five words might well have suggested the approach of a British capital ship (it was in fact the *Duke of York*); he could then have ordered the *Scharnhorst* to break off the convoy operation and return to her fjord on a course which would have taken her beyond the reach of the British. Instead, she went on to her end. As Rear-Admiral Bey went down with his ship when the *Duke of York* and its destroyers sank the *Scharnhorst* later that day, it is not known what he made of the aircraft's signal. But Doenitz himself suggests that he too would have been led by the missing five words to break off action and so save a ship which had always been more effective in what she threatened to do than in what she could in fact perform.

Even in ships bearing every device of modern detection – radar, D/F equipment, listening apparatus – the prejudice in favour of what the 'watchkeeper' has seen remained strong. Yet imagination could play tricks with the eye even late in the war, when victory at sea seemed virtually certain. For over two years NID had been receiving from various sources reports of new Walter boats, with high surface speed and capable of partial submersion. Correctly, the German Section (I) had sent the information only to the technical department of the Admiralty for study. There was no point in alerting and alarming the Fleet about a weapon which was still in the experimental stage.* When it was known early in 1944 that trials of these boats had taken place and production had begun, a signal was sent out 'promulgating' the information and saying that Walter boat operations might begin at any time. Within twenty-four hours, the head of NID* recorded at the time, the first alleged Walter boat was 'sighted' and further reports were received for months, all of them false but made in good faith.

Sightings made in bad weather, or under fire, or by airmen not trained to recognize ships silhouettes and assess types could therefore be baffling for the intelligence officer who had to assess them. Against the certainty that something had been seen he had to balance the possibility that the airman had mistaken a cruiser for a pocket-battleship or a main unit with minesweepers for a big merchant ship with escort. When there was a general hunt on for a particular ship, as was so often the case with units of the German Fleet, it was easy to think that any warship must be *the* ship. Witness the brief attack by the Fleet Air Arm planes from the *Ark Royal* on the British cruiser *Sheffield* in May 1941 while searching in mid-Atlantic for the *Bismarck*.

Agents

High in the list, naturally, comes the good agent. A reliable and devoted person long planted inconspicuously in the right position, with secure and effective channels of communication, is hard to beat, particularly for intelligence of certain specialities. One of the most remarkable successes in Naval Intelligence in the last war was the reporting of the movements of the *Tirpitz* and other big ships from Altenfjord, Trondheim and other ports in Norway. So reliable was this service, provided by two or three Norwegians from the armed forces, that the OIC in London had complete faith in their accuracy and regularity. Likewise, an agent watching a stretch of coast which enemy ships must inevitably use, or sitting in an office with access to important documents, can be of decisive importance.

In fact, naval intelligence proper was not assisted in any way by either German or Japanese traitors, if that word is used in its full sense. There were defectors among prisoners of war, some of whom were very useful for the information they gave and also for the information they extracted from their comrades in the prison camps. Otherwise, it can safely be said that the inveterate suspicion of the German naval security services that their vessels and dockyards were infested with traitors was unfounded, whereas their feeling that every move in the U-boat bases of Western France was being watched and reported was fully justified.

It has to be remembered that the pre-war agent organization, controlled by the British Secret Service and Allied services, suffered a disastrous blow in 1940 when the Nazis unexpectedly overran Europe. Indeed, it took at least two years for satisfactory networks to be re-established and to solve the communication problems that arose in reconstructing espionage in occupied territory. By the time the Allies went over to the offensive, good service was coming from networks of agents; but by then alternative forms of intelligence were giving equally valuable results.

The quality of reports from an agent was circumscribed by various factors. In North Norway, a sparsely populated area where every suspicious movement attracts attention, the agent would be able to transmit information only at certain hours of the day and night. Conditions for W/T communication are about the worst in the world and this imposed further limitations and uncertainties. Wherever the agent was, communications were the limiting factor.

How valuable his information would be depended on the extent to which he had been briefed. To realize what is 'suspicious' in enemy activity, he must know what is 'normal'. To know what he need or need not report, he must know something of the extent of what is already known at headquarters. Ideally, the source should have as complete a knowledge as those who control him and will then be able to correct any false information and fill in gaps in their knowledge. But as headquarters cannot be omniscient, the source must know in what particular fields it is most important for them to be fully informed. Since, however, the headquarters controlling the agent wishes to know the unknown, it can never give fully specific requirements.

So a continual two-way exchange is necessary: the agent will report the unusual and as a result headquarters will speculate as to its meaning, will then ask questions to confirm or disprove a hypothesis and from its better knowledge suggest lines for the source to follow up. By this means new trends will gradually be discovered.

It has to be stressed that DNI never controlled agents; that was the function of the Secret Intelligence Service with which Room 39 maintained close contact. Sometimes one of his officers would help to brief an agent, but such contact was, quite properly, rare. Likewise, it was not the function of groups of individuals controlled by the Special Operations Executive to seek or send naval intelligence. Sometimes incidental information of value was picked up; but experience showed that collecting intelligence and organizing resistance and sabotage did not go happily together, each activity requiring a different type of mind and personality.

The use of an agent to report on detail which cannot be ascertained by other means is illustrated by the Bruneval raid of 1941. The RAF wished to check on the German radar system which was part of local defence against British bombers. One radar station was on top of the cliffs near Fécamp conveniently close across the Channel. A small raid was planned by Combined Operations and NID was asked for the necessary intelligence.

Ten days before the date fixed, CCO in person sent for the head of the NID section, Lt-Cdr Gonin, and pointed out that the latest air photographs revealed a suspicious black spot on the cliff edge. Was this a machine gun or a gorse bush or what? Gonin put fresh interpreters onto the pictures, had them blown up in size, all to no purpose. No one could be certain. The only possibility was that the Secret Service might send in an agent. They said it might be possible, but CCO must accept the responsibility if he was captured and the target revealed to the enemy.

Just in time – there was only a week to spare – the report came in. There was no machine gun on that cliff – and the raid took place with complete success. Later Gonin was told how the agent had contacted a tradesman in Fécamp who visited the lonely radar station regularly. This man left his bicycle one day by the cliff edge and when he went over to pick it up was able to take a complete view.

By far the most remarkable of the agents who served NID abroad was young Lieutenant Pettersen who arrived in Britain from Norway in June 1943. After training he was smuggled back into North Norway by submarine as a member of the team of wireless operator agents which watched and reported the movements of German capital ships in Altenfjord. He managed to instal himself at the tiny village of Elvebakken, at the south end of the fjord, in the German base itself. His job as a second cashier with the road-making authority gave him a reason for regular travel by car to pay men at their sites, often passing the *Tirpitz* at her anchorage. In order to get local people used to the absences from work which enabled him to transmit his reports at fixed times to England, he acquired the reputation of a drunkard.

From November 1943 onwards Pettersen was able to report the movements, state of repair and date of readiness of the battleship. The Fleet Air Arm attack of February 1944 was based on his intelligence which included information on radar installations, high tension cable and flak. Just before the attack he was providing two-hourly weather reports. After the attack the Germans made an intensive search of the area for wireless equipment and Pettersen reported that he might have to try and escape. But he was persuaded by London to stay on while three more attacks were prepared, which did not take place. He escaped from Norway into Sweden in March 1944 and was later awarded the DSO.

Prisoners of War

Prisoner-of-war intelligence grew more and more valuable as it grew in volume. The reason for this lies in the process by which knowledge breeds knowledge. An experienced inter-rogation officer concentrating on, say, U-boat crews or Italian frogmen would become acquainted with the whole background of the men's life, names of well-known officers and other per-sonalities, details about bases and rest camps (including names of favourite girl friends), gossip about new equipment or about losses, or about what was going on at home. By skilful handling of these fragments of information it was frequently possible to disarm the security sense of the highly trained officer or rating and make him feel that to dissimulate or remain silent was useless. The officer talking – generally young and sympathetic – appeared already to know so much that there could not be much point in refusing the opportunity to talk and smoke a cigarette and drink a glass of beer.

When prisoners of war were talking to each other in what they imagined to be privacy, they would often mention facts and persons and places which would be recorded. The intelligence officer who subsequently studied these conversations from the 'bugged' room could never be certain that the prisoners, especially if they were officers, were not saying inaccurate and misleading things in the full knowledge that they were being overheard.

As a source of information about weapons and technical matters, prisoner-of-war information was outstanding.

Wireless Traffic Study

Valuable though this was as a warning of impending movements of naval units or of the direction to be taken by a ship making for base, it is an example of the kind of intelligence which is truly significant only when related to other items. Expertise in this department is also a double-edged weapon; for nothing is more easily simulated, in order to deceive any enemy, than the kind of special wireless activity that precedes a big operation. Indeed, the deception of the Germans in the summer of 1944 about the exact landing places of the Allied invasion forces was largely achieved by the simulation of tremendous operational activity in the area opposite Calais – where it was *not* our intention to land. The subject is treated at greater length in Chapter 4.

Press and Radio

Quite high in the ranking of sources came the enemy's communiqués and propaganda statements, by press and radio. Not only were omissions significant in the light of our own knowledge, but what was included was determined by a known line of propaganda. For example, U-boat commanders after the early months of 1942 became increasingly worried by air attack, which was now occurring in waters where they had up till now thought themselves safe; it was even developing at night. German programmes and articles for home consumption therefore emphasized, whenever possible, the success of U-boats in fighting off air attack. Likewise propaganda would stress the efficiency of the U-boats' listening apparatus, when it was, in fact, doing them more harm than good.

42

The Admiralty was often and bitterly criticized for insisting on taking its time over the wording and publication of communiqués and stories about action at sea. Unreasonable or over-cautious it certainly was at times, but their Lordships had good reason to know how much could be given away by those who had no understanding or experience of intelligence work. To give one simple example: an official statement of loss or damage made in a country with a free press and Parliament was treated by the enemy as A1 information. The more quickly and fully it was made, therefore, the more trouble it saved enemy Intelligence. The Admiralty in its communiqués dared not lie and had to take every precaution against exaggeration.* A German Naval communiqué, however accurate the information reported back by the commander at sea, was always liable to be interfered with or indeed transformed by Dr Goebbels' propaganda machine, not in order to deceive the British but in order to mislead their own people about the course of the war and Hitler's management of it.

Incidentally, such exaggerations were often used by the Germans in their propaganda to Britain and the rest of the world in order to provoke the Admiralty into admitting – say, the loss or whereabouts of some important ship, like the aircraft-carrier *Ark Royal*. In London, American and other neutral newsmen would use the claims of Goebbels, in the early days of the war, to nag the Ministry of Information into recommending disclosures which the Admiralty refused to make.

What can be gleaned and deduced from the communiqué, news story or propaganda feature is illustrated by a memorandum which the DNI circulated in March 1942. This was meant to help Admiralty operations and press divisions, by showing them what NID was being given on a plate by the Germans.

For example, a simple and quite discreet announcement by the enemy of tonnage sunk could be the first clue to the nationality of U-boats in certain areas. The Italians, anxious as allies to show their mettle to the Germans outside the Mediterranean, could not forbear announcing successes in the West Indies and American areas. This was the first indication, and a most valuable one, that they were there. Likewise, a German announcement that their boats had sunk shipping south of

43

Freetown was useful, because the number of U-boats capable of operation at such long range was known. If two or more were in the South Atlantic, the number left over able to operate against the tankers sailing to and from the West Indies would be all the smaller, and therefore the more easily detectable.

It was normal for successful U-boat commanders – especially in the days of such heroic figures as Prien and Kretschmer – to be welcomed at base in France or Germany with bands, crowds, wreaths, microphones and perhaps the presence of Doenitz himself. The scene would be recorded and reported by the German radio in the breathless, emphatic style that our own television reporters now use, and more often than not the fêted commander and one or two of his petty officers would be questioned. Presumably they did not know that these programmes, every word of which was taken down by the BBC monitoring service at Caversham and sent by teleprinter to the Admiralty, gave clues and details of the following kind:

Length of cruise and time spent in base;
Names of merchant ships sunk and descriptions of incidents in convoy battles helped to reconstruct the cruise, about which other intelligence would be available;
Boasts and questions threw light on capabilities and idiosyncrasies of commanders and the general strategy of the U-boat command.

If the German naval censors had suppressed the names of the commanders, more than one mention of an incident during the cruise, the names of ships sunk and patrol areas, and the date of the jamboree, NID would have lost valuable information.

It is not difficult to imagine with what questions Goebbels' Ministry must have nagged at the Kriegsmarine, a far less powerful body in Berlin than the Admiralty in London. 'How can we maintain the morale of our U-boat men unless their successes are publicly proclaimed?' 'Why should the German people and the world outside believe our claims unless we give confirmatory details in the form of ships' names and commanders' names?' 'How is the Navy to be built up in the eyes of the Party and the other Services unless it has its share of war-reporting from the front line?' These must have been the

44

arguments that the propagandists used against the naval officers; and in Germany, where opinion control was fundamental to the political régime, their power to get their own way was greater than in London.

Communiqués and war reports were eagerly studied also for admissions of damage by air attack or mines. Because the Germans kept quiet about the damage to *Scharnhorst* and *Gneisenau* done by Bomber Command's mines during their dash from Brest to Wilhelmshaven in February 1942,* some weeks passed before agents' reports enabled the Admiralty to announce that the ships had been damaged severely enough to be out of action for months. Yet for all that time there was bitter criticism by Press and Parliament of the failure of our forces to prevent a dash up Channel to a home port where they were less of a menace than at Brest.

Censorship

Censorship of letters and cables, both in this country and in British possessions abroad was a useful source of detailed information about foreign ship movements and breaches of the blockade. It could even give clues to enemy agents or to sabotage and subversive plans in places like Brazil and Mexico. As a source of facts affecting naval operations it could be most important.

Topographical Intelligence

It might be assumed that all topographical intelligence was open and public. That is not so. Much of it was available in books or in ordinary people's minds; but the particular, specialist information that would be required for a raid by land or sea might have to be secured by secret and dangerous methods which will be described in a later chapter. All up-to-date information about areas occupied by the enemy against which operations were being planned became *ipso facto* secret. For nothing would give away military intentions more surely than to concentrate the minds of a large number of civilians on a particular area. As a source, therefore, the Inter-Services Topographical Department at Oxford and the sister organiza-

45

tions in the Middle East and Far East could rank in every category from top secret to unrestricted.

Old hands would recall how the planners of 1914–18 had assumed, quite wrongly and disastrously, that the Gallipoli Peninsula would provide the forces landing there with all the wood, fuel and water they would need. Younger hands knew how the troops so hurriedly landed in Norway in 1940 had no accurate information about the snow and road conditions they would find around Narvik. No one knew, even in 1942, that fifty miles inland from the Tunisian coast vehicles of the 'Torch' operation which got bogged down for weeks along the coastal road could have found firm if not hard going; had they known this, Rommel might have been disposed of a few months earlier by this threat to his rear. And so on.*

The eye-opening lesson in Norway was salutary, and steps were at once taken to cure the dismal ignorance that had marked that operation. The amount of detailed intelligence required for the successful landing and maintenance of an expeditionary force with modern weapons and with modern standards of feeding and equipment is prodigious. Even if the landing is unopposed, the Navy has navigational, coast defence and other requirements which cannot be taken for granted. If it is opposed, the most meticulous preparation by air photography, raiding parties, agents' inquiries, cross-examination of people who know the landing area, underwater reconnaissance and geological survey is required.

Both the methods of acquiring such information and the immensely varied nature of it became disguised after 1940 under the word 'topographical'. The ISTD, which did indeed produce in its Handbooks a great deal of valuable straight topography, was also responsible for finding 'contacts', that is to say, people with specialist knowledge of areas and places, perhaps across the Channel in Normandy or far away on the coast of Burma;* for preparing operation orders in hundreds of copies with the help of printers of the OUP; for searching the great libraries of the country and the learned institutions for every kind of botanical, geological, mineral, agricultural, medical detail that might affect the efficiency of a force operating abroad.

Friendly Observers and Refugees

Throughout the war refugees in thousands reached this country by all kinds of means, and a whole department of military intelligence (MI 19) was concerned with their screening and interrogation. To it were attached representatives of other interests eager to gather information from inside Occupied Europe. Through this source came the latest news of German security and administrative arrangements, precious detail of daily life (rationing methods, state of rail and road transport, fashion and slang, etc.) which were needed by those in SOE who were training our own agents to land and operate in Occupied Europe. The BBC learned about the listening habits and conditions of its captive audience; MEW checked on the raw material and petrol shortages.

The screening process did not concern the NID man who worked with MI 19 at the Royal Patriotic Schools, Wandsworth. It was only when this was over – and it caught more than one German agent posing as a refugee – that people were set aside for intensive questioning in the naval interest. There would be, for example, a member of the Todt Organization who had worked on the construction of U-boat shelters in Lorient or Trondheim; a Frenchman who had seen signs of the first V1 sites; Breton or Norwegian fishermen who knew the habits and routes of German coastal shipping supplying garrisons and bases. Their information would be studied and filed in the NID section interested and sometime later would come the query which could be answered from this source.

A curious and striking example of how valuable intelligence can be provided by a routine operation through a neutral source occurred in Sweden. NID was always pressing for information about the movements of U-boats and identification of their numbers. This was difficult to obtain because no boat had its number anywhere discernible and the crews identified their ships only by the field post number. However, the captain of a U-boat when signing for fuel, completion of repairs, taking on stores, etc., had to sign a form giving its actual number. Through the Norwegian and Polish intelligence networks NID was able to obtain copies of some of these forms from Swedish tankers which carried out bunkering in Danzig and from the dockyards in Bergen and Trondheim, where U-boats were frequent visitors. The amount of fuel taken on was an indication whether the U-boat was bound on exercises or on an operational cruise; and this information provided very useful additions to the Admiralty's U-boat mosaic.

Technical and Tactical (Our Ships)

The signals and Reports of Proceedings sent in to the Admiralty after any action or contact with the enemy would be examined for useful technical information (weapons, ammunition, mines) and tactical lessons (destroyer and E-boat behaviour, handling of a U-boat pack).

Sightings by Merchant Ships and Coastal Watchers

For tracking down the German armed merchant raiders the reports of ships attacked by them or of survivors from them were often the only concrete evidence about their appearance and methods. In narrow waters everywhere on the periphery of occupied Europe and Asia, the coast watcher or fisherman could turn out to be a useful source. Outstanding was the secret watchers' organization in Norway.

Survivors

Eye-witness information about the armed German surface raiders (already mentioned), which would suddenly pounce on ships sailing independently in the most distant seas where U-boats could not patrol, would reach the Admiralty in the most roundabout ways. Survivors of a British or allied merchant ship might be picked up, say, in the South Atlantic by a Brazilian ship, having been given a few minutes to take to the boats before their ship was sunk by the raider days before. Landed in a South American port, they would be immediately contacted and questioned by the nearest naval attaché, who would send to London what provisional estimate he could get out of them about the enemy's appearance, the position where she was met and on what date, the tactics she followed and so on.

But this interrogation would be, at best, a poor substitute for the expert questioning which would be brought to bear some weeks later in London. There an officer carrying in his head every fragment of intelligence about these evasive and mysterious ships could glean details which might lead to the identification of this particular one. Already he had in his room over his desk an estimated plot of the last known positions of every raider and from that he could assist the survivors in finding the clues. Some of what they said might be graded up to A1; some of it downgraded to D5.

Again and again DNI had to stress to those at sea that preliminary interrogation even for tactical and local purposes might do more harm than good. It was almost always true that inexpert questioning in the earliest stage could spoil witnesses for later examination. They would be pressed to be more specific than their observation justified; ideas would be put into their heads; and they would be biased in favour of those explanations that the first officer they met seemed to prefer. The classic case was that of the *Rawalpindi* survivors very early in the war, when the drill in these matters had not been established. On 23 November 1939, when the exact whereabouts of the German battle-cruisers was still a mystery, this British armed merchant cruiser reported sighting the battle-cruiser *Scharnhorst* between Iceland and the Faroes, and then a few minutes later corrected *Scharnhorst* to the pocket battleship *Deutschland*. This caused much confusion in the Admiralty and when survivors of the sunk *Rawalpindi* were questioned the bewilderment grew worse. Here I quote from Godfrey:

> It was of vital importance to discover the name or at least the class of ship that had sunk her. Our only sources were the survivors. The senior one – a Chief Petty Officer – was sent to the Admiralty and, after being questioned several times en route, was sent for by Admiral Pound, who asked a series of leading questions. By the time he reached the NID the man was confused and, as an objective witness, useless. So many suggestions had been made to him in the meantime that the mental image of the shape and size of the German ship had become blurred.*

Other Services

It took time for the British to learn – and the Germans and Italians never fully grasped – that the intelligence of one

49

fighting service could be invaluable to another service; or indeed that co-operation between the operations branch of one service and the intelligence branch of another would produce special results. For example, the intelligence won by the RAF about Luftwaffe movements and strength pointed again and again to enemy naval intentions, whether in Norway or the Channel, in the eastern or western Mediterranean. For the defence of ports, for the interception of a blockade runner making for a Biscay port on its way from the Far East, for the protection of Arctic convoys, this exchange of naval and air intelligence was routine; likewise of course RAF mining operations depended on the Navy's intelligence about swept channels and convoy routes.

Information about movements and indiscretions of agents of the Abwehr would give clues to future intentions of the German Army; and leakages from German Army plans, for example, about movements to and from Rommel's Army provided useful intelligence for the British submarines operating against his convoys between Italy and North Africa. Most sensational of all, perhaps, was the information about the British 8th Army gleaned by German cryptanalysts who broke the diplomatic code in which the United States Military Attaché in Cairo was informing Washington of British plans and dispositions.

The Admiralty's interests were world-wide and unpredictable so that NID had to be kept posted with Foreign Office, War Office and Air Ministry intelligence which made intelligible evidence which would otherwise mean very little. The development by an enemy of new types of aircraft might appear as a matter only for the RAF; but they might be intended for anti-shipping operations and provide the clue to other reports received by NID. Information about the German Air Force made it possible to foretell the intentions of the German Army in 1940. Likewise the Germans, trying to assess the strength of the Allied forces preparing for the invasion of Normandy in 1944, found useful clues in intercepts of RAF traffic and from the Gestapo watching the French resistance groups.

Double Agents

For reasons that should be obvious, any detailed discussion of the part played by double agents in securing intelligence is impossible. The technique is as old as the hills; what was new in the last war was the development of it made possible by sophisticated wireless communications. How and when the game was played and who played it remains a secret but its use in securing positive information is interesting and little known.

The instructions sent to a double agent who has built up a good reputation for himself will sometimes give away the intentions of his original masters. The priorities they give to certain items of information they ask for – for example about bomb damage – will reflect their tactical thinking. If the double agent was sent with alternative sets of instructions, an inquiry from him suggested by his new masters should bring an answer telling him which to follow. At the time of the invasion threat to this country in the autumn of 1940 it was an exchange of this kind between an enemy agent in our hands and his controls in Europe which convinced DNI that Hitler had postponed Operation 'Sea-Lion' indefinitely.

Naval Attachés

Naval attachés are dealt with last in this chapter because each representative of the DNI abroad, if he is in an important capital, virtually becomes himself in wartime the centre of an intelligence system, drawing on many different sources. For that reason there is no good purpose in comparing or grading him with any one of the varieties of source that have been discussed. At various times NID was receiving through naval attachés the products of a neutral secret service, of intercepted German communications with Berlin, of visitors from Japan and Italy and occupied eastern Europe, of neutral journalists, of friends among the shipping, fishing and trading communities. All was grist to their mill; and some of the booty that came out of it is described in a special chapter.

It was in the neutral capitals, where enemy and Allied representatives were operating cheek by jowl in bitter but correct rivalry, that our naval attachés did their best work. As a source of naval intelligence Stockholm was certainly the best of them, because of its proximity to the Baltic and to occupied Norway and Denmark. Madrid with its unique political background and as an observation post for Gibraltar, the western Mediterranean and North Africa imposed rather different duties and offered very different information. Ankara and Istanbul were more like Madrid than Stockholm. There the prize was Turkey's participation in the war on the Allies' side; as in Madrid, the work of the naval attaché had more to do with politics than with intelligence, although the information about conditions and personalities in the Balkans which came out through Turkey was to prove very valuable after 1944. Moscow both before and after June 1941, yielded virtually nothing because of the suspicious attitude of the Soviet Navy.

In the United States the particular status of Naval Attaché Washington was soon lost to view once the collaboration between Navy Department and Admiralty began to grow. His particular duty of informing the Admiralty about American naval affairs was more and more taken over by a team of specialists, communicating through NID 18; and the informing of the Americans about British experience and intelligence came through the British Admiralty Delegation which began to function openly in Washington after Pearl Harbor.

In Latin America the duties of naval attachés were largely concerned with keeping a check on German activities, whether in espionage or blockade-running or anti-British propaganda. Once the Americans came into the war, their organizations tended to take over this area of activity.

It was only rarely, and then mainly from Madrid and Stockholm, that naval attachés were able to send operational intelligence of importance, although the coast-watching organization run by the Norwegians in the Kattegat often gave warning of German warship movements. Of great value would be the information and gossip that Swedish and Spanish and Turkish naval officers and others would bring back from Berlin, Rome and Paris, some of it deliberately planted by the Germans in the belief that it would reach the Allies, some of it just useful indiscretion or the result of observations made on conducted tours of ships, establishments, dockyards, etc.

3 From cold to hot war

To compare the Intelligence Division taken over by Godfrey on 3 February 1939 with what he left behind him four years later would be most unfair to his predecessor's efforts unless the difference between the wartime and peacetime status of the work were understood. Indeed, any peacetime government faced, and still faces, a serious difficulty when trying to decide whether money and effort should be permanently devoted to Intelligence. When there was no enemy it languished; its time was spent in collecting obsolescent information; its strategic functions were only vaguely apprehended by a generation of officers with no experience of its role in Operations, yet among them were some of the best minds in the Service.* It would have been lucky if it had even kept up with weapon developments abroad. Whereas Intelligence is concerned in wartime first and foremost with the movements of hostile or potentially hostile ships, and the protection of our own shipping and lines of communication, there was nothing of that kind happening at sea between 1918 and 1936 – at least, nothing comparable to the cold war operations which kept NID on its toes after 1945: Abadan, Korea, Palestine and later Suez, Malaysia, and the watch on Africa, east and west. Nothing except the Abyssinian episode and the Spanish Civil War.

Above all, as a deterrent to initiative and inquisitiveness until the mid-Thirties, there had been the annually renewed reminder from the Cabinet to the three Service Departments, originated in the Twenties by, of all people, Churchill:

It should be assumed, for framing revised estimates, that the British Empire will not be engaged in any great war during the next ten years, and that no expeditionary force is required for this purpose.*

While Chatfield was toiling to rebuild the Navy with inadequate funds, it was not to be expected that NID would be treated as anything but the Cinderella of the Naval Staff.

How bad were things? Probably no worse than lack of money and staff, and absence of clear direction by Ministers made unavoidable. But why be enthusiastic and assiduous, if you were a Commander or a Major of Marines with no prospect of advancement before you, and no clear indication of priorities in your work? Who could tell on what coasts of the wide world the British should be landing or which ports they would need to use? Who could foresee that the Channel coast of France, the chief ally, would become the highest priority of intelligence towards the end of a war in which the British Army had been pushed out of Europe, or that Japanese naval aircraft would be bombing Colombo? Why initiate comprehensive studies when there were not sufficient draughts-men* to keep existing files up to date? It would be enough to watch the navies of Germany and Italy and, if possible, Japan – all to become increasingly security-conscious police states; record what the naval attachés sent – which was not much; and leave the Secret Service to spy out what they could with their special expenditure limited to less than £500,000 a year. In all minds, even in those of the eight Directors* who sat in 'Blinker' Hall's chair between 1918 and 1937, was the knowledge that the Division was a shadow of its old glamorous and powerful self.

Fortunately one man who had been in Hall's team was still in a position to cast a stone into this not quite stagnant pool. In 1935–8 the Deputy Chief of Naval Staff was Vice-Admiral Sir William James, who had been Deputy Director of Intelligence after 1918 and had been in charge of the Room 40 where German naval and diplomatic signals were decoded and studied. In 1936, worried by the Abyssinian crisis and Italian behaviour in the Mediterranean, he sent to the Directors of Plans and Intelligence the question: 'What would happen if war were suddenly declared?' and asked for comments. He was not counting on the code and cipher-breakers repeating their feats of 1916; they were not there to do the work; indeed, to be

dependent on such sources was dangerous and also unnecessary. 'There is a great field of work', he wrote in his
minute, 'with directionals, reports from agents, own ships,
etc., and if astute men are put on to this work, there is no
doubt in my mind that very soon a valuable form of operational
intelligence will be built up.'

What had specially worried the Admiralty lately was the
need to identify beyond doubt Spanish Nationalist or other
submarines, which had been sinking merchant ships in the
Mediterranean. The methods and staffing of the tiny Movements Section, where reports of ships were filed, were quite
inadequate. So the DCNS went on prodding, and in June
1937 it was decided to bring Paymaster Lt-Cdr Norman
Denning* into NID to work out the organization that would
be required for a wartime operational intelligence centre.
Denning quickly realized that the set-up was pathetic and that
the information coming in fell far short of what the Board
wanted. So he arranged to spend three weeks with the wireless
traffic and cipher experts at Station X to study how they
worked and what they might with extra effort provide. Returning to the Admiralty, he found out what priorities between
navies were indicated by Naval Staff thinking, and then got
down to producing a proper card-index system. The pre-
cedence at that time was Italy, Japan, Germany – the last
standing third, because the negotiations for the London Treaty
limiting German warship building were then in train.

The next urgent task was to get the direction-finding (D/F)
and interception (Y) organizations strengthened so that a
closer and wider study might be made of the wireless traffic
of potential enemies. This happened just at the time that
Italian submarines were taking a hand in the Spanish Civil
War; they were identified with fair success, although Denning
wrote in January 1938:

Even now we are ignorant of the names of most of the submarines
concerned . . . and are still unaware of the actual identity of Italian
submarines which were subsequently turned over to the Spanish
Nationalists . . . A record of German and Italian submarines within
their own territorial waters is essential to discover the identity of
pirate submarines by elimination.

C*   55

As the British Fleet in the Mediterranean could only patrol and not take offensive action against the pirates, there was no point in making elaborate efforts to keep it fully informed; but enough was seen of the difficulties of promulgating information on which action could be taken for Denning to urge that the existing devious system of passing intelligence to ships and other departments was intolerably cumbersome. He therefore devised, with the backing of James and despite the misgivings of his Director, Rear-Admiral Troup, and the civil servants, the nucleus of an Operational Intelligence Centre entitled to communicate directly to authorities inside and outside the Admiralty all information of operational value. After intense badgering of every senior officer and civil servant in sight, Denning finally secured three rooms for his section where he was joined by a signals expert. In one of them a current plot of ships' movements was kept on maps and charts, and in another direct communication by pneumatic tube and scrambler telephone was established with the War Registry, through which passed all incoming and outgoing signals. By peacetime standards this was luxury. The OIC as it was to be known, had arrived.

The Munich crisis of August–September 1938, during which the section was joined by some of the officers later allotted to it in wartime, provided a useful running in; so successful was the work that Denning was able to report: 'We had all the German units outside Germany and a great number of her larger merchant ships taped the whole time.' The known movements made it clear that at this time the German Navy was not intending or expecting major war in the immediate future. The disposition of the German Fleet from the morning of 28–29 September was accurately given.

This was perhaps Rear-Admiral Troup's greatest achievement as DNI. With support at the highest level he wrote to the senior civil servant concerned:

The underground OIC should be developed to produce perfect communications at as early a date as possible. Mr Le Maitre may take the instruction about communications as a Board decision.

Now that Munich had loosened the purse-strings a little, the wireless experts were allowed to order some new American receivers and to buy better D/F sets direct from Marconi's. Despairing of the Post Office, the DNI bought two MF/DF sets with secret funds and set them up at two sites in the North. More important still, just before Godfrey joined as DNI in February 1939, approval was given for an independent communications system of teleprinters, bringing signals into War Registry from outside with direct connection to the underground headquarters to which OIC was to be moved. This system had to cope with variety as well as volume of incoming material. Material gleaned from enemy signals from Station X (headquarters of the cryptanalysts and wireless traffic experts) came by teleprinter to the teleprinter room, and delivered thence by hand into the various sections. All D/F bearings picked up in England were co-ordinated at one or two points and passed by teleprinter and tube to OIC. D/F bearings from abroad came in by signal to War Registry and were sent by hand to OIC. Results of air reconnaissance came in from three Coastal Command headquarters at Plymouth, the Nore and Rosyth. Reports from local naval units and coast watchers were collated at area HQs and sent by teleprinter. Reports from agents were telephoned, if urgent; otherwise they came by teleprinter or handborne letter. Naval reporting organizations signalled by cable and telegram; and reports from Lloyd's and merchant ships came by special line. Where one man had operated with a trickle of fact there was now an organization as large as a great news agency.

In effect, what were to be known as NID 8 and 9 went underground in mid-August 1939, and by the beginning of October the battle of brains with Raeder and Doenitz had begun, with sixteen officers of Commander's rank and above, eleven below Commander's rank, eleven civilian officers, and two clerks. 'By autumn 1939', says Denning, 'we had enough for war with one power.' That such a revolution could be achieved in less than three years reflects credit on the Admiralty's staunch and helpful civil servants.

What precisely was the difference between OIC and other intelligence departments? Day-to-day operational intelligence* is to long-term intelligence (say, about the size of the Chinese submarine fleet in 1970, or the obsolescence of Soviet aircraft operating with the Indonesian navy in 1972) what the front

57

page news of a daily paper is to the comment and feature articles of a Sunday paper.

In planning the shape and working of the new centre, the few who could remember Jellicoe's day and the Grand Fleet had to guard against repetition of the stupid incompetence which snatched from him at Jutland what might have been a decisive victory. The story is told by Marder* of how on 31 May 1918 a certain Captain Jackson of the Operations Division sent to the Commander-in-Chief a signal locating the German fleet at base, when it had in fact sailed several hours earlier. Jackson had asked in Room 40, where the German naval signals were deciphered, a question about the German flagship without telling them why he wanted to know or subsequently telling them that he had passed the misunderstood answer to the Grand Fleet. Worse still there was the failure, later the same day, to let Jellicoe know about signals which showed clearly the homeward course of the German fleet.

These failures, later described by Jellicoe as disastrous, were due to three faults of organization. First, Room 40 was not allowed to interpret and present intelligence in the light of its extensive knowledge of German practice gained from signal breaking. Secondly, Operations Division asked only for raw material, the bare facts of signals made in varying circumstances and with varying delays. Third, the intelligence men were told nothing about their own fleet's operations which would enable them to relate their knowledge of the enemy's intentions to those of Operations Division or the Commander at sea. Room 40 was treated as a first-aid chest, to be used only in an emergency and kept secret from all but a very few.

If luck should come our way again in Hitler's war – the sort of luck which presented Room 40 with the ciphers contained in a German special agent's luggage brought from Persia – then it was important to rule out such difficulties. From the first, OIC must be accessible to Operations and Plans, and they must be accessible to it. There must be a full exchange of signals between Intelligence and operations, and interpretation must be the former's and not the latter's job. Even if information from enemy signals were not obtained on the scale of 1916, none the less all other intelligence was also to be studied, interpreted and passed on in this way. Thus the Naval Staff, in September 1939, found themselves ready to go into action with a highly trained organization for centralized control of the war at sea.

Ideally, such an operational intelligence centre should reproduce the enemy operations room. Only rarely can achievement rise to such heights; but the ideal is precisely that – to reproduce the enemy's mental processes by participating so far as possible in *his* information and bringing to bear on it one's own complete information about the intentions and strength and position of one's own forces. Whenever the Director of Anti-Submarine Warfare or C-in-C Western or Northern Approaches, or the First Sea Lord or the PM himself rang up, he must be sure of getting a clear, accurate and brief answer to the question 'What are they up to now?' Just as rival commanders came to know each other's idiosyncrasies, the wireless operators to recognize the touch of one operator among a hundred U-boat transmitters, so a good operational intelligence man would read his enemy's intentions. The technique was applied not only to U-boats but also to the big ships, the E-boats in the North Sea and Channel, the raiders, the minesweepers, the blockade-breakers, the Luftwaffe's attacks on shipping and minelaying, and the movement of enemy merchant shipping in the Baltic and the North Sea and Channel.* So it was that Chief of Staff, Home Fleet, would ring up Denning several times a day when in harbour. The lady in 8E watching the movements of E-boats and other small units in the Channel would ring up the Staff Officer Intelligence at Plymouth and suggest a night's hunting for our own motor gunboats. And the First Sea Lord at a critical moment could put a simple decisive question to the officer studying the daily movements and habits of ships like the *Bismarck* or the *Tirpitz*.

The working of the submarine tracking room, which was only one section of the whole OIC, is described in a separate chapter. The organization of the adjoining sections is dealt with below, but it is more convenient to give examples of its work on particular occasions in the course of a later chapter in which the chase of the *Bismarck* is analysed from the intelligence point of view. (See Chapter 7.)

As the war developed, specialisation grew, the methods and ideas were transplanted overseas, and new men came in. Denning, having given over the tracking of U-boats, had become responsible for the German main fleet, the armed merchant raiders, all coastal craft like E-boats and mine-sweepers, photographic reconnaissance of German bases, minefields and swept channels, and also all enemy air activity connected with naval operations. Sub-sections dealing with each of these reported to him and it was in his mind that the significant patterns formed. Along the corridor were sections dealing with wireless traffic and interception, watching over the security of our own signals, ruses and stratagems of all kinds to be worked out with the Signals Division. A tiny Italian section fed all relevant intelligence from Station X and other sources to a similar OIC in Alexandria, and later in Algiers and Caserta, as C-in-C Mediterranean changed his headquarters.

The Italian and Japanese sections fed intelligence sub-centres abroad with the kind of intelligence available only in Britain, but were much more remote from the control of operations. In the main their task was to keep the Admiralty staffs and Cabinet war-room informed about current enemy operations in their areas of operation. They, in fact, provided the hot news of the Mediterranean and Pacific wars.

The sight and sound, even the smell, of this headquarters on a busy night might have been transmitted item by item from a newspaper in Fleet Street only a mile away. There was an untidy, clattering bustle; hardly one of the small rooms had less than two telephone conversations going on; officers and civilians and 'secret ladies' moving about the narrow corridors with heavily labelled folders and dockets, teleprinter flimsies or illegible sequences of decoded signals. There was a smell of rooms never empty for more than a few minutes, used all round the clock. The Citadel quarters were admirably clean, ventilated and warmed by the standards of those days, but cut off by twenty feet of steel and concrete from the fresh air of St James's Park and the Mall. Indeed, it was probably the best bomb-proof headquarters in London.

Six hundred yards away to the south in Storey's Gate, the Prime Minister might sometimes wonder during the Blitz whether a direct hit might not bring the Thames flooding into his basement shelter. Not so the hundred men and women of the OIC working in the Citadel, described by Churchill in his memoirs as that 'vast monstrosity which weighs upon the Horse Guards Parade'. They had the assurance of safety from even a direct hit – and a bracing assurance it was – but for it they paid the price of complete exclusion from the outside world: no windows, no daylight, no sound of traffic or birds or wind, only the noise of the work being done. It was the engine room of NID.

For 18 months before Godfrey took over, his predecessor Rear-Admiral J. A. G. Troup had been interviewing and retaining suitable civilians.* By April 1939 there were one hundred and fifty names to choose from, and thirty to forty vacancies to fill. The new DNI now recalled Hall's success with choices that were 'outlandish, unorthodox and inspired'. Some volunteered out of the blue; most were recommended by friends, interviewed, told they would be informed if wanted, vetted by the Security Service, and then put on the call-up list. But one thing that Troup clearly could not have done for his successor was to select the personal staff that would be needed in Room 39 in war. So Godfrey began early in 1939 collecting the kind of civilian talent that the stockbroker Claude Serocold had collected for 'Blinker' Hall twenty-five years earlier; indeed Hall was very close to Godfrey's ear in these preparatory months. Retired RN officers of good quality; barristers and solicitors; writers and journalists were vetted. As his personal assistant he chose a young stockbroker (Ian Fleming*) who had trained at one time for both the Army and the Foreign Office and as his private secretary a solicitor (Edward Merret) with a taste for drawing and a genius for friendliness and reducing tension.

The principle he followed in selecting and using his staff was to take them into his confidence and then throw on them full power and responsibility, avoiding any appearance of inter-ference. This, he realized, was diametrically opposed to the tendency of some senior naval officers to 'usurp the functions of their subordinates', but it was the way of doing things that he had learnt as a young officer from Commodore Rudolf Burmester, Chief of Staff to the Mediterranean Command

61

during the First World War, whom he greatly admired.

Many amusing stories were told of how and why people came into their jobs. There was the marine biologist who had volunteered at a Labour Exchange, had been recorded as an expert on *cryptogams* (plants which have no stamens and pistils) and so ended up in the section studying enemy wireless traffic. There was Winn the barrister who offered his talents as a cross-examiner for interrogation of U-boat prisoners-of-war, and ended up as head of the U-boat tracking room. There was Todd, head of Thomas Cook and Sons Berkeley Street office, an expert on Egypt who took over the Scandinavian section; and Charles Mitchell, the historian of fine art who collated and studied all the information got from prisoners-of-war. Only in one section did the job seem tailored to fit the recruit; in the Information section with distinguished writers like Charles Morgan, Hilary Saunders (librarian of the House of Commons), William Plomer and later the editor of *The Times Literary Supplement*, Simon Nowell-Smith.

Godfrey spent much time getting to know newspaper editors and proprietors who might be helpful with the information and censorship duties which would fall on the Division in wartime; he also took soundings in foreign embassies and in the City about contacts who would advise on the diplomatic, financial and social problems liable to surprise an Intelligence department. Here Godfrey was consciously walking in the footsteps of Hall, who had always assumed that everything was and must be the DNI's business: the Admiralty with its seniority and its world-wide interests must have its own trusted sources of information, at any rate until other sources were found and tested. There is some substance in the charge of 'empire-building' that was heard among Godfrey's critics in these early days, but it is fair to say that it died away as soon as joint service bodies were providing the services to which the DNI believed the Board of Admiralty to be entitled. If an analogy from journalism is permissible: every quality newspaper takes the home news service of the Press Association and the Foreign service of Reuters but each still prefers to have its own specialist sources for the really important stories.

A typical example from June 1940 of the use of these personal, contacts is told by Godfrey as follows:

I was introduced by Reggie Hall early in 1939 to Lord Tyrrell who, after being British Ambassador in Paris, held the post of Permanent Under-Secretary at the Foreign Office for many years. He was old and frail and an invalid, but these disabilities in no way impaired the shrewdness of his judgement about European affairs. He encouraged me to go and see him in his flat in Chesham Place, and this I did at frequent intervals. In spite of his infirmities he seemed to be remarkably well in touch with what was going on and his prognostications were usually correct, although it was the fashion at the Foreign Office to make light of his warnings.

When France was collapsing and A. V. Alexander (First Lord) and Admiral Pound were about to make a final effort to get in touch with the French Minister of Marine (Darlan) at Bordeaux, Tyrrell rang me up and asked me to come and see him urgently. It was to warn me that Admiral Darlan was likely to be a twister. He had formed this opinion years ago when he was in Paris and knew Darlan, who held the post of Naval Chef de Cabinet. I got back to the Admiralty just as Admiral Pound was leaving for France and gave him the message; but he was incredulous. To him it seemed unbelievable that Darlan was anything but an honest, straightforward sailor whom he had met and talked shop with a year or two before.

It was, of course, one thing to plan on paper an intelligence divison and assemble its staff in time for hostilities; it was quite another to get the machine working under the stress of war, with a world-wide blockade being imposed on enemy ships, and every allied merchant ship at once exposed to the menace of submarine, air and mine attack. There was at first much crashing of gears, stalling and erratic steering.* Here, from his unpublished Memoirs, is Godrey's own picture of the Admiralty at work in the last months of 1939:

In 1939 the green line and other secret telephone systems did not exist, and much time was wasted in running backwards and forwards between the First Lord, Mr Churchill, the First Sea Lord, Admiral Pound and the Deputy Chief of the Naval Staff, Vice-Admiral Tom Phillips, my own room and the OIC. The idea that Pound and Phillips should come down to the OIC on arrival each morning and find out what was going on never materialized and the special door provided remained unused by them.

The incidence of responsibility between the operational planning, trade and anti-submarine directors was as yet ill defined; neither

63

was it possible to adjust the frontiers between these divisions and correlate them with Intelligence needs within the framework provided by the Admiralty buildings in 1939 and 1940. Much more elbow room was needed.

There were interminable conferences about propaganda, censorship, publicity, and problems connected with the work of the Ministry of Information, which was having much worse teething troubles than the Admiralty, and was being pestered by the Press and House of Commons and nagged at by all departments.

When any 'naval occasion' took place, or showed signs of breezing up, everyone concerned crowded into the small conference room in the underground OIC, with the First Lord and other Sea Lords coming and going. There we used to wait for news to come in during such episodes as the Battle of the Plate and the sinking of the *Rawalpindi*. The hours spent during the night, sometimes for long periods in complete silence in the fuggy, thickening, gloomy atmosphere, were not the best precursor to a fruitful day's work. Sometimes one had just time to have a bath and breakfast and return to read the telegrams and prepare for the daily staff meeting in the same room. Neither the room nor its nocturnal inmates started the day well, and the atmosphere at the 09.30 meeting was frequently stale, frowsty, peevish and petulant.

Priority in NID war preparations went to OIC and Room 39; but there were other important and near-operational activities to be manned. Geographical sections dealing with Germany, Italy, Japan and the United States needed to expand. A section for prisoner-of-war interrogation had to be formed. The Assistant Director's (ADNI) organization*for supervising the security of the Fleet had to go on a war footing. All RN personnel, whether at sea or on land, officers, petty officers and ratings, men and women, had to be informed at their different levels about the progress of the war. It had been Godfrey's experience in 1914–18 that information collected was not efficiently pumped out to those who needed it. Officers and ship's companies, especially abroad, were starved of news of the war's progress. But if this were to be put right in Hitler's War, certain difficulties had to be overcome. Information had not only to reach its destination speedily but under proper security conditions; the more valuable the information and its source, the more care had to be taken over the form of its distribution. So with much labour and lobbying during the

64

spring of 1939 the Secretary of the Admiralty's approval for an Information section (NID 19) was secured.

The idea of providing the Fleet with a well-informed candid account of political and military happenings was not without risks. It was liable to be read by the wrong people. The weekly Summary of Naval and Political News (SNPN) was mildly confidential and intended for commissioned, subordinate and warrant officers and attachés. Through the last-named it became known to the foreign officers who visited our missions abroad, and so a copy of SNPN containing a frank account of the difficulties and precarious situation of M. Daladier, the French Prime Minister, reached his desk in the spring of 1940. The British Ambassador, paying a courtesy call, found himself confronted with the offending article which the Prime Minister produced from a drawer of his desk with words and gestures of considerable irritation.

Within a few weeks French resistance to the Germans collapsed and the incident was forgotten; but the time between was filled for DNI 'with the poisonous dust of acrimony'. He found himself being rebuked by a Foreign Office Counsellor, then by the head of the Foreign Office, Cadogan, and finally by the Prime Minister via Dudley Pound. 'They were all', writes Godfrey in his private memoirs, 'determined to have DNI's guts for a necktie', using a favourite expression of *Britannia* cadets in 1903.

In spite of this reverse, NID 19 persisted in its admirable effort to keep the Fleet informed and produced a new, smaller and highly professional periodical called Weekly Intelligence Report (WIR) which would fit into the pocket of a naval monkey jacket. The colour of this authoritative and reliable weekly was different for each issue and it was hoped that in the welter of changing shades the identity of the old SNPN would be forgotten. Meanwhile it was necessary, if the facts of life were to be told to the Royal Navy, that naval attachés should be told that the old periodical no longer existed.

It is not easy to find out for certain whether the Fleet properly understood or welcomed the great effort made in the Naval Intelligence Division to keep officers and men informed of what was going on in the world. Certainly the more thoughtful of them appreciated it. If nothing had been done from the beginning, they would perhaps have realized what was being done. The quality and regularity of what was provided by the Information Section may have been too much taken for granted.

Credit for recognizing and anticipating this future demand goes without qualification to Godfrey himself. As in other branches of his work, he was drawing on memories of what it was like to be a young officer at the heart of naval affairs in 1916. The BBC news broadcasting service apart, the information problem would be much what it was then. Ships' companies and their officers would not see a British newspaper for weeks at a time; the newspapers they saw were under censorship and limited in size and could not give all the background that an officer needed to form his judgement or inform his men. The balanced view of our successes and failures – where was that to come from? What was the true state of affairs in occupied Europe? Why were the Russians so unco-operative whenever they met British units? How far were the war aims of the allies changing?

Hence the demand was for something between an intelligence summary and a newsletter, for a fair, well-informed and confidential view of the world at war and how the British interest in it was faring, recounted in a way that would be private to the British. Then there was the demand for facts about the enemy and discussion of the latest intelligence about his U-boat losses and new building, about the location of his main units, about weapons and tactics. There must be air photographs, too, of his bases showing how much we knew and could find out, and occasional contributions of good quality about actions on land; the tracking and sinking of a U-boat by a Coastal Command aircraft, a pioneer flight across Africa from west to east by the new air route to the Middle East, the spirit in which the Maltese faced the great bombings by the Luftwaffe, the dangerous coastal operations by which the Eighth Army was kept supplied in Libya. Material of this kind, well presented week after week in the Weekly Intelligence Report, must have given many officers and officials some pattern into which to fit their own isolated experiences, some fund of knowledge from which to answer the questions they might be asked by their men, one might even say a *raison d'être* for the fighting man.

66

Those who did this work were very proud that the highest civilian standard might be applied to what was a Service operation. The writer William Plomer has depicted for this book what the civilian doing such work felt like, in touch with all that was most secret while not being of it.

A civilian officer on the Naval Staff recruitment had a phantasmal unreality, like a horse-marine, but the ambiguity of his position had its advantages. Wearing no uniform he was able to maintain a degree of independence, and perhaps more tolerance than a certain major of Marines who had been heard under the Admiralty roof to declare that he couldn't stand civilians or understand them either. (One much hoped that his mother, for instance, had avoided the stigma of being civil rather than military.)

We civilians in the Information Section had been taken on, I suppose, because we were thought fairly responsible and articulate. It would be pleasant to believe that the supposition made up a little for our inevitable ignorance of naval technicalities. Whatever our failings, we were almost priggishly conscientious, perhaps at times even more conscientious, about security for example, than some persons in uniform. In conversation one or other of our naval superiors would occasionally give us a quizzical look, as if wondering whether the NID could be kept afloat with such a crew; but, for better or worse, we were all in the same boat together, and they never treated us with the least asperity or discourtesy.

I spent most of the War in a series of small enclosed spaces, more suitable for submariners than claustrophobes, with Marjorie Napier, a still youthful veteran of the previous World War, with Simon Nowell-Smith and later Dudley Massey. I seize this chance of saying what a pleasure and privilege it was to be with them and to learn the extent of their patience and amiability, qualities conspicuous elsewhere in NID. As everybody knows, living and working in London, especially with some inside knowledge from day to day or from hour to hour of the War and its more menacing possibilities, was no picnic, but good temper and good manners in the NID made it much more like one than it would otherwise have been. The German paranoiac who had put us all to such trouble might have procured the deaths but one couldn't imagine his weakening the morale of, say, Cicely Stanhope or Walter Meade, or of Commander Lister-Kaye, who presided over our little cell with unruffled fatherliness and urbanity.

The function of our Section was to learn all we could, from all available sources, about political and economic developments

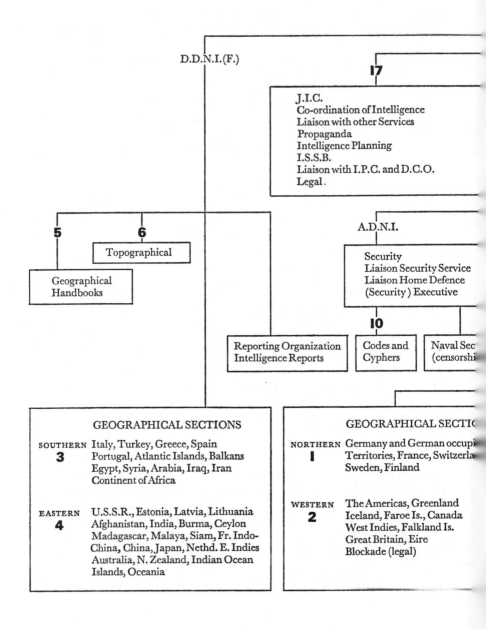

D.D.N.I.(F.)

17

J.I.C.
Co-ordination of Intelligence
Liaison with other Services
Propaganda
Intelligence Planning
I.S.S.B.
Liaison with I.P.C. and D.C.O.
Legal.

5

6

Topographical

Geographical
Handbooks

A.D.N.I.

Security
Liaison Security Service
Liaison Home Defence
(Security) Executive

10

Reporting Organization
Intelligence Reports

Codes and
Cyphers

Naval Sec
(censorshi

GEOGRAPHICAL SECTIONS

SOUTHERN **3** Italy, Turkey, Greece, Spain
Portugal, Atlantic Islands, Balkans
Egypt, Syria, Arabia, Iraq, Iran
Continent of Africa

EASTERN **4** U.S.S.R., Estonia, Latvia, Lithuania
Afghanistan, India, Burma, Ceylon
Madagascar, Malaya, Siam, Fr. Indo-
China, China, Japan, Nethd. E. Indies
Australia, N. Zealand, Indian Ocean
Islands, Oceania

GEOGRAPHICAL SECTI(

NORTHERN **1** Germany and German occupi
Territories, France, Switzerla
Sweden, Finland

WESTERN **2** The Americas, Greenland
Iceland, Faroe Is., Canada
West Indies, Falkland Is.
Great Britain, Eire
Blockade (legal)

ORGANIZATION OF NAVAL INTELLIGENCE DIVISION

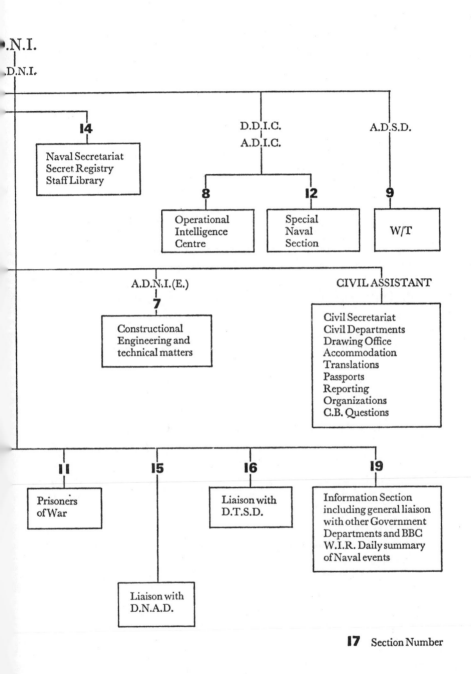

.N.I.

D.N.I.

14
Naval Secretariat
Secret Registry
Staff Library

D.D.I.C.
A.D.I.C.

A.D.S.D.

8
Operational
Intelligence
Centre

12
Special
Naval
Section

9
W/T

A.D.N.I.(E.)

7
Constructional
Engineering and
technical matters

CIVIL ASSISTANT

Civil Secretariat
Civil Departments
Drawing Office
Accommodation
Translations
Passports
Reporting
Organizations
C.B. Questions

11
Prisoners
of War

15

16
Liaison with
D.T.S.D.

19
Information Section
including general liaison
with other Government
Departments and BBC
W.I.R. Daily summary
of Naval events

Liaison with
D.N.A.D.

17 Section Number

throughout the world; to condense it; then, with the help of persons with special knowledge and qualifications, to estimate its truth, value and implications; and finally to get the information we had collected into print, in a form and style useful to naval officers. What we hoped was that, by doing something to dispel fogs of ignorance and uncertainty, we should be helping them to know better what the enemy was up to and his good and bad fortunes, as well as those of our allies and of neutral nations, and in general to improve visibility.

I learned anew, every day, that in the processing of official information several heads are as a rule better than one. And in looking back over the five-and-a-half years I spent in NID I feel it was no loss to me as a writer to have a great deal of practice not only in composing plain English but in extracting from masses of various papers their gist, drift or main points – an exercise with which, before and since those days, my life has been much occupied.

In order to maintain the candour and high standard of the Report, great care had to be taken to see that copies did not leak in the wrong directions. It was distributed without inhibition to the Americans but to no one else. Persistent efforts were made by the Soviet Mission in London to get hold of copies; they seemed uncertain of what it contained but they phrased their requests for weekly summaries so as to bring it within the scope of DNI's promise to give more information.

NID was resolved that this valuable production must not be emasculated to please our Soviet allies, who would certainly have protested at some of the judgements and analyses contained in WIR. Experience had shown that however much the British missions in Moscow and North Russia adjusted themselves to Soviet susceptibilities, there would have been a stream of complaints and minor acts of retaliation. A solution was found by giving Weekly Naval Notes, which already went to all embassies, to the Russians who then dropped their inquiries about WIR.

Even so difficulties were sometimes run into with senior officers who took exception to some remark or fact printed in WIR, a sunk U-boat claim disputed, an operational report questioned in detail, political or topographical information challenged. When the *Prince of Wales* was sunk off the coast of Malaya after having been hit by six Japanese torpedoes, the fact was so recorded in WIR and somehow found its way into the notice-board version of the Report which could be read by ships' companies. As the ship had been constructed to withstand a dozen torpedoes, it was read firstly as an affront to the Controller and Naval Constructors and secondly as a threat to the morale of her sister ship the *King George V*. A personal and incredulous call from Admiral Tovey, C-in-C Home Fleet, who had seen the offending version ashore at Scapa was the first that Godfrey knew of the matter. The point was conceded and the notice went no further.

There had been some difficulty in convincing the Board of the need to have an Information Section. Men at the top, who can see everything they wish and ask questions anywhere, will always underrate the difficulty for those lower down of seeing the wood for the trees. From WIR the junior naval officer who wanted to know in his minesweeper or overseas station how the war as a whole was going, if only to be able occasionally to explain things to the men under him, could get the kind of survey and detail that no newspaper would have been allowed to publish. Likewise in the BBC (with its vast propaganda operations to enemies and occupied territories), in Whitehall departments, in the offices of friendly attachés, this weekly survey of the war at sea kept the eyes of VIPs on naval essentials. Thus a great deal of useful and important, if not highly secret, intelligence was spread abroad in a reliable, readable and retainable form. There was a moment when Hilary Saunders and Charles Morgan, the co-editors, wanted to brighten up their weekly with a few illustrations, jokes, book reviews and perhaps a serial story. The 'new look' pleased the ward-rooms and the captains, but the admirals, notably C-in-C Plymouth, were not amused – and that was that.

That security – the guarding of secrets – is part of Intelligence and that censorship, and its reverse side publicity, should therefore be controlled by a Director of Intelligence is, in principle, incontrovertible. If they are separated there will be muddle; but *a fortiori* if they are kept together under one man, he will be grossly over-burdened. Godfrey, in February 1939, was not to know this. He was attracted, as is every intelligent staff officer at some time in his career, by the idea of 'handling' the Press, taking editors and correspondents into his confidence,

71

seeing that they get all the information they need and hoping that in an emergency he can call on them to do something for him. It is a reasonable calculation and sometimes it works; but only if political masters and Service superiors will give the Director complete discretion. Godfrey in 1939 overrated the possibilities, and the story of what happened contains much of the essence of what is a perennial problem between Fleet Street and Whitehall, even today.

Traditionally the DNI had been responsible for censorship and publicity, as well as for security,* in the broader sense. When Godfrey took over, there was a move to remove the Press Section from him to the Secretary of the Admiralty and to eliminate NID as the Admiralty liaison with the Security Service. But this was resisted by Godfrey who believed that these matters all closely concerned the Chief and Deputy Chief of Naval Staff whom he represented. With a war coming on, this was not a job for permanent civil servants. The idea was dropped and the Director set about his own plan: having got to know all editors and some proprietors personally, he would gain the confidence of reporters by frank and informal press conferences and then build up a service of naval war correspondents afloat.

The disaster to the submarine *Thetis*, while undergoing her acceptance trials in peacetime, gave the Admiralty a taste of what was to be expected in war. The organization for dealing with a major naval event was shown to be inadequate and nobody was certain where lay the responsibility for getting communiqués issued and questions answered. Their Lordships took a hammering from MPs, the Press, Parliament and the public. Godfrey writes:

The public demand for information and capacity for criticism seemed to be insatiable, and for a while everybody remotely concerned had to 'drop everything' and concentrate not so much on salving the *Thetis* as on stemming the torrent of words and newsprint which threatened to drag the Admiralty from its moorings.

The episode had the effect of securing for Captain Brooking in the Press Division an adequate staff, and convinced everyone that informal press conferences should begin. To learn something of the technique, Godfrey attended two or three

briefings in the Foreign Office News Department conducted
by Charles Peake. Having consulted editors of the national
newspapers, the heads of Reuter and the Press Association and
others, Godfrey began the weekly meetings in the library or
big conference room. They lasted less than an hour, and once
war had begun directors of anti-submarine warfare, trade
operations and other divisions would attend and explain their
work. At the third of these conferences Mr Churchill appeared
and presided, more – some thought – as an old journalist than
as a First Lord.

Already sensing the time-consuming nature of this task and
its distracting effect on intelligence work, Godfrey had placed
information and the press section under the retired Rear-
Admiral Macnamara. As a senior, wise and imperturbable
character Macnamara was invaluable; but he was suddenly
snatched away to join C-in-C Nore, who felt that he needed
two or even three Chiefs of Staff. In his place Vice-Admiral
Theodore Hallett was appointed (the choice was Dudley
Pound's), a much more lively and impatient temperament,
who underrated the First Lord's intense personal interest in
handling the Press and suffered the consequences.

Hallett used to talk with the Press at the Ministry of Information on Monday afternoon. The choice of day was
dangerous, for Mr Churchill liked to do his BBC broadcast on
Wednesday, and to keep for it any cheering, colourful tit-bits
which might come up in the signals. The first time that Hallett
filched the tit-bit, he should have seen the red light, even if it
was only a twinkle. But the second slip brought a 'steady beam
of admonition' (I quote Godfrey's account) and the third 'a
pyrotechnic display':

It was more than Mr Churchill could bear. There was a lively
scene in which a deluge of wrath descended on my head. The next
morning I had to ask Hallett to see me and told him that the First
Lord was appointing him to sea and that the Press Section would
become a Press Division with a director responsible to the First
Lord.*

Sorry though Godfrey was to lose Hallett, this storm and
the decision it provoked were a blessing in disguise; for Admiral
Hallett went on to make a great reputation in charge of com-

73

bined operations training. His place as the Navy's spokesman was taken by Lieutenant-General Tripp, Royal Marines – whose khaki uniform greatly puzzled foreign correspondents at the Ministry of Information – and the tide of trouble with the Press began to turn.

Not least of DNI's troubles in these opening weeks and months of war was the insistence of the First Lord, burning with the pent-up energy of his years 'in the wilderness', that the Naval Staff should get on with planning 'Operation Catherine'. What he proposed was that the old R class battle-ships, fitted with extra armour, should make a raid into the Baltic under the very noses of the German Air Force. The assumption, surprising in the light of Spanish Civil War experiences, was that the anti-aircraft guns of the fleet would cope with bombing and dive-bombing attack without assistance from fighters. Believing as they did that the proposal was utterly unrealistic, the Director of Plans (first Danckwerts and then Daniel) fought hard against the Prime Minister, but without real support from Pound. In this dispute DNI had to offer his advice; indeed, he had to give up the entire services of his deputy for the planning of 'Catherine' just when he needed him most.

But there remained in addition to this most delicate security task the Director's general responsibility for security, which he exercised through a special deputy and Staff. Once war began DNI had found himself dealing with some unfamiliar security matters: ensuring that MI 5 was not too hard on high-grade technicians with rather pink political antecedents whom the Navy wanted to recruit; indiscretions by officers of all ranks, including one of the heroes of the First War; sabotage in ships and naval establishments. (By July 1940 thirty-one cases had been reported in ships, forty in factories and twelve in establishments working for the Navy, but only seven of them were established as true sabotage 'in the interests of the enemy'.) Whenever the Security Service had a case against a naval person it was DNI's job to put its proposals to the Board of Admiralty and see that they were carried out if approved. Dangerous talk or gossip was always a major worry. In June 1940 Godfrey felt obliged to circulate to sixty-five addresses in the Admiralty the following rebuke:

In the course of investigations during the last three months, the Security Board has been impressed with the large number of individuals who have been informed, or have acquired knowledge of, impending secret operations, and by the deplorable amount of irresponsible chatter that goes on about most secret matters. The elementary rule, to inform no one unless his ignorance might cause a breakdown, is often not observed.

4 The wireless war

Before considering some of the operations in which NID was
to find itself involved, we must examine the nature of the
'wireless war' that began on 3 September 1939 and the working of the U-boat tracking room.
The battle of wits by wireless which was fought for six years in
the Atlantic and other oceans began, curiously, in the Red Sea
in 1936. Just as the Spanish Civil War was used by the
Germans and Italians and Russians to try out and study the
effects of dive-bombing, new infantry tactics and the latest
ammunition, so the Italian attack on Abyssinia offered the
cryptanalysts of the German B Dienst their first bite at the
signal systems used by the British Fleet. It is no exaggeration
to say that the Admiralty's preparations to execute sanctions
against Mussolini – that is to say the British Government's
preparations, however half-hearted, to do its duty to the
League of Nations – led directly to a state of affairs three years
later in which the Royal Navy and the Merchant Service
began the war against Hitler under the most grievous disadvantage. For much of what their warships and convoys
planned to do – their routes, their positions, their departure
and arrival times, their changes of mind – was read by the
B Dienst, studied and collated by German Naval Intelligence
and passed to operational headquarters for U-boats, surface
raiders and long-range aircraft to direct their attacks. True,
this tragic and shocking failure of signal security had been
completely overcome by the summer of 1943; but for nearly
four critical years Admiral Doenitz reaped a rich harvest of
sunken supply ships – 11½ million tons in the North Atlantic

alone, to say nothing of the humiliations and losses of the Norway campaign of 1940, and other episodes.

How did this happen? Between October 1935 and June 1936 a squadron of the Mediterranean Fleet based on Aden kept watch on the Red Sea and the Italian preparations for invading Abyssinia. Being virtually on a war footing, the ships had ceased signalling to C-in-C Mediterranean at Alexandria in plain language and had begun using the codes and ciphers that would be available to the whole Navy in wartime. Gathered in a limited area, for an obvious purpose, their ships' names easily found out by agents ashore (or even from the London Press) producing a daily flow of material for interception and study, they offered a cryptanalyst's feast. Call-signs were easily identified; key words and phrases regularly repeated. A Paymaster Lieutenant-Commander sent down from Alexandria to Aden to help in the organization of base supplies was switched onto the job of clearing up the chaos into which ciphering and deciphering had fallen under the unfamiliar pressure of security rules long unpractised. But then, as later, codes and ciphers were so little changed – and change at frequent intervals is the first rule for protecting code and cipher against the cryptanalyst – that telegraphists and officers knew portions of them off by heart. 'To this day after thirty years I can remember them,' said one officer to the author: '7761 equals new paragraph; 4834 equals full stop.'* Repetition, which had sunk these clues into their minds, had sunk them also into the files of future enemies, as the Lieutenant-Commander was to see for himself in 1945, when he studied the German records.

It was just about this time, in the middle Thirties, that the Americans were giving up hand-made ciphers for machines which offered complete security against anything but the most elaborate electronic analysis; and it will be a crucial task for the naval historian of the Thirties to find out precisely why, and with what degree of care and thought, the Naval Staff of those days rejected a similar change for the Fleet. The soldiers and airmen had already begun experiments with a Type X machine of British invention; indeed, it was in limited production for the RAF by 1937. But it was nobody's business in those days to ensure that all three Services should pool their technical ideas, or use uniform wireless equipment, or indeed join together in protecting their signals from enemy scrutiny. Our own code and cipher makers had been, it is true, under a form of overall control and which took account of the needs of all Service Ministries; but it seems probable – and it is highly understandable – that they were less interested in their defensive duties than in their attack on the signal security of other nations. Miracles of cryptanalysis had, after all, been achieved against the Germans in the First World War (largely under the control of the Director of Naval Intelligence) and there was a reputation to be kept up.

Be that as it may, the impression one has is that signal security was considered by many senior officers as an aspect of defence neither important nor interesting. Lord Mountbatten, himself a distinguished signal officer and innovator in these matters, tells the story of his attempt in 1936 to change the Admiralty's mind. He was then a Commander in the Naval Air Division. He tried to interest other divisions, both by formal representations and by informal talk, in the idea that the Admiralty security methods were certainly obsolescent and probably unsafe. He did not suspect leakage on any large scale at the time, but he was thinking of the war that probably must come within five years. Getting nowhere 'through the usual channels', he decided to tackle the Controller of the Navy, Admiral Henderson, privately. One week-end in Sussex, after long argument, Mountbatten convinced his senior officer that the Americans were forging ahead with their cipher machines, that the Admiralty should overhaul its own signals policy, and that the best way to start would be to buy four or five of the Type X machines with which the RAF were experimenting. The Controller did this, and ordered that the machines should be tried out at sea; but he was soon told from all quarters that they were unworkable in bad weather, that they might break down, that they were too complicated and so on. Mountbatten is now convinced that the experiment was the victim of sabotage. That old, disastrous conservatism of the Admiralty in technical matters had reasserted itself and no real progress was made. Little wonder that the Americans, when they came into the war five years later, were embarrassed and annoyed at the systems which the British

78

proposed to share with them ('slow, old fashioned and dangerous', said an American staff officer to one of DNI's emissaries). None the less the British cipher in question was accepted as safe even if it was cumbrous.

In fairness to their Lordships, it must be said that few of the senior officers of that time had seen with their own eyes the havoc that cryptanalysts could play with the secrecy and safety of a Fleet. The methods and results of Room 40's work in the first war against the Germans had been known to only a few; here and there a senior naval officer would wonder whether the same could be done again if there were another war – but all this work was no longer under exclusively naval control. Moreover, there was a general feeling that if, during an operation, wireless silence were maintained by ships at sea, then most of what could be done to cheat the enemy and his 'Y' stations would have been done. When Godfrey took over as DNI in 1939 one Signals officer of his own seniority contested the need for an operational intelligence staff with this very argument; that the Germans and Italians would keep wireless silence in wartime and that would be the end of all plans for D/F fixes, plots and so on. These attitudes now seem stupid, if not purblind; but when one hears intelligent laymen still scoffing in the Sixties at the intelligence uses of satellites circulating and televising in space, one understands the attitude.

Once war began, it changed. Coding and ciphering, decoding and deciphering, became part of the day's and the night's work in hundreds of British warships and merchant ships all over the world. Failure of security could now mean death and disaster, not merely reprimand, at the end of an exercise. It was not a question whether the enemy was or was not listening and intercepting – he was quite certainly doing so. When submarines were sent (like the *Seal*) into dangerous waters where they might be sunk and salvaged or crippled and boarded, NID had to make sure that they took as few confidential books with them as possible, and that the ciphers they used for communicating with base could be instantly withdrawn if enemy action should compromise them. In April 1940, after being crippled and beached on the south shore of Ofotfjord in the famous destroyer battle of Narvik, the destroyer *Hardy*

D

was known to have been boarded by the Germans. In a fever of anxiety – this was not the first case of its kind they had to deal with* – NID 10, the section responsible for signal security, caused long and painful dislocation to naval communications by the orders it caused to be sent out, for it had to assume that a full set of flotilla leader's codes and ciphers had been seized and were now in the possession of the B Dienst. The German Naval Archives show no sign that a 'pinch', as it is called, was in fact made; but in the Admiralty of 1940 the only safe course was to assume that they had. Incidentally, the measures taken on this occasion caused the B Dienst their first serious in-convenience since the outbreak of war: but on this as on other occasions hundreds of British ships at home and abroad had to be supplied by courier with thousands of fresh code and cipher books in order to perplex and frustrate – if only for a matter of days or weeks – Kapitän zur See Kupfer and his fifty odd back-room men in Berlin.

NID was well aware that British low-grade ciphers were likely to be broken, just as they were knowingly broken on both sides in land and air operations. Where action is urgent, where the situation is a tactical rather than a strategic one, where many recipients in lower headquarters are involved, attempts to enforce high-grade signal security are not practic-able. Consequently the overhearing and recording of barely disguised conversations and orders whether in merchant ships, or tanks, or aircraft, was taken for granted and allowance made for it. One danger to be constantly guarded against was that subordinate commands might pass on in low-grade cipher operational or intelligence information of a top secret kind that had reached them in high grade forms. This kind of error might enable any cryptographic service with sufficient man-power to work back over a period of time from the low-grade to the high-grade material with disastrous results to the latter. This happened on both sides during the war and the Admiralty cannot fairly be blamed for risking this margin of error; although when the great operations after 1942 took place, in which surprise was essential and enormous masses of ships and men were exposed to enemy attack, even this pardonable security risk seems to have been eliminated by a tremendous tightening up of procedures and techniques.* So successful was it that the Germans were as surprised as they were baffled.

From early 1940 the staff of NID 10 became increasingly aware that the tools they had inherited were quite inadequate for the job. They were not themselves cryptographers – to make and break codes and ciphers was not the Navy's duty – but they could, with the help of their colleagues in Operations and Intelligence look for and analyse episodes which suggested that the Germans had knowledge of British movements and intentions which could not have come to them through air reconnaissance or sightings at sea. Obviously, those in charge of the U-boat and other operations of the Kriegsmarine would take the utmost trouble to avoid flaunting such advance knowledge; none the less coincidences accumulated. The arrival of a U-boat, capable of only six knots, on the course of an independently routed fast ship doing fifteen knots, and which had kept wireless silence since leaving port; an attack by aircraft on Home Fleet cruisers in circumstances which had made their previous detection by air reconnaissance un-likely; a huge concentration of U-boats waiting in the path of a specially well-escorted convoy – this was the kind of co-incidence which set NID officers wondering time and again what was happening. The temptation to believe in coincidence rather than carelessness was strong. No clue, so far as the author has been able to find out, ever came through prisoner-of-war interrogation, the source most likely to reveal the German naval officer's pride in his intelligence sources; nor was anything found, until very late in the war, from captured documents. The activity of the B Dienst was as secret as it was brilliant.

Quite apart from the constant discussions of this risk that went on in Signals Divisions and OIC, there was the occasional officer with cryptographic talent who spent quiet hours on duty breaking the ciphers his battleship was using but it was the challenge of combined operations that led to rapid and spectacular improvements. New devices and ruses were found to make life more difficult for the B Dienst and for later offensive operations of the highest importance naval communications were made – as is now known from German documents – completely secure. Outstanding was the case of 'Torch', the landings in November 1942 in North Africa. If ever an operation seemed unlikely to achieve surprise it was this one. To land first 90,000 men, and later another 200,000, with all their supplies and weapons, on probably unfriendly territory, across 1,500 miles of sea from Britain and 3,000 miles from America, within easy range of German and Italian air reconnaissance from Sicily and with convoys forming up and aircraft being assembled under the eyes of the Spaniards in Gibraltar – this was possible only if the enemy were left guessing up till the last moment about the ultimate destination of these Mediterranean-bound forces. That they were there or going there could not be concealed; but what was the objective? The slightest hint could have given that vital clue away; and only complete signal security could ensure that it was not given away.*

But what was done then for 'Torch' and later on an even vaster scale for 'Neptune' in the English Channel could not yet be done in the earliest years for the whole of allied naval operations; and it is necessary now to go back in the narrative and trace the main stages in the wireless war of wits between the two navies.

The story begins with the code used by the Navy for administration – not operations – since 1934 and compromised by the Red Sea episode already mentioned. By 1938 the Germans had largely reconstructed its contents for themselves. They had, however, too few men on the job to grapple effectively with the cipher used for the Navy's operational messages and suffered a setback in August 1939, because of precautions taken by the Admiralty ten days before war was declared. Yet in the next six weeks they had made sufficient progress to be able to read a small proportion of the messages which interested them, namely those concerning North Sea and Skagerrak traffic. They knew the closely guarded secret of the use of Loch Ewe as Home Fleet base. When their big ships went out into the Atlantic and when the *Rawalpindi* was sunk in November 1939 by the *Scharnhorst*, they were able to read a number of signals dealing with the Home Fleet's counter-measures.

Much worse was to come. In the spring of 1940, the moment of Nazi triumph in Norway and later in France, work on the Navy's codes and ciphers enabled the B Dienst to learn virtually everything connected with operations in and off Norway by reading between thirty and fifty per cent of the naval traffic. Above all they could estimate accurately the correct dispositions of the Home Fleet.* Never again were they to have it so good, because in August 1940 both the administrative code and the operational cipher were changed.* This meant delay and more hard work for the B Dienst, which was now increasing its staff. Gradually it began to master the new systems, but in January 1941 there was fresh trouble for them when a change in procedure suggested by NID 10 was introduced. For four weeks the enemy read nothing; after another month back they came into the game but with nothing like their old success. Unfortunately, further changes in September 1941, designed to make things more difficult for the B Dienst, seem to have made things easier. By 1942 they were back to their highest standards and giving Doenitz and Raeder invaluable service.

It is now established from the German records that by the time the Admiralty changed its codes and ciphers U-boat headquarters were receiving from their B Service the following information, based on reading over 2,000 messages a month.

(a) The times of arrival of Atlantic convoys in British coastal waters and distribution of ships among ports of destination. This made possible far-reaching conclusions about the timetables of convoys.
(b) Information about their escorts' successes, about attacks on U-boats and about damage to or sinking of U-boats at sea.
(c) Approach points for convoys and independently routed ships.
(d) Insight into the number of independently routed ships.
(e) Weather reports from all oceans.

Before taking the story further this point should be made: to ensure security over a broad field and to stop proven leakages was an enormous week to week, month to month, administrative task. For instance the printing of codes (which kept part of the Oxford University Press busy throughout the war) is a large scale business, and every book and table has to be distributed by courier in strict security conditions to all the ships of the fleet. This was part of the work of the Military Branch of the Admiralty (M), and to achieve wartime distribution in a matter of weeks to a fleet scattered across the seven seas is a feat of organization and timing which any criticism must take into account. To do it unnecessarily was therefore unthinkable. Indeed, members of the German B Dienst, when discussing British difficulties after the War, sympathetically referred to this very point.

None the less the story of the cipher mainly used for Atlantic convoy operations is deplorable. The traffic using it naturally grew rapidly in volume after the US began playing an active part in these operations in October 1941 and the Germans soon noted its importance. It was distinctive by its call signs and was used almost exclusively for convoy escorts. The B Dienst called it the Convoy Cipher. By February 1942 they had made very substantial progress in their reading; the greater proportion of signals yielded their secrets 'after the briefest of intervals' and not only in the North Atlantic. Between this date and June 1943, when this fatal system was dropped and another which the Germans were never able to break introduced, they read regularly the Admiralty's widely distributed daily U-boat disposition signal, which gave them some insight into what the submarine tracking room in the OIC were thinking of Doenitz's plan and possibilities. Fortunately, there was a more detailed and secret series of signals from the Admiralty which reached those who needed them in a cipher system which the B Dienst could never break. These special ciphers were brought in for Admiralty signals to and from Commander-in-Chief Home Fleet and Commander-in-Chief Western Approaches, and were immediately and finally effective.

Meanwhile another cipher, also used in the Battle of the Atlantic, had succumbed to the brilliant team in Berlin. By October 1942 they had reconstructed most of it and were reading convoy traffic so quickly that Doenitz sometimes had information ten to twenty hours in advance of movement. What was gleaned here was supplemented by the much easier reading of routine signals from Western Approaches and Halifax, and unfortunately the Merchant Ships' Code. This last was a typical victim of the Government parsimony and the mood of 'no more war' which ensured that our great merchant fleet faced the U-boat campaign with no sure method of concealing its communications.

Nor was that the end of the intelligence which reached Doenitz and his U-boats from this source. Until June 1942, there had been no special inter-service cipher available for combined operations like Norway and later Dieppe and St Nazaire. Instead a cipher system linking the Services posts and Foreign Office, Dominions Office and Colonial Office was used. The Germans got quickly into this and, as it was used by consular offices for reporting shipping movements from neutral ports, they learned from it routes of independently routed ships (not in convoy) and some details of the Navy's measures against their armed merchant raiders. In July 1941, this fortunately became suspect in Whitehall and a new system which was used only by naval authorities ashore was introduced with some success.

In fairness, it must be stressed that the success of the B Dienst against the Royal Navy's tactical code was very variable, since it depended on how much traffic from an operation they could obtain for study within a reasonable period and between changes of cipher. Thus they seldom, if ever, gained *advance* operational information about warships. In the 'Torch' landings of November 1942, a special edition of this code defeated them completely; and during the Home Fleet operations leading to the surprise and sinking of the *Scharnhorst* off Norway in December 1943, they read nothing.* Some thirty Home Fleet signals were intercepted but, although the code was in its last few days of use, not one was unravelled. As late as 10 January 1944 they were still trying to unravel the mystery but without success. Another notable example of success was in the Anzio landings of January 1944, when a special edition again defeated the B Dienst which intercepted 158 signals, but were not able to achieve a break.

By the closing stages of the war, however, the Germans were doing better with the tactical code. This was perhaps due to the greatly intensified surface and air effort in the Atlantic battle with consequent increased number of contacts with U-boats. Many more tactical messages were passed which enabled the Germans to obtain valuable intelligence about anti-U-boat operations and coastal convoys from the 1,500 signals a month which they claim to have been reading, a figure which our experts find astonishingly high. But in the summer of 1944 another valuable source of German intelligence on convoy routes was stopped by the introduction of a new and improved cipher for communication with ships in convoy. This defied all efforts of the Germans to break it.

How this kind of intercepted wireless intelligence (by NID graded A1) was used and its value to Doenitz and his Commanders is best studied in the specific instance of convoys HX229 and SC122 which fought a prolonged battle with a huge pack of U-boats from 16 to 19 March 1943, just before the tide of the Atlantic battle turned in the Allies' favour. Up to the first day of the attack, U-boat headquarters had been able to read sixteen signals giving advance information of the movements of both convoys. Notable among them were the messages at 22.10 on 4 March giving ocean routes and stragglers' orders for HX229, and a signal from Halifax at 19.32 on 13 March giving diversion orders for both convoys based on the Admiralty OIC's estimate of U-boat whereabouts. This action, in which forty U-boats assembled from far and wide on instructions from their well-briefed headquarters, lost us twenty-one ships of 140,000 tons and the enemy only one U-boat. It was, says the British official naval history, 'a serious disaster to the allied cause'.* Indeed, Captain Roskill in that chapter of his book quotes the British Naval Staff as writing that 'the Germans never came so near to disrupting communications between the New World and the Old as in the first twenty days of March 1943'.

If that period of mortal crisis changed with amazing speed into the triumphant counter-offensive which by June had driven the U-boats off the North Atlantic trade routes, it was due not least to the failure from this time onwards of the B Dienst to give the intelligence service the U-boats had come to expect; and it was precisely in the month of June that the new system which solved the Navy's problems was introduced. The Admiralty's steadily improving precautions had had their effect. According to Doenitz, his acceptance of the defeat of his U-boats in the Atlantic dates from 24 May when 'I ordered them to proceed, using the utmost caution, to the area southwest of the Azores'. His monthly rate of losses as a percentage of boats at sea was climbing steeply, from 3·9% in the first half of 1942 to 9·2% in the first quarter of 1943.

Doenitz, unlike other Commanders of the Second World War has not concealed or minimized his tremendous debt to A1 intelligence, especially in view of the Luftwaffe's failure to give adequate long-range air reconnaissance. He writes in his memoirs:*

I have had repeated occasion to mention the remarkable work done by the German B-Service, our cryptographic section, which time and again succeeded in breaking enemy ciphers. As a result U-boat Command received not only the British signals and routing instructions sent to convoys, but also in January and February 1943 the British U-boat Situation Report, which was transmitted to Commanders of convoys at sea and which gave the known and presumed distributions of U-boats in the different areas.

These reports, Doenitz goes on to point out, were of great value to him in the effort to find out what British Naval Intelligence – that is to say the OIC – knew about his own dispositions and what degree of accuracy they could attain. That is to say, the Admiralty signals to the Fleet containing the intelligence resulting from the brainwork of NID were used by the Germans to check the security of the U-boat Command's own signals system. Directed as every U-boat in the Atlantic was from a central point on land, using as Doenitz was, tactics of concentrated attack based on reports from his boats, his operations room ran every hour of the day the risk that its wireless traffic, with its lavish and regular patterns of behaviour, might be as valuable to the British as British signals had been to them. Amid their brilliant work of offensive intelligence, his small staff of six officers kept a constant defensive watch on British movements, whether by escort vessels or support groups or by convoys being diverted from a waiting pack or by escorting aircraft. They were watching for any sign of British foreknowledge of German whereabouts that could not be explained simply by first-rate HF/DF intelligence and air reconnaissance, or by the calculations and guesses of NID's experienced staff keeping day and night watch on the North Atlantic plot.

This watch convinced the German staff that their cryptographers had beaten the British cryptanalysts and were as good at devising safe codes and ciphers as they were at breaking them. On this subject Doenitz is worth quoting at length:

Except for two or three doubtful cases British conclusions are based on data regarding U-boats which are readily available to them, on U-boat positions and on their own plotting of the boats' movements, combined with a quite feasible process of logical deduction. The most important result that has emerged from our investigation is the all-but-certain proof that, with the assistance of his air-borne radar, the enemy is able to discover U-boat dispositions with sufficient accuracy to enable his convoys to take evasive action.

That was written in 1944 when the U-boats had been mastered. In 1941 his staff, less successful then than they were later with their reading of the British traffic, were less certain about their own security: referring to the period around 1941 Doenitz writes:

Whether and to what extent the enemy reacted to radio transmissions was something which, try as we might, we were never able to ascertain with any certainty. In a number of cases drastic alterations in the course of the convoy led us to assume that he did. On the other hand, many cases occurred in which, in spite of U-boat radio activity in the area, enemy ships sailing independently, and convoys as well, were allowed to sail straight on into the same area in which only shortly before sinkings and even convoy battles had taken place.

Later in the war, when its own attack on British signals was faring badly, the B Dienst became more worried about its defences. Smarting under the complete failure to anticipate where the allied attack of June 1944 on France would fall, they naturally became more conscious of the possibility of an enemy success against their own signal systems, which had so far been more up-to-date and mechanized than the British. Moreover, the U-boat crews were becoming disturbed by their heavy losses. We can read in the German archives the following admission by B Dienst in July 1944, a month after the Normandy landings:

The present situation is characterized by disquiet in the U-boat command resulting from the course of operations, but without there being any special evidence of insufficient cipher security. . . . The cases of betrayal which have hitherto occurred and been discussed in the Navy have not been concerned with the main cipher methods.

Indeed, a description of the immense success achieved by the Allies with HF/DF ends with an almost cocksure declaration of confidence in themselves: 'The fundamental limit of successful cryptographic activity has been reached.' Considering that this extensive inquiry into naval signal security had been conducted under the chairmanship of a naval signals specialist, the boast is not surprising. It is always difficult for experts to prove themselves wrong.

Another factor comes into the causes of this confidence. The Germans always lagged behind in the development of radar and tended to credit British ships and aircraft with limitless powers of long-range detection. Likewise, their Navy was denied by a jealous Goering anything like our own fully developed Coastal Command, carrying out Admiralty requirements.*

The most important result that emerged from this investigation is the all-but-certain proof that Doenitz's staff overrated what air photography and reconnaissance could do. For all these reasons they were loth to believe that the British – or the Americans – had at any time broken into their signals traffic on any serious scale. They retained confidence in the Enigma machine, which was used throughout their Navy and took great pains with their changes of ciphers: minor ones each day and bigger ones over longer periods as a double check. Thus it was that the NID, from March 1942 to early 1943, knew nothing from this source about the Atlantic U-boats. It is no coincidence that this was the worst period of the whole campaign.*

Lastly, it has to be remembered that the Navy, virtually immune though it was from Nazi party control or influence, shared the obsessions of the day. Germany lived under a régime in which treachery and disloyalty were more dreaded than error or inefficiency. Its military intelligence service under Admiral Canaris (who turned out in 1944 to have been a long-

89

standing opponent of Hitler) was spotted with intrigue and personal rivalry. There were at least four rival intelligence systems. The result was that the work of the Naval branch of the B Service was surrounded (as it was in Britain) with the greatest secrecy and any errors it might make or be blamed for were attributed to treachery after investigations in which no one outside Naval operations and intelligence was allowed to take part.

Doenitz (pp. 326–8) declares:

That a widespread spy network was at work in our bases in occupied France was something we obviously had to assume. An efficient enemy intelligence service must in any case have been able to ascertain the distribution of U-boats among the various bases, the dates of their sailing and return to port, and possibly also the sea areas allotted to boats proceeding on operations.

Here is revealed that deep respect for the British Secret Service and Naval Intelligence (no clear distinction was made by Germans between them) which the German Navy had inherited from the first war and from the deep study of its lessons made by their naval staff. In fact, it was not until the later stages of the war that British agents' reports from U-boat bases, and especially from naval bases in Norway, were good enough to enable the OIC to track individual U-boats with their help.

There, for the historian, the matter must for the time being rest. We can be quite certain that had their archives not fallen into our hands, the Germans would have made public nothing of their success. They would have hoped that at least the cryptographic weapon – perhaps the most valuable of all to a defeated country – would escape the scrutiny of the Allied disarmament controls. (No. 30 Assault Unit created by NID found on Capri in 1944 an important secret service cipher which the Italians had failed to give up as promised under the surrender conditions they had accepted.) The post-war co-operation between friendly German staff officers and British and American historians and researchers might have led to disclosure of some of the B Dienst's secrets and thus to knowledge of our own shortcomings; but that is far from certain. In any case, it is most unlikely that British Naval Intelligence, run down as it was from four thousand persons to eighty by 1951, would have found the resources to carry out the lengthy research needed to prove by analysis and deduction what the German Archives gave up, so to speak, on a plate.

Likewise there is no reason, despite occasional hints and leakages – more of them in the United States than in Britain – why allied cryptographers should reveal just how far and by what methods they were successful.* Obviously they must have had their successes: the traditions of the first war and of Room 40 had been preserved after a fashion. The capture of books and machines from ships and U-boats provided cryptographic material which was bound to give them periods of success, even if the German machine ciphers defied their efforts over the main field and for most of the time. There was a great deal of low-grade tactical wireless traffic in the air and on land which the enemy must have realized would not escape scrutiny. German naval wireless traffic, when a special operation was preparing – whether by U-boats or battleships or small surface craft in the Channel – made patterns of activity which men and women in NID with memories and files and imagination could make sense of. Some U-boats were immensely talkative and costly errors could be made like that of the *Bismarck* (see page 158). Even in 1940 the German invasion of Norway might have been detected a day or so earlier had the warning of a young student of W/T patterns at Station X been heeded in the OIC. But it was early days yet and there was no real faith in such techniques of intelligence. That is to say, the young man was believed by the senior officer he spoke to on the telephone, but the senior officer knew he could not convince the men above him in charge of operations that the vast enterprise of sending out the Home Fleet should be set in motion on such slender evidence. Intelligence that cannot be sold to the user is, for the time being, useless.

To understand the values of the world of cryptographers working for their Defence Ministries and services, it is useful to compare them with researchers in mathematics or medicine. The latter form a genuinely non-political, international community, free and eager to exchange information and ideas through journals and institutions founded for that purpose, able from slender clues to deduce what men and women in other countries are doing or trying to do. Cryptographers, in contrast, are charged both with the preservation and the breaking of secrecy. Their researches are both offensive and defensive. Their professional sentiment has to be jealous and nationalistic. Their task is to devise the methods by which a Government can communicate secretly and quickly with its allies, its forces abroad, its diplomatic representatives, its agents and even its home departments. At the same time, they are trying to penetrate the methods used by other countries for precisely the same purposes; and one effort assists the other. Thus, if one country's cryptographers are allowed to boast of past successes at a particular date in a particular area against a particular enemy, the clues thereby released can be of current value to actual and potential enemies.

British and American knowledge of all the German crypto-graphical achievements in six years of war has been shown to have been of immense value. How, in the particular sphere of naval signals, was it gained? To gain access to the B Dienst cryptographers was one of the main targets of the NID units in the field as the allied armies advanced in the spring of 1945 towards the Baltic ports, where German naval headquarters were concentrating. Other considerations apart, it was un-desirable that the Russians should capture German experts with an extensive knowledge of the Royal Navy's signalling methods. The Soviet attitude to proposals for a three-power seizure and occupation of the German Navy's Headquarters in Berlin did not suggest very co-operative intentions. Kupfer and his men had been ordered by Doenitz to leave Berlin for Flensburg on the Baltic and to co-operate with the British and the Americans by giving all the information and help that was asked of them by the special interrogators sent over from the Admiralty. Fact by fact, document by document, the evidence accumulated that the German success against British codes and ciphers had been greater and lasted longer than was suspected. Eventually the British – and American – security measures had triumphed, notably in the great offensive combined operations of the second half of the war; but it had been a very long run.

Back in London that summer of 1945, the officer who had visited Aden nine years earlier and sensed that all was not well with the Fleet's signalling methods (see page 77) was pre-paring to leave NID 10 where he had been working since 1941.

Deeply interested by the reports reaching him from junior officers interrogating the Germans in Flensburg, he asked that his return to the Fleet should be postponed for six months while he found out from the German Naval Archives, then arriving in London, what precisely had happened in the duel between his section of NID and B Dienst: what changes and ruses devised by his colleagues had worked, how and when the Germans had got into high-grade codes and ciphers, what convoy or fleet disasters could be directly traced to the excellent German wireless intelligence, what resources it had at its disposal. He was seconded to the Signals Division for six months and settled down to a job of research, the sensational results of which have already been described.

For most of the war, it was discovered, the B Dienst numbered no more than the fifty working cipher and code breakers who turned up in Flensburg in June 1945. With more staff they could have achieved even better results, and much material was discarded. They had enjoyed the special protection of Doenitz, after he became Commander-in-Chief in 1944, otherwise they were not specially favoured. They owed very little to captured documents or machines; the odd 'pinch' they did make told them little that they did not know already. They were full of self-confidence and doubtless hoped that their co-operation would encourage similar confidences from their opposite numbers in Britain.

In five months the report was ready. Two copies were made and sent to DNI and Director of Signals Division. What happened after that is not clear. Certainly only very few in the Admiralty read the report, and it was not readily available for post-war Directors of Naval Intelligence to read as a warning of what could happen to signal security. War weariness, a change of government, the changes and reductions of NID staff were creating an atmosphere in which post-mortems roused little interest. Above all, of course, it could be claimed that the report was as much a success as a failure story. In NID 10 itself, which could not be held in any way responsible for the deplorable state of affairs that was inherited from peacetime, it was felt that they had mastered their job. Indeed, the head of the section had played a leading part since late 1944 in setting up, under Cabinet authority, a central organization which

93

would ensure that all Government departments – not merely Services – would have secure cipher systems in future.

The layman may permit himself two comments. First, it seems likely that the reorganization of 1922, which removed all cipher matters from Service to civilian control, did not pin responsibility for security of ciphers clearly enough in one place. So far as naval communications were concerned, it was clearly the duty of Admiralty Signals Division to provide quick, clear and efficient methods, and of the Intelligence Division to watch over the security of confidential books, the keeping of wireless silence during operations, and the skilful management of wireless traffic in order not to give away the time and direction of ship movements. But both divisions were entitled to assume that the codes and ciphers given to them in the first place were up-to-date, technically as good as they could be, and proof against enemy scrutiny. Indeed, it is hard to understand why, in the stormy years between the Spanish Civil War and the invasion of Poland, there was not set up by Whitehall a small cryptanalysis unit to test the Fleet's security and demonstrate to officers what signal behaviour at sea could reveal to an inquisitive and hostile 'Y' service.

It has been shown how the Air Ministry took the initiative in trying out a machine cipher and how efforts were made to interest the Admiralty in it; also how the Americans as late as 1941 were surprised and irritated at being asked to share what they regarded as obsolete methods. The Navy had been warned; and the pre-war Admiralty must take some of the blame for the loss of hundreds of ships and the failure of a dozen operational plans.

A possible explanation may be that the Navy's use of grossly inadequate cipher systems for so long after war had started resulted from the lack of proper co-operation between the Admiralty and our own cryptographers who, we must assume, were engaged in attempting to break the ciphers of the enemy and so could surely have devised secure ciphers for our own use. Perhaps the security which rightly covers this kind of work was so strict that the right hand did not know what the left was doing – and our own interest suffered in consequence.

This chapter has dealt so far only with the most sensitive and secret aspect of the wireless war; the effort of each side to

94

intercept and read in their entirety the most important operational signals of the other – the *summum bonum* of all intelligence work. But there is another branch of this craft, no less fascinating but far less secret, with which NID 10 achieved some brilliant defensive results. It is the systematic study of wireless traffic from important centres such as a base like Scapa Flow, a headquarters like Western Approaches or the Mediterranean Fleet in Alexandria to see what patterns are created by the intention to go to sea, to receive returning ships, to organize air reconnaissance and so on.

For example, operations initiated by the navy of Heartland cause a rise in the number of long and high-priority signals in naval cipher which will be observed by Fringeland which is plotting all signals intercepted by its 'Y' stations. Counter-moves laid on as a precaution by Fringeland will cause reactions by Heartland resulting in a rise in the number of its *short* and high-priority messages in naval cipher. In the first case Heartland is sending out detailed but not immediate orders about movements and behaviour which the enemy is supposed not to know; in the second case it is sending out brief and urgent orders to seek or elude the enemy in positions probably known to him.

Within a few days of the outbreak of war every operational signal in and out of the Admiralty was reaching NID 10 for scrutiny. The volume was at first overwhelming. To help him the head of the section had recruited a team of civilians in uniform, none of whom had any previous experience of what they were to do. 'I chose men trained in habits of analysis and of an adventurous turn of mind,' said Commander Wilson: a biologist who was an expert on the Great Barrier Reef, a geologist, a solicitor, a pharmaceutical chemist, an accountant, and the Keeper of the India Section of the Victoria and Albert Museum. They were turned straight on to studying what patterns they could find in current and past W/T traffic in the Fleet; and their first recorded success had to do with the hunt for the *Graf Spee* in the South Atlantic culminating in the Battle of the River Plate in December 1939. They showed how German Intelligence could, without great difficulty, have found out that the cruiser *Achilles* was coming round from New Zealand to join in the search. Their reasoning was as follows:

Study of traffic through the Admiralty wireless station at Rugby over a limited period showed that signals addressed to the Pacific Ocean area off the west coast of South America never contained delivery groups other than HAP or PSH and that these two never came together. This fact established that only one ship was concerned. From other messages it was possible to deduce that on 2 October the ship was in the Cape Horn area on passage from the Pacific into the South Atlantic. This followed the movement, of course known to the Germans, of a German warship in the Pernambuco area. That the ship addressed was a light cruiser could be assumed, as the Germans would know that two such units were in New Zealand when war began. As the Commander of the Squadron was in the *Leander*, which could be picked out by the characteristics peculiar to signals addressed to flagships, it would follow that the other must be the *Achilles*. This having been established as fact, the *Leander*'s delivery groups would be compromised – that is to say, they would be recognized and read if used again wherever the ship might be. Just to rub it in, the NID 10 men pointed out that before 3 October the transmissions to the *Achilles* had been less than two a day; but on 4 October there were fifteen, on 5 October eighteen, and on 10 October when she was leaving Valparaiso, twenty-two – all adding up to a clear indication of intention to move, followed by operational contact with the Admiralty.

There was no question in this case of asking whether the Germans were in fact reading and understanding what was sent to the *Achilles*; almost certainly they were not. What was being demonstrated was the amount of information that could be given away simply by 'going on the air' at a time of emergency when every signal was likely to be intercepted and plotted by the enemy. This relatively new and perplexing problem of security had to be grappled with by DNI and DSD before anything else.

In a guide to these matters for the Fleet written later, NID 10 drew attention to the varieties of information that can be quarried from a statistical or merely scholarly study of signal traffic. First of course, the frequency of waves used, which gives in the long run a clue to the identity of the ship; then the geographical location of the transmitter, which can be found by direction-finder; the methods of communication used – for example, repeated broadcasts from one station or repetition back from a second; details of delivery instructions, giving a clue to the identity of the recipient; the date and time of messages, giving clues to the ship's rate of movement and direction; priority, giving a clue to urgency; length of message, indicating a damage report, intelligence report or special instructions. The diligent filing and collation of all such facts – which is what the Germans were already doing in 1936 – could over a long period produce a most impressive body of operational intelligence.

To elaborate a little; an increase of high priority messages from a ship or a command is a sure sign of operational movements beginning. The preparations of an E-boat flotilla for night operations, for example, might be marked by an unusual number of messages alerting other ships, like minesweepers, the Air Force, adjacent naval commands and so on. The movement of a big German ship from a Norwegian fjord with its attendant escort vessels nearly always gave some opportunity to the British 'Y' stations listening eagerly for a whisper. The signal patterns from Scapa, until strict wireless discipline had been achieved, must have given the Germans ample notice of the Home Fleet's pending movements. Having been alerted to an enemy movement by its 'Y' service, the intelligence division can ask for an air or ship reconnaissance to contact the enemy. The resulting visual information of his movements, if passed quickly to the cryptographers and movements experts, will assist in making further deductions about the content of messages. It was demonstrated that operations ordered in advance by us – say a sweep by a Home Fleet squadron against German shipping along the Norwegian coast – caused a rise in the number of *long* high-priority messages in naval cipher; whereas in cases where operations were ordered in response to enemy action – say a sighting of the Italian fleet sailing to intercept a convoy in the central Mediterranean – there would be a rise in *short* high-priority messages. In other words enemy intelligence could distinguish between an operation which was initiated by the British and an operation which was a reaction to one of their own.

It is apparent that this kind of analysis without an enemy

97

to study must have been virtually impossible in peacetime, though something might have been attempted during the operations of the Mediterranean Fleet in the Nyon patrols against pirate submarines in 1937. The conditions leading to wireless betrayal could hardly be simulated in sufficient detail without actual operations against a secretive enemy. But if the Germans could be provided in peacetime with sufficient material to enable them to read much of our naval traffic in 1939, it is hard to believe that some British research could not have been organized by the responsible authorities to study in peacetime the likely patterns of wartime signal traffic.

It hardly needs to be pointed out that in the heat and press of war, the interests of Operations, Signals and Intelligence might clash. The Head of NID 10 said:

It was always in the back of my mind that the security precautions which we had to take might cause communication delays which could lead to some operational failure at sea. This alone could be serious enough, but I had the added fear that such an incident might make it even more difficult to achieve the standards of security which I knew to be so essential.

A serious failure of this kind would certainly have led to an inquiry in which gunnery officers might have had the chance to urge that the intelligence fanatics had been given too much rope – the school of thought which might be described by the phrase 'signal and be damned'.

Enough has been said to demonstrate that the work of NID 10, side by side with OIC, was among the most vitally important of the functions directed by Godfrey and Rushbrooke. The evidence of the 'turn of the tide' in the summer of 1943 is enough to show that signal security was a war-winner just as cryptanalysis looked a war-winner to the Germans up to that date. For one side the breaking of codes and ciphers was a way of saving lives, economizing in time and money, ensuring surprise at sea, achieving concentration of forces. For the other side it was a killer of convoys, the ever-lurking spy on the Home Fleet, the eavesdropper on the plans and thoughts of the Naval Staff in London. Neither side knew at any moment whether the roles were being reversed.

For a time after the war this subject was taboo with historians

98

and commentators for good reasons arising out of the cold war of those days. Since then technological progress has made many of the methods of Hitler's day obsolete or unimportant. The public has learned from the memoirs of commanders and statesmen, from spy trials and from unofficial and official narratives that interception in every form is practised by military powers – even by neutrals – against one another. Of the British official war historians Captain Roskill alone, writing in the Fifties, allowed himself to refer to the B Dienst's successes. Yet, if the history of the war were being reconsidered in the light of what could now be said, people would understand better the tremendous handicap under which the Fleet and the Merchant Navy went to war in 1939 and the narrow margin by which we escaped defeat at sea or at best stalemate. Indeed, it is important that not only the Servicemen of the future, but also the civil servants and politicians and formers of public opinion should realize how important is this branch of intelligence to the organization of peace, whether by power working against power, or by international groups. No military power can afford to neglect it, either in its offensive or defensive aspects. To share this work is the greatest sign of confidence that ally can give ally.

If British wireless intelligence recovered as well as it did against the brilliant and thorough preparation of the enemy, some credit must be given to those who fought the battle of manpower in pre-war Whitehall.

To give a fair example of the delays that might accompany preparations in that lowering summer of 1939, the author decided to investigate in detail one small but important – and at the time highly secret – piece of recruitment by Rear-Admiral Troup, Godfrey's predecessor. This was Whitehall's handling of a proposal to set up a new naval service of civilian W/T operators who would perform 'Y' duties – that is to say, watch and intercept and record foreign signals – at stations in Britain and abroad. Without a sufficient supply of reliable men, thoroughly trained in this specialized art, a branch of intelligence vital for operations could not begin to function. On their work would be based the whole system of locating and following enemy ships and submarines by HF/DF fixes

99

which was to dismay and surprise the Germans with its accuracy and scope. On it, too, depended the supply of raw material for our cryptographers and later those of the Americans. Even with thirty or more active service telegraphists from the Fleet working for them, the 'Y' stations in 1938 were undermanned – the Gibraltar station, for example, was closed owing to lack of men – and to meet future requirements more stations were being built. If war came, there would certainly be pressure to pull out from 'Y' stations and into ships at sea every telegraphist who could be extracted from the Director of Signals and the DNI, who had joint responsibility for this work.

A meeting at the Admiralty in May 1938 agreed that the best remedy would be to form an Admiralty Civilian Shore Wireless Service with a total strength of about one hundred and eighty, along the lines of the existing Air and Army Services. It was hoped by this means to release at home twenty-nine active service telegraphists and abroad – if accommodation could be found for their civilian substitutes – three PO telegraphists, nine leading telegraphists and thirty telegraphists for the Fleet.

The Admiralty's civil servants got to work at once and reported that the Air Ministry service was recruited from retiring and pensioned RAF operators only, who were paid £4 a week rising by annual increments of 2s. to £4 16s. 0d. The weakness of the precedent was that these ex-airmen had no specific obligation to serve abroad – and this the Navy would require.

When the Admiralty put up the proposal to the Treasury in early July two months had passed; four members of the Board had to see the docket on this secret and vital matter, and some ten other officers or officials in the Admiralty were consulted. Now five weeks passed before the Treasury replied. Broadly speaking, it saw nothing to object to in the idea, provided that the naval scheme was like that of the Army and Air Force. (The Treasury, in its running battle with Service departments, is naturally always watching for attempts to establish new precedents in expenditure or to modify existing ones.) So it fastened on two features of the Admiralty's letter.

First, the strength of one hundred and eighty* planned for the CSWS eventually was 'seriously out of scale' with the thirty to forty strength in the other Services. No matter of principle here, but it had to be explained that the Navy functions on a world-wide scale and that the new service would be manning station in places like Aden, Trincomalee, Stonecutter's Island in Hong Kong and Malta. What did raise questions of principle, however, was the proposal that a special allowance of 3d. a day should be paid for 'special duties in Japanese Morse'. The Admiralty argued that the Navy's active service telegraphists already received this little extra, and it seemed reasonable that the civilians working side by side with them should receive it too. It is not, after all, everybody that can get the hang of Morse handled by Japanese. No, said the Treasury – on the day that Chamberlain met Hitler in Munich – this 3d. extra might embarrass the War Office whose uniformed personnel receive no allowance of this kind. The Admiralty, presumably sensing that this was an invitation to battle on ground where it could not win, quickly decided to drop the idea. The scheme went through and the leaflet offering terms of service and inviting recruits was published early in January 1939.

It had taken eight months to put forward, discuss and take action on a most urgent and secret intelligence requirement involving at the first stage not more than a few dozen men. This tiny, but not trivial, instance of the prevailing attitudes will be recalled in a later chapter which describes the brilliant work of these stations. Godfrey had reason to be grateful to his predecessor for waging these wearisome struggles against what would be called nowadays a rearmament freeze; and also for undermining the belief in certain quarters of the Admiralty that men in plain clothes could not keep secrets as well as men in uniform.

5 In the tracking room

*'These are much deeper
waters than I had thought.'*

(Conan Doyle, *Adventures of Sherlock
Holmes:* 'The Reigate Squires')

Introduction

It fell to one of 'Blinker' Hall's men, a Paymaster Commander
who had tracked U-boats in the famous Room 40 of 1916–18,
with its running flow of decoded German signals, to launch the
tracking room (known as NID 8 (S)) on its course. Thring,
then already over sixty, re-joined in 1938 to develop and extend
the work described in Chapter 2 started by Denning, who now
devoted himself to surface ships. With invaluable experience of
an arduous and subtle art, Thring brought that staunch
scepticism which is the true virtue of the Intelligence man. He
knew how hard it was to be certain that a U-boat had been
sunk; he would snort at most of the claims sent in by escorts
and Coastal Command pilots, some of them in most colourful
language. The novelist and critic, Charles Morgan, who was a
member of NID from 1939–43, recorded his impression of
Thring at a time when his caution was under fire from another
veteran of Jellicoe's day – Churchill in the First Lord's room.

There were those who raged affectionately against him. He lay
sceptically at the centre of his web, unimpressed by oil, unpersuaded
by a corpse floating, according a reluctant 'probable' to what
others might regard as overwhelming circumstantial evidence. He
doubtfully growled over any German submarine that was not
visibly in the bag.

But it was Thring's training and advice that made it possible
in January 1941, when the strain on his health became too
great, to choose as his successor the barrister Rodger Winn.

To appoint a civilian to such a responsible post so early in the war was a daring decision, which was supported by the Director of Anti-Submarine Warfare at the time, Captain George Creasy. Creasy recalls discussing the choice with Godfrey and the relief he felt at finding that the Director shared his view that Winn was the only man for the job. They agreed that, although regular officers must supervise the work of the Operational Intelligence Centre, the best kind of civilian brain would do the job just as well, provided there were one or two skilled sailors to consult.

It was about this time – the end of 1940 – that the new technique of analysis and deduction of German movements began to show results. During the first year of war 8S, as this section was called, had been little more than a repository of accumulated information about past episodes and current movements of U-boats at sea. Its files and charts told more about the past than about the present or – most important – the future. Then one day, so the story runs, the Director of Operations Division Home (DODH), then Captain Edwards, said to Thring: 'This is all very interesting and instructive; but why not try to tell us what the enemy is going to do next week or tomorrow?' Thring was dubious about what he called guessing, but his deputy, Winn, thought this uncertain art might at least be attempted.

So the day came when Captain Edwards, standing over the charts, put the following problem to Winn. 'In this position are two very valuable tankers south-east of Newfoundland, unescorted, on a Great Circle course and bound for the North Channel. Tell me what you would do with them in the present state of U-boat dispositions?' After studying his plot for a few minutes, Winn said: 'I have a definite view to offer here. At midnight last night, from a point 200 miles east and 100 miles south of the tankers' present position, there was a long U-boat signal, more than 300 groups of it. Either that boat is homeward bound at the end of her patrol and sending in her sinking claims to U-boat H.Q., or she has suffered mechanical damage or faults which she is describing. I feel ninety per cent certain she will be bound north and the tankers should therefore be routed to the south.'

Edwards then went to Trade Division movements room and

put the proposal to the Commander in charge, who scoffed at the calculation and suggested that the tracking room should not be trying to take over Trade Division's job. But after pressure from Edwards it was decided to experiment with a compromise diversion; one tanker was ordered to take a NE course and the other SE. The next morning Edwards, having read only his incoming signals, came down to the tracking room worried and irritated, and said to the men around the plotting table: 'Well, that's the end of our precious experiment: one tanker sunk out of two.' Winn, not knowing what diversion had been ordered, asked 'But what course was she on, sir; presumably northward?' Unable to reply Edwards went next door to Trade Division, checked the Out signals and returned ten minutes later to apologize to Winn who, he admitted, had been right in his calculation. It was the northbound one.

It was as a result of this and similar incidents that DOD(H) recommended to the Board that routing of convoys according to OIC intelligence calculations should be tried as a regular practice; even if it were only fifty-one per cent successful, it would be worthwhile. But before pursuing this development we must look more closely at the problem that the tracking room had to grapple with.

The decisive argument for the convoy system is that it makes possible the planned routing and diversion, *as well as* the protection of valuable shipping. That it also makes possible the concentration of air and surface escort forces against the enemy U-boats or aircraft is an offensive argument in its favour; but it is valid only if the escorts exist in sufficient numbers and have the range and endurance to operate over the convoy's whole journey.* That was not the case until 1943; thus, during the crucial first four years of the war, when everything for the future war-winning offensives in Europe had to be brought across the Atlantic or sent from Britain to overseas theatres, it was on the diversion of shipping that the Admiralty's chances of outwitting Doenitz largely depended. The successful handling of convoys and independent ships needed good intelligence allied to skilled calculation of speed, direction, weather and enemy intentions.

Here operational intelligence (its origins are described in

Chapter 3) came into its own. Here NID and Trade Division worked side by side, in neighbouring rooms at the bottom of the Admiralty Citadel in the quarters allotted to Captain Clayton's OIC. Commander (later Captain) Rodger Winn, RNVR, plotted and tracked the U-boats; Commander Richard Hall, RN, plotted the mass of allied shipping in the Atlantic and gave it the orders for evasive action. Hall gave Winn estimated positions for all merchant ships in the Atlantic from the Admiralty Plot; Winn gave Hall known and suspected U-boat positions. Their motto was 'Never the twain shall meet'. No ship – not even Churchill's – left Britain without a route from Hall in the lower war room which had been checked in Winn's. This was one of the great and most cordial partnerships of the war – the two men even shared transport to the Admiralty at seven each morning; and when Admiral Edelsten took over from Admiral Moore as Assistant Chief of Staff U-boats and Trade the latter said to him, 'If those two ever stop bickering we shall lose the war.'*

To make clear the nature of this operation, it is necessary to explain not only the defensive methods imposed on us but also the opportunities created for us by Doenitz's tactics. For what follows the author is indebted to Admiral of the Fleet Sir George Creasy, who was Director of Anti-Submarine Warfare at the time when the tracking room was laying the foundations of its success.

The key to understanding convoy tactics is the difference in speed between the merchant ship and the submerged U-boat. The average speed of convoys, even in good weather, was somewhere between seven and nine knots. A U-boat, until the Schnorkel was fitted in 1944, had an average speed submerged of two to three knots. If she put on speed, say, to six knots, her batteries would be quickly exhausted and she would be forced to come to the surface to recharge them. Thus, the pre-Schnorkel U-boat should be thought of as a slightly mobile mine, with its contact antennae limited to the running range of its torpedoes and the visibility of its periscope.

To attack a single ship moving at high speed the U-boat must have the luck – or the good intelligence that Doenitz had up to 1943 – to be in a position more or less ahead of the target when it is first sighted. Even then a sudden zigzag by the ship might make a firing position impossible. To attack a slow-moving convoy, likewise, the submerged U-boat would need a good sighting position, preferably somewhere on the bow and certainly not abaft the beam; and except in fine weather and bright moonlight she could not see well enough by periscope to attack at night submerged. Nor could a U-boat, once she had fired her torpedoes submerged, reload and overtake the convoy for a second attack.

These were the simple facts which led Doenitz to abandon operations by single submerged U-boats and to adopt the so-called Wolf Pack tactics, operating in groups *on the surface* at relatively high speed and only diving when forced to do so. U-boats ceased to be submarines properly speaking and became submersibles.

For Admiral Doenitz the inescapable problems attending such tactics – which gave OIC its opportunity – were first the finding of the convoy. In the vast areas of the Atlantic the most unwieldy convoy is only a speck. Even if intelligence gave him its chosen route and time of departure, diversion of the convoy by the Admiralty created impossible problems of calculation. A piece of research done for Commander Hall showed that two of his staff, given all the diversion signals sent to a convoy on Winn's advice, were unable to estimate its correct position at any later time and date within five hundred miles. Thus, if U-boat headquarters were getting the best possible intelligence about a convoy's date of departure and its planned course but could not break in time the Admiralty's top secret signals changing the course, a concentration of U-boats taking several days to bring about might be rendered futile.

Doenitz's second problem was to ensure that a convoy that had been sighted by one of his U-boats should be immediately reported, and that the reporting U-boat should shadow the convoy while other U-boats were summoned to join it. The resulting wireless traffic was at once intercepted by the Admiralty's direction-finding network and a comparison of the fix that they achieved (plotted on Winn's charts) with the planned course and estimated position of the convoy (plotted on Hall's charts) provided the material on which a diversion could be planned. In other words, by sacrificing the invisibility that was given to it by remaining silent and submerged, and by operating in close touch with base, the U-boat accepted much greater risks of being seen and heard.*

For the British Naval Staff the facts that emerged, says Admiral Creasy, were that the surfaced U-boat could not normally be located by the Asdic detection device, on which so many hopes had been pinned in the Thirties; that the U-boat, with her tiny silhouette, especially when trimmed down, was almost invisible at night to the human eye; that the British 130 cm radar in small craft used against surface targets was less helpful than had been hoped; and that two things were vital: RF/DF, especially if escort ships could carry it with them, and escorting aircraft, which could force U-boats to submerge and drop bearing — eventually losing touch.

We knew, Admiral Creasy insists, even in the winter of 1940–1, that the new U-boat tactics (which at first took us by surprise) could be beaten given sufficient strength and training in escort vessels and Coastal Command aircraft; but that would take a long time to achieve. Meanwhile until escorts and aircraft were ready the only answer was evasion. This was the vital, twenty-four-hour-a-day job of the men in Rooms 8 and 12 in the Citadel. What, then, did this critically important HQ look like?

If you walked straight into Room 39, you did not take the same liberty with the top secret room occupied by Winn's team. You knocked and waited and stated your business. What you first saw inside was like a large billiard room, with human figures dotted around at tables in corners. The light, day and night, was concentrated on a centre table, seven or eight feet square, over which stretched a massive chart of the North Atlantic. Clusters of pins with tabs on them and stretched elastic cords showed where a convoy battle was in progress or in preparation. At any moment the table was recording the history of several fifteen-day journeys by great convoys of merchant ships loaded with food and raw materials and equipment of war in one direction, taking back the products of British factories for the world outside in the other – and of the long voyage of U-boats sailing from Baltic or Biscay ports to shadow and sink them. What happened on this plot or central chart?

Incidents of all kinds were recorded with date and time on

the plot in pencil; sightings, signals, sinkings, D/F fixes – anything that showed the presence of a U-boat. Radiating from the Coastal Command bases were red circles showing within what range patrols could search or attack. U-boats would be marked by symbols; these would add up to letter codes which kept track of the boat according to information coming in. The pinheads marking the details varied in colour according to the intelligence source; red for a fix, white for a sighting or firm contact, blue for reliable wireless intelligence and so on. Other flags recorded the convoys themselves and their escorts, the times of attacks and sinkings, the routes of our own and enemy air patrols, the possible pattern of a U-boat wolf pack concentration.

Around the walls of the room there were graphs of sinkings and new construction and on a side table the German naval grid, on which the vast ocean spaces were squared off into numbered and lettered sections. The total picture, let it be said, meant nothing to the outsider who might have business in this secret room. What was totally clear in the minds of at most three officers in the room looked a muddle, like someone else's game of Halma.

Each day by noon the U-boats plot had been finalized and recorded for circulation in the daily situation report sent out by 8(S). Likewise Hall next door would have sent four pages of foolscap with the latest convoy dispositions for recording on the Prime Minister's War Room map. Once a week during the night a watchkeeper would transfer the whole plot, item by item, to fresh sheets – a tricky job, for Winn would unfailingly spot any error.

Much of the working day (7.15 to 9 at night or later) was spent by Winn or his deputy working at this table, chin on hand, plotting movements, measuring distances, planning with Hall diversions for hundreds of thousands of tons of shipping, preparing for the inevitable battle in a few hours' time (which he had sometimes seen boiling up days before the escort vessels and their charges), or pondering for days ahead about the effect on our plans and dispositions of an appearance of U-boats far to the south of the Azores, around the Cape, or away in the West Indies.

To this room came a ceaseless flow of facts: urgent bits of

paper torn off the teleprinter run, flashes from Station X where intercepted signals and the patterns of wireless traffic were being studied; bearings of enemy signals from 'Y' stations followed by fixes from the D/F experts; signals from escort vessels making contact with U-boats thousands of miles out at sea; situation reports from Western Approaches, Liverpool, or other operational commands in contact with the enemy; information from the Trade Division plot next door about sailings and arrivals of convoys; extracts from captured documents; detailed interrogation of U-boat prisoners.

With all these sources it was possible to construct at least the skeleton of a U-boat's life story. When it first appeared in the Baltic to work up, its number and other details would sometimes become known on the low-grade cipher traffic between escort vessels, local shore authorities, lightships in the Bight or the Baltic. These, as the Germans must have known well, were intercepted by our 'Y' stations and relayed to Station X. There they were deciphered and sent by teleprinter raw to the OIC, there to start the biography of yet another boat and its commander. There might even be on occasion fragments of completely reliable information deciphered from the U-boat's own signals made available for a limited period after operations of the *Lauenburg* kind (see page 272).* (When such a capture enabled Station X to read signals for a period, it took time to catch up with the current situation at sea. If reading then stopped, Winn and his plotters returned to calculation and guesswork. When it resumed the first messages would mean nothing because they referred to happenings of which nothing was known. Then reading might catch up to date, only for the thread to be lost again.)

The same process was repeated when the U-boat left for its operational cruise and was escorted through the Belts leading from the Baltic to the North Sea; and again when it arrived in its Biscay or Norwegian base, or back home in its German base. With these fragments of completely reliable information there was at least a framework within which to make shrewd guesses at a U-boat's whereabouts. If it left the Belts on a certain day it might be expected to signal its arrival in the patrol zone within a certain time. The speed and endurance of the type would be accurately known, and its leave and refitting cycles.

Certain characteristics of U-boat signals were known; for example, those of the sighting report sent to headquarters when a convoy was sighted, or of the weather report or of the long (though generally indecipherable) damage report. Likewise, the limits of an average cruise were known. A boat could not stay at sea for more than a month, and would stay less than that if damaged or without torpedoes. It could return to base only through three sea passages which were more and more closely patrolled by ships and aircraft as the war went on; the Biscay route, the Iceland-Faroes route and the Norwegian coastal route down to the Baltic. So much was known or deduced that it could truly be said by 1942 that most U-boats were to some degree followed throughout their lives.*

The most pressing of these facts came through to the men at the table raw; the great majority of them came processed – that is to say, in a sifted form in which they could be recorded and plotted at once into the general picture. Watchkeepers all round the clock were plotting D/F fixes before passing them to the main chart; others at the side tables were handling coast watchers' reports, ships' reports of sightings and attacks with position, evidence of missing ships, reports from air reconnaissance, deductions from enemy broadcasts. Much of this was dross; and only gold was useful at the centre table.

What had been collected and deduced had to be promulgated – and that meant consultation. Every morning not later than nine o'clock there would be a 15–20 minute telephone conference with the Chief of Staff of C-in-C Western Approaches in Liverpool and with the Chief of Staff Coastal Command and 15 Group. Winn or his deputy would describe the main news of the night, how the previous day's threats had grown or waned, and what new developments seemed likely, what errors had been made. They would talk about attack possibilities, diversion problems, comparative strengths of U-boats and A/S forces. Later in the war, when Normandy was being invaded, ANCXF (Admiral Ramsay, Allied Naval Commander to the Supreme Allied Commander, Eisenhower), and C-in-C Plymouth would join in a six-line link-up, the main battle having moved for some months from the Atlantic to the Channel and its approaches.*

The complexity of the tracking room operation is best

brought home by setting out the duties of the twelve people normally working in Winn's room:

Civilian watchkeepers: They received all messages and kept the signal log; kept the plot of our own convoys with facts provided from next door; recorded our own warship movements. Signals of operational importance were passed on to the Naval Officer watch.

D/F Plotters (8X): In this team there was only one Naval Officer. They were in touch with the central collecting station for D/F reports which came through by telephone. Having plotted the fixes or bearings of U-boat signals in their own charts, they would inform the Duty Officer at the central table what they were.

Naval Officer watchkeepers (8S): They kept the plot of all enemy warships and U-boats movements and maintained a 24-hour watch on the total picture. When an important situation seemed to be developing on the central plot, they would inform Winn or his deputy; and he would in turn inform the Director of Anti-Submarine Warfare and Operations Division. Also on duty was an officer representing the Director of A/S Warfare who was responsible for training, tactics and weapon development.

Day workers: Civilian researchers only, compiling records, combing the prisoner-of-war interrogations, studying U-boat building, etc., and keeping card indexes.

The core of all this work, with whatever Station X might provide, was the D/F fix. Every day at 11.30 a.m. the D/F plotters would change, the watch taking over being first briefed by the watch going off. Their chief attention was on the principle northern W/T station which collected bearings from all the British D/F stations*. There the work of a dozen different stations was collated in minutes and telephoned direct to the Admiralty. All bearings were noted in a log with time of interception, origin, indicator groups and so on. During a wolf pack attack, with up to a dozen U-boats concerting their movements and reporting sightings and sinkings to base, bearings would pour in at the rate of thirty to forty an hour, so giving a fair picture of their dispositions. The frequencies and routine of the U-boat signals were familiar to the D/F expert, Lt-Cdr Peter Kemp (8X) from long study, and both he and the operators at the D/F station had learnt to give the approximate area from which a signal had come by merely looking at the bearings before plotting them. Of course, as soon as a U-boat was fixed near a convoy, the Admiralty plotters sent an immediate signal to the escort commander.

A 'good' fix was reckoned to be within forty to fifty miles of the transmitting U-boat; a 'very good' one would get within ten to fifteen miles. Bearing in mind the low speed of U-boats submerged (on average not more than three knots and on the surface not more than eleven knots in favourable weather conditions), it is obvious that frigates and destroyers, especially in heavy seas, had a fair chance of making contact if given without delay a good fix of a U-boat position. Radar-equipped aircraft had an overwhelming advantage. One plotter recalls how a U-boat plotted by D/F bearings was found within three miles of the established position in the Baltic and sunk by a Coastal Command aircraft, all within half-an-hour of the U-boat's signal being intercepted.*

'A plotter has above all to have conscience,' Winn used to say. Positions could be rigged, if it were wanted; but the show-down would come sooner or later. That is not to say that the experienced man could not have valuable hunches, which could be checked against the evidence of other sources.

From long experience the D/F plotter could even tell from the type or length of message that had been intercepted by the 'Y' station whether the U-boat had just surfaced or not. He could also estimate whether it had been reporting the sighting of a ship, reporting the weather or sending a routine message about state of fuel and torpedoes. As the war went on, a refinement of the plotters' work was introduced by having junior scientists to sit with them. They could advise how to distinguish fixes from scatter sources or skips and could also record bearings and then work out errors. This enabled OIC to evaluate the work of individual D/F stations and improve their accuracy and training.

The most arduous mental detective work began after the clue had been given – that is to say, after the U-boat had given its position away. This was Winn's speciality: in which direction would it go next? Towards a convoy, obviously, if it had sighted and signalled one, or was putting other boats of a pack on to it. Then the course of other U-boats to meet the convoy could be estimated and the time of contact with the convoy fairly accurately predicted. How accurately would depend on weather conditions and on how up-to-date our knowledge (gained partly from study of convoy actions and partly from prisoner-of-war intelligence) of their tactical doctrine was. It was therefore quite often possible to forecast where the next attacks would be and to warn convoy escorts.*

The author has reconstructed with former members of the tracking room what would happen in a typical emergency. During the afternoon a signal might come in from a Coastal Command aircraft, based on Iceland or on Northern Ireland, reporting a U-boat on the surface at a position which, on the plot, was bare of pins or symbols. 'Look, Rodger,' one of Winn's assistants would say, 'here's a new one. I wonder where she's come from?'

Then began the calculation with pins and dividers and card indexes to decide whether this was indeed a newcomer or a U-boat already tracked – but wrongly. This one might have covered the distance from its last reported position in the time available; but it seemed unlikely in the known weather conditions. That one might have changed direction since the last bearings were plotted. Which was it?

That point settled – and sometimes, thanks to Winn's uncanny flair for guessing a U-boat's behaviour, it was settled very quickly – there were other questions to ask. 'Where is this one going – now?' That is to say, straight in the direction of such and such a convoy, or not? 'Are there any others?' That is to say, is this U-boat one of a patrol line; if so, what distance does the line cover in each direction? While these possibilities were being worked on, Winn might say, 'We'd better have Hall in quickly.'

Hall comes hurrying in from next door and asks 'Which one is this about, Rodger?' 'HX42', comes the reply. 'Here's a U-boat we didn't expect, only fifty miles away to the south. There may be others. How is your convoy doing?'

Hall looks carefully at the plot as Winn points out the threat. 'Couldn't be more awkward,' he says, 'HX42's escort is low on fuel and I simply can't order a long diversion. How sure are you, Rodger?'

'Sure! You know as well as I do, Dick, nothing is sure in this

113

game. But my hunch is that your convoy's running into trouble on its present course.'

'All right,' says Hall, 'I'll talk to Western Approaches and tell them the worst' – and leaves the room. Twenty minutes later he is back, good news beaming from the fresh and plump face in which a majestic nose recalls the features of his famous Admiral father, the DNI of Jutland. 'That's saved us,' he says, 'Western Approaches say they've got a support group* handy which they can send to join the convoy when we divert it, and the present escort can refuel in Iceland.'

'All right,' says Winn, 'that's better; now let's work out the course.' And the argument begins again, dividers in hand. If the U-boat were going in that direction surfaced at an average speed of ten knots – say a bit less in the rough weather – she'd report the convoy at such and such a time and position. If she were part of a patrol line, the U-boats in it would be able to concentrate in five to six hours. So, to make quite sure, Winn would order HX42 to make a 90° turn east for four hours, then bring it half back on course for another four. 'It may be cutting things a bit fine,' Winn would say, 'but with a fresh support group joining up we can risk a fight.'

So the advice is argued out; and once the decision is reached, the rush begins to get out the signals through C-in-C Western Approaches with Trade Division's signature on them. Then the familiar, painful, important wait begins. All that can be done has been done. As Winn and his men go on working at a score of other U-boat and convoy problems, they look at their clock from time to time and wonder whether the diversion of HX42 will do the trick, whether they have guessed right, whether once again Doenitz has been outwitted or whether there'll be another bloody battle on those cruel seas. If there is, then at least the best possible counter-measures have been called in; the enemy will not achieve surprise. Intelligence has done its life-saving work.

It may be imagined that the intense intellectual labour that went into this battle of tactics was tolerable to the human beings engaged in it only if it became for them virtually like a game of chess or bridge. During the five years that Winn and his principal aides were at it, they had to keep in check any leap of the imagination which would have pictured in terms of appalling human suffering their failure, say, to extricate a tanker convoy from the assailing pack. Otherwise the strain would have been too great. There was one occasion, however, when the imagination could not be stifled. A certain Commander Boyle, who had been a much-liked RN colleague in the room for many anxious months and had then returned to sea, was commanding the escort of a convoy of eleven tankers from Trinidad. (His wife was actually working at the time in the room as a secretary.) They watched helplessly day after day in 8S, with aching hearts, as that precious and vulnerable convoy was picked off ship by ship until there was only one left – but Boyle himself was safe.

Typical of their skill and confidence and luck is the following story. Hall was routing a valuable merchant ship on its own through the Bay of Biscay and wished to make sure that it would avoid a U-boat shown on Winn's plot as probably moving eastward, at three knots submerged. Winn said that there was no danger of their meeting provided that he could be certain of the precise position of the ship. Hall thereupon ordered the ship to break wireless silence and signal its position. When the reply came Winn was able to demonstrate that, from this position, the ship would pass on its present course safely under the U-boat's stern. Ten days later the ship's master arrived at the Admiralty and demanded an interview with the Assistant Chief of Naval Staff responsible for convoys. He complained indignantly that he had been ordered by the Admiralty to report his position, so endangering his ship and breaking the strict orders given to him about wireless silence. Only with great difficulty was Commander Hall able to convince him that had the Admiralty not ascertained his position and ordered him to proceed as arranged, he might not have been alive to make his complaint.

The authority acquired and asserted in the Admiralty by the tracking room was, considering the predominant part played in it by uniformed civilians, remarkable. Certainty, more often than not, was impossible in this work because of the speed at which events developed. But, as Winn himself has put it, a 'working fiction' was evolved. 'What could only be an estimate and a guess was to be taken as a fact and acted upon.' No one was in a position to override the room's interpretations; it

115

could not and need not consult at a higher level because it had all the information. Its head was protected from the very beginning by DNI and the DDIC (Clayton) against the pressure of higher authority – which was sharply contrary to the naval tradition that the senior officer must always be right.

Lt-Cdr Patrick Beesly, Winn's RNVR deputy from 1942, recalls one example of the method by which the room would win a case with senior officers. Dealing one evening with one of their more difficult convoy problems, Winn and Beesley had concluded that the intelligence available allowed two deductions, neither more convincing than the other. To take action on one, course A, would give the Fleet a lot of trouble in changing routes, reorganizing escorts and so on, whereas course B would give none; and Winn had persuaded Beesly with some difficulty that A must be the answer even if the Naval Staff would not like it.

To Beesly's astonishment, when the 'gold braid' came down to the tracking room to discuss the decision, Winn launched into a detailed and forceful exposition of the case Beesly had made to him for the less troublesome course B. Having concluded this, he went on to point out in his best forensic manner that there was of course another point of view, which in all fairness he must state because it was held by colleagues whose judgement he respected – to wit, course A. But he realized, he said, that this was out of the question because it would involve for the Naval Staff difficult changes of plan and movements of ships. Delighted at the chance to show their indifference to such considerations and for once to disagree with Winn, the senior officers plumped for course A – the one he in fact favoured.

The following vivid picture of 8S in action was given to the author by one of Winn's RNVR officers:

Senior officers in the naval staff changed from time to time, and it was fascinating to see their first reactions to Winn and the way in which a close and friendly working relationship was established, often after some initial distrust and scepticism on the part of a regular naval officer recently returned from sea. Winn was always correct and respectful, treating his seniors much as I imagine he behaved as a barrister towards a judge in court, using his legal technique to the full to win over his audience to his point of view, often by presenting an unpopular theory in such a way that the Assistant Chief of Naval Staff, or whoever it was, came to believe that he, and not Winn, had first stumbled on the truth of the matter.

He was very much an individualist and, although we all worked as a team, Winn had to see every scrap of evidence himself and would not rely on his staff merely presenting him with ready-made solutions of parts of the jigsaw. I think this was natural to him and that he could not have worked in any other way, but it is fair to say that it was also essential. The man in charge could not afford to neglect any clue; he had to consider each and every item carefully himself, he had to study every part of the puzzle, not just the centre piece.

This imposed a tremendous strain on him. Not only were his hours long – rarely less than eleven hours a day and frequently much more at times of peak activity – but he was also working under great pressure. Minutes lost in assessing evidence, advising on a diversion or drafting a signal could well cause the loss of several ships and even more valuable lives. He always managed to remain calm and in full control of himself and the situation, but only with the expenditure of great nervous and physical effort.

To a remarkable brain and supreme self confidence, Winn added great moral courage. The decisions he gave could, and often did, have far-reaching consequences. It is always tempting to give one's superiors the advice they would like to receive, but he was never guilty of this failing. His views on whether an attack on a U-boat had been successful or not, on where Doenitz would next concentrate his efforts, on the rate of building, on the possibilities of the Germans carrying on the U-boat war from Norway after the subjection of the Fatherland, and so on, often made him unpopular, at least temporarily, with those who had to take action as a result. His decisions, or guesses, if you like, were usually proved or disproved within days, sometimes within hours, and to recognize this also required a great deal of moral courage when so much was at stake.

Two episodes remain in my memory as particularly good examples of his readiness to take a decision and stick by it. One was the initial determination to try and plot U-boats on from their last known position even if further evidence was scanty or non-existent. The other was his hunch, it was not much more, that a U-boat attack was planned, in 1943, off the Cape of Good Hope. There was very little concrete evidence for this, but day after day we plotted those boats out from the Bay of Biscay, across the Equator and down into the South Atlantic. No one would say we were wrong but most people were surprised when we were finally proved right.

Such a man was not always easy to work for. He drove his staff extremely hard and had a pretty biting tongue when he felt he was getting anything less than the very best. Nevertheless we all recognized that he demanded even more from himself than he did from us and he always gave all of us his full support and backing over decisions taken in his absence. The effect of this was that the 'high-ups' came to place almost as much reliance on the advice of the RNVR Sub on night watch as they did on Winn's prognostications during the day. As a result, although the limelight was always on him, and quite rightly so, we all felt that we had contributed our part, and were extremely proud of 'The Room' and its reputation. Maybe we even felt that we were winning the war on our own.

Winn always insisted that his room would express one view and one only. The staff could argue, criticize and disagree as much as they liked; but once an outsider came in, one official view must be given to avoid confusion.

By 1943 Admiral Edelsten, then ACNS (UT), laid it down that without reference to him no ship or convoy was to be routed against Winn's advice. Sometimes, for operational reasons to do with the requirements of the Minister of War Transport or other higher level direction, the room would be pressed to change its mind. Winn recalls how in December 1942 he was told that the White Star liner *Ceramic*, carrying urgently needed airfield specialists to Takoradi, should be detached from her convoy because it was urgent to get her to her African destination. She was in a convoy routed well to the south. Winn had recommended Halifax–New York–Hatteras –Caribbean–Recife, and then a short hop across the South Atlantic. For four days Winn refused to detach her, because he believed the convoy to have been shadowed and reported, but he finally yielded to the pressure of the Ministry of Shipping and agreed to her peeling off from the convoy with two destroyers, in view of the urgency with which her passengers were required. Having left the convoy, the *Ceramic* oustripped her escort within an hour or two and was later sunk – with only one survivor who was rescued by U-boat and lived to tell the tale. Winn took full responsibility for a decision which he feels he made against his better judgement under considerable pressure.

In the tracking room, as in other rooms of the OIC, the

strain was intense. Partly the work itself was responsible; partly the long hours of underground work by electric light; partly the effect of London life with its bombing and shortages and other difficulties. As another of his younger officers told the author:

> Winn spared no one in getting himself briefed for his work and conferences, for at these the reputation of the room and its methods were at stake . . .
>
> He was a merciless driver. Watchkeepers, tired and dazed by the strain of a night's work, were harried for condensed and accurate reports on every happening during their turn. Any mistake was dealt with with brusque severity and no excuse was taken.
>
> But Winn made personal friends of his staff. Christian names were used off duty, and everyone was treated as an equal. He never failed to give the credit for good work to his subordinates in the presence of senior officers. And Admirals like Henry Moore and James Edelsten came to accept the informal spirit of the room and work with it.*

Was there nothing wrong with this most secret brain-centre of the Atlantic battle? In naval circles, among those who knew, a reference to the tracking room prompts immediate praise, like the mention of a great cricketer or a great actor – the repute is beyond challenge.* Yet Winn and his colleagues never concealed the fact that errors, costly errors, were made; and the question is whether these errors could have been averted.

The author's judgement, based on some personal knowledge of Citadel conditions and questioning former OIC staff, is that avoidable mistakes were made. First, too great a burden was allowed to fall first on one man, and later on two men. In late 1942 Winn had been so affected by the strain that it was thought his doctor would not allow him to return; his departure at that juncture – six months before the tide turned in the U-boat war – would without question have been disastrous. Too much of the understanding of the play of Doenitz's judgement was in one man's mind and his only.

Secondly, senior officers should have given more attention to the amenities and manning of the section. By comparison with the old Admiralty, it is true, the Citadel was safe, warm, clean and quiet. But the overcrowding was dire; there were no proper places to sleep for any but the highest; Denning slept

E*   119 under his table during the hunting of the *Bismarck*; his woman assistant slept in a bunk that was seldom empty for more than an hour or two – what the navy calls a 'hot bunk'. The medical attention for such key personnel was perfunctory.

Lastly, office arrangements and management and catering were primitive. When the Americans were eventually persuaded by the British to set up an OIC, it was done with a wealth of equipment and staff which made the visitor from London sick with envy; silent typewriter, all message-passing mechanized, lavish filing systems and photographic equipment, every kind of aid to orderly work. By comparison ours was a Heath Robinson affair.*

OIC in general was not an unfriendly, uncomfortable place. If it had not required a pass to get one past the Marine sentry at the door between Admiralty and Citadel, it would have been a great gathering place of gossips and news-hunters. But entry to its various rooms was the privilege of very few people; only those with 'need to know' were admitted. 'Top brass', Dudley Pound himself among them, working late at the Admiralty or sleeping there would drop in for a chat and for a fascinated look at the plot on which, in the first three years, everything depended; and the Duty Captain would ring up of an evening to inquire whether there was any item of hot news, good or bad, which could be given to the Prime Minister for his trans-atlantic 'phone call to Roosevelt. The Assistant Chief of Staff (U-boat Trade) might look in night after night, morning after morning for three weeks – and it would still be the same price-less convoy of weapons or food or oil battling its way home, or the one and only armoured brigade with its tanks plodding to Egypt round the Cape. It was like watching a precious patient fighting hour by hour for life.

From time to time, rather as the layman sometimes wishes he could understand the data from which the weatherman makes his forecasts, a senior officer would insist on knowing the facts and argument on which some advice given him by NID was based. Not surprisingly Admiral Sir Max Horton figures in an incident* which took place about a year after he took command of Western Approaches in November 1942. He complained of cases in which ships had been lost in situations where the advice of Winn had been followed. Masterful and

120

ruthless character that he was, he felt sure he could show the backroom men in the Citadel a point or two, and asked to have explained to him the methods and reasoning by which they drew their inferences about enemy movements. Winn politely suggested that this would be best done on his next visit to the Admiralty. When Horton arrived he found waiting for him the mass of signals, D/F fixes and other fragments concerning the episode of which complaint had been made, together with the plot. It was explained to him how the contradictions and uncertainties had been dealt with and why one course of action had been preferred to another, and then the Admiral was left to it. After a few hours' work he was baffled and, according to his biographer, admitted the fact. 'With the old familiar smile which some called catlike and others benign, he held out his hand and said "Goodbye, Rodger, I leave it to you." And thereafter he did.'

To those who knew the story of Winn's initiation into these mysteries the episode had its comic side. Needing practical experience of the difficulties that faced submarine commanders and of the training they were given to overcome them, he had asked Horton (then Flag Officer Submarines) in the early days of the war to give him some instruction. This he did, Winn firing questions at him up at Northwood during the Admiralty lunch hour, imbibing according to the pupil wisdom and gin in equal quantities. Neither man could know or even imagine that within two years the RNVR pupil would be virtually telling the RN master just what he should do with his ships to outwit and overcome the German submarines. Horton up in Liverpool knew he was dealing with a strong man and one who was not under his authority; so the relationship was workable and not disagreeable.

In December 1944, Rushbrooke the Director who saw the back of the U-boat campaign broken, was able to pass on to Clayton, Winn and Beesly and others the congratulations of the retiring Assistant Chief of Naval Staff in charge of the anti-U-boat war, Admiral Edelsten:

After two years' very close association with the Tracking Room, I feel it would be most ungracious of me not to record my very great appreciation of the work carried out in this section of your department.

Admiral Clayton has been admirable at keeping his finger on the U-boat pulse and I have found his ever-ready advice and counsel of the greatest help in appreciating the anti-U-boat war and in many difficult decisions which I have had to make.

For the Tracking Room staff itself I can only speak in terms of the highest commendation. Under the masterly leadership and guidance of Captain Winn, this section works as a team in perfect accord and co-operation under difficult conditions.

I have seen, time and time again, convoys and independents guided out of danger as the result of the intelligence, anticipation and foresight of these officers, ably assisted by Commander Hall and his hard-working movements staff belonging to Trade Division.

Finally, I should like to thank you most sincerely for all the willing help I have received during the last two years from all sections of your department concerned with the many aspects of the anti-U-boat war.

NID.2699   31 December 1944

It is interesting, though hardly surprising, to learn that on the German side, there was a comparable concentration of work in a few minds – but minds of regular Naval officers. Doenitz had with him at BdU headquarters (whether in Berlin or Paris or Lorient) a group of five who lived at their work, were on duty day and night, and discussed every move in the 'tonnage war' together. There was his Chief of Staff, Godt, an operations officer, another in charge of 'enemy appreciation', another responsible for the escorting of U-boats going on patrol and returning and a signals specialist. Kapitän zur See Meckel, who filled the last role from 1939 to 1943, has described to the author the intensive research and thinking which lay behind the orders sent to the U-boats. Every commander returning from patrol was interrogated by Doenitz himself and these four officers on every detail of his operations. Meckel would have ready an analysis of all signals sent by and received by this officer; his log would be checked; his tactics would be elucidated and criticized; any information about British anti-submarine methods and tactics would be recorded; every loss of a U-boat was the subject of meticulous inquiry.

Dependent as they were for nearly four years on information derived from Allied signals, this little U-boat staff was constantly worried by the possibility that the British might from time to time be reading their own signal traffic. This was so voluminous, because of the central direction insisted on by Doenitz, that some leakage seemed inevitable. The question was, how much? In 1943, and not before, an officer was added to the staff with the duty of examining all suspicious circumstances; the evasive routing of an American or British convoy away from the U-boat patrol line waiting for it; the rounding up of U-boat tankers; the clever anticipation of sudden switches of U-boats from one sector of the ocean to another – all the tracking room's work. Again and again the question was asked, not least in the B Dienst headquarters itself, but the answer was always negative.

In November 1966 the author asked Admiral Doenitz whether he felt during the battle of the Atlantic that he had opposed to him a single commanding mind reading his own. Not, he replied, until Horton took over the conduct of the anti-U-boat operations at Liverpool in November 1942. It seems likely that the working of operational intelligence as understood in the Admiralty was not known to the German Naval Staff. Doenitz and his officers received their intelligence material in digested form on the end of a teleprinter, they tried to combine in one office the conduct of operations with the study of the enemy's intentions and forces; which is a very different thing from having intelligence and operations working closely together but separated in command and organization.

6 Churchill and Godfrey

That there should be a clash of mind and will between Winston Churchill and the new DNI at the outset of the war seems now, looking back, to have been inevitable. The growing Division had to establish and defend its standard of working and truth-telling; the First Lord wished to put heart into the nation at a time when the service under his authority was the only one actively engaged with the enemy over a wide area. In the autumn and winter of 1939–40 it was not yet the moment for offering nothing but blood, sweat and tears. What the public required during the 'phoney war' was evidence, of a kind that they could understand in figures and pictures, that Britain, having failed to save Poland, was not standing by doing no hurt to the Nazis. Churchill intended to find and publish it, both for the Navy's sake and his own.

It has to be recalled that Churchill had taken no direct part in the administration of naval affairs since 1915–16 and that he may still have associated Naval Intelligence with the kind of horse's mouth, sensational but factual evidence from enemy signals that Room 40 had given the Admiralty and Foreign Office when he was First Lord twenty-five years before. Such operational material, in 1939, was neither available nor expected: cryptography, like everything else in defence, had been allowed to run down after Curzon in 1922 had secured its transfer from Admiralty to civilian control. Where the Cabinet and Chiefs of Staff demanded hard complete fact, quickly available, only bits and pieces of evidence assembled by arguing and guessing could be got. The deeply trenched bed of knowledge from which certainties would grow so luxuriantly in later years had not yet been dug. Thus, when Churchill set out to establish and publish to the world precise but hopeful figures of U-boats sunk and new U-boat building he ran into difficulties.

He encountered the DNI on two fronts: first as the member of the Naval Staff responsible for getting those figures and keeping them secret and second, as the officer supervising the work of Press Division, which was responsible under Captain Brooking for getting as much information as possible out of the Admiralty for the satisfaction of the public and the guidance of the national newspapers. DNI was later relieved of this double duty as gamekeeper and poacher, but it was an arrangement which is logical and, on paper, looked practical. Who can judge better than the DNI – in touch with all knowledge about the enemy, with all operations and with all security requirements – what can and cannot be said to the Press or by the BBC? In fact, as has been shown in Chapter 3, this was work which had endless political implications, demanded constant consulting of the other Services, was liable to interference from the official censorship, and therefore exposed the DNI and his officers to distractions which could do Intelligence no good and might do it much harm.

Here was a situation as certain to attract Churchillian attention as any in the Admiralty. For the First Lord frequently – and quite rightly – thought of himself as a journalist, indeed, the most inspired and effective publicist in the Empire. He claimed the right to approach the British people in his own way; he did not hesitate if it suited his conception of the interest of a nation at war to twist the truth or to paint a rosy picture that had no connection with veracity. To increase the confusion and the certainty of clash between Admiral and politicians, there was the teething trouble which the Ministry of Information was suffering between 1939 and 1941, bringing much public criticism of the censors and their struggles to get out what war news there was. The Admiralty, reputed to be the most silent service, was in the thick of bitter controversy, in which the First Lord wanted to win.

Instead of being free to put all his effort into going out to look for information rather than waiting for it to come in – what he called 'the aggressive side of intelligence' – the DNI

125

was pinned down by Press troubles and by the First Lord's prayers, those brief inquiries and demands for action which began 'Pray inform me' or 'Pray why has . . . not been done?' Godfrey wrote in his private memoirs:

These were dictated last thing at night and one found them hot from the press when one arrived in the morning. The wording was insistent, frequently harsh, and an answer was usually demanded by a certain time, say 5 p.m. . . . . They put one on the defensive and added greatly to the strain of those early months.

These Churchillian prayers had somehow in a few hours to be answered fully and convincingly and not in a way that would provoke a come-back. Here DNI began to see the special value of Ian Fleming, the Lieutenant RNVR behind the door of Room 39 who was his Personal Assistant. Fleming's experience with *Reuters* had given him the 'feel' of the Press and he took over the prayers in his long and jaunty hurdler's stride, undeterred by their awesome wording. By lunchtime or soon after there would be a draft on Godfrey's desk with the boldly scrawled initial 17F – or just F. After talking it over with others concerned Godfrey would approve it. Then Miss Cameron, credited with typing the best-looking memoranda in the Admiralty, would do a fair copy and away it would go to the Private Office – there to be presented to the 'former naval person' who had enjoyed a refreshing sleep between lunch and 5 p.m. such as his naval staff seldom achieved until well after midnight.*

In these 'prayers' the emphasis at first was always on publicity, seldom on intelligence. Yet, when it switched to the question of sinking U-boats, it was the intelligence aspect that gradually prevailed. But before passing on to the complicated argument that raged between First Lord, First Sea Lord and DNI, let it be recorded that Godfrey once watched the composition of one of his master's largely maritime broadcasts to the nation. It was in October 1939 that the First Lord, very late at night, sent for him to be present while he dictated the first draft of a broadcast – to see to it that the facts were correct. Again I quote Godfrey's memoirs.

My recollection is of a most efficient secretary-typist, a completely silent typewriter, three copies on half sheets of foolscap, two long drinks and two enormous cigars, and Mr Churchill walking up and down dictating, clad in a dishevelled dinner jacket and dropping cigar ash and spilling whisky and soda over his waistcoat. The sentences seemed to emerge without any effort.

From time to time there was a correction which by some magical process was incorporated in the draft. My interruptions and minor suggestions were welcomed and acted on. Within two minutes of the end three beautifully typed copies had been produced, sorted out and strung together; one was for me to take away and fill in details by 10 a.m. next day. The whole was then reduced to a sort of blank verse, which I have seen since in the BBC records, and it was from this that he addressed the world.

This was the only occasion when I was privileged to witness the evolution of one of those speeches, which brought hope and inspiration to countless millions of human beings.

Precisely when the dispute began is not clear, but on 12 November 1939, only ten weeks after the outbreak of war, Mr Churchill claimed in a broadcast that 'the attack of the U-boats has been controlled and they have paid a heavy toll'.* What was the basis of this heartening assertion? Since 3 September DNI had issued a weekly tabular statement of U-boat losses based on the conclusions of the submarine assessment committee, which made searching examination of all claims against U-boats sent in from the Fleet. He sat on this body with the Director of Anti-Submarine Warfare, the Director of Naval Air Services, the Director of Torpedo and Mining, Coastal Command's representative and a French naval officer. The statement at first, though secret, was given a wide circulation inside and outside the Admiralty, the sources of our knowledge being then neither extensive nor particularly secret.

The companion return, a *monthly* estimate of the number of U-boats likely to be built, was in the nature of a 'best guess', to be modified periodically upward or downward as information from agents, prisoners, air photos and Ministry of Economic Warfare expert research became more detailed and reliable. By studying these two returns, it was hoped in time to form a forecast of how quickly the Germans would be able to replace lost boats (and of course their experienced crews) and what kind of shipbuilding effort would be required if the British and their allies were to hold and master the U-boat offensive. As the whole future of the war, of Britain's ability to counter-attack and of her capacity to rearm and feed her people depended on that mastery, the effort to ensure the accuracy of these figures was to have the highest priority in naval and economic intelligence.

It could be argued – indeed, it was argued by politicians like Brendan Bracken – that there could be in the situation of 1939–40 two kinds of truth about Germany's U-boat strength: one as accurate as possible, for the experts and the War Cabinet, and another – a cheering guess – for the public and Parliament. If so, it would be necessary to ensure that so few persons knew the first that the frailty of the second would never be detected, even by the Fleet.

Up to 12 December the number of *known* sinkings was only eight; but mention was made in DNI's summaries of 'probably sunk' eighteen, 'probably seriously damaged' five, and 'probably slightly damaged' ten, together with the name and number of the Allied ship or aircraft. This was done for two reasons. First, to keep the nature and scale of the problem, with all its perplexing shades of doubt, before the minds of the Naval Staff and the technical departments which should be increasing and improving our anti-submarine effort; and then, hardly less important, to encourage all at sea who took part in these attacks.

So it was with such figures in mind that the First Lord claimed 'a heavy toll'. We now know from the German naval archives that the state of the U-boat score on the day of his broadcast was six boats lost out of fifty-seven in existence when war began (which does not mean 'operational', as two thirds of available boats were generally on their way to and from their patrol area, or repairing damage, or resting). The NID estimate was six out of sixty-six: in other words, the number of boats claimed sunk was right, but the number of boats estimated to have been in existence was nine too many. Six out of sixty-six could hardly be represented as 'a heavy toll', but perhaps six out of a score or so actually at sea could be. At any rate, it was.

Then came the suppression. On 24 November, Churchill minuted on his copy of this Weekly Return of U-boat Casualties, No. 6, 21.11.39: 'This information is not to be circulated except to First Sea Lord, Deputy Chief of Naval Staff and First Lord.

A monthly statement should be prepared for wider circulation and I will see it before it is issued.' DNI then suggested that the member of the Naval Staff directing anti-U-boat warfare (DAS/W), because he was chairman of the Assessment Committee, should prepare these returns and, when necessary, initiate an Admiralty letter to senior officers and the C-in-C concerned about attacks which had been judged successful. Thus the Fleet would learn of individual kills but would be denied totals. This was agreed to before the year was out, and the monthly return was officially seen by only very few people.

The next cheerful guess to be imparted to the public over the BBC was in Churchill's broadcast of 20 January 1940: 'It seems pretty certain tonight that half the U-boats with which Germany began the war have been sunk, and that their new building has fallen far behind what we expected.'

This was, by any standard, an astonishing assertion. To say that initial estimates of U-boat building capacity were proving to be exaggerated would have been correct; but to give the impression that new building had for some reason slowed down was quite another matter. To explain the background to Churchill's treatment of the facts – I fancy that 'misprision' is the kind of word he would have chosen in the context – it is necessary to go back a little way into pre-war history.

The Admiralty had been misled before war began by reports or rumours inspired from Berlin into the belief that Hitler had a larger number of boats than in fact existed.* The Germans boasted on the one hand that they were not exceeding the quota laid down in the Anglo-German Naval Treaty; on the other hand, they spread rumours during the Munich crisis and in the spring of 1939 that boats were already at war stations in the South Atlantic, even on one occasion that a couple of U-boats were lurking off Portsmouth. A picture of looming disaster was therefore formed in the minds of Ministers which it took many months of work and argument by NID to correct.* Curiously Churchill allowed part of the myth to survive in his memoirs. In vol. 1, page 282 of *The Second World War* he writes that Hitler had 'always been building U-boats as fast as possible irrespective of any agreement'; whereas the Germans did not really exceed the number of U-boats allowed by treaty, although they did cheat over the size of the *Bismarck*.* As is explained in an earlier chapter, Hitler's naval construction plan, stretching to 1944, had assumed no war with Britain for some time.

It was for such reasons that the Admiralty's estimates of sixty-six U-boats in existence (instead of the correct fifty-seven) in September had been acceptable. Oddly enough, this exaggeration was to some extent corrected by the strong temptation to add together 'known' and 'probably' sunk; so that by chance the number of U-boats at Germany's disposal in January 1940 was correctly assessed at forty-nine – but it was a fluke and not known at the time to be the truth.

By the date of Churchill's broadcast, it was certain that nine U-boats had been sunk. By adding in sixteen probables, he got the number up to twenty-five, and later by calculations of his own or of Lindemann's statisticians up to thirty-five. This brought the total of 'claimed sunk' up to more than half of what the Admiralty thought existed when war broke out. No wonder the First Lord could make a cheerful broadcast! Let us look in more detail at the argument that was now developing.

On 18 January DNI had circulated a paper in which he gave an opinion on U-boat numbers:

Existing 1 September 1939	66
Increase 1 September 1939–1 January 1940	9
Known losses	9
Plus probables	17
Probable future increase by 1 July 1940	48
Anticipated total on 1 July 1940 without allowance for losses between 1 January 1940 and 1 July 1940*	109

Four days later Churchill criticized these figures in a personal minute (22 January 1940). From Godfrey's notes made at the time it is possible to reconstruct the form in which the comments and DNI's replies would have been seen by the Board on the relevant dockets: to simulate this they are shown on page 131 and 132 printed side by side.

Between the lines one can hear the Intelligence men bristling in the remarks: 'it would be unwise to base our policy on wishful thinking', 'it is important that the probabilities as seen by the Naval Staff should be presented without bias or wishfulness'. Upstairs in Plans Division, where they had been

First Lord's Remarks, 22.1.40

DNI's comments to Admiral Phillips, Deputy Chief of Naval Staff, 26.1.40.

DNI paper is really intended to announce the good news that the previous forecast of NID about the new building of U-boats was excessive.

In September 1939 our estimate was a 'best guess' which would need monthly modification. MSU series (which was suppressed by First Lord on 24 December) gave monthly estimate of numbers, buildings, and losses. Object not to convey good or bad news but to state the truth as fully as possible. Views based on NID and Ministry of Economic Warfare investigations.

To predict the figure 109 in July 1940 it is necessary to assume that not more than 26 U-boats have been sunk before the end of 1939, whereas 35 is the lowest figure that can be accepted.

35 is an over-estimate, and it would be unwise to base our policy on wishful thinking.

1939-1940 Absurd to present figures on the assumption of no further losses; at least 5 probables have occurred since the beginning of new year. (Note by J.H.G. – Actually none were sunk between 1 and 18 January.)

Obviously possible to scale down the number 109 depending on how optimistically or pessimistically one regards our effort in the spring and summer of 1940. I think 5 probables is an over-estimate.

If we assume the same rate of loss for the next six months as characterized the first four, namely 2 per week, 52 would have to be deducted from 109 making a total of 57 on 1 July.

2 per week probably an over-estimate. Most unwise optimistically to assume that Germans will lose 52 U-boats in next 6 months.

131

First Lord's Remarks, 22.1.40

DNI's comments to Admiral Phillips, Deputy Chief of Naval Staff, 26.1.40.

(Note by J.II.G. in 1948: DNI, DAS/W, MEW estimate was 9 known and 17 probables in 18 weeks; actually 9 are known to have been sunk, i.e. *one a fortnight, not 2 a week.*)

A new statement should be prepared which gives due consideration to all the factors at work. This should be discussed between First Sea Lord, DCNS and myself before being widely circulated. The statement of U-boat losses is a matter of high policy.

I feel somewhat doubtful regarding the efficacy of this statement, as it is based on assuming knowledge of unknown factors, but unless we assume that the Germans are going to make a considerable effort to increase their number of U-boats there will be no incentive to make the corresponding effort ourselves to overcome the menace, and this will sooner or later have an effect on our preparations. I feel strongly that it is important that the probabilities as seen by the Naval Staff should be presented without bias or wishfulness.

wrestling with some of the First Lord's offensive projects, the advice would have been underlined, once if not twice. How often was this to be said later about the first plans for a second front, about Bomber Command's claims of damage to U-boat yards and shelters and battleships in Brest, in that warning voice of scepticism which makes the fighting commander or politician as resentful of Intelligence as of a nagging doctor.

By the end of the next month (February) inflation had set in. When a rather gloomy monthly report reached the First Lord, he insisted once again that only a few should know. He minuted: 'I am sorry that we sank no U-boats in the two months between 4 December and 30 January. This gloomy view of our A/S activities will be circulated only to 1 SL, DCNS and myself. WSC.' Although it was not known at the time, the NID estimate in February of fifty-six U-boats available was too high by seven; but a report from the Hague mentioned eighty-eight· Incredible as it may now seem, by deducting the figure of fifty-six from this new hypothetical figure of eighty-eight some-one gave rise to the notion that thirty-two boats were 'un-accounted for'. As three had been successfully attacked since the date of the report, the First Sea Lord added them on to make a total of thirty-five sunk. Churchill went one better and on 17 February remarked: 'A working hypothesis but I think forty-five will be nearer the truth.' (In fact only eleven had been sunk and the DNI's estimate at that date was ten.)*

Godfrey was understandably dismayed that this piece of gross exaggeration should have been allowed to pass without challenge and that the First Sea Lord should have made his own contribution to myth in his neat green handwriting. Steps were taken to see that the paper had no further circulation. It was the DNI's first encounter with what he later called 'wishfulness in high places' (see Chapter 15).

Two months later, on 15 April, light was shed into these dark places by an authentic U-boat order of battle recovered during the sinking of U49. It showed that the Germans then pos-sessed only forty-three U-boats and that twenty-two had been sunk up to date, compared with the First Lord's 'working hypothesis' of forty-five sunk up to February 1940. Here was A1, undeniable evidence.

Incidentally, although DNI had long given up the pre-war idea that the Germans might be deceiving us by a system of duplicate numbers, Churchill himself returned to it in the last minute he wrote on this subject as First Lord: 'It does not follow that sunken boats have not been replaced by others of the same number.'

It was one thing to get A1 intelligence about numbers of U-boats built from a captured boat; it was quite another problem to find out for certain the scale of building. Much better photography from the air and a great increase in photo-graphic reconnaissance aircraft were required before the early guesswork and the rare contributions from agents could be improved upon. So Admiralty estimates remained on the high side. Indeed, as Prime Minister, Churchill commented on 15 July 1940 that sixty to sixty-five U-boats in existence was exaggerated; and we now know that the Germans had completed and commissioned only twenty-two boats since war began, instead of the thirty-eight with which we credited them.

The practice of surrounding U-boat estimates with the greatest secrecy continued until January 1941, when it was decided to revive the old procedure of 'promulgating' to the Fleet and to departments concerned the known and probable losses of U-boats. So for fourteen months of the growing U-boat offensive detailed and secret information was officially denied to the Plans and Operations Divisions, the Assistant Chiefs of Naval Staff, Home and Foreign, the Controller and the Fourth Sea Lord, whose job it was to build the ships and supply the stores and weapons to fight the Battle of the Atlantic. By word of mouth and other means the information was got around to them and may, indeed, have attracted more notice for having been thus smuggled; but it is the motive behind the politician's ban that is interesting and, from the Intelligence point of view, significant.*

While Churchill's personal responsibility for these minutes is beyond doubt, it is not certain that the calculations which they reflected were his. It is possible that Professor Lindemann's special section, then accommodated in the Admiralty, had something to do with them. He had taken over the statistical department which DNI had been trying to form, with the Board's approval, so that shipping losses, U-boat casualties and so on might be presented in easily understandable form. The idea was inspired by the statistical department started in 1917–18 by Geddes as First Lord, with George Beharrel in charge. This had succeeded in putting right some gross misconceptions which underestimated our shipping losses and exaggerated our shipping potential. Godfrey had consulted Beharrel, now the Chairman of Dunlop, and learned from him what was needed to start such an organization and how it should be run. But Lindemann, with Churchill's approval, took over the idea and what was to have been a general utility department for naval matters became a private piece of machinery covering all aspects of the war operated first by the First Lord and then by the Prime Minister. Whether the explanation of a piece of mystifying distortion is to be found in this fact or not is uncertain. What is certain is that this episode enabled the Intelligence Division to state its principles and to make clear to the Naval Staff the standards that must be maintained.

The distortion of intelligence by politics which has just been described did not last long. Shortly after Churchill became Prime Minister realism prevailed, although the new First Lord, Mr A. V. Alexander, took office believing firmly that by July 1940 at least thirty U-boats had been sunk. Nor did the illusion have serious effects in the long run, for the U-boat war quickly climbed to a scale which could permit no illusions about the future. But a second example of a comparable process, with which Churchill had nothing to do, is worth detailed scrutiny. It had serious long-term effects on our choice and design of battleships and led at the time to a sequence of credulities which would be hard to believe if the record did not prove what happened.

Many men conspired, if not always deliberately, and many events linked up to induce the Admiralty to be content with the 14-in. gun *King George V* in face of the 15-in. gun *Bismarck* with its greater size, endurance and protection. The error, as it turned out, was not fatal; but it might have been, as the official account of the chase of the *Bismarck* in 1941 shows. Wishful thinking, that ever lurking temptation for politicians dealing with military affairs – and for serving officers involved in politics – is even more conspicuous in this episode than in that of the U-boat sinkings.

The story begins with the Anglo-German Naval Treaty of June 1936 which released the Germans from the limits set to their navy by the Treaty of Versailles. As this had been repudiated by Hitler in March 1935, it was thought wise in London to start afresh with the new régime in the hope that the German Navy could be kept to an agreed fixed percentage of the British. So the Admiralty argued. Considering the attitude towards Britain then uppermost in Hitler's mind, the calculation was not unreasonable; for it is now known that he was not planning an early or direct challenge to our naval predominance in Europe and hoped to avoid war with Britain. The weakness of the arrangement was that Britain had

135

already been restricted in its naval construction by an agreement to which the Germans were not parties when the *Bismarck* was laid down – the Washington Naval Agreement and the later London conference which had limited battleships to 35,000 tons. If the Germans were to build bigger ships, so that two or three or more British major units would be needed to pursue and destroy one of theirs, then the principle of the treaty – which was that German strength should never exceed thirty-five per cent of the British – would lose its value. It was doubtless on that calculation that Admiral Raeder ordered that the *Bismarck* and *Tirpitz* should both be of 45,000 tons and deliberately cheated on his Government's undertakings.

How precisely was the game played and at what points were the British outwitted? On 1 July 1936 the German Embassy informed the Foreign Office in confidence that the particulars of battleship F would be 35,000 tons, beam 36 metres (118 ft), calibre of largest gun 38 cm. (14·8 in.), mean draft 7·9 metres (26 ft). The Director of Naval Construction is on record as commenting (5 September) some weeks later that the large beam (15 in. more than that planned for the *King George V*) was presumably dictated by the comparatively shallow draft of the ship, which in turn was made necessary by the shallow water in the Kiel Canal and the Baltic. The same month Plans Division in London, which had been closely involved in negotiating – and therefore believed in – the various treaties limiting naval armaments, made their comment. Captain Tom Phillips, later to be Churchill's first Vice-Chief of Naval Staff, remarked: 'The present design of German capital ships appears to show that Germany is looking towards the Baltic with its shallow approaches more than in the past.' In other words, they felt, these battleships might be regarded as aimed more at the Russians than at ourselves. Yet Phillips was by nature a sceptical, aggressive man.

In the German section of NID, however, there were suspicions of the German figures, partly inspired by secret reports that they were inaccurate, partly by a reasonable assumption that Nazis might lie. But at a meeting to discuss the *Bismarck* in early 1937 a split in opinion was revealed between on the one side the technicians, represented by the Director of Naval Construction and the NID technical section, and on the other side the non-technical officers. The Director of Naval Intelligence, with his advisers divided, was in no position to be tenacious for scepticism against optimisim; and later that year on 5 August DNC wrote:

The figures given are not in themselves sufficient to warrant the conclusion that the standard displacement of 35,000 tons is being purposely exceeded ... From our experience with *Gorizia* it is probable that in these countries the designers are not pressed to be meticulously accurate. To put this into more precise terms, taking into account displacement variations of completed British ships before displacement by treaty was laid down, the designers of the 35,000-ton ship would not be blamed if the displacement on completion was 36,000 tons, and such a figure would be more in conformity with the length and beam reported than 35,000 tons.

This reference to the *Gorizia* should have alerted the Board to the risks of optimism about *Bismarck*. For physical examination of the Italian cruiser while in dock at Gibraltar had shown that she had an armoured belt and exceeded the permissible treaty 10,000 tons by between two and four thousand tons. There was no reason to believe that Hitler's capital ship policy would be notably more honest than Mussolini's. Yet the Director of Plans allowed himself to write: 'Our principal safeguard against such an infraction of treaty obligations lies in the good faith of the signatories'.*

Who is to blame Phillips for this attitude when the Whitehall line, set by the politicians and by what they believed to be the mood of the voters, was to hope for the best and give the dictators a little more rope to hang themselves? Plans Division's job was not to argue against the treaties, but to make the best plans they could within their limits.

Is the Director of Naval Construction's department entitled to that particular defence? It appears that the mystery of the *Bismarck*'s shallow draft was not investigated as thoroughly as it should have been by those who were designing and building the equivalent British battleships. On the other hand they were hard pressed with the new programme and deeper probing of the German design would almost certainly not have led them to a change in our own designs which would mean breaking treaty limitations. When, in 1941, information from the survivors of the sunk battleship and from the Russian Admiralty confirmed NID's suspicions that *Bismarck*'s tonnage was nearer 45,000 than 35,000 tons, it became clear, even to DNC, that the 'mystery' of her shallow draught was a mystery no more. The *Bismarck*'s draught was in fact not very different from that of the British capital ships and its shallowness was simply a device to give colour to the gross understatement of her displacement.

What irked Godfrey at the time was the readiness of his colleague at Bath to believe immediately from the Russians something that he would not accept from NID.

From the German naval documents we know what was going on behind the scenes in Berlin while the Admiralty hoped and guessed. On 11 February 1937 the Plans Division of the German Admiralty wrote to Admiral Raeder:

> In view of the difficult conditions in our harbours, a displacement of 42,000 tons should be the limit of ships to be built, unless we widen the harbours and channels and also the curves of the Kiel Canal. . . . Politically it must be decided if the displacement should be still further increased above the treaty limits.
>
> The Constructional Office considers that no further increase should take place as long as we are tied to the 35,000-ton limit which we have already exceeded by 7,000 tons, so that a further increase could hardly be concealed . . . The Constructional Office would like to build an extra ship rather than exceed the 35,000-ton limit.
>
> Even if other Navies renounce the limits of the London Agreement or go in for calibres above 38 cm . . . we should be reluctant to increase them owing to the state of our channels and our Treaty obligations . . . a decision cannot be reached till the various aspects including the military factors and the clauses of the Treaty have been considered.

Here, clearly, someone was trying to be honest; but the argument which counted in his mind was the technical rather than the moral one. Indeed, the morals of the matter were not his business.

For German Plans Division it was a different matter. They stated in a memorandum to the Chief of Staff dated 18 February 1938 that the *Bismarck*'s true displacement was twenty per cent greater than that announced to the British; but they argued that it would be wrong to indicate a greater tonnage than had

138

already been announced to Britain, Russia and Japan because 'we shall be accused of starting an armament race'.

What, then, was the British Naval Attaché doing? Was he too misled and if so, by what methods? Were the suspicions of NID due to anything reported by him? On 23 December 1936 the yearly report of Captain Troubridge, Naval Attaché in Berlin, to the Foreign Office (copies to DNI and C-in-C Home Fleet) said:

> The Anglo-German naval agreement was one of the master strokes of policy which have characterized Germany's dealings with her ex-enemies since the war. *When the time is ripe, as history shows, it will unquestionably go the same way as other agreements: but the time is not yet.*

The italic passage was omitted from the printed version of the Ambassador's annual report (Sir E. Phipps to Mr Eden dated 12 January 1937 C357/357/18) and the Director of Plans already mentioned in this chapter, Captain Phillips, wrote a minute on 1 January 1937 on the NID docket sent to him with Troubridge's unexpurgated report: 'It would be of particular interest to know the basis for the very definite statement on page 2 of the memorandum.'*

This general expression of scepticism seems to be as far as Troubridge got and there is no doubt that the intelligence coming to the Admiralty from Germany was thin and poor. Why that should have been so is not clear; the Nazis after 1934 never tried to conceal their successful rearmament and were always anxious to show what they could do. For example, the French Air Attaché, Stehlin, was given the fullest opportunity to see what the Luftwaffe would be able to do to France (see Chapter 15). It seems likely that the Secret Service was not specially pressed to find out the state of German naval building just because of the official optimism about the working of the treaty.*

Ten years later, Troubridge was asked by Godfrey if he could explain how we had been so misled and he wrote as follows:

> I fancy that generally speaking the reason that we were 'fooled' by the Germans, both as regards submarines and the battleship tonnage, was that we were inclined at the time (after the Anglo-German agreement) to trust them in these matters.

I confess that Raeder's earnestness and apparent sincerity, assuring me that Germany meant to adhere strictly to the agreement, may well have influenced DNI when my reports of these interviews came through. I started my time pretty well open-minded, though having studied *Great Britain and the German Navy* by Woodward, I was pretty well on my guard.

As evidence of my state of mind in 1936 I mentioned in the NA's annual report, which is annexed to the annual report of the Ambassador, something to the effect that the Anglo-German naval agreement remains the cornerstone of German naval policy. It will unquestionably be torn up when the moment seems propitious, but the time is not yet.

The boys in the Chancery refused to put this paragraph in, but it will remain on the record none the less in the copy sent to DNI and Commander in Chief Home Fleet.

Doubt about the tonnage of the *Bismarck* came shortly after the launching, when information from Williams, the vice-consul in Hamburg, indicated that she was drawing a good deal more than she should.

That Raeder lied to me and also to my predecessor is undeniable. Muirhead-Gould [Naval Attaché Berlin before Troubridge] always said he had, but I fear I was lulled to a certain extent by his apparent sincerity. Moreover I found it hard to understand why he found it necessary. But then to understand is to understand the tortuous workings of the Teutonic mind. Sometimes they lie just for the sake of lying.*

It will be interesting to see, when the records are opened, whether historians can find out the reason for this significant excision by Sir Eric Phipps from his Naval Attaché's despatch. The fairest presumption is that he thought his subordinate should stick to naval facts and abstain from political generalization.

The lies, the realities and the contrast between them are most easily grasped in tabular form on p. 141.

The mistakes and omissions here recorded were made for the most part in the pre-war NID which faced difficulties of getting information and staff which have been described elsewhere. But there is this to be said in their defence. The Naval Staff in peacetime were strongly disinclined to accept from their intelligence advisers any views or facts that might be 'awkward', that is to say, in sharp conflict with current strategic doctrine or political appreciation. They probably felt that if Germany was in fact cheating and could be proved treacherous, no one in the Foreign Office or Downing Street would handle the accusation effectively; why then make it?

But there seems too to have been reluctance among our own technical experts to believe that the *Bismarck* could combine

Facts about the *Bismarck*

Authority	German Embassy Official Statement	*Bismarck* survivors and notebook	Russian Admiralty	German Records	*King George V*
	Apr. 39	Oct. 41	Oct. 42	Oct. 44	
Displacement ..	35000*	41150*	45000	53000† 45000*	35000
Length	792	792	792	792	745
Beam	118	118	118	118	103
Draft	26	33¾	34	34	34
H.P.	80000	150000	150000	150000	111000
Armament ..	8–15″	8–15″	8–15″	8–15″	10–14″
Thickest armour ..	9″	13″	13″	12½″	15″
Full speed	27	30¼	30¼	30¼	28¼
Endurance ..	?	?	17500 miles at 18 kn	17500 miles at 18 kn	14500 miles at 10 kn
Fuel stowage ..	?	?	8500 tons	8500 tons	3860 tons

* Standard displacement.
† Full load.
Definitions:
Full load displacement with all oil stores, ammunition, etc., on board vessel fully equipped and ready for sea.
Standard displacement – as for full load, but excluding all fuel and reserve feed water.
Normal displacement – figures may differ in different countries but generally cover the condition of vessel fully equipped and ready for sea but with a portion only of stores, fuel and reserve feed water.

the high speed, long endurance and good protection with the mounting of 15-inch guns; just as there was reluctance to believe that U-boats could dive as deep as they did dive, or that underwater speed could be increased to the degree that it was by 1944. Perhaps the British underrated the tremendous advantages of starting again, as the Germans did, from scratch and were inhibited by too many decisions already taken and too many economies rigidly enforced. Be that as it may, they were disinclined to listen to uncomfortable truths of intelligence.*

Godfrey himself looks back on this episode as illustrating three lessons for the craft:

1 The unwillingness of authority to believe information that has awkward political implications.

2 The tendency of naval officers and others who have taken part in negotiations to become advocates of the integrity of the persons with whom they secured agreement, and to lose the scepticism which is part of vigilance.

3 Our technicians may not be the best judges of enemy intentions and achievement. They find it hard sometimes to believe that what they cannot do or have not thought of doing has been done by the other side.

7 Who betrayed the *Bismarck*?

*'The accuracy of the information supplied by
the Admiralty and the speed with which it
was passed were remarkable; and the balance
struck between information and instruction
passed to the forces out of visual touch
with me was ideal.'*

(Admiral Tovey)

(*To understand the tremendous excitement and interest aroused all over
the world by the pursuit and sinking of the* Bismarck, *one has to
recall that Britain had by 27 May 1941 lived through many weeks of
unrelieved bad news. Rommel had forced Wavell back in Cyrenaica; the
Germans had invaded Greece and Jugoslavia on 6 April; there followed
the surrender of those countries and the evacuation from Greece of British
forces with the loss of twenty-six ships to the Navy; then the German
attack on Crete and more reverses. The Russians and Americans had
still to be drawn into the war. The Home Fleet's prompt extinction of the*
Bismarck's *ambitions meant that the Mediterranean Fleet could be
relieved after two ordeals by evacuation; but what counted was the
public demonstration of British sea power against the most powerful
ship afloat.*)

In the masterly narrative of the *Bismarck* operation given by
Captain Stephen Roskill in his official naval history there are
brief references to the part played by intelligence on both sides,
including the tribute at the head of this chapter. They are quite
properly made incidental to the complex and thrilling story of
the movements, pursuit and fighting which, as we now know,
shattered once for all the original German plan for achieving
temporary command of the Atlantic trade routes with surface
ships. Yet the intelligence staffs on both sides played a crucial
part in the whole episode, and it is possible now to study in some
detail the British effort to calculate the intentions of the Germans
and the Germans' effort to read the minds of the British.*

F

During the decisive phases of the week-long chase the Admiralty – that is to say the War Room and Operational Intelligence Centre working together – had the advantage for most of the time of reliable and full sighting reports, first from the cruisers *Suffolk* and *Norfolk* shadowing the *Bismarck* and the *Prinz Eugen* with the help of radar, then from the *Prince of Wales*'s shadowing with them, and then from aircraft sightings and further reports from shadowing cruisers. Only during thirty hours between 25 May and 26 May, when contact was lost, was the Admiralty forced into calculation and appreciation with no positive naval intelligence to work on save one D/F fix from *Bismarck*'s signals to base which gave a rough but decisive clue to the direction she had taken. The German operations and intelligence staffs, in contrast, were ill-served by air intelligence and remained for much of the time blind, owing to the wireless silence kept by their two ships. Judging from the log of the heavy cruiser *Prinz Eugen*, their 'Y' service was able to give no accurate information about the Home Fleet's movements to correct the errors of the Luftwaffe.

One can detect in the German Naval Staff's appraisal of what led to the sinking of the *Bismarck* the tendency to wishful thinking which is examined elsewhere in this book as a major cause of intelligence failure; and there is striking evidence of the fallibility of the air reconnaissance from Norway on which the Germans had largely to rely for their estimate of the Home Fleet's available strength at any given moment. If this chapter invites more interest in the German than in the British intelligence view of the operation it is because the material available reveals so strikingly the mediocre quality of our own NID's opposite numbers, the hazards of operational intelligence working in the vast spaces of the Atlantic and the deep respect of the Germans for the agents of that amorphous and omniscient monster, the British Secret Service – who, in fact, played no part at all in the operation.

The German Naval Staff's inquest on the lost battleship during the summer of 1941 was anxious and protracted. To have sunk the *Hood* was a matter of great pride, even for those German officers who recalled that she was twenty years old; but Raeder's fleet could not afford a one-for-one exchange of capital ships with the British. That way the ability of the half-dozen German surface ships to harass, still more to threaten to harass, the Atlantic trade routes would soon be crippled. Their raids must, if possible, avoid such costly engagements. It must be discovered why the *Bismarck* and *Prinz Eugen* had not achieved surprise when they broke out, why they were caught where they were, and why the whole web of supply and reconnaissance ships spun out like bases over the ocean in advance of their departure from the Baltic on 18 May had been broken up by the middle of June with the loss of nine ships, six of them precious tankers.

As time went on the mystery of the supply ships exercised the mind of Godfrey's opposite number more than the loss of the *Bismarck*, and a further inquiry was held in July 1942, including with the nine ships already mentioned three others not directly connected with 'Operation Rhine Exercise' (*Rheinuebung*) as the sortie of the two ships was called. The explanation put forward, which is analysed later in this chapter, exonerated those responsible for the security of the Kriegs-marine's codes and cipher tables. Indeed, as in the case of the *Bismarck* itself, no individual or department was found to be blameworthy.

The evidence on which the German intelligence investigators had to work was confined to the log of the *Prinz Eugen*, which had been in company with the *Bismarck* until the early evening of 24 May; the evidence of her officers and wireless ratings; the signals to base received from Admiral Lütjens after he knew that he was being shadowed; a certain amount of material intercepted on board the *Prinz Eugen* from British tactical signals; and the accounts released by the Admiralty of the manner in which the *Bismarck* had been spotted, tracked and sunk. One thing no one could do; read the mind of the late Admiral Lütjens, commander of the squadron. His intentions and calculations, like those of his pursuer, Admiral Holland, in the *Hood*, remained forever a mystery.

The failure of the German ships to reach the high seas unnoticed was quickly and easily explained. As they moved out of the Baltic with destroyers and minesweepers through the Kattegat and Skagerrak between six and eight in the morning of 20 May, the Swedish cruiser *Gotland* proceeded with them, close to its own coast. Admiral Lütjens assumed at once that the British would therefore learn of his movements and sent a slightly plaintive signal to headquarters to that effect. He judged correctly: for the next morning at 6.45 the German 'Y' service intercepted a British 'aircraft radio station' order to aircraft to look out for two battleships and three destroyers reported on a northerly course. Just after 7 o'clock the look-out on the *Prinz Eugen* saw four unidentified aircraft for a short while in the distance. Later that day the two ships were identified by Coastal Command in Korsfjord south of Bergen, where they fuelled. How had this come about?

Captain Denham, then Naval Attaché in Stockholm, has told the author how, on the day of the *Bismarck*'s sortie, he happened to be having one of his twice-weekly evening meetings over a drink with the Norwegian Naval Attaché, who was a close friend of the Chief of Staff to the head of the Swedish Secret Service. The latter had received the *Gotland*'s signal as a matter of routine and had mentioned it as material of no particular secrecy. Denham informed the Admiralty the moment he got back to his office, grading his report A1 – 'Most Immediate: Kattegat today 20 May. At 15.00 2 large warships escorted by 3 destroyers, 5 escort craft 10 or 12 a/c passed Marstrand course north-west.' By 3.30 the next morning OIC 'not altogether surprised and much excited' had alerted Coastal Command.*

The comment of German Naval Intelligence on events up to this point is revealing. The staff study claims:

> It is quite certain that the *Bismarck* squadron was observed proceeding through the Great Belt and Kattegat by agents of the enemy coast-watching organization and of the Secret Intelligence Service, so famed for its efficiency, and that this intelligence was passed on to the enemy via the communications centre, the British Naval Attaché in Stockholm.

It does not appear to have occurred to the writers that the Luftwaffe, at the Kriegsmarine's request, had been unusually busy making visual and photographic reconnaissance flights over Scapa and paying special attention to weather conditions in the narrow Denmark Strait between Iceland and the edge of the icefield off Greenland's eastern shore – all of which had been noted by British Intelligence,* which alerted the Commander in Chief Home Fleet.

The Germans were really more interested – and this preference, almost an obsession, appears repeatedly – in the theory that the operation had been given away by treachery and carelessness. There had been discussion of plans over the telephone between the Naval War Staff and the operational control offices in Paris and Kiel. Supply preparations had involved many people. Security had not been all it should be. The wife of an officer on board the *Bismarck* had 'spread it around among civilians' that the ship had sailed; and while the battleship had cast off from Gdynia the band had played '*Muss i' denn*', a ballad of grief and parting.

Yet in all technical matters under naval control great efforts had been made to maintain security. Flag Officer i/c of Baltic Defences had suspended all merchant traffic through the Great Belt and Kattegat for the night of the 19–20 May and next morning – perhaps a rather conspicuous precaution. To cover any unusual increase of wireless traffic arising from the squadron's departure, simulated traffic had been put on to deceive the British 'Y' Service. Moreover the battleship key for ciphers had been brought out for the first time, so ensuring that, with this foolproof system, signals could be exchanged only between authorized persons with an operational interest in the undertaking; and of course at sea wireless silence had been duly observed until Admiral Lütjens knew that he was being shadowed by two British cruisers.

What more could have been done? A tone of irritated helplessness runs through the report, a sense of being caged in, of the German fleet always having to run the gauntlet of British intelligence hovering over the outlets to the North Sea. But again the signals specialists were given a clean bill of security: 'According to renewed and very extensive inquiry, the possibility of the enemy's being able to read signals by deciphering them has been unanimously discounted by all the experts.'

And quite right they were: not one signal from and to the *Bismarck* squadron could be read back in England – which deepens still further the mystery of her 'betrayal'.

The naval officers and civilians responsible for this report would have been less than human had they not tried to hint at failures by other services, for which the Navy could not be held responsible. For example, they said that the counter-espionage wireless service of the OKW believed that a strong and clever organization of radio transmitting British agents existed, especially in Norway. The places most dangerous at the moment 'were thought to be the Gironde Estuary, Brest, Cherbourg, Flekke Fjord and Trondheim – all departure points for German warships, of course. Furthermore, although the telephone service used by the German Naval Staff between Group West and the BdU (C-in-C U-boats) was on a naval transmission network, these lines ran via booster transformer stations in occupied territory which could not be manned only by Germans. 'The tapping of these lines by British agents', it is pleaded, 'is very probable.' (In fact nothing of the kind was achieved.)

So much for the failure to reach undetected the Atlantic or even the North Sea, which can be counted a failure of German security only if every success by British intelligence receiving neutral help is to be put down to some German omission – which is absurd; so let us turn to a real failure in intelligence by the Luftwaffe. We have to remember that the German Navy suffered severely throughout the war from its inability to train, inform and control a reconnaissance service not under its own command. The delays and irritation suffered by the NID before it achieved its happy and fruitful relationship with Coastal Command were mild compared with the experience of Raeder and Doenitz.*

In the first place the reconnaissance of Denmark Strait (the way out to the Atlantic) with its hazards of ice and bad visibility, had been inefficient: just enough to alert the British that something was brewing, but insufficient to detect that the Home Fleet's cruiser watch on this passage was never relaxed. Then the reports on Scapa Flow were misleading about the location and strength of the British main units, on which the intelligence given to Admiral Lütjens was incomplete. The *Hood*, for example, one of the only three ships capable of single combat with the *Bismarck*, had been placed as either in Gibraltar or at Scapa. Most important of all, the whereabouts of the carrier *Victorious* were uncertain and the cruiser strength was underrated. So neither German Naval Intelligence nor Admiral

Lütjens knew that Admiral Tovey, commanding the Home Fleet, could bring to bear not only the *Hood* and *Prince of Wales* but also the battleship *King George V*, the aircraft carrier *Victorious* to say nothing of Force H at Gibraltar.

Compare this with the good intelligence work by Home Fleet and OIC consulting together which had alerted Tovey to the possibility of a break-out from Norway, even though the *Gneisenau* and the *Scharnhorst* were pinioned in Brest by Bomber Command. Thus, when he heard on 21 May that Coastal Command had found the *Bismarck* and the *Prinz Eugen* in Korsfjord, he had sent the *Hood, Prince of Wales* and six destroyers to Hvalfjord in Iceland, where they could refuel and move to intercept the German squadron on whichever of the two possible routes it chose. In Denmark Strait the *Suffolk*, with her new radar equipment, was on patrol with the *Norfolk*, while two other cruisers, the *Birmingham* and the *Manchester* covered with the help of trawlers the alternative route between the Faroes and Iceland.

Thus, when Tovey heard at eight o'clock in the evening of 22 May that the German ships had now left Bergen, he was ready for what he rightly assumed, with OIC agreement, to be a break-out into the Atlantic. Within three hours he had sailed from Scapa with his main fleet in support of the *Hood*'s squadron. Thanks to the wireless precautions taken by the Fleet this movement seems to have passed unnoticed by the German B Dienst or 'Y' Service.

Just about this time Group North (the command under which the German ships were operating until they came under Group West for their attempted dash to France) reported to Lütjens the latest intelligence about the British. Recorded in the log of Captain Brinckmann of the *Prinz Eugen* is the information that no photographic reconnaissance of Scapa Flow had been possible owing to bad weather; but the presence of four heavy ships had been confirmed visually. To this was added the advice that 'the enemy, it seems, has still no knowledge of the sortie'.

This advice was based on a report from Fliegerfuehrer Nord (the responsible air command co-operating with the Navy) that visual reconnaissance on 22 May showed the forces in Scapa to be the same as those shown on 20 May by photographic reconnaissance. Weather conditions had made it impossible to take pictures. So the presumption was, on the word of a Luftwaffe air crew, that four battleships, possibly an aircraft carrier, and what appeared to be six light cruisers and several destroyers were even now still in the Home Fleet base. In fact, of course, by this time the *Hood* had already left and the rest of the Home Fleet was on the way to intercept the German squadron.

In the evening of 22 May Fliegerfuehrer Nord corrected his previous report drastically as follows:

Scapa Flow is not occupied as previously reported by visual reconnaissance by three battleships and three cruisers, but by two probably light cruisers and a gunnery training ship.

And later that night:

After thorough second-phase interpretation only one light cruiser and six destroyers as well as smaller vessels and merchant ships could be distinguished.

The change of mind was spectacular.

Further intelligence was transmitted by Group North to the effect that 'nothing worth special notice' had been observed in aircraft wireless traffic. There was no operational wireless traffic and they were unable to observe any result of the *Bismarck*'s putting to sea or of the British order to search for her – only reinforced air reconnaissance in the north-eastern sector of Norway. As a statement of intelligence available this cannot be faulted; as an appreciation of the likely disposition of the Home Fleet it seems to show wishful thinking and lack of understanding.

From the *Prinz Eugen*'s log it sounds as if this reassuring news from home was taken on board with a grain of salt. It was, after all, negative intelligence; and, valuable though negative information can often be, fighting men generally distrust it. One can feel only sympathy for a staff and a commander receiving such baffling clues. It says a lot for the self-restraint of the German NID that it did not comment more harshly on the Luftwaffe's competence.

The Naval Staff view after the inquiry reads as follows:

Subsequent confirmatory reports prove that the visual reconnaissance of 22/5 according to which four battleships were lying at Scapa Flow was incorrect. By transferring back the position of the British ships on 24/5 it becomes evident that the main body of the Home Fleet must have sailed out of Scapa early on 22/5, probably immediately on receiving the report from the aircraft which had searched the fjords around Bergen, had found them empty and therefore confirmed that the German squadron had put to sea.

It was shown on 24/5 how little one can rely on *visual* air reconnaissance alone in unfavourable weather conditions. In the afternoon, *after* the battle (in which the *Hood* had been sunk), Flieger-fuehrer Nord reported 'Visual reconnaissance only possible through gaps in cloud but berths were examined. Three battleships among them probably the *Hood*. It could not be made out clearly whether an aircraft carrier was also there. Apart from these three cruisers, probably light ones.'

But the German NID did not allow itself to observe that Admiral Lütjens at sea on the morning of 22 May must have assumed that the main body of Admiral Tovey's forces was still at Scapa. He might have calculated that if it had then put to sea and set course straight for the southern end of Denmark Strait at full speed it would have to cover 1,200 miles, or exactly the distance already covered by the *Bismarck* and *Prinz Eugen* by that time.

There seems to have been no great surprise on either bridge as the German ships made their way in the mist and snow through Denmark Strait when the 'Y' service on board the *Prinz Eugen* intercepted the *Suffolk*'s first report to the Admiralty that she was in contact. That was at 19.22. At 20.46 the 'Y' service reported another unit. Misled by the cruiser's call sign, they thought it was the battleship *King George V* – a suggestion which must have alarmed and puzzled Captain Brinckmann. At 23.53 there was another report: 'operational activity by the enemy discernible'; and at three the next morning it is recorded that radio intercepts showed the shadowers to be getting course, speed and alterations of course very quickly. In other words, despite the weather and the zigzagging and the poor visibility the British ships were hanging on. Two and a half hours later the *Hood* and the *Prince of Wales*, guided to their prey by the *Suffolk* and *Norfolk*, joined battle.*

Not until four hours after it was over, and the chase had been

resumed, did the captain of the *Prinz Eugen* record his impression that the British must have a location gear of remarkable
range and accuracy, although it was not out of the question
that D/F bearings were being got from *Prinz Eugen*'s own radar
apparatus. Presumably the captain of the victorious *Bismarck*
came to the same conclusion: if such shadowing were possible,
then the only escape from it was for the ships to separate, the
Prinz Eugen being the rear ship and the one being tracked.
Neither of these officers had been warned that their high speed
and the helpful weather conditions might be neutralized by
the British radar. It is hard to criticize German intelligence for
this ignorance, for they gained little access to British technical
secrets. Indeed, the efficiency of our radar became an obsession
with the German naval and air staffs.

Then at 4 a.m. on 25 May the *Suffolk* lost track of the German
ships and for thirty hours – hours of anxious and intense calculation and argument between OIC and Operations in the
Admiralty Citadel – the *Bismarck* was lost in the vast spaces
of the Atlantic. (Not until a Catalina aircraft saw her at 10.30
the next morning steaming south-east towards France was
there any real certainty about what to do next.) Yet at 10.45
a.m. Admiral Tovey received D/F bearings from the OIC
which, owing to a mistake in plotting, led him in the wrong
direction – north-east – while the *Bismarck* steamed south-east.
And at 11 a.m. the next day the OIC was able to advise Force
H, coming up in the south from Gibraltar with the carrier *Ark
Royal*, that the prey might be making for Biscay ports. The
same advice was given to Admiral Tovey seven hours later,
probably as the result of unusual wireless activity observed
by Station X in the area of Group West (France) caused by
German naval and air force preparations to aid the *Bismarck*.
At this point, visual contact by aircraft and ship again took
over from wireless intelligence, calculation and inference. The
narrative must return to the German squadron.

Once the battle was over and the *Hood* sunk, Admiral
Lütjens could expect no more intelligence help from base. The
Luftwaffe could but scour the high seas to find them. He must
assume that every unit the British could muster would be sent
to avenge the loss of their most famous big ship. Nor, indeed,
could he ask for information or orders or advice once he had

shaken off his pursuers. For any signal would be picked up by the British D/F network or by 'Y' operators in the Home Fleet; the approximate area in which he was operating would then be plotted and known in a matter of minutes. He had to make up his own mind in which direction to turn.

Unfortunately he overrated British powers of pursuit. Seven hours after the *Suffolk* had lost contact at midnight, it was still believed in the *Bismarck* that she was being shadowed. It was therefore decided that no harm would be done by reporting at length to Germany what the situation was. Anxiety there can have been no less than it was in the Citadel in London. For a whole day had passed without news.

This half-hour long signal that the *Bismarck* sent out at 08.52/25 was a godsend. It gave her position away when she had been lost by the British for over eight hours. As the bearings were picked up by the British 'Y' stations and reached the Citadel in London, the excitement that morning was intense. Every allied D/F set had been alerted and was taking bearings: indeed, they began to stream into the Admiralty over tele-printer and telephone even before the *Bismarck* had completed her message. What happened then is clearly recalled by Lt-Cdr Kemp who was in charge of plotting all fixes on the OIC charts both for Winn and Denning. He writes:

As plotted on the chart the bearings showed the *Bismarck* as well to the *east*ward of her known position when the *Suffolk* lost contact. Unfortunately, it was a very vague cut and quite impossible at this stage to pin down to an exact position.

Admiral Clayton, Captain Edwards and Denning all came along to have a look at these bearings on the chart, and we all agreed that it showed unquestionably that the *Bismarck* was some hundreds of miles more to the eastward of where we would have expected her to be had she continued her break-out course towards the Atlantic or the homeward route.

In the mistaken belief that the Commander-in-Chief in the *King George V* had with him some destroyers fitted with direction-finding sets, and might thus have obtained a cross-bearing, the individual bearings were signalled out to the fleet instead of the position which they indicated on the Admiralty chart. I remember arguing the case for sending the position most strongly with Clayton, and I believe Denning backed me up, but Clayton was adamant that the bearings should be signalled as they stood. I feel that this was a mistake on the part of the Admiralty, since it was unfair to ask the C-in-C in the midst of a big operation to interpret the raw material of intelligence rather than receive our own interpretation of it. In fact there were no destroyers with the C-in-C fitted with D/F.*

As plotted in the flagship the bearings gave a position far to the northward instead of the eastward. This gave the misleading impression to C-in-C that the *Bismarck* was making for the North Sea and home. Later, when the operation was over, I put the bearings on a navigational chart and it became obvious what had happened. The 'Y' officer in the flagship had plotted them on an ordinary navigational chart and not on a gnomonic chart.* As plotted on his chart the bearings showed a position nearly 200 miles too far north.

Denning now agrees generally with this account of the change of direction which might have lost the *Bismarck* to the Home Fleet. But he thinks it may have been at the flagship's special request before sailing that bearings only were sent by OIC. He confirms that Admiral Clayton insisted on the action that was taken in the belief that the Fleet would get better fixes where they were than could be got from the land stations.

Cruise of the Bismarck – May 1941

18 May Left Gdynia in the Baltic with *Prinz Eugen*.

20 May Admiral Tovey alert in Scapa. German ships sighted in Kattegat and reported to Admiralty.

21 May Intensive Coastal Command search started and found ships at Korsfjord near Bergen where they fuelled.

22 May Making for Atlantic via Denmark Strait. Evening, naval aircraft from Hatston, Orkneys found fjord empty. Tovey sails with Home Fleet.

23 May Spotted at 7.22 p.m. by *Suffolk* and shadowed by cruisers.

24 May a.m. after losing contact in snowstorm cruisers just after midnight in touch again. Sinking of the *Hood* follows 6 a.m. Cruisers keep up chase.

24 May 6 p.m. *Bismarck* and *Prinz Eugen* part company, the cruiser westward and the battleship south-eastward towards France.

25 May 3.06 a.m. *Bismarck* lost by Admiralty for thirty hours with Home Fleet searching part of the time in wrong direction. Sends long signal home at 8.52 a.m. which enables Admiralty to fix her rough position and advise Home Fleet eventually to change on to right course.

26 May 10.30 a.m. Catalina aircraft guided by the OIC sights *Bismarck*.

26 May 8.47 p.m. Fleet Air Arm attacks from the *Ark Royal* in Swordfish.

27 May 8.47–8.49 a.m. Final attacks by Home Fleet and Force H began.
Bismarck sunk at 10.36 a.m.

So although the *Bismarck* betrayed herself, the mistake was nearly made up for by an understandable error of technique both in the Admiralty and in the flagship.

It must have been soon after this that the naval wireless network of Group West in France began to take over on the frequency used by Group North in Germany, so creating a volume of sudden and unusual traffic which was at once observed in London. Added to other clues and arguments, it pointed to the Bay of Biscay as the *Bismarck*'s destination.

As for the German naval staff, the *Bismarck* for the time being was the only source of intelligence quickly available to them to form any conclusion about the next step: what the U-boats should do – if anything – what aircraft might be sent to give the ship cover and bomb the British pursuers when they came within range of France. On the decision by Lütjens to send his long informative signal the Naval Staff commented:

The W/T traffic lasting over half an hour seems to have provided the latter [the enemy] with rich opportunities for taking exact bearings by D/F. Gibraltar and Iceland give a cross-bearing angle of approximately 90 degrees for the position. The British Commander in Chief knew from this that he was already *west* of the *Bismarck*, ordered *King George V* and *Rodney* to turn back on a north-easterly course and then in the afternoon, when he was on the

Bismarck's route, steered a parallel course. After these bearings had proved that the *Bismarck* was steaming a south-easterly course in the forenoon of the 25th, no other conclusion could be drawn than that she was heading for the west coast of France.*

In fact, of course, the British C-in-C received from the Admiralty a signal pointing out the error that had been made.

It is possible with the help of the German archives to reconstruct with some verisimilitude the kind of arguments that led Admiral Lütjens into the trap of Home Fleet and Force H (and which, *a fortiori*, enabled British intelligence – the OIC – to advise that the *Bismarck* would go south). The German Naval Staff must have discussed incessantly the dangers and advantages of operating from the Baltic or from Norway, from the Bay of Biscay or from the North Sea. The successful cruise of the *Scharnhorst* and *Gneisenau* must have been mulled over time and again, and it is known that at the conference on board the *Bismarck* the day she sailed, the question of using or not using Denmark Strait and of the kind of weather needed to do so was gone over again. So the reconstruction made after the event is, not surprisingly, much like the appreciation made by the OIC during the event.

Rear-Admiral Clayton, Commander Denning and their helpers, familiar with every move of the big ships after two years' study and familiar with the problems of Commander in Chief Home Fleet in his Scapa base, did not find it impossible to read the mind of Admiral Lütjens. But it was important they did not know at first the extent of the damage the *Bismarck* had suffered from the two hits scored by the *Prince of Wales*, one of which caused the oil leak which produced a wake spotted by a shadowing aircraft.

Here then is how the German Naval Staff read Lütjens's mind as he considered the alternatives open to him after sinking the *Hood*. First there was the question of distance. If he made straight for St Nazaire the distance would be about 1,700 miles, but if he hauled off for half a day or so to shake off his shadowers, it would be at least 2,000 miles. If he turned north for Norway, Bergen was 1,150 miles away; Trondheim via Denmark Strait 1,400 miles.

The greater distance to the French ports would not matter

156

so long as the fuel leak caused by one of the *Prince of Wales*'s hits was not made worse by rougher weather or further gunnery action. If she did make Brest or St Nazaire his ship would be in position for further Atlantic forays, perhaps in company with the *Scharnhorst* and *Gneisenau*. To choose this course would be to show the offensive spirit.

The shortest way home, to Bergen, led quickly into an area where the Luftwaffe could offer help; but it also passed close to British sea and air bases. If, as reconnaissance reports suggested, part of the Home Fleet was still in Scapa, the route between the Faroes and Shetlands would lead straight into its arms. The same was true of the route to Trondheim south of Iceland.

In favour of the Denmark Strait route was bad visibility on the ice boundary and reduced danger from aircraft in the predictable weather conditions. Above all, along this route *Bismarck* was most likely to avoid meeting the main body of the Home Fleet moving in the direction of the battle that had taken place that morning.

Why then did Lütjens not turn north? It seems possible, the argument continues, that the *King George V* was believed, on board both German ships, to be with the shadowing cruisers. If that were so and if the *Prince of Wales* had suffered only minor damage, then the odds against the *Bismarck* without the *Prinz Eugen* would be too great. (Lütjens could no more know that the *Prince of Wales* had suffered serious damage than Captain Leach could know that his guns caused serious oil leakage to the *Bismarck*.) Moreover – and this was probably the decisive consideration – it is apparent from the signals sent by Lütjens and from the log of the *Prinz Eugen* that they had been deeply impressed by the British tracking equipment, against which the conditions in Denmark Strait had already been shown to offer scant protection.

To shake off the pursuers by separating the ships and then strike south was clearly the right answer. It appears that during the night of the 25th the naval staff, not then knowing the nature or extent of the damage done to their ship, had considered ordering Lütjens to head southward and west for the Atlantic convoy routes; but they decided that 'it would be wrong to influence him in any definite direction' – the man on the spot could judge best.*

157

The naval staff drew the conclusion that Admiral Lütjens followed above all his sense of duty:

It can safely be assumed, however, in view of Admiral Lütjens's personality and sense of duty, that the deciding factor at this point was not so much the question as to which port the ship could reach with the greatest degree of safety, but his task . . . to put the battle squadron into action against the enemy supply routes in the Atlantic.

They did not know, it seems, as the Admiralty did not then know, that worsening weather and the second exchange of fire with the *Prince of Wales* between 6 and 7 in the evening of the 24th had aggravated the fuel leak. So there was in fact no choice whether to make for France or not. Where there is no freedom of choice intelligence ceases to have decisive value; and with Force H maintaining wireless silence as it moved up to meet the *Bismarck* and the German B Dienst unable to unravel the mass of operational signals between Admiralty and Home Fleet, the German NID had had nothing important to offer. If only it had known, or been able to calculate, Admiral Tovey's decision that if by midnight on the 26–27 – the night before the final action – *Bismarck* had not been slowed down, he would break off the chase owing to shortage of fuel and the danger of U-boats and bombers coming up on a slowed-down *King George V*!

What, meanwhile, had happened to the *Bismarck*'s companion and satellites? Early in the morning of 24 May, the *Prinz Eugen*, having parted from the *Bismarck* at 6 p.m., was fuelling from the tanker *Spichern*.* (Her tanks had only 250 cm available against the 3,233 cm with which she had left Norway.) Her plan was, with the assistance of the scouting ships *Gonzenheim* and *Kota Penang*, to make a sweep over the southern part of the HX convoy route. Captain Brinckmann hoped that the pursuit of the *Bismarck* would have drawn off British heavy units from the convoys and that he might reasonably expect to meet either an independently sailing ship or a lightly escorted convoy. To organize this, an exchange of wireless messages between the cruiser and the supply ships at her disposal went on during the next three days. This fact alarmed Captain Brinckmann, who notes in his log for 27 May 'It should be

158

mentioned here that the unnecessary signalling, since bearings would have been taken, would certainly have given our position away.' Fortunately, perhaps, for him, serious trouble with the *Prinz Eugen*'s engines forced her to make for Brest where she arrived on 1 June.

This entry from the cruiser's log is recorded because, curiously, it seems to have been ignored by those instructed to inquire into the loss of the supply ships, three of which at least were in active contact with the *Prinz Eugen* only to be sunk soon afterwards: the *Gonzenheim* (scuttled 4 June when intercepted by *Esperance Bay* and naval aircraft), the *Esso Hamburg* (scuttled 4 June when intercepted by the cruiser *London*) and the *Friedrich Breme* (sunk by the *Sheffield* on 12 June.)*

Even in the second inquiry of July 1942, provoked by information said to have been given by British prisoners of war from the ocean-boarding vessel *Malvernian*, there seems to have been a determination not to regard excessive signalling or any other breach of communications security as the cause of the June massacre of supply ships and weather-reporting trawlers. The main clue seemed to be the capture on 4 June by the *Marsdale* of the supply ship *Gedania* (of which the Germans learnt details from the survivors of the *Malvernian*). Secret papers in this ship would have shown the British (*a*) what the Germans knew about their dispositions; (*b*) the operational area of U-boats in the North Atlantic (south of 42° N, east of 30° W and north of 05° N); (*c*) the exact position of a weather-reporting trawler; (*d*) the prescribed route for prizes taken; (*e*) routes to the Bay of Biscay and swept passages to the ports there. This, in itself, would be a valuable prize for British intelligence (perhaps furnishing information used in the raid on St Nazaire in March 1942), and invaluable material for NID's replica of the German squared chart of the Atlantic battle. But the *Gedania* carried as well full instructions for supplying surface units like the *Bismarck* squadron, the rendezvous point with the *Egerland* (sunk on 6 June by the *Brilliant* and the *London*) and the cruising route to be taken to it. Material captured in this ship therefore might explain some of the British success of the next few days.

Then the British had captured the tanker and reconnaissance ship *Lothringen* (15 June) and would have confirmed from

159

her documents what had been learnt from the *Gedania,* with the bonus of an additional rendezvous point.

The conclusions of the German DNI were therefore as follows:

1 Betrayal by Norwegians probably accounted for the loss of two weather-reporting ships, *Freese* and *Muenchen.*

2 The capture of the *Gedania* 'may have offered the enemy an insight into the operational documents, which later probably led to interception of the *Egerland* and *Esso Hamburg* at "Red" in square ER, the rendezvous mentioned in *Gedania*'s operational orders and perhaps to the loss of the *Lauenburg*'.*

3 The *Gonzenheim* and the *Friedrich Breme* were lost almost on the prize route towards the Bay of Biscay as stated in *Gedania*'s orders. But the dates (both were sunk on 4 June) excluded the *Gedania* documents from being the cause of the *Gonzenheim*'s loss. As both were sunk by a battleship* it may be assumed that this loss was due to the enemy's measures for intercepting the *Prinz Eugen* on the prize route, compromised at an earlier date.

4 *Belchen* (sunk by naval forces on 3 June) must have been sighted in the course of aircraft patrols searching for the *Bismarck.*

5 The *Lothringen* was 'probably lost during a search along the prize route or near the supply area of the central Atlantic, due to *Gedania*'s documents falling into enemy hands. As the location of the loss is unknown, no conclusions can be drawn; but the fact that aircraft were used points to a systematic search of the area in question'.*

6 Regarding the *Babitonga* (supply ship for armed merchant raiders in the South Atlantic) and the *Alstertor* (supply ship for armed merchant raiders in the Indian Ocean), nothing was known about the cause of their loss*, but it was thought that the *Alstertor* might have been accidentally sighted during the search for a British general in a missing 'plane. 'There seems to be no connection between the loss of these two ships and that of the other two.'

There follows a summary showing the difficulties facing German naval intelligence as it tried to find out what mistakes, whether at sea or at base, had led to the break-up of this valuable and carefully planned supply network, one of the most decisive and comprehensive naval operations of the Battle of the Atlantic.

By analysing the causes of the losses, connections between five cases become apparent. For the remaining seven ships unlucky circumstances, encounters with convoy escorts, reinforced patrolling of the approaches to the Bay of Biscay must be taken into account; and it is not necessary to put the blame on a breach of security as regards the code and cipher tables.*

The lessons of the *Rheinuebung* for British intelligence are clear. It was the skilful combination of various intelligence sources, each serving and supplementing the other, that was decisive. The enemy's departure known at once through contacts developed by the NA Stockholm; the smooth working co-operation of OIC and Coastal Command which led to the immediate alerting of our air reconnaissance with indications of where to look; the daring search carried out by the airmen; the sighting reports to OIC and Home Fleet from the cruisers made possible by their radar, the effectiveness of which surprised the Germans; the working of the 'Y' stations to establish the *Bismarck*'s direction after she had been lost; the judgement made in OIC that she must be making for France; the briefing of the Catalina aircraft for the final sighting. To expect that German naval intelligence should foresee such efficient guarding of the approaches to the Atlantic trade routes was unreasonable after the ease and secrecy with which the *Scheer* and the *Scharnhorst* and *Gneisenau* had made their earlier raids. The work of NID had greatly improved in twelve months and in intelligence, as in other skills, practice makes perfect. No wonder that the head of the German 'Y' Service visited Doenitz on 8 June, just after the sinking of the *Bismarck* and recommended stricter rules about the use of wireless at sea.

Since this chapter was written there has appeared a remark-able account of this episode by Lieutenant-Commander Peter Kemp, head of the Naval Historical Branch of the Admiralty, which includes some new details. Among them a description of an intelligence error made in the Admiralty during 25 May, when the *Bismarck* was 'lost' – an error which, however, turned out fortunate. At 13.20 on that day the signal of a German U-boat from mid-Atlantic reporting, as we now know, her sighting of the *Victorious* was intercepted and the position fixed and plotted in the OIC. It fitted in with the course that the German ship would take if she were making for the Biscay ports. It was assumed, 'against all experience and the known German wireless procedure, that this might be the *Bismarck* giving direct orders to U-boats, using the frequency reserved for them'. This position was signalled to C-in-C Home Fleet, but there followed a few hours later another signal from the Admiralty to all units at sea, to act on the assumption that the enemy was making for the west coast of France.

8 Prisoners of war

The situation in which a prisoner of war finds himself is humiliating and, to sensitive minds, distressing. He has lost his liberty, his privacy, almost his status as an individual. To exploit his plight by getting information out of him which must, if it is accurate, endanger the lives of his former comrades can be seen as a shabby business. Indeed, that is how some British naval interrogators saw it; but those who saw it most clearly were among the best interrogators. Is it surprising? Perhaps some prisoners sensed this attitude and responded to it; certainly it had a lot to do with the reasonable and intelligent way questioning was conducted. If there was on both sides of the interrogation table the feeling that war was a sad business which imposes its own standards of behaviour, then it would help to account for the remarkable success of prisoner-of-war intelligence – a success which could not have been achieved by brutality, brain-washing, drugs or other forms of coercion.

But it has to be understood that the success of the interrogator was rooted in work in which he himself never, or seldom took part, much of which has been described in previous chapters. This was done in the German Section of NID, (NID 1/PW) drawing in to itself every kind of information about the enemy, sifting it and passing it on in a form which would help the interrogator. From the same source came the questions which the men at sea and the staffs directing operations wanted to have answered. Likewise, when interrogation was complete, it was the specialists in prisoner-of-war intelligence of the German section who put results into a form suitable for passing on to those who could use them; it was they who advised DNI on what signals should be sent promulgating urgent information and who really assessed the morale of the enemy seaman and his officers. The same has to be said of Italian and Japanese prisoner-of-war intelligence conducted far away in Egypt or Ceylon and Burma. Success at the confrontation of prisoner and questioner was rooted in scholarly, thoughtful and sometimes inspired staff work.

Whatever discipline, detailed instruction and warning could do to prepare the German and Italian naval prisoner for the wiles of his captors had been done. He knew his rights under the Geneva Convention on Prisoners of War: he need give only name, rank, number and date of birth. He had been warned that any talk he might have with a comrade in a cell or dormitory might be listened to and recorded; and that the comrade might have been put there as a stool pigeon by the interrogators. He knew that German-speaking refugees from Hitler were helping the enemy and could be indistinguishable from good Nazis. It had been explained to him how the lives of other German and Italian seamen might be risked by any lapse in his silence. Above all, until well on into 1943, he believed that Germany was winning the war and that captivity would not, therefore, last long. This, perhaps, was the most important element of all in the stubbornness with which he faced his questioners; and an arduous business some of them found it, month in and month out, breaking this resistance down by patient and rational treatment.

As he came to attention in front of the interrogating officer's table, the first thing that the U-boat prisoner noticed was that the questions were coming from a man of his own age. This was not the intelligence officer of the seaman's imagination, not the kind of person he had come up against in his training but apparently one of his own kind, speaking good but not perfect German or Italian. Nor did the interrogator take notes or pursue questions like a querulous lawyer; for he was trying first to find out two things: whether the prisoner was likely to be obstinate or co-operative in more detailed questioning and – unless he knew it already – the number of the U-boat. Without the latter the interrogator was 'thrashing about in the dark', unable to apply his carefully filed knowledge to impress the prisoner. But once he had it – more often than not quite quickly – he would become relaxed and chatty, ask at first apparently trivial questions, and then gradually reveal an astonishingly detailed knowledge of the boat's life history, the latest gossip at base about commanders and operations, the off-duty and leave haunts provided for the crews. Such leisurely, discriminating methods were not possible at sea.*

At the sinking of the *Scharnhorst* in December 1943 the Home Fleet flagship *Duke of York* picked up 36 survivors. The Staff Officer (Intelligence) on board wished to respect the rule that interrogation should not be attempted until they reached the CSDIC; but the gunnery officer of the *Duke of York* was understandably anxious to ascertain at once whether it was one of his early salvoes, if not his first, that caused a critical reduction in the German ship's speed. The difference was referred to the Chief of Staff who asked for a ruling from Admiral Fraser. The SOI, who had been accused of a short-sighted attitude and warned that the prisoners' memories would have been blunted a week later, was told to get on with his questions. In fact he was able to get nothing out of them: 'they were punch drunk with their terrible experience and if ever there was a case for leaving prisoners alone to be com-petently dealt with in due course this was it'.

The secret of success was quite simply that knowledge breeds knowledge: a prisoner is induced to talk by making him think he is saying nothing new. An interrogator who knows seven out of ten relevant facts in a logically appreciated situation will successfully use them to elicit the other three from prisoners who think he knows them already. Here let a member of NID 1/PW speak for himself:

The old guard of interrogators who, month in and month out, mixed in with all ranks and ratings of the U-boat service came to live and breathe the German Navy, and smell it, and even talk the special jargon and slang of 'U-boat Deutsch'. (That all-pervading stench of oil and fug which all U-boat prisoners carried about with them is with me yet.) We certainly came to know vastly more about the German Navy than we knew about our own service and we also came to assemble more knowledge about the U-boat arm than most of those we had to deal with. You could have asked any of the old guard to think of a number between one and a thousand, and without a second's hesitation he would have given you the U-boat's captain and probably the names of his first lieutenant and engineer officer as well.

Kretschmer, the U-boat ace, had precisely this impression when he was interviewed after capture in spring 1941 by the Director of Anti-Submarine Warfare, then Captain George Creasy. 'The British,' he told Harald Busch, author of a book on the U-boat war, 'were extremely well-informed . . . To them the U-boat service was more than a label; it was a living entity. To us, on the other hand, the enemy was no more than an anonymous mass.' Germans who listened to the short-wave radio programme for the Wehrmacht run from England by Sefton Delmer (first known as *Kurzwellensender Atlantik* and later as *Soldatensender West*) were astonished by the detailed knowledge shown in its programmes of what was going on, for example, on board the blockade runners waiting in the Gironde River or of how Doenitz's staff were having trouble with their research scientists about radar.

In face of this expert approach it seemed pointless to stick firmly to the phrase drilled into all German naval personnel by their security officers: *Ich darf es nicht sagen:* I am not allowed to tell you.* Why say 'I don't know' if the British showed an amused and ribald interest in the whereabouts of the red-haired waitress at the Café de Rennes in Lorient? Why deny that Lieutenant Commander Z had the reputation of being scared stiff of mines, whereas his own commander, now captured, was a dare-devil? Why not accept the probability that comrades *had* talked?

Naturally, if the prisoner made no response to such well-informed questions, the manner of the young officer with the wavy stripes of the RNVR might change suddenly. He might point out – in the early days of the war – that imprisonment would be lasting a very long time, that some but not all prisoners were sent to Canada (across what the prisoner believed to be a U-boat infested Atlantic), that no one had ever succeeded in escaping from the British Isles, and that life was easier for realists and decent chaps than for obstinate Nazis. No third degree, hypnotism, truth drugs, threats of violence, starvation diet or solitary confinement. That kind of treatment was not only forbidden under the Geneva Convention, but was also regarded as useless by good interrogators and hankered after only by lazy and bad ones.

While a U-boat crew were being interrogated – indeed, from the moment their capture was known in the Admiralty – the interrogators would be reading and digesting everything already in their files about the boat, its commander and the officers of his term, the type of equipment it might be carrying, its known performance, the details of the attack. They would also have by them standing briefs from various divisions of the Admiralty to inquire about torpedoes, search equipment, wireless techniques, tactics of attack and evasion, endurance and fuelling. If this or that boat or commander promised points of particular interest, urgent and special requests would come down from technical experts, and sometimes the answers to them meant the difference between life and death for the men of the Atlantic and Mediterranean convoys.

But caution and restraint had to be practised in this priming of the interrogator and the prisoner. If the former knew too much, he might merely put into the prisoner's mind a fact or an idea taken from another source; and no one would then know whether the result was or was not prisoner-of-war intelligence, with all its known limitations. On the other hand the interrogator on technical matters did require a thorough briefing from other Admiralty departments to do his job well. The interrogator might ask: 'How long have you known about the Type C search device?' The prisoner might reply 'three months', never having known before that the mysterious piece of apparatus in his U-boat was called Type C. If this led to the conclusion that this boat certainly had a Type C device, it would be a piece of bad intelligence work.

Prisoner-of-war material is sharply distinguished from other sources by its ability to explain in detail what things are done by which people in what manner – in other words, tactical methods of commanders, technical methods, design and performance of weapons and equipment. It took the Admiralty some time to understand this; for in the first three years of the war the NID sections by which technical questions were being asked and answered were manned by older officers more interested in engines than in the newest developments in radar, torpedoes, mines and other weapons. Indeed, one of the main tasks that faced Godfrey's successor in 1943 was to improve the service of technical intelligence. On the urgent advice of the German section, Rear-Admiral Rushbrooke appointed, in that summer, a Cambridge-trained engineer with some knowledge of German to join the interrogators, and this immediately brought results. By visiting British experimental and research establishments to find out what problems they were working on, he was able to equip himself for questioning suitable prisoners; and by knowing the general principles and language of engineering and other applied sciences he could provoke from the various divisions of the Admiralty better questions. He could also assist his colleagues at the interrogation centre with any technical problems they came across.

After the summer of 1942 and up to 1944, rapid progress was made in the quality and amount of intelligence secured. One interrogator got out of a prisoner a full description of the *Pillenwerfer* which produced a submarine bubble target (SBT). A device operated from inside the U-boat created a false target for the British Asdic apparatus and enabled the U-boat to escape behind a screen of misleading noise. SBT was a nuisance but never became a menace, thanks to our good knowledge of it. In the same year full details were secured of the search-receiver which had been specially designed to give U-boats warning of radar contact by allied aircraft and ships. This enabled the Admiralty to change the wave-lengths of the radar used by the Allied forces at sea and so fox the Germans. The most valuable information of all on torpedoes was also given by prisoners, who became more co-operative as German defeat became more likely, and the Admiralty was in two or three instances able to devise counter-measures before the new types became operational. There was no single aspect of the technical specifications and performance of the successively more sophisticated German torpedo types – acoustic, homing, magnetic, etc. – which was not made available in detail from this source.

There is a striking story to be told about the acoustic homing torpedo, the Gnat, on which Doenitz set such high hopes in the summer of 1943, when the Atlantic campaign had obviously failed. The Gnat was first used in the great five-day battle around convoys ONS18 and ON202 between 18 and 22 September.* Thanks to NID's warnings that the new weapon was now available to the enemy, counter-measures were ready, though still rudimentary. But they had not been applied when the Canadian destroyer *St Croix* and the corvettes *Polyanthus* and *Itchen* were sunk, all by the Gnat, as part of the deadly new tactic of attacking escort vessels instead of merchant ships.

On the day that the news of these sinkings came through, it happened that the RNVR Lieutenant who was the technical interrogation specialist was visiting the Admiralty establishment working on torpedo development. He learned that they had solved the problem of making a British acoustic torpedo but had not gone on with development because the Naval Staff was not interested in it at any speed under 30 knots. Yet experiments had shown that at over $24\frac{1}{2}$ knots the noise of its own propellers would deafen the torpedo's acoustic apparatus. The Germans, who it was learned later set their torpedo at $24\frac{1}{2}$ knots precisely, had achieved a striking success by accepting the lower speed.

It was, however, short-lived, for the simple device of the Foxer – a noise-making contrivance with two steel bars rattling against one another which was towed behind a ship – attracted the Gnat away from the ship's propellers and exploded it at a safe distance. Foxer had the disadvantage that it spoiled the performance of the Asdic – still the main U-boat detection device – in the ship towing it, and that it could not be towed over 15 knots. So that any escort vessel wanting to pursue a U-boat at high speed would have to give up its protection. However, the combination of technical ingenuity with good advance intelligence did frustrate at the earliest stage a dangerous German stratagem.

Intelligence helped to find the answer to other ingenious German experiments. Advance information about the Schnorkel* had come from the Naval Attaché in Sweden, who had it from a Dutch source; and with this help interrogators were able to persuade knowledgeable prisoners that its main features were already known. Sometimes NID had to persuade our own commanders and specialists that it was right and they were wrong. One interrogator tells the story of how he and a colleague – both Lieutenants RNVR – were sent up to see the redoubtable Admiral Sir John Tovey, then commanding at the Nore. He was worried about reports of two-man submarines likely to operate in coastal waters (it was the spring of 1944) and his staff had been sending to ships instructions which in NID's view were wrong. The two young officers were charged with explaining to him just what was known about German intentions and capability.

On arrival they were escorted into a vast operations room by what seemed to them a posse of gold lace and led up to the Admiral's desk. There, to their surprise, they were cross-examined by Tovey himself, with great skill and courtesy, 'as if they were three-ringer specialists'. When Tovey had found out all he wanted to know he turned to his staff and said, 'Take care of these gentlemen and do just what they say.' And they did. That, it should be said, was not always the attitude of Operations to Intelligence. Nor was it the normal attitude, at first, of technical departments. The minutes they sometimes wrote on dockets containing prisoner-of-war intelligence about, e.g., resistance to depth charges, speed of training, speed and diving capacity and calibre of guns in 2 class destroyers betrayed that wishful thinking which only accurate intelligence convincingly presented can expose.

For example, interrogators repeatedly obtained strong evidence that U-boats could dive to 600 feet and more. The Staff of Flag Officer Submarines refused to believe this and so did the constructors, until the capture of U570 and her trials with RN personnel proved that the interrogators were right. She turned out to be so well constructed that diving to such a depth presented no difficulties. Had this fact been accepted earlier, British depth charges would have been set to explode below 550 feet, which was the maximum ordered in the first part of the war.*

A similar case of incredulity occurred over the German destroyers active in Norway and in the Channel-Biscay area. Prisoners repeatedly asserted that they had 15 cm (5·9 inch) guns. As the men had no reason to exaggerate, the information seemed sound. But the Admiralty's constructors declared that no 2,400-ton ship could carry such armament; and so the information that the so-called 'Narvik' class carried such heavy armament was not promulgated to the Fleet. Even after an

Admiralty signal was sent out with a very high probability grading, many refused to believe it – until in July 1944 one of these ships went ashore in Brittany, fell into our hands and proved the constructors and gunnery experts to be wrong. There was similar incredulity about their anti-aircraft armament and the traverse of their torpedo tubes.

Prisoners were, of course, not the only source for such material – it could be deduced or found out about by other means – but it was only the prisoner of war who could give the full descriptive material which satisfied the technician. Indeed, that was the best thing he could do for his captors: tell them what it looks like, how it works, what he did with it. But as the war moved into the summer of 1944 so much equipment, books and documents were being captured that one subject after another could be dropped from the questioning. The war at sea moved much closer to the British Isles. Prisoners were now coming in from the Channel, the North Sea and what were to us virtually home waters. Instead of U-boat men being of overwhelming importance, it was now the E-boat men, the crews of small battle units that were wanted; for it would be they, if anybody, who might cause difficulties with the lines of communication of 'Overlord'.

This meant that PW intelligence became more and more operational and tactical. By bringing survivors from explosive motor boats, midget U-boats, controlled torpedoes, within hours to interrogation at the beach-head or at a Channel port in France, it was found possible to keep the Fleet abreast of all the latest developments in German ingenuity and daring, which never flagged even at this stage of the war. Above all the Admiralty was passionately interested in the Schnorkel boats, which seemed likely to give the war against our trade a new lease of life.* By now enough was known of their equipment and armament; wanted now was information on tactics, flotilla locations and expansion in training. These were quickly in NID's possession.

To speed up the flow of information, forward interrogation units manned by men specially trained for Admiral Ramsey's team were operating in France and moved forward with the Army as it seized one by one the Channel and Biscay ports. The RN Forward Intelligence Unit was formed in time

171

for the invasion and in the first months operated under Lieutenant-Commander Ralph Izzard, RNVR, over a wide field; three teams around the prisoner-of-war cages in the British beach-head, one in Cherbourg and the Cotentin Peninsula, another in the Brittany ports down to Brest. Then they joined Patton's forces for the entry to Paris and occupied with No. 30 Assault Unit the headquarters of the German Admiral Commanding France at the Palais Rothschild in the Bois de Boulogne. Thence, armed with a white pass signed by the Supreme Commander, entitling them to requisition anything and requiring military formations to give them assistance without question, they ranged far and wide in their Humber staff cars: first to the invested Channel ports, then to Walcheren and eventually into the North German bases.

Brian Connell, later a well-known TV commentator, was Izzard's No. 2 as Lieutenant RNVR. 'What we were really looking for in the U-boat line after D-day,' says Connell, 'were the two types of Walter hydrogen-peroxide-propelled boats. Heavy water plants were at the top of our intelligence target list. We did not appreciate the additional application of this search to atomic bombs until very much later. Hydrogen-peroxide and alcohol also provided the fuel for V-2s.' Never, probably, have intelligence officers been given such a free hand and such a front seat – at any rate by the Royal Navy.

Now to return to the methods used. The obstinate man who was believed to know nothing of special interest would be quickly discarded from the intelligence centre to an ordinary prisoner-of-war camp. But if he had valuable specialist knowledge or was one of few survivors from an important ship or U-boat, he would be kept back and allowed to think that he had got the better of his young interrogator, perhaps receiving as his companion a helpful prisoner. 'What', the latter would ask, 'did they try to get out of you?' And the obdurate character would be more often than not tempted to boast of how he had misled the British officer and to confide in his companion, who might well be a specialist like himself from the Navy or from the Air Force and would lead him expertly on. Such a conversation might not at once bring pickings for the listening monitors, but it could be the beginning of future confidences which could then be used in interrogating others.*

In other cases, especially when the interrogation centre was fully equipped with recording and listening aids, it was not necessary to introduce the stool pigeon: officers and petty officers and men, given the chance, would talk freely together, longing to chat and confide and share fears and hopes. For some of them, certainly, there was a clear if subtle distinction between answering the enemy's questions and talking freely when he was not actually present. Sooner or later bits of information or clues would emerge which might mean nothing to the listening monitors and very little to the gossiping men; but the single remark recognized in its context, might be a clue to valuable details.*

There was another factor of unique importance: this was an ideological war. From the first, Germans in the armed forces could be divided into Nazis and non-Nazis, however few relatively the latter might be. Captivity gave some of the latter their first opportunity for years – or ever – to curse the Nazis and discuss politics freely, to read non-Nazi newspapers, even to think, if they were the thoughtful argumentative type. Few of them were as intelligent or felt as strongly as the petty officer from Socialist Hamburg (now dead) who had been in a concentration camp and who co-operated completely with naval intelligence out of deep conviction that his country deserved to lose the war – and was fully aware of the risks that he ran. He was the only one to volunteer to co-operate. The others were persuaded by interrogators. But a man had only to show symptoms of an anti-Nazi attitude to be put together with others of the same persuasion. They would then gain courage from their collectivity – and information would result.

Information offered willingly and intelligently, whether out of conviction that Hitler must be defeated or out of cynicism about war and politics in general, was always worth incalculably more than anything that might be induced by bribe or favour. Indeed, in British practice such inducements were forbidden. The co-operative prisoner would be given special quarters, partly for security reasons, but the only luxury there was a much-cherished degree of privacy. He was allowed to listen to the radio and trouble was taken to find him the right books and records. Never, whatever the circumstances, was special treatment after the war promised; and those who

173

had been helpful returned to Germany eventually in a manner which attracted no attention.

Apart from these small privileges no reward was offered, but sometimes a likely convert would be taken for the day to London, there to be convinced by his own eyes that Nazi newspapers and radio propaganda had lied to him. After a fixed price lunch at Simpson's in the Strand, the quality and quantity of which never failed to surprise, he would be given his own choice of the sights he wished to see in the city which the Luftwaffe had claimed as mortally damaged. The spectacle of St Paul's standing virtually intact amid the ruins around it, of whole districts apparently untouched and of business life energetically going on, while people and newspapers argued openly about the conduct of the war – all this would move deeply an intelligent and sensitive man who had half decided to help his 'enemy'.

Now that it is known how valuable was the information given by co-operative prisoners of war, one reads with mixed feelings the warning sent by the DNI to the interrogators in October 1944 about money spent on entertainment. They were warned against 'outlay at the average rate of two pounds per diem', and reminded that 'it would be most difficult to make a case for such continual expenditure'. Several items were described as objectionable, for example: 'entertaining at the Ritz and the purchase of considerable quantities of gin. If these facts became known, there might be good cause for scandal'. 'Furthermore,' wrote the DNI rather plaintively, 'I and many others are quite unable to enjoy these luxuries and it is out of all proportion that our enemies should. An occasional outlay of this kind is a different matter but the objection is to the continuity of this treatment.' On which the interrogators' comment was that they had been spending, mostly, their own pay on the occasional drinks, claiming only a fraction of it back, and that it had been well worth two pounds on one occasion to convince a sceptical U-boat commander that the Ritz was still standing, despite the VI attacks and what Goebbels might claim for them.

An important factor in persuasion was the satisfaction some otherwise patriotic German and Italian naval men felt at being free to discuss things rationally. In this respect captivity was for them a sort of liberation from the restrictions and double-talk they had grown up with under Hitler or Mussolini. Likewise for the interrogators, most of them young professional men still in the first stage of their careers, the opportunity to persuade and convert ('to liberate from Hitler's spell') was compensation for the distasteful side of their duties. 'With most of them,' said one interrogator, 'we were just playing a confidence trick to get information; but now and then there was straightforward rational persuasion.' On this kind of basis, during walks in the Buckinghamshire countryside and over beer and tobacco, confidences – even friendships – were formed which might be as fruitful in ideas to the German side as they were productive of information to the British.

It cannot be too strongly emphasized, however, that this was exceptional. The average German naval officer, petty officer and rating was staunchly patriotic if not Nazi, well-drilled in security (every device mentioned in this chapter would be known to him) and convinced up till the summer of 1943 that there was hope of winning the war.*

Then, for a time, as a result of the heavy losses in the Atlantic, morale in the U-boats weakened badly, only to recover in the most dismaying fashion as Nazi propaganda branded into German minds its own version of what was meant by the 'unconditional surrender' demanded by Roosevelt in January of that year.*

The Admiralty was always reluctant to pronounce, let alone to assume, that the morale of the German fighting man or civilian was weakening. For it believed that too much had been claimed on this score already on behalf of Bomber Command. A typical example of its cautious assessments is dated 12 March 1944 when the First Sea Lord, advised by DNI, sent the following reply to a Minute from the Prime Minister:*

Generalizations can be misleading [but] the following comparisons can safely be made between prisoners taken during the heavy U-boat sinkings last summer (1943) and the large number captured during the past three weeks:

(i) Their age is progressively but not sensationally lowering.
(ii) The standard of efficiency of each U-boat has declined. This is due more to lack of training and experience in the officers than to

G   175 the youth and inexperience of the majority of the crews, who are generally well led by a few seasoned senior ratings.

(iii) The interrogators think seventy per cent of survivors are willing to admit among themselves that the war is lost and about twenty-five per cent admit it to a British officer. Six months ago only about fifty per cent were convinced.

(iv) The number of men who express a wish to go to sea again in U-boats becomes less and less.

(v) None the less the prisoners show much higher security consciousness than six months ago. There is a general belief that those who divulge information will be punished after the war.

The final judgement was cautious: it said that there was 'no marked deterioration in the fighting spirit of either officers or men while still engaged in war'. Nor was there 'any proven case of refusals to carry out orders by commanding officers or by crews'.

It was a long time before any useful intelligence was secured from officer prisoners. Certainly none of them was ready to co-operate to the extent that many ratings were. Early in 1944, the first naval officer was completely 'converted', largely because of his family background; and after that it became possible to form at the interrogation centre a small permanent staff of officers with different kinds of technical knowledge, among them U-boat commanders.

Those British officers who did this work are still convinced, twenty-five years later, that skilful use of normal human means of persuasion would not have been helped in any way by the use of drugs, threats or psychiatry. Examination by trained psychologists was found useless except for their own statistical purposes. Although alcohol would loosen some tongues, no one can remember its securing important information that a man did not want to give away. Likewise drugs: their possible use was studied early in the war and interrogators submitted themselves to experiments – but the idea was soon dropped. The Geneva rules for the treatment of prisoners were, in fact, strictly observed because it was right to do so, because prisoners would appeal to the protecting Power and because any suspicion of ill-treatment would be held to justify the Nazis in maltreating British and Allied prisoners in their hands.

A comparison of first with second war methods of obtaining

176

intelligence from prisoners of war throws up interesting illustrations of some of the general points made in Chapter 1, in particular the constant danger of wishful thinking and disregard of the accepted rules of evidence. In 1914–18 the approach was often haphazard and unreflective. The DNI, Sir Reginald Hall, would sometimes disappear to a mysterious house in Cromwell Road and carry out personal interrogations – not always of Germans. Prisoners arriving at ports would be questioned by those who knew less about intelligence than they knew of German. English-speaking prisoners would be asked to help. Experience showed that the untrained interrogator without experience has these weaknesses:

1 He generally puts ideas into people's heads without knowing it.

2 He has no benefit from the work of other interrogators and so may not know what are the right questions to ask. He is ignorant of the mosaic into which his bits fit.*

3 Prisoners who have once been formally questioned and know what interests their captors most, become very wary of further questioning by the trained interrogator when his turn comes.

4 Talk between prisoners and interrogators whose knowledge of the language is poor leads to misunderstanding and false deductions.

The secret of the successful direct interrogator was the ability to assert his personality over that of the prisoner. The impression had to be given that he knew more about the German Navy than the man standing in front of him, that lies or exaggerations would be immediately detected and that to refuse co-operation was futile and time-wasting. It was, of course, fatal to relax the strict discipline which Germans expected, but friendliness always paid, once the limits had been firmly set. It need hardly be pointed out that such methods of interrogation would not succeed if carried out through an interpreter.

The practice of segregating prisoners as soon as possible also had important and interesting psychological aspects. The purpose of it was to prevent them comparing notes about questions and answers, and to stop officers and petty officers maintaining

177

control over ratings. To take such precautions, say, in the cramped quarters of a destroyer when a score or more had been captured was very difficult. Not only was complete segregation impossible, but fraternization with the British ship's company would begin; and prisoners searched on arrival at the camp would sometimes be found to have in their pockets the addresses of British seamen or their families.

The War Office (MI 19) at one juncture asked the Admiralty (NID) what was the point of insisting on segregation in camps if the Navy could not enforce it in ships and drew attention to the strict orders against fraternization. The reply pointed out that at most it was possible to separate officers from POs and both from ratings. As for fraternization, it cited the following episode on board the destroyer *Maori* which took part in the final attacks on the *Bismarck*. When she had left Plymouth some of her ship's company had been bereaved in air raids and swore that if they sank a U-boat, there would be no ———— survivors. Yet when the opportunity came to save men from the blazing German battleship, struggling in the oil-covered sea, several men of the *Maori* dived in to rescue them 'and there was visible consternation and grief' when rescue efforts were ordered to be abandoned because of danger from approaching U-boats. 'Is this subversive?' the DNI asked. 'A sailor is incurably romantic and would neither think nor see evil in swapping yarns or addresses with a prisoner to whom he had offered a cigarette.'

Following instructions a number of prisoners, both Italian and German, tried to pass information back in their letters home. German naval officers had been given, by Doenitz, a simple code which was broken very early in the war by a civilian expert on commercial codes. This was based on the Morse Code as applied to the first letter of each word: A to H were dots; I to K were spaces; and L to Z dashes. A simple message could be composed (for example 'three Wabos at fifty metres' meaning that the U-boat had been sunk by three depth charges at about fifty metres depth) which would be helpful to German intelligence. It was decided to allow the code to be used without interference in the hope that sooner or later it would reveal something really important.

In 1942, while Lt-Cdr Ralph Izzard RNVR was in

Washington training American officers as interrogators, he received from DNI Ottawa a letter written by Doenitz himself to a Commander called Heyda, who was a prisoner at Bowmanville. As Izzard had to give a lecture on the letter code to his course, he decided to use this Doenitz missive as illustrative material. To his astonishment and everyone else's the letter, which on first scrutiny did not look like a coded message, told Heyda that if an escape could be arranged a U-boat would be ready at a specific point in the St Lawrence to pick up escapers. The date was to follow.

On the strength of this decoding an elaborate trap was laid for the U-boat, two prisoners found it possible to get out of Bowmanville – but unfortunately the Canadian coastguards were not in the plot and spoiled it by seizing the prisoners as they were waiting on shore for the U-boat's dinghy.

For similar reasons a close watch had to be kept on all applications for repatriation. The Admiralty well remembered how in the first war Doenitz, then a U-boat commander, had got himself back to Germany in 1918 by feigning madness. Returned officers and specialists would have been invaluable for training purposes, quite apart from what they might guess or know about interrogation methods. Indeed, Churchill when he was First Lord, ruled that no U-boat officer should be repatriated in any circumstances, and the instruction was followed until it became no longer important to deprive the Kriegsmarine of personnel.

No section of Naval Intelligence had a more detailed and intimate knowledge of its subject than the NID sections which handled all the information from German and Italian prisoners coming into the Admiralty, presented it in special long-term reports, or passed it on for promulgation to the Fleet in the form of new and urgent intelligence about performance, tactics, weapons and so on. The sections, small though they were in numbers (one never exceeded five), were great junctions of intelligence traffic. They received and replied to requests from every division of the Naval Staff and every section of NID. NID 1/PW was in touch by telephone with C-in-C Western Approaches on U-boat intelligence, and with the east coast and Channel commands on surface ship information. It had to keep in touch with SOIs (Staff Officers Intelligence) at ports who attended to the segregation of prisoners, prepared lists of names and sent useful preliminary hints. It had to assist branches abroad.

For nearly five years the total results of interrogating each separate ship or U-boat were composed and published as a secret Confidential Book or CB. This would be edited, proof-read and published within four months. But by 1944 a hundred separate issues of this CB 04051 had been put out with distribution to five hundred recipients. Publishing on such a scale with limited staff became quite unmanageable. More important, the results were just not reaching the officers and specialists fighting the U-boats, whereas the CB was reaching cruisers. Useful individual items of information were, of course, passed out on a day-to-day, even hour-to-hour basis. After the middle of 1943 a weekly summary was prepared instead by a Wren officer in the section and 130 issues of anything from six to fifty foolscap pages were got out. These give a remarkable picture of German naval development even though they were only a compilation of raw material, without comment. They did something to ensure that the watchkeeping officers in smaller vessels and the aircrew of Coastal Command learned as quickly as possible what the Admiralty knew.

How much the German Navy knew of British methods and how strict its security standards were is best read straight from this Standing Order of 1943:*

Above all and first of all Silence. The enemy tries every method to get out of the prisoner all possible information. Everything that the prisoner gives away can be used directly against his comrades, and one brief unconsidered remark can do serious damage to those fighting in the field.

There follows advice on how to behave when rescued:

Then, generally speaking, the U-boat man is treated in a comradely manner. He may say in voluntary chat things he would never say under interrogation. Therefore, from the moment you are on board the rescuing ship keep the strictest watch on yourself, in what you say not only to the enemy but also to one another.

The warning against British interrogation methods is thorough and well-informed:

1 Normal interrogation. Don't let yourself be bluffed. The enemy often knows in astonishing detail about the service and private life of the person being interrogated. Sometimes he will pretend to have all kinds of military knowledge, when he is in fact bluffing. To all questions of that kind give no answer.

2 Listening rooms. The enemy has good built-in listening apparatus which cannot be seen, and which will pick up the slightest word. He brings several prisoners together into such a room and hopes that their conversation will reveal things which he cannot find out in any other way.

3 Stool pigeons. You must be on the look out for stool pigeons who make approaches to prisoners under a mask of comradeship and try to lead talk on to secret matters. As long as a prisoner is not in the general prisoners' camp he must practise complete reserve towards everyone friend and enemy.

4 Threats. From time to time the enemy threatens prisoners with shooting, electric chair, sending to the Soviet Union and similar things. No case is known in which the threats have been carried out.

5 Favours. Accept no favours because these always lead to greater readiness to talk. In no circumstances accept alcohol.

Stick it out! Stick it out! Demand vigorously to see representatives of the protecting power.

Only give name, rank, birthday and address. Never speak in the enemy's language.

The less a prisoner says and the more obstinately he behaves the quicker he will be let out of the interrogation centre and reach the end camp.

9 The Attaché's art

'The King has been graciously pleased
to approve your appointment as Naval
Attaché to His Majesty's Legation at
——— You should bear in mind that
you form part of His Majesty's Mission
and that you do not hold an independent
post . . . You should take the greatest
care to avoid any action liable to create
the suspicion that you are attempting to
procure secret information by illicit
means. You must have no relations or
communications with persons acting, or
professing willingness to act, as spies
or secret agents . . .'

(Extracts from Foreign Office Letter
of appointment to a Naval Attaché)

The story is told of an Embassy in the Balkans where explosives
had been stored by a certain department in the cellars, next to
the Ambassador's wine but without his knowledge. The idea
was that in case of a German advance in that direction it
could be seriously impeded by demolition work in a narrow
passage of the River Danube. A moment came in 1940 when
the Naval Attaché felt obliged to tell the Ambassador the truth.
'Why didn't you tell me when you put it there?' asked His
Excellency furiously. 'Because, sir, you would not have allowed
it.' 'Then why', came the reply with spluttering expletives,
'tell me now?'

The Naval Attaché is reminded in the instruction at the
head of this chapter that he serves two masters; his Ambassador
and the Director of Naval Intelligence. His loyalties are placed
in that order, because his first duty in a foreign capital is
clearly to serve the mission of which he is a member. He must
advise its head on naval matters, keep him informed of anything
important that he learns through his professional and social

contacts, co-operate with Chancery and other attachés, and play his part in the representative social role of the diplomatic team. If the Ambassador and the DNI in London take the trouble to get to know one another, the division of duties can be fruitful. Too often in the past they did not.

But the officer has also a duty, through the DNI, to the Admiralty; his future career in the Navy will be largely determined by what is thought of him there. His quality will be judged, in peace, not only by the information he supplies, but also by the ship and weapon orders he helps to win, by the advice he offers, by what is said about him by the naval mission in London of the foreign power to which he is accredited. What looks at first sight like a straightforward representative post can become the centre of a complex and delicate web of diplomatic, intelligence and commercial relationships.

In peacetime, generally speaking, the most important Naval Attaché posts are in potentially enemy countries; Washington from 1936 onwards was an obvious exception. In the late Thirties Berlin, Rome, Tokyo and Washington were regarded as the key capitals and the Admiralty seems to have overlooked the fact that, in case of war, the key positions must rapidly change. Suddenly Stockholm – as an observation post for all of Northern Europe and a capital with numerous contacts with Germany – became outstandingly important while Paris became useless.

Whether he was in an enemy or neutral capital when war broke out, a swift transformation came over the Naval Attaché, as indeed over many of his diplomatic colleagues. In the neutral capitals the Naval Attaché gained overnight quintupled importance. There (Washington) was a potential ally; here (Stockholm) was a window on Germany, Russia and the Baltic; here (Madrid and Lisbon) one of the lock gates of the Mediterranean in which the Royal Navy hoped to keep in war the predominance it had built up in peace. In Ankara, next door to Russia and the Balkans and the Middle East the Naval Attaché's office became a centre of inquiry, influence, information and even of intrigue. Staff, money, communications, which had been grudged, were now quickly granted; it was sufficient for the Naval Attaché to report to London the vast retinue and expensive habits of his German colleague, with whom he was now competing for the favours of the local naval staff, of the local intelligence chiefs and of influential politicians, editors and businessmen.

Not the Navy's business, one might think; but a hundred years of naval attachment had built up a special position for its representative abroad – varying of course with personalities. The Royal Navy had been the chief symbol of British power and wealth; indeed, almost the only one, because the British Army was not taken seriously abroad between 1815 and 1914 (there the German Military Attachés – and before them the French – had the whip hand, notably in Stockholm and Ankara). Moreover, everything to do with ships had to do also with trade and banking and insurance and precious raw materials like oil and wolfram. Through these channels, especially in Spain and Scandinavia, information and influence passed back and forth as smoothly as they did through the diplomatic ones. A naval officer's training especially in the Mediterranean and in the Pacific, had prepared him to be an instinctive and diligent intelligence bee.*

The Naval Attaché system is reciprocal: DNI controls British representatives abroad and looks after the interests of foreign representatives in London. The obligations of eating and drinking, calling and talking that fall on the DNI and his staff (and their wives) are almost gargantuan.

True, the Naval Attaché representing a country in London will have his requests and questions dealt with by the officer in charge of the geographical section of NID to which his country belongs: but the responsibility for observing the behaviour and views of foreign Naval Attachés who are known (friendly or unfriendly) to be seeking information by every legitimate means lies with the DNI.* And the nature of that responsibility varied enormously between the activities of, say, the Soviet and Swedish and Japanese Naval Attachés. If he thinks it necessary, he must advise the Foreign Office that diplomatic status is being abused for illegitimate espionage.

In the intelligence game that is played by international Service Attachés there are certain acknowledged rules and accepted penalties. The running of covert espionage organizations is taboo, although there are probably few Embassies in which espionage is not represented. Excess of zeal in overt activities may lead to a warning or a request for withdrawal. If it is pressed, the government making it must expect to find in reprisal its own NA being declared *persona non grata*. On the other hand, the indiscretion or misbehaviour of a foreign naval attaché may by its direction and motives furnish useful counter-intelligence clues to the host country. Whereas in Britain it would be quite exceptional in peacetime for him to be watched by the police or the Security Service, such surveillance would be normal in a certain kind of totalitarian country. For example, before the war it was taken for granted in Japan, in the Soviet Union and intermittently in Spain; it was almost non-existent in Portugal and Norway. In pre-1941 Japan all diplomatic cars were lettered and numbered, indicating the nationality of the mission and the rank, viz. GBI 1 for the Ambassador and GBI 4 for the Naval Attaché. It had to be assumed too, in such countries that servants and drivers were potential informers. Even in democratic, tolerant Switzerland the watch on foreign intelligence networks was close and expert. The situation in Dublin was unique, as one would expect. The Irish wanted the advice of a senior British naval officer but found it politically unwise to employ one. The British Naval Attaché filled the need. During the war the Dublin authorities, without pressure from London, made life difficult for the German mission, for obvious reasons.

In wartime conditions changed drastically. Spies were attracted to neutral capitals as pigeons are to crumbs, and neutral Governments therefore became very security conscious. They were under pressure from each side in the war to suppress the intelligence and sabotage the activities of the other. (It need hardly be said that German bullying for the first three years was often more outrageous and effective than our politer pressures, even though the British blockade was a weapon of decisive power against an industrialized country.) On the other hand, there were in every neutral country well-placed persons who had strong and non-neutral sympathies one way or the other. In Stockholm intense feelings of pity for the Norwegians and Danes under Nazi occupation competed against traditional German influences in the military and intelligence staffs and civil service, as well as against a persistent fear of what Russia might eventually do. As soon as it seemed likely that Britain and her allies would win in the long run, the current of feeling underneath the strict official neutrality began to run in our direction, to the great benefit of Captain Denham, DNI's representative in the capital. Stockholm became by far the most important overseas source of naval intelligence.

In Madrid things were different. The work of the Naval Attaché had been neglected before the war, even during the civil war, with all its naval activity and experiments in modern warfare. The office was run from Paris and the Naval Attaché's visits to Spain were irregular and the service inadequate. When Commander Alan Hillgarth was sent there in August 1939 as Assistant Naval Attaché, he was subordinated for a short time to NA Lisbon, which irritated the Spanish Government even more than the idea of Madrid's being regarded as an outpost of Paris. Contacts had to be built up virtually from scratch at a time when the Spanish attitude to the all-conquering Nazis was of crucial importance. Nothing could illustrate more clearly the danger of neglecting contact in peacetime. As Hillgarth put it: 'Where there is no predecessor, there is no position of strength to work from.' It was only because he himself had built up a personal position with the Spanish Navy at Palma during the Civil War that the leeway was made up.*

In Ankara the naval representation was complicated, but worked well. Because of the perennial British hope that Turkey would come into the war against the Axis, the skeleton of a naval mission had been sent there to prepare, so far as was possible with a strictly non-belligerent Government, future naval co-operation. The head of this, Admiral Sir Howard Kelly, was therefore in Ankara from 1940 to 1944 as Commander in Chief Mediterranean's personal representative. He had no diplomatic status – which worried the British Embassy – but was treated by the Turks as a distinguished visitor. Being on very friendly terms with Marshal Chukmuk, he often secured inside information denied to the Naval Attaché. Indeed, it is clear that whereas the Admiral had the run of the NA's files, the service was not reciprocated. There was therefore always a risk that the advice given by the NA to the Ambassador and DNI might be different from that given by Admiral Kelly, a possibility that would make life difficult for intelligence officers back in London. The First Sea Lord and Admiral Cunningham, however, liked the arrangement because of the high-level personal links it provided – and so it went on.

It may be imagined how keenly the Foreign Office feared lest the safety of Sweden or Spain – or indeed of any neutral country – should be put in danger by any British activity to which the Axis powers could effectively object. The risk was threefold. At worst the Germans might use a pretext furnished by the activities, say, of SOE in Spain to march into the country (a German plan for the invasion of Spain existed from 1940 to 1943). Less disastrous but still grave, important commercial or intelligence arrangements with the country might be suspended as a reprisal for some subversive or irregular operation.* Again, the Service Attaché or other Embassy specialists might be declared *persona non grata* with a consequent loss of his personal contacts, special knowledge and experience.

Nor was this the only chapter in the recurrent nightmare of the country departments back in London. If an NA was suspected of having tapped sources in the neutral government itself or in its intelligence and security services, he might be watched and followed and the surveillance extended to the whole of his Embassy. It is fair to say that some British Ambassadors were stout-hearted enough not to let these prospects worry them; others looked askance, as some still do, at all covert activities that might be traced to or associated with their missions.

Naval Attachés sometimes found to their dismay and surprise that some British diplomatic representatives either had no training in security (that is so say, in the ways in which information can become available to and be used by an enemy) or did not understand the difference between the requirements of peace and those of war. NA Washington had to complain that information given by him to a member of Chancery had been passed on to a Junior, who 'dined out on it'. An Assistant NA in Istanbul reported to London:

The insecurity of numerous personnel, senior and junior, attached to embassies . . . lacking even the normal discipline of career officials, is a constant source of danger. Long separation from womenfolk at home induces, moreover, a state of affairs which is not lost on the enemy, who make good use of it in Turkey.

187

Outstandingly unconventional in this respect, perhaps because he was not a career man, was Sir Samuel Hoare in Madrid. He realized the importance of the intelligence aspect of his mission's work and very sensibly put the Naval Attaché in charge of the Embassy's security, which was virtually non-existent. Generally speaking, the principle followed was 'I do not want to know what is going on, so that I can say in case of trouble that I know nothing of it. But I rely on my staff to be discreet while doing all they can to win the war.'*

Captain Hillgarth, in some notes he wrote for the NID after the war, recommended NAs to pay particular attention to the gathering of business intelligence, and to relations with the Embassy commercial staff:

He will seldom find here any difficulties of jealousy but a ready wish for collaboration of which he should take full advantage. Economic and commercial matters are closely tied up with maritime affairs . . . Not only warships and dockyards and naval supplies but also shipyards, both naval and commercial, armament factories, steelworks, mineral resources, shipping lines, port facilities and a hundred kindred matters touch both the NA and the commercial staff.

Common to all three key neutral capitals in Europe was the readiness of well-placed civilians sympathetic to Britain to provide useful and sometimes vital information. Shipping firms in Norway, and later shipowners and captains in Sweden with access to occupied Denmark, Norway and Germany itself, were examples of this. From these sources too, came channels into and out of occupied Poland and the Baltic States. The Assistant Naval Attaché in Istanbul regarded his civilian sources as better than the paid agents. In the United States, then as now, unofficial contacts counted for everything.*

NAs had to be very careful in accepting such help that they did not compromise their friends in the eyes of the government or secret police, or injure their business interests. For at least half of the war, the Germans had or seemed to have the whip hand, and it was only the British control of the blockade at sea or the volume of British investment abroad that offered a counter-balancing factor to the commercial communities in such countries. There was always the risk that a neutral government would so tighten up security regulations that straightforward and overt intelligence gathering would become impossible; and there were ways of isolating a Naval Attaché from his contacts without infringing his diplomatic immunity. He could, for example, be compromised in several different ways.

Whatever Foreign Offices and Ambassadors might say, their naval members – indeed all Service Attachés – would be suspected of controlling secret service and sabotage organizations. For example, the German NA in Washington (whose work can now be examined in the Archives) was credited by the Americans with many activities which were far beyond his capacity. In Copenhagen, on the other hand, the pre-war activities of the German NA were so crude that the Danes, greatly daring, asked for and obtained his withdrawal. During 1942 the Swedish Press reported the case of a convicted gangster who was accused of sabotaging German shipping. At his trial he stated that he had been interviewed by one of the British Naval Attache's 'sabotage department'. The publicity given this statement caused great embarrassment to Captain Denham, and of course to his Ambassador. The Special Operations organization had tried to persuade Denham that one of their staff should enjoy 'cover' as a member of his staff. Very reluctantly he agreed, on the strict condition that he should not take part in any violence and should be discreet. The undertaking was not honoured and after the trial Denham was regularly watched by the security police.

Lest the impression is given that the neutrals did not do everything in their power to maintain the reality and appearance of neutrality, let Denham be quoted on the Swedes:

Reticence was brought to a fine art in conversation of every Swedish officer or Foreign Office official. They were unwilling to discuss any subject which might have some professional savour . . . It was most disheartening to find that all doors expected to lead to sources of intelligence were literally slammed in one's face. It took many months to find a soft spot.

All over the world the security of British and Allied ships against sabotage (a very real risk in wartime, and a costly one, when ships were being sunk at the rate of millions of tons a quarter) had to be supervised by the Naval Attaché's office. In Spain, for example, there was a port security officer in each major port, who was generally the British vice-consul or one of his staff. Security guards were provided for each ship from a pool of watchkeepers in Gibraltar which was replenished from Britain. Special lighting was installed on board while the ship was in port; special searches were made and periodically divers would be sent down to examine ships' bottoms.

The Spanish port authorities had received from their Government a general directive to watch for saboteurs, but it was not always rigorously enforced. Hillgarth in Madrid had to enlist the help of the local police, stevedores and dock-watchmen against the numerous German agents. He was well informed about most of these agents and, by representing sabotage as being contrary to Spain's interests, he was able to anticipate much mischief. Of course there were successful bomb attempts; and in cases where attempts were frustrated, reports that they had succeeded would sometimes be circulated so as to cover the tracks of our own counter-measures.

To be a Naval Attaché to an ally could be the most arduous and delicate post of all. The United States in the early days of the war; Portugal during the days when it was thought the Germans might seize the Azores and we had an expedition ready to forestall them; above all France during the years before war broke out. After the years of calculating or pretending that war was unlikely for ten years – the period being shifted forward after review each year until it became a habit that was very hard to break – the British were thrown together with the French in the Mediterranean by the Abyssinian crisis, in which Italy seemed for a while likely to become the common enemy. The relations then established led to exchanges of information about the dispositions of warships, base facilities, fuel supplies, aerodromes and W/T stations. Plans were made for an inter-allied cipher and the exchange of liaison officers, but by April 1936, as the crisis waned, nothing more was happening than swapping whereabouts of warships.

In November 1936, the French Chief of Naval Staff, Admiral Durand-Viel, approached the First Sea Lord, Chatfield, through NA Paris, with the suggestion that closer relations should be established. He anticipated, quite correctly, incidents in the Mediterranean arising out of the Spanish Civil War and suggested naval staffs should collaborate. This approach was countered by Chatfield's pointing out that a proposal of this kind must have higher authority behind it. It appeared that Admiral Durand-Viel had acted without reference to his Minister of Marine or to the Quai d'Orsay. Chatfield's instructions were quite firm: Britain was rearming in a mild way, had given up the ten-year rule, and was being guided by the Chiefs of Staff's plea 'Keep us out of war until 1941'.

The French were of course anxious to tempt us into an alliance or a private understanding, but – astonishing as it may seem – no question of future war operations was ever discussed. The information given to Paris was restricted to details of our forces available in Home Waters, with and without mobilization and technical details about ports, and so on.

The influence of Duff-Cooper who was First Lord in 1938, was in favour of full and frank discussions. The only argument against having them was that they would upset the Germans and Italians. This, Duff-Cooper maintained, would happen however restricted they were. But in the event NA Paris was severely restricted in his instructions:

Such contacts between the two staffs should be clearly understood on both sides not to give rise, in respect of either Government, to any political undertaking, nor to any obligation regarding the organization of defence forces . . . political assumption should be confined to the obligations undertaken by HMG towards France and Belgium under the Treaty of Locarno. . . . Germany alone being assumed to be the aggressor.

Admiral Darlan, understandably, did not like this last clause because he wanted to talk about what was happening in Spain and Italy. But one practical and important outcome of these talks in June 1938 was agreement to compile an Anglo-French cipher which would take a year to produce. In conditions of utmost secrecy – the Governments would have been highly embarrassed had the fact been known – a certain French Signal Officer, Lieutenant Toulouse Lautrec, came to London to 'learn the language' and spend his time with two cipher experts of NID elaborating a wartime means of communication.

A formidable and very intelligent officer in Plans Division,

Captain Victor Danckwerts, was very cautious about the talks that had been approved by his seniors. He felt, perhaps recalling the events of 1914, that a hard and fast line must be drawn beyond which we could not go without morally committing ourselves to act with France in war. To allow that to happen would be to make nonsense of the assumption on which he and the other Joint Planners had been ordered to work by the Chiefs of Staff and the Cabinet – a further three years' expectation of peace.

However, in January 1939 Godfrey, as part of his preparations for taking over the NID, went to Paris to work out ways and means of collaboration with the French DNI, Rear-Admiral de Villaine. It was 'a very cordial and co-operative occasion' and they agreed to exchange information about intelligence centres abroad and about Axis war and merchant ship movements. This meant revealing to the French, what they most probably knew or suspected already, that we had a world-wide system of ship reporting by consular officers.

Godfrey on this visit met Darlan several times and was shown round the Operations and Intelligence Room deep below the Ministry of Marine. He found it much better equipped than the Admiralty equivalent and he had no doubt at the time that Darlan was wholeheartedly in favour of working with the British.

The fall of France complicated the naval intelligence task in Spain as much as the fall of Norway and Denmark complicated it in Sweden. But between the work done in the two countries by two of the most enterprising Naval Attachés of the war there was this profound difference; although the Germans might threaten Sweden with attack and had powerful friends in the higher ranks of government and the Forces, there was never any question of the country joining the Axis. The mass of opinion was democratic and friendly to the West even when Hitler seemed sure to win. From Spain, on the contrary, there was always the danger that she might be brought into the war – certainly not on the Allied side — either by pro-Axis elements, especially in the Falange; by British errors in the use of the blockade against the Axis or in anticipating German action in North Africa and Morocco; or by the ability of the Germans in occupied France to push across the Pyrenees, establish themselves on the Atlantic and Mediterranean coasts, and perhaps bomb and starve us out of Gibraltar.

Looking back now, Captain Alan Hillgarth is confident that there was never any serious risk of Spain becoming a belligerent enemy, hostile and provocative though some individual Spaniards were in the earlier stages of the war, but on the one condition – that we did not lose Egypt to the Germans. Had that happened, Franco would have reckoned that Britain had lost the war and that it was time to join the winning side. Nor does Hillgarth believe that an attack on Spain, after 1941, would have brought the Germans anything but an exhausting extension of their vast commitment to defend the coasts and feed and fuel the people of Europe. Spanish resistance would have been intense; it would have been supported by the British and later by the Americans; and the Navy might well have had its task in the Atlantic and Mediterranean made easier by being able to use some Spanish and all the Portuguese ports and move into the Canaries and Azores at an early stage.

So the real danger was that a few Spaniards, some high up in Madrid, others lower down in important ports such as Ferrol and Vigo, would play along with the Germans by sending them raw materials which Britain needed, allowing U-boats and tankers to fuel at their ports, giving them footholds in Morocco, and hampering in every way possible our own attempts to organize intelligence sources and, in particular, escape lines out of occupied Europe for pilots and other prisoners of war. Above all, it was feared that German and Italian agents would be allowed such opportunities for spying and even sabotage in the Straits, that nothing of importance could be assembled or even planned in Gibraltar without the enemy knowing about it.

On the other hand, there were men in important positions in industry and shipping, banking and insurance, as well as in the Services and the Government, who desperately wanted for their country a long period of recuperation. 'They were by no means alone,' Hillgarth writes, 'in resenting the constant German pressure, with its threats of invasion and occupation; but they were exceptional, at least in the earlier stages, in recognizing that German victory would mean servitude for Spain, and an end to the individual freedom which is as neces-

sary as air to most Spaniards'. Using 'liberal' in the English
sense their point of view might be described as liberal monar-
chist. They preferred the British way of politics to the German
and the Italian, even though they found it convenient to support
Franco against the Republicans of their own country. Among
the more outstanding personalities was Juan March, of whom
more in due course.

Whereas neutral Stockholm was a magnet for intelligence
(from Norway and Denmark, from Holland and Poland, from
Finland and even Russia) and by far the best observation post
into Hitler's Europe, non-belligerent Madrid was a place for
action. Much of Hillgarth's work might be fairly described as
counter-intelligence; although like Denham he was collecting
information hard, his chief work had to do with preventing the
Germans getting away with infringements of Spanish neutrality.
He would represent day in, day out to the Ministry of Marine –
rather more friendly to Britain than some of the other Ministries
– that German mischief-making in the ports, their infiltration
of the Spanish police and abuse of hospitality were against the
national interest. Was it not apparent that Spaniards needed
peace after the ordeals of the Civil War? The British, and not
the Germans, could let the Spaniards have the oil and wheat
they needed. Sooner or later the British mastery of the Mediterranean would be reasserted – especially after the Americans
joined the war – and the Italians, incidentally much looked-
down on by the Spaniards, would be defeated.

This, it may be thought, was work for a diplomatist rather
than for a naval officer, but Hillgarth had been in close touch
with the Spanish Navy for a decade and was fortunate in having
an Ambassador and Minister who saw their whole staff as one
team, each doing his bit of the supreme job of keeping Spain
out of the war. Sir Samuel Hoare had been convinced by
Admiral Tom Phillips, in 1940, when he was Vice-Chief of
Naval Staff, that he must take on Madrid, not as a diplomatic
assignment but as a fighting post of the greatest strategic
importance. 'If the Atlantic ports of the Peninsula, and with
them the coast of northwest Africa go over to the enemy,'
Phillips had said, 'I do not know how we shall carry on.'*
Moreover, Hillgarth had been recommended to Hoare both by
Churchill and by Dudley Pound because, from 1932 to 1939, as

British Consul in Palma, he had been a valuable source and contact for the Foreign Office and the Admiralty, and for one period was the only channel of communication between the British Government and the Nationalists.

The first two years, vividly described in Hoare's book, were difficult. The Germans, who were given much franchise in Spain, did everything they could to embroil its government with the British. After the fall of France they infiltrated, or tried to influence, all branches of the civil service, police and business. Their tools were to be found even in the Ministry of the Interior. At one moment large formations of German soldiers, calling themselves tourists, were seen as far south as Valladolid. U-boats took refuge in Spanish coastal waters and bought fresh stores. But the Germans played their cards clumsily and soon became as much disliked as the French had been before the war. They tried to force port authorities to allow un-neutral facilities to U-boats, organized escapes of German merchant ships to French ports, paid Spaniards to sabotage British and Allied ships.

These incidents merely made Hillgarth and his colleagues intensify their vigorous and persistent protests. The Ministry of Marine, understanding the food and fuel needs of the country and the stranglehold which the British had on overseas supplies, were throughout insistent on maintaining neutrality. If Hillgarth could prove mischief and identify mischief-makers, he could generally get something done, sooner or later; and NID was kept constantly informed of the state of affairs in the ports, where Hillgarth relied on the British reporting service and especially on the personal reconnaissances made by his assistant attaché, Don Gomez-Beare, a native of Gibraltar, who, as an RNVR officer, rendered Britain most remarkable service of the true cloak-and-dagger kind.

At the same time it was part of Hillgarth's job to prevent any irregular British activity about which the Ministry of the Interior could legitimately complain. When SOE began to take an interest in Spain, it was strictly limited to planning measures to immobilize ports and give other assistance in case of a German attack.* Meanwhile, in spite of all that the Embassy could do, the Germans maintained elaborate watch on the Straits, which had to be countered by Spanish agents in British pay and organized from Gibraltar – so that His Majesty's Naval Attaché in Madrid could disown them.

The success of this tactic of vigilant appeasement depended on intelligent understanding in London, especially by the Ministry of Economic Warfare and the Admiralty. Hillgarth had a staunch supporter in the Prime Minister and also A. V. Alexander, the First Lord, whenever he came back to London to argue the case for an easier hand with Madrid; although the planners in the Admiralty, from time to time, wanted to take a tough line with General Franco. In fact, as he was able to show, the Madrid Ministry of Marine did deny the Germans most of the invaluable services and privileges they wanted in Spanish ports and merited some confidence, whatever might be true of the other Spanish Ministries.

As Allied war prospects improved, so the job of the Madrid Embassy became easier. Egypt was the battlefield the Spaniards watched most carefully – Rommel's successes and the inability of the British to force convoys through the Mediterranean or part of it without heavy loss and effort. They watched too for any sign of Allied designs on the Canary Islands, where a German occupation might have made the U-boat war, at any rate for a time, even more difficult for the Allies. But the German Navy wisely advised, as in the case of Iceland, against any lengthening of the communications it had to guard. Both in Washington and in London there were those who would have preferred to make quite sure of the Canaries, but Pound was convinced by Hillgarth that it would be criminal folly to strike such a blow at national pride and unite opinion behind the influences hostile to us.

'Torch', in November 1942, was the turning point; the Spaniards, like the Germans, were taken completely by surprise. Hoare and Hillgarth, having been fully admitted into the planners' confidence, were able, on the very morning of the North African landings, to explain in Madrid the scale of the operation, its targets and scope, and reassure General Franco about Spanish interests in North Africa. This sudden arrival of American as well as British military power in the middle of the Mediterranean made a profound impression on Spanish opinion and led to the disgrace and withdrawal of the hitherto very formidable German Ambassador, Dr Stohrer.*

196

None the less, mischief-making between the Spaniards and Germans and Italians did not cease because of the swing in Allied fortunes. One day a historian with access to the Spanish and Italian archives will be able to ferret out the whole story of the 5,000-ton tanker *Olterra* and its use as a human-torpedo base against ships in Gibraltar. When Italy entered the war, this ship was detained in Gibraltar Harbour and scuttled herself in shallow water, but in November 1940, Spanish engineers refloated her and she was towed into Algeciras Bay. There the Italian master and crew rejoined her and stayed on board. A certain Italian naval officer, Lieutenant Lino Vinsintini, hit on the idea of using this ship sitting opposite Gibraltar as a starting point for attacks that had hitherto been made from Italian submarines. Using tools sent from Italy by land, camouflaged as machinery for the ship, the tanker was fitted with a special compartment in the forepeak, from which a hinged trap-door below the water line provided a launching point. Trained naval personnel arrived from Italy, also by land, and joined the ship by mingling with the crew returning from shore leave, departing after each attack if they returned safely.

On the night of 7–8 December 1942, they made their first attempt against two aircraft carriers and two battleships in Gibraltar Harbour. Of the three craft launched, only one returned and that with one of its two operators lost. Victims of inaccurate intelligence, they found themselves facing defensive depth charges dropped every three minutes instead of every ten, as reported. They had expected to be able to lift the harbour-net and swim under it, but found the bed of the sea defended with barbed wire. One crew scuttled their torpedo and were taken prisoner. When interrogated they declared that they had come from a submarine and gave no clue to the *Olterra*. In April 1943 a more successful attack damaged three merchant ships, totalling nearly 20,000 tons in Gibraltar and in July they damaged 24,000 tons of shipping.

In spite of prisoners' denials, Intelligence in Gibraltar suspected that there was a ship or land base on the Spanish side of the bay, and Hillgarth was asked to investigate and protest. The Ministry of Marine had the *Olterra* searched from top to bottom, without discovering any trace of the alleged saboteurs, and a senior officer gave his word that the suspicions were without foundation. (As there was no access to the compartments from inboard, nothing was found. Hillgarth realizes he should have asked for an inspection by divers.)

However, after Italy capitulated, Hillgarth was able to persuade a member of the Italian Embassy in Madrid to reveal that there had been all along a compartment in the forepeak of the ship from which torpedo men had operated. Armed with this information, Hillgarth was able to insist that the Minister get to the truth of the matter by having the ship towed to Cadiz and there examined by carpenters until the secret compartment was found – as it was. Understandably embarrassed, the Spaniards expected the Admiralty if not the British Government, to deliver a thunderous protest about what must be either connivance or gross carelessness. Wisely, the Admiralty decided that the best policy would be to let the facts speak for themselves.

I know of no better example, from the history of NID, of intelligence in action than of the way in which his duties could lead a Naval Attaché from simple diplomacy to intelligence inquiries; thence to counter-intelligence; and so back to a diplomatic call and successful action – but in this case of course too late.

Among the useful naval intelligence that reached Hillgarth was news of the German-controlled Vichy French Navy, which for three years was the cause of constant acute anxiety to the Admiralty. It was part of his wartime job to keep a watch on North Africa. He had a private arrangement with some French officers that he should be told at the last moment of ships' movements; the idea being to avoid incidents at sea and to keep in some kind of touch with both sides. Usually the news they passed was unimportant, but on 10 September 1940, just before operation 'Menace' to capture Dakar for General de Gaulle was to take place, he heard that three French cruisers and three destroyers were leaving Toulon and making for Dakar through the Gibraltar Straits. Dashing to the Embassy, Hillgarth got off an Immediate signal to the Admiralty, repeated to Flag Officer Gibraltar, reporting that there was certainly a movement, the destination of which Hillgarth had not been given but could guess. He knew the move must have some strategic meaning (though he knew nothing of the plan against Dakar) because it could not have been made without German agreement. Unfortunately, neither the duty officer in London nor the OIC grasped the importance of the signal or the merits of the Naval Attaché's source and the First Sea Lord was not informed until the next morning. What then happened in Gibraltar is well known from the whole controversy over Admiral North.*

From this incident Hillgarth draws a conclusion, discussed elsewhere in this book, that too much security about operations can be stultifying, and even dangerous. If he had known that an operation was being planned against Dakar, he would have referred to it in his signal and understood even better the importance of his information. He also points to the failure of the Foreign Office and the Admiralty (this would be NID's business) to alert posts and agents abroad – for example, the Consul-General Tangier – to the need for the fastest possible reporting of Vichy ship movements in the then existing situation. In fact, so far as is known none of them received such warning. Later in the war such a failure of operational intelligence would have been unthinkable.

If a streak, or more than a streak, of the 'Blinker' Hall conception of intelligence shows itself in this chapter, it is not least because the Ambassador in Madrid had been head of the British Secret Service in Russia during the First World War, and because Hillgarth had spent seven of the pre-war years in a role which confused diplomatic, naval and intelligence functions in the best Hall style. Both men had the deep understanding of unofficial activity which made it possible to talk convincingly to moderate Spaniards about their country's neutrality and the damage that might be done to it by German machinations. But it has to be stressed that Hillgarth's conception of his role in Madrid made it essential that he should not only observe the proprieties, but be seen to be observing them. For the secret of dealing with the Spaniards was the same when we were strong and winning, as when we were weak and apparently losing; to win genuine confidence by understanding and representing in London their point of view, with due regard to their national pride and their dislike of most foreigners. His skill was perhaps most highly tried during the

199

deception operation known as 'Mincemeat', an episode which reveals, as clearly as any one story could, the complexities of Anglo-Spanish relations.

It has been fully described in the book by Ewen Montagu (NID 17M);* and it is only necessary to recall here that the purpose of the plot was to convey to the Germans through their agents and friends in Spain a piece of what would appear to be high-level and first-hand intelligence (the written equivalent to the wireless intercept) about the direction in which the Allies would move next from North Africa, in the winter of 1943. The papers in question were on the body of a British Marine officer, whose body (presumably from a shot-down aircraft) had been washed ashore near Huelva. It had in fact been launched at sea from a British submarine.

For the success of the deception it was vital that Spanish local authorities should allow German agents enough time to photograph the papers in detail and check quickly the identity of the body and any clues as to its origin: the more thoroughly they did this, the more likely that German Intelligence back in Berlin would swallow the whole story told by the contents of the dead Marine's brief-case. On the other hand, it behoved the British Naval Attaché – who had sent the energetic and resourceful Gomez-Beare down to handle the affair on the spot – to insist energetically on the earliest possible access to the body and its papers, and to demand that no unauthorized person, especially German agents, should be allowed near it. Fortunately, everything worked out right, because the German agent did not want to attract attention by taking too long over his task, the Spaniards with whom he was secretly dealing did not want to get into trouble with Madrid, and Madrid did not like being hurried.

Nothing required of the Naval Attaché – and of his Ambassador – more tenacity of purpose than the handling of complaints and allegations that Spanish Ministers or officials were assisting the Germans, as indeed they were likely to, in the circumstances of 1939–43. With their hundreds of miles of northern coastline alongside the Bay of Biscay route to the Atlantic or Mediterranean, they were in a position to offer U-boats valuable opportunities to refuel, to buy fresh provisions or to repair damage. They could also cause the

Admiralty anxiety by shipping precious iron ore in a few hours sailing to ports in occupied France or fruit and other supplies from southern ports to Marseille and Genoa. The use of this traffic by enemy intelligence could never be excluded; many ships had a German Secret Service agent on board. The important thing to ensure was that British Intelligence should get its facts right so that the Madrid Embassy could complain effectively. Sometimes, doubtless, the Foreign Minister did not know what the Navy Minister was doing; or Madrid did not know what its employees in Cadiz and Corunna were allowing or stopping. Spanish port officials did not always carry out as they should have their obligations as neutrals, even in those places were the British were known to keep a sharp watch.

For some reason that was never clear, rumour pointed early on to Vigo, a commercial port in the far north-west of Spain, as a port much used by U-boats. Early in May 1940, the Embassy in Rome reported the American journalist Vincent Sheehan to London as telling a 'reliable' friend that Vigo was a German base and that some twenty boats were using it. This caused quite a stir and on 18 May the First Lord told the War Cabinet that reports of the increasing enemy use of Vigo were being checked. This, it will be recalled, was the time of catastrophe in France, the very week that Churchill had taken Chamberlain's place as Prime Minister, when people felt that anything now might happen.

Careful and detailed inquiries, in which NA Madrid had played his part for some time, convinced NID that this was yet another misleading – perhaps deliberately planted – series of rumours about U-boats, and on 5 August it reported to First Sea Lord that much of the evidence was 'unsupported by positive facts' and conflicted with what was known of U-boat movements in the OIC. No British authority had actually seen U-boats there and 'If they have been making use of Vigo it can be stated with reasonable certainty that they have not operated from that port. In all probability one or two U-boats have made calls there for some special purpose, but no regular operational use has been made of the port.' That was the end of the Vigo queries with which Godfrey had been badgered.

Enemy activities in Spanish ports continued to cause concern and complaint in the Admiralty until 1944, although the

German naval archives now reveal that things were not nearly so bad as was feared in the first three years. After the war began, for example, no U-boat actually refuelled or took on supplies in Vigo or any other port until 30 January 1940 when U25 refuelled in Cadiz. The records refer to the 'smooth way in which this, the first U-boat supply operation to take place outside home waters, was carried out'. Again, on 19 February 1940, the German Naval Attaché reported to the High Command that' When the Ambassador of Hitler was visiting the Spanish Foreign Minister the latter told him with a laugh that the British Ambassador had called to inform him that it was intended to fuel a U-boat from a tanker in Vigo between 16 and 18 February. He agreed to send the British Naval Attaché to Vigo to see for himself.'

However, in the following month the *Altmark* incident made Spaniards much less willing to take risks and German records show the German Naval Attaché reporting that they were unlikely to 'concede Pontevedra or Arosa as supply points'.* In April he told a representative of the German Naval War Staff that if secret supply operations became known the Spaniards would probably stop any passive condoning of them.

None the less preparations had been made to exploit Spain's blind eye. For example, in February 1940 there were one hundred tons of lubricating oil in the ships *Brake* and *Nordatlantik* at Vigo; two hundred and seventy tons of fuel oil and provisions for two U-boats in Corunna; and eight hundred tons of fuel oil, four tons of lubricating oil and provisions for one U-boat in El Ferrol. A letter from the German Naval War Staff to its Attaché on 6 June 1940 describes in detail the arrangements made for refuelling U-boats alongside German merchant ships during the night and states that this would be done entirely without Spanish co-operation. 'In every case it is carried out within the harbour, alongside the German ship during the night in such a way that unobserved entry and exit is ensured (under water if necessary).'

Indeed, the Germans always insisted that all they wanted from Spain was a blind eye. Sometimes, however, they ran into resistance from individual Spaniards which could be either spontaneous or inspired by British agents. In November 1939 they had arranged a supply operation from the merchant ship

Landro which had to be abandoned because the Spanish captain refused at the last minute when threatened with virtual mutiny by his crew. And crew trouble was experienced also in the case of a sailing vessel which was bought by German agents and taken to Puerto Sta Maria for modification. Fitted with three 7-ton capacity tanks she was to be filled at Ceuta and then sent to the mouth of the River Guadalquivir where a small boat-house was fitted up ostensibly to build rowing boats for the fishing population. Here she was to be fitted with three or four more tanks giving a total capacity of 40–50 tons, which would be useful for U-boats in need.

It was a curious evidence of Hitler's unreadiness for war with Britain in 1939 that so many German merchant ships were caught in neutral ports. In March 1940, when the British blockade had really got a grip, there were 222 ships of nearly 1,100,000 tons spread over Europe, China and Japan, and the Indian Ocean and East and West Africa. As Allied shipping losses mounted and German needs grew more urgent, these vessels became more and more valuable, whether as prizes for the Allies or as potential blockade runners or saleable assets for the Axis. In Spain alone there were fifty-five ships of 219,500 tons, some of them tankers, which Churchill as First Lord longed to get hold of by fair means or foul. Much energy and paper were expended in Room 39 trying to find a way of getting these ships which was legal, but would not make the Germans a present of scarce currency.

In September 1939 Godfrey had received a visit from Don Juan March, a Mallorquin banker and industrialist who had made a large fortune from modest beginnings, and was one of the richest men – if not the richest man – in Spain. He came to remind DNI that he had helped in maritime matters in 1914–18 and said he hoped to be even more helpful now. This, formerly, was because he 'admired the British institutions and outlook', and because he saw no future for his country and for businessmen like himself should Germany win the war. This meeting led to an intermittent but always invaluable collaboration with Whitehall over the war years. Señor March had large interests in oil and shipping, among other things and he was often able to help the Embassy, both by putting it in the way of information and by using his considerable influence to persuade people that a British victory was in Spain's interests.

Now we come to perhaps the most important piece of business tackled in Spain by DNI and which brought Room 39 into alliance for the moment with the new SOE.

It is tempting to add to the thousand and one 'ifs' of history by asking what would have happened to plan 'Torch' (the landings in North Africa of November 1942 which were the first step in the return to Europe) if Mountbatten's Commandos had been used in the spring of that year to destroy the German and Spanish detection posts overlooking the Straits of Gibraltar. Where they were was known exactly. Would an assault on them have given the Germans an excuse for coming down into Spain and seizing air and sea bases for use in the Atlantic and Mediterranean campaigns? If so, would it have brought in retaliation British and Americans into Portugal and the Atlantic Islands? Almost certainly.

How long had this Gibraltar plot been hatching? On and off since the fall of France agents had been busy around Gibraltar but in 1941 the effort was intensified, and it was after many weeks of reports from agents and other sources that Room 39 had produced, in March 1942, a detailed account of the German organization of observation posts on both sides of the Straits, and on Alboran Island, from which direct wireless touch was maintained with Berlin and Paris via Madrid. The British in Gibraltar, by using the hours of darkness and various deceptive tactics, had been holding their own in the intelligence struggle in which Canaris (head of the German Abwehr) was personally engaged; but the Germans were now preparing a site on Spanish territory slightly west of the Bay of Gibraltar, and another on the African coast opposite, to instal a combination of infra-red apparatus and radar.

A number of ways in which the enemy might use the site were discussed at the Admiralty. But here detailed information was needed. So it was decided to send a Scientific Officer to look more closely into the possibilities and a photographic reconnaissance of the site was ordered; but this was to be carried out in such a way that the enemy would not guess that we knew what he was up to. In fact, the preparations were known to many people; roads were being built, sites prepared, much money spent on compensating evacuated residents.

In pressing for action to stop the Germans Ian Fleming played a leading part and he was able to assure his Director that Plans Division and the Directors of Operations were on his side. It was vital that what he called 'the detailed and deadly watch' of the enemy on the Straits of Gibraltar should be frustrated by one means or another. Even the cautious Military Branch* (dealing with the international implications of Admiralty operations and with legal matters) which fought many of the Navy's battles with the Foreign Office, thought diplomatic action might be futile. The First Lord (Alexander) strongly favoured at least drafting an operational plan; but it was eventually the Chairman of the Joint Intelligence Committee, Mr Cavendish-Bentinck, who persuaded the Admiralty to bring the whole problem before the Chiefs of Staff, whence it would reach the War Cabinet.

On 19 May they decided against armed action. The old argument, it seemed, had prevailed: there was danger of throwing the Spaniards into the arms of the Germans by increasing the influence of the pro-Nazi Ministers around General Franco and giving them a chance of rousing national pride against British interference. The Foreign Office was able to point out, what NID well understood, that it was not in Spain's economic interest to exasperate the British and – since 1941 – the Americans by turning a blind eye on German abuse of Spanish neutrality. So it was decided that the Ambassador should try again.

Hoare received instructions on 23 May 1941. He immediately asked to see Franco personally and urgently, but without telling the Foreign Minister on what matter. This caused alarm in high quarters and on the same day Hoare was summoned to the Prado. The interview, so the story runs, lasted for over an hour, Hoare being careful not to give the impression of threatening any sort of ultimatum, Franco insisting that the British were seeing a mare's nest in what he contended were only Spanish coastal fortification works. Hoare said he assumed that what was really going on was unknown to the Caudillo but stressed that there could be no possible doubt about the British information. The Ambassador even hinted that he knew of a German proposal that Spanish uniforms had been provided for the technicians manning the sites and suggested that

205

Spanish neutrality was being dangerously threatened. Hoare also pointed out that scarce petrol – the supply of which depended on British and American forbearance – must have been used in the building and transport operations on the site.

General Franco promised urgent and personal inquiry. Three days later the Minister of Marine admitted to the British Naval Attaché that the Germans had offered a radar station for instruction, which the Spanish Air Force and Army had been foolish enough to accept without realizing what it might portend! He, the Minister of Marine, was of course in favour of shutting it down; the Service Ministries in Madrid knew all about the affair and so did the Senate. Powerful personalities were against taking such risks with neutrality.

We now know from the German archives that less than a month later Admiral Canaris was interviewed by Franco and told that the entire undertaking must be cancelled and his agents removed. Spanish watchers and Italian agents remained but that was the end of an operation which might have had incalculable effects on the whole Mediterranean strategy of the Allies. It is also pleasing to think that Canaris suffered a personal defeat at the hands of British intelligence in the very country where he believed his reputation and influence to be most effective.*

The interest of this episode lies in the way Godfrey found himself bridled and delayed by the very system of joint consultation he had done so much to encourage. 'Blinker' Hall twenty-five years earlier, would certainly have found for himself the money, the men and the authority to deal with the Gibraltar threat. The DNI of 1942 could do no more than urge action in his dual role as the member of the Naval Staff responsible for both intelligence and counter-intelligence. But counter-intelligence was something NID could not practise on its own. He found himself, moreover, up against a reluctance in high quarters to understand why detection apparatus in that area was a highly dangerous weapon, not just another gimmick in the boffins' war. If radar was allowed why not a long-range gun on railway mountings to bombard Gibraltar airfield? Shore-based torpedo tubes might be the next move. With an effective reporting system (covering for example the movements of Force H or the Malta convoys), the German and Italian

U-boats from Bordeaux could bottle up the Mediterranean. The use of intelligence by one country's organization to outwit that of another is a delicate and sometimes dangerous matter. It is useless to protest on the strength of such information to a foreign power, as Hoare protested, unless one can prove one's case or at any rate give hints about it sufficient to convince the other side that what they have been concealing has been detected. But this is to run the risk of giving away sources and of thereby doing, in the long run, serious damage to one's own intelligence. This was especially the case in Spain, where British sources of information being usually anti-Nazi might therefore be represented (only three years after the Civil War) as anti-Franco. To show too much knowledge of what was going on in Spain was to court the charge of interfering in her internal political affairs. Needless to say, the British were scrupulously careful to avoid meddling even though the Germans, at any rate up to 1944, were doing so flagrantly and overtly, as Hoare describes in his book.

Just as Spain on the map hangs watchfully over the Straits of Gibraltar and North Africa, so Sweden looks straight down to the naval bases and ports of north Germany, to the Baltic exits to the North Sea, and up to the northern waters which provide Russia with her only quick and direct sea passage to the Atlantic and her wartime Allies. It was a key position for operations, had Sweden been fighting on either side; and it was a key position for information, not only about Germany and Russia but also for occupied Europe, so long as she remained neutral. Within the Baltic itself trade could go on unhampered by the British blockade, although the RAF's mining operations created constant delays and hazards; and to and fro with trade flowed information, and sometimes people, from Poland and the inner depths of eastern Europe.

Captain Henry Denham in Stockholm spread a wide net to cover most aspects of naval and general war intelligence. His sources were to be found not only in the Allied missions, of which the Norwegian one under Colonel Rosher Lund was outstanding, and had the closest contact with the Swedes, but also among pro-British individuals. These men and women, sometimes at great risk to themselves, turned to our advantage information they gained through their professional positions

H   207 about German warship construction, U-boat building, movements of military transport, industrial and scientific developments. Only rarely, however, could the Naval Attaché expect to provide London with the highest grade of intelligence, the kind which leads to immediate operational action. For example, advance information about German attacks on Arctic convoys could be obtained only from Swedish 'Combined Intelligence' or by subterfuge from 'Secret Intelligence'. The chiefs of both these organizations were men of the highest integrity but, although their loyalty to Swedish interests never wavered, they had an unmistakable sympathy for Britain which events were to justify.*

Before recounting some of the difficulties that sprang from Sweden's exposed position between Germany and Russia – most vulnerable between 1939 and 1943 – it is fair to explain their roots. Whereas the Swedish people as a whole were far from being pro-German, and made a clear distinction between their historical experience of Germans and their attitude to the Nazis, in the officers' corps sympathies with Berlin were strong. They showed themselves in many of the higher posts of the ministries in Stockholm; but they were, unfortunately, most pronounced among the higher admirals, and the Swedish Admiralty made some foolish concessions to German pressure. Denham, of course, made it his business to know about them and the action he took to protest cut both ways; the officers and officials concerned were compelled to cease their unneutral action, which was a score for Britain; on the other hand, they felt their authority being undermined and their actions spied upon. Understandably their relations with Denham became complex.

The British had taken little pains to cultivate Swedish goodwill between the wars; Stockholm was treated as an outlying parish of NA Berlin, whereas links were close between the Swedish and the newly reviving German Navy. There was already enough here to cause the Royal Navy difficulties when it added to them in a flagrant and much-resented fashion. In June 1940, four Swedish destroyers proceeding to Sweden by an agreed route were challenged by a superior British force and called upon to follow them to port. This grievous blow to the pride of the Swedish Navy was long remembered.*

As the German Naval Attaché recorded in his diary at the time 'either anger or depression, according to individual temperament, was apparent'. There followed the obstructive attitude to Sir George Binney's ore convoys at Gothenburg (see Chapter 12), the permission given to the Germans to lay an anti-submarine net off Hälsingborg to prevent our submarines from entering the Baltic, the escorting of German transports in Swedish territorial waters and the sweeping of British mines in neutral waters.

When Denham's information was used with operational effect, then German protests were to be expected. How the message from Stockholm on 20 May 1941 started the hunt for the *Bismarck* has already been described in Chapter 7. The Germans were furious about the use of the *Gotland*'s report and made serious complaints to the Swedish Government and to the Swedish Naval Attaché in Berlin about 'unneutral behaviour'. Denham was warned by various staff officers, not for the first time, that he had been meddling in matters outside his 'recognized scope of interest', and he began to be conscious of a close watch kept on his movements, and on the personal contacts which were his most useful means of obtaining information.* During that year the Swedish police measures were not very effective, but later they were intensified and threatened to impair his usefulness to London.

By November of the next year, 1942, he realized that the security police had not only taken a flat in the building opposite his own block, from which they watched and photographed everyone coming in and out, but must also have installed a microphone in or close to his sitting-room. In spite of many searches he was unable to locate it, until he took expert advice and traced it to his chimney into which it had been hung from the roof.

An unfortunate sequence of unconnected happenings led to this intensification of Swedish police measures. First there was the visit of a former NID colleague, now working with the Secret Service, who had come over to assist in some particular business about Italian naval officers who were planning to desert. He naturally visited Denham and was quickly identified by the Swedes as someone about whom the Germans would be sure to protest. By this time, too, Denham's association with

Colonel Björnstierna of Swedish Intelligence had been discovered and the Colonel had been dismissed; and other Swedes
had been actually arrested and sentenced for their assistance
to the British.

It was not only Denham's intelligence activities that caused
the trouble. Like Hillgarth in Madrid, he had the chore of
nagging the Government and its officials about un-neutral
behaviour. A keen eye had to watch for incidents like the
following. Because of their labour and material shortages, and
the bombing of their shipyards, the Germans were by 1942 trying
hard to get ships built for themselves in neutral and occupied
countries. In the autumn of that year the British Embassy
learnt that forty-five fishing boats were being built in a certain
Swedish shipbuilding yard for delivery to Germany, where
they were likely to become minesweepers. Details having been
obtained, London protested to the Swedish Government
(15 February 1943), pointing out that these ships were not to
be equipped for fishing before delivery by their Swedish
builders, and that their specifications were identical with
those of minesweeping vessels being built in occupied countries.
The Swedes rejected the protest, arguing on technical grounds
that the vessels could only be used for fishing.

Denham was then allowed to take a hand and visited the
department of the Swedish Foreign Office concerned. He was
given an assurance that a German order for a further forty-five
vessels of the same type had been countermanded, but failed to
satisfy his visitor about the ships which were the subject of the
first British protest. Denham, well-informed as usual, protested
strongly in writing that he was being misled, and made it
clear that he knew the bank and the bank director behind the
deal. The next stage in the long argument was that one of
these ships was inspected by a mixed committee, including a
representative of Lloyd's Register; but this was fruitless from
the point of view of the British, who stuck to their contention
that these ships, whatever they looked like while still in Sweden,
would be completed by the Germans as ships of war. The
British lost the tussle; but sure enough Denham was able, after
the war, to identify thirty-eight out of the forty-five ships in
northern ports, all fitted as minesweepers. His satisfaction
scarcely needs recording.

On a smaller scale, but more serious from the strictly naval point of view, was the affair of the tankers. The Germans were painfully short of small tankers for fuelling U-boats and other warships. It was learnt in mid-1942 that Swedish tankers on charter were being used for this purpose. The Ministry of Foreign Affairs was apprised of the facts and was later again told that further tankers were being sold for the same duties. An official denied that this was so but promised Denham that no licence to export would be granted; later, however, two small tankers were identified as leaving Sweden for German bases. Not until late in 1943 did persistent representations from London persuade the Swedes that it would be wise to withdraw these tankers from German waters.

Another experience shared by the two Attaché's in the widely separated capitals of Madrid and Stockholm was the occasional failure of the Admiralty to act on the information they sent. For example, on the night of 22/23 September 1943 British midget submarines attacked the *Tirpitz* in Altenfjord, the new fleet anchorage in the far north of Norway from which the German capital ships could dash out to attack the Arctic convoys to Russia. This very gallant surprise attack crippled the mechanical gear of the battleship's main armament and put her main propeller shafting out of alignment for many months to come. The attack had, however, very nearly failed because one of the X craft became entangled in a bunkering net about which its crew had not been briefed. Fortunately they were able to free themselves and were able to complete the operation. Denham, who had been plying the Admiralty with microfilmed reports, brought to him through Norway over the mountains by young resistance men facing great danger and hardship, was dismayed and angry at this mishap; for he had been pressed to report on the net defences at Alten-fjord and had sent details of what looked like an A/T net (purpose unknown) about 200 metres long and 50 metres wide, with its position shown on a sketch map. A later report said that it was a bunkering net of double mesh with two gates, which was used when naval vessels were oiling from the *Altmark*. Subsequent inquiry at the Admiralty did not reveal why the information intended for the midget submarine crews did not reach them.

Another example of the same kind, more deplorable because there was a serious loss of men and aircraft as a result, was the failure to inform the leader of a low-level attack by RAF bombers on the *Tirpitz* in Trondheim in April 1942 that there was efficient smoke apparatus close to the ship. Wing-Commander Bennett (later Air Vice-Marshal and leader of the Pathfinder squadron) complained that the loss of seven heavy bombers by heavy A/A fire was caused by his not knowing of the smoke danger. Denham had, in fact, sent particulars of it in a report of 16 February which appears to have been promptly passed by NID to Air Ministry, Coastal and Bomber Command, Home Fleet and MI 15. Someone blundered, but it is not clear who. Let the episode stand, at any rate, as an example of what may happen when intelligence is not distributed to those who need it.

At the beginning of 1943 Denham was seriously worried about his declining usefulness in securing high grade intelligence and knew that the head of the Swedish Foreign Office had tried hard to get him withdrawn. But soon he saw an opportunity of improving his position. His friend Colonel Björnstierna had been succeeded as Chief of Combined Intelligence by Kommandör Landquist, from the Operations Division of the Naval Staff. For reasons explained below, it was a time of crisis in the Swedish Staff and Denham was regarded with great suspicion by the pro-German Commander-in-Chief, General Thörnell. Indeed, Denham at that time could not enter the staff building for an interview without the C-in-C telephoning to know why this had happened. But, even though Landquist was under the direct supervision of the C-in-C, there seemed to be a chance of making a new start.

Landquist had been invited to visit Berlin, where he was entertained by senior officers including Admiral Canaris, chief of the Abwehr, and had presumably been impressed by what he had seen and heard, despite his known sympathy for Britain. On his way back he had also visited Helsinki. Denham therefore proposed to the Admiralty that the Kommandör should be given an invitation to London, which he could hardly refuse in view of his visits to two 'enemy' capitals. The suggestion was accepted and immense trouble was taken by NID and the Foreign Office over the visit. The result was that the new

Swedish intelligence chief returned in excellent spirits and full of optimism about an Allied victory. He had also, in response to DNI's parting request, promised to do what he could to get the security measures against Denham lifted.

He did not at first succeed in this, because the head of security in Stockholm was notoriously pro-German and a personal friend of the German Intelligence chief in Stockholm, Colonel Wagner. Indeed, he was Denham's evil genius in dealings with the secret police. At last an opportunity occurred for action of a different kind. Denham invited the head of the Foreign Office to lunch in his flat, with his Minister and others, and during the meal it was pointed out to him that the police observation post in the opposite building could be clearly seen from the table. This hint to the embarrassed official was sufficient to get this particular supervision stopped.*

The next stage in Denham's duel with the security authorities came after the withdrawal of Count Oxenstjerna from London, of which more later. He knew by now that a portable microphone was being operated in his chimney and he planned to make a public scandal about it. However, the Minister forbade such action and instead himself made a formal protest to the Security Chief and obtained an apology. Then an attempt to get into Denham's confidence was made by an *agent provocateur* who was a security officer, only to be promptly detected and exposed. Then he was able to prove that the Swedish Navy had placed on board Sir George Binney's coaster the head of German Telefunken in Sweden for no other purpose than to get information about his radar set. This revelation, says Denham, led to the Chief of Naval Staff giving him one of the most expensive lunches he has ever eaten.

The pressure for Denham's withdrawal continued without result until in July 1944 the Foreign Office gave the Embassy in Stockholm the strongest possible instructions to defend him. They spoke of the 'extremely serious impression' that the Swedish request had made and to the obvious wish to take reprisals for the removal of Count Oxenstjerna. The request would therefore be regarded as only the last of a whole series of unfriendly and un-neutral acts by the Swedish Navy, and they threatened to make public the reasons for requesting the withdrawal of Count Oxenstjerna.

The story of the removal from London of Count Oxenstjerna, several times referred to already, really belongs to the record of the precautions taken to seal Britain off from Europe in the months preceding the assault on the Normandy beaches; but its intelligence significance stands out more clearly in the context of Denham's difficulties in reporting from Stockholm.

The difficulty that faced the Government in early 1944 was that neutrals, however friendly and trustworthy, whether they were diplomats or businessmen or journalists, might, without intending to give anything away, be the means of giving the Germans some vital piece of information. Neutral service attachés, for example, might be expected to observe and report home as part of their duties, facts about our preparations. No service attaché after all, has any overriding loyalty to the country in which he is serving; whatever his sympathies, it is his job to pass on everything he thinks important. He is an intelligence officer first and foremost. This convention, with its curious code of obligations, was perfectly well understood in Room 39, in touch with naval attachés all over the world, used to lunching and dining with agreeable gentlemen from abroad of insatiable curiosity.

The Swedish Naval Attaché, Count Oxenstjerna, was an engineer of wide technical knowledge, much liked and respected in London. His sympathies were undoubtedly on the Allies' side. But it had been reported to the Admiralty that during a facility trip in a cruiser from Portsmouth to Rosyth he had shown much interest in the stabilizer equipment and had spent a lot of time talking to engine-room artificers. This he was entitled to do; but it was evidence of industry and curiosity backed by expert knowledge. The head of the NID German section, Commander Tower, had also been impressed by the kind of questions that the Count would ask. It was therefore decided between the Admiralty and the Foreign Office that ways must be found of removing this expert eye for the period when preparations for 'Neptune' would be most conspicuous; specially in mind was the risk that he might see and report experimental Mulberries for artificial harbours in the Thames Estuary which he had in fact tried to visit.

After long and difficult discussions the matter was referred to the Prime Minister, who agreed that the life and death circumstances of the day justified a request through Denham in Stockholm that Count Oxenstjerna should be recalled. There was some anxiety lest this should lead to the expulsion of Denham in retaliation; but as the Count had not been declared *persona non grata* (only a source of understandable anxiety) it was hoped that the Swedish Navy would not take too deep umbrage. The removal was at last arranged, everyone was full of regret, and Lt-Cdr Todd, the head of the Scandinavian section, went to see the Count off at King's Cross, still protesting his loyalty to our cause and unable to understand why this was happening. There was a friendly sequel.

After the war Todd was invited to join a goodwill visit by the cruiser *Birmingham* to Sweden, the Navy's first since the war. At a party given in Stockholm Oxenstjerna was present and Todd was able to explain the fears leading to his departure. To make his point clear he told the story of how Beatty after Jutland had got most valuable information from sitting at dinner in London next to the Swedish Naval Attaché, who had just returned from a conference in Stockholm. There he had met his colleague from Berlin, who told him that the Germans were recounting with great relish how a number of British shells at the battle of Jutland had not exploded on impact. This remark gave Beatty, who had been urging that our shell fuses were not adjusted to ranges opening at 20,000 yards, just the material he needed to insist on the thorough test of the Navy's shells that he believed necessary. It revealed a deplorable state of affairs which might otherwise not have been discovered until much later.

When the Count realized that his departure was to be interpreted as a compliment to his powers of observation he declared that he understood. Indeed, Todd clearly recalls his saying that the Admiralty was right; if he had seen a Mulberry he would have guessed its purpose and would have reported it to Stockholm. Whence, of course, for reasons which are apparent from an earlier chapter, the facts might quickly have reached Berlin.

10　Showing the Americans

It was probably at the suggestion of 'Blinker' Hall that Godfrey had paid special attention from the first to his contacts with the American Embassy in London. It would be in any case an important – and very demanding – part of the duties of DNI to cultivate the friendship of the US Naval Attaché and his staff and to look after their interests by providing information and arranging visits to ships and establishments. But in the particular case of the Americans there was on both sides of the Atlantic the still vivid memory of how Hall had worked with Page to bring the United States into the First World War, and the conviction that the Americans – even though they might remain neutral, if the Axis let them – would never be potential enemies in the way that had seemed for a short time possible twenty years before.* From the very first day of the 1939 conflict it was in the mind of the Admiralty that the Americans might be our allies sooner than we expected, and that whatever preparations for working together could be made within the limits of neutrality laid down by Congress should be set in motion as soon as possible. This was to mean more than two years of tactful, secretive, assiduous and above all personal wooing and salesmanship. In this diplomatic and military game NID played a leading part, if only because it was for some time the only formal meeting-point for the American Naval Attaché in London and the British Naval Staff.

By the summer of 1939 the DNI had already seen a good deal of Captain Alan Kirk, who held that position and was to become DNI Washington in 1941.* Whether as Naval Attaché or later as Chief of Staff to the United States Naval

216

Heaquarters in London in 1942, Kirk was found to be entirely co-operative and 'invariably met the DNI more than halfway'. Emotionally highly strung, he had gone through tortures of doubt during Dunkirk and the Battle of Britain. In June 1940, he told Godfrey that Britain would be defeated before 4 August unless the Americans came in on her side – only one symptom of the defeatism then prevailing in Ambassador Kennedy's Embassy. Godfrey countered by betting him half-a-crown that he would be proved wrong.

The help of this 'modest, shrewd and kind-hearted man', as Godfrey's memoirs describe him, proved invaluable in the summer of 1941 when the DNI paid his first visit to Washington. The object of his mission was to persuade the Americans to pool their intelligence with ours, to adopt those of our methods which had been proved by nearly two years' experience and to accept all we were prepared to offer.* As early as 1940, during the disasters of the Dunkirk summer, Room 39 originated a proposal that the Admiralty should offer to Washington an extensive revelation of naval secrets. Although American isolationist sentiment was then very strong and it was not even certain that Roosevelt – our main hope for the future – would win a third term of office as President, the paper argued that such an offer could do nothing but good if it led to most secret and informal contacts. It used the perennial arguments for what was to be called in the post-war years the 'special relationship'; they are now well worn but then they seemed unfamiliar and even daring. The Americans would certainly not come into the war against us. The intelligence we could give them would make them far more effective allies if they should eventually join us. Indeed, the giving and accepting of intelligence and other information would create a number of semi-official contacts which would help to counter the influence of the isolationists; and from this effort would result personal collaboration and friendships between officers and officials which would be invaluable in war. Extensive inquiries had shown that American security was on the whole as good as the British; our secrets would be safe from the Germans with our opposite numbers in Washington.

It was part of DNI's plan that collaboration with American intelligence might bring a much-needed reinforcement to

217

British resources. It was known that Washington's cipher experts had had considerable success with Japanese signals. The Secret Service network in Europe had not yet begun to recover from the effects of the German occupation, with its huge and ruthless counter-espionage system. So long as the United States remained neutral, it could gather first-hand information from Germany itself, where it had consuls over all the country, and from occupied Europe and Italy. In particular, we might be able to get up-to-date information from the African colonies under Vichy control. Those in Africa had ports and anchorages – Dakar and Madagascar were the most important – which if held by the Germans or by hostile French forces or by the Japanese could threaten our convoy routes to the Middle East and the Cape as dangerously as U-boats and surface ships based on the French Biscay ports could threaten our Gibraltar convoys and the south-west approaches to Britain. Possibly an exchange – so far as intelligence was concerned – would work out as favourable to us as to the Americans.

The Board readily agreed and the Americans accepted; progress was then fast. The US Naval Mission in London, which had been six strong, grew in a few weeks to forty. Its members came into NID (Section 2) to be introduced to divisions of the Naval Staff in which they were interested, and to have visits and liaison arranged for them. The painstaking friendliness shown in those days must be rated as one of the most valuable achievements of the Division; and the contact enabled a civilian head, Peter Wilding, to build up remarkable expertise about the American Navy and its men. Indeed, it was partly through his section's work that the Board of Admiralty's scepticism about American ability to build the largest Navy in the world in a couple of years was gradually overcome – an interesting example of the value of good intelligence about allies.*

This is the moment to digress and explain more fully a point of principle in Intelligence work touched on already in Chapter 2. It was foreseen that the contacts in London between the NID and the American Naval Mission – to say nothing of those that were to grow up in Washington between the intelligence section (NID 18) of the British Naval Mission there and the Navy Department – might cause confusion and foolish competition between individuals. Godfrey insisted that there should be no 'trading' of intelligence and no suspicion in anyone's mind that 'trading' would be possible. To ensure this, he gave orders that officers responsible for passing intelligence to the Americans should so far as possible not be associated in any way with receiving it. Those who gave should ask for nothing in return. Someone foresaw that American officers quite inexperienced in operational intelligence matters might introduce competitive business methods* into its practice, with disastrous effects on security. Security, it must be pointed out, was in those days almost as much directed to keeping the Anglo-American collaboration out of the American and British press as to guarding its secrets from the Germans. Publicity which might alert the rivals and critics of Roosevelt could mean disaster, at any rate until the presidential elections were over and the American C-in-C for the next four years was firmly installed. Trouble was therefore taken to systematize the methods used by both sides in passing information and to provide clear Admiralty guidance about what was and was not to be revealed. So the Navy Department asked for information through the London Mission, and the Admiralty asked for its material through the British Admiralty Delegation in Washington.

Matters were taken much further between January and March 1941, when there were long staff conversations between an American staff committee and a British delegation representing the Chiefs of Staff. The Admiralty representatives in these highly secret talks were Rear-Admiral Bellairs and Captain Danckwerts, both in close touch with NID and friends of its Director. Their purpose was to determine what would be the best way of defeating Germany and her allies (Japan of course being specially in mind) 'should the United States be compelled to resort to war'. Far-reaching basic decisions were agreed, although decisions about the general strategic concepts of the associated powers were deferred; for example, a 'sustained air offensive against Germany' would be among the principal offensive policies; the Atlantic and European theatre was to be regarded as the decisive one; and if Japan came into the war, Allied strategy in the Far East would be at first defensive.

As a result of these talks, against a background of steady personal pressure on the President by the Prime Minister in their private correspondence, a Joint Staff Mission went to

219

Washington in June 1941. This included a naval mission under Admiral Sir Charles Little and Captain Danckwerts. Because of the neutrality of the United States, it was attached to the Embassy under the cover title of Advisers to the Supply Council, which was openly organizing American sales and aids to Britain. Within this mission was a picked intelligence staff of four, henceforth to be known secretly as NID 18, the Washington counterpart of NID 2 in London. As it happened, Godfrey was on the spot when the section arrived and was able to introduce them personally to the Office of Naval Information where he had had consultations.

This mission, on which Godfrey left London on 24 May accompanied by his personal assistant, Lieutenant-Commander Ian Fleming (17F), was to prove so important in later history that it is worth tracing back its origins. The suggestion was made by an assistant director of Naval Intelligence, Colonel Neville, that someone should go to the United States and lecture on security in the great ports, where huge supplies vital to the British war effort were being handled, where our warships might be repaired or refitted and where German and Japanese Intelligence must certainly be active and well-organized. This kind of work was ADNI's special responsibility, but he was not to know at that stage that American naval authorities then, and even more later, already paid almost fanatical attention to security at the expense of some aspects of its work. Discussion of the project determined Godfrey – possibly with encouragement from Fleming – to suggest that direct contact should be made with *all* branches of American Intelligence.

On 28 April, Godfrey had taken a second initiative with the bold suggestion that if the best use were to be made of the American forces, with which collaboration would soon be essential, they must get the best intelligence. To send them summaries and telegrams was not enough. The aim should be 'complete fusion of the British and American intelligence services'. He wrote:

What I have in mind is not liaison but complete co-operation, with US officers attached to NID sections and vice versa. In certain special categories this co-operation exists already and we have derived benefit from it in the Far East. It is up to us to return their services in the Atlantic.

As Kirk, now head of the Office of Naval Intelligence (ONI) in Washington, could not come to London, it was suggested that Godfrey should go to Washington and help Captain Danckwerts, Rear-Admiral Pott and Kirk 'with a mandate to set up a combined intelligence organization on a 100% co-operative basis'.

Rear-Admiral Bellairs, with all the authority of one of the original participants in the Anglo-American staff talks, welcomed this idea. He suggested more ambitiously that Godfrey should represent the views of all three Chiefs of Staff and be briefed by them before leaving. That this proved readily acceptable is shown in a minute a few days later from the VCNS, Vice-Admiral Sir Tom Phillips, saying that the Chiefs of Staff had discussed the project, and his naval and air colleagues had agreed. So when Godfrey arrived in Washington it would be as the emissary of all three services with the authority of the Chiefs of Staff and the Joint Intelligence Committee behind him.*

What state of affairs was he going to find across the Atlantic? On their air journey via Lisbon and Bermuda he and Fleming again went over the kind of departmental structure that could best be recommended to the Americans. Unity was the important principle and the condition of that was inter-service co-operation. The Americans should avoid the mistakes, as NID then regarded them, made in Britain where subversive activity and resistance movements abroad (SOE), political warfare (PWE) and economic warfare (MEW) had been put under different political masters and divorced deliberately from both Services and Foreign Office Intelligence departments. But they must take account of American politics and of the risk that powers which could be given to a *combined* intelligence organization in wartime – never yet in peacetime – might be refused to Britain in peacetime America, even if it were as close to war as it was in 1941. Even more important, the British must not appear to be interfering; not only would this be understandably resented, but it would also give a handle to our numerous critics and enemies in the United States and weaken Roosevelt's ability to help us.

All in all, Godfrey decided, he had been given as tricky a diplomatic mission as could fall to a naval officer. If it failed, some people back in London would be only too pleased; for the persistent taking of the initiative by the Admiralty in Intelligence matters had hurt feelings and irritated departments in Whitehall – the same kind of feelings and departments as were to be mobilized against Admiral Mountbatten twenty years later, when he began his drive for an integrated Ministry of Defence. Godfrey decided it would be wise to use Fleming whenever he could as intermediary for the most daring but informal approaches.

The prospect was not clear or inviting for other reasons. On 5 May 1941 Rear-Admiral Pott had sent for NID's guidance an impression of the Intelligence set-up in Washington. The technical neutrality of the United States enabled its representatives to circulate in enemy or enemy controlled territory, but with decreasing ease. Reports from American Consuls lacked precision and detail; reporting was irregular and communication back was difficult. The most serious difficulties, Rear-Admiral Pott reported, were raised by the State Department which controlled these representatives. 'It is far more closely wedded to forms and proprieties, which are ludicrous in view of the Government's policy, than are the Service Departments.' One or other of the British Embassy's first secretaries would visit the State Department daily, where he would be permitted to see a selection of telegrams and reports – but not to take any notes. 'Such reports as they bring back are lacking in detail, lacking in accuracy and sometimes miss the essential points altogether.' It could take five days, Pott concluded, for the report of an event in Dakar to get via the State Department to the British Embassy. Even there in Washington the organization for handling intelligence was still bad. Three separate authorities were receiving it from the Americans and six people were communicating separately with London. There was no single point at which all intelligence could be collected and submitted to a comprehensive view by one person or department.

In the Navy Department, on the other hand, Pott reported great improvements, probably owing to Kirk's influence and NID's help. 'Practically every item of importance was passed to our Naval Attaché' and Rear-Admiral Pott's staff were allowed to coach the Department about British needs. Special orders for information requested from London had been passed on. Lieutenant Otway Smithers, RNVR, assistant naval attaché in Washington and Mexico, by assiduous social and diplomatic efforts of the kind which DNI encouraged, had got himself invited to various sections of the Office of Naval Information. He had even visited the cipher-breaking organization and was allowed to copy some of their intelligence about the Japanese and pass it on, in the strictest secrecy, to London, where not even the First Lord might see it. But vague memoranda were still preferred to hard facts, and appreciations to the brief categorical judgements favoured in London. The Americans still had no system of grading intelligence (see Chapter 2) and Pott had strongly recommended them to adopt, with other service departments, a uniform system such as the British had so far failed to achieve in spite of the strongest representation by the Naval member of the Joint Intelligence Committee. The result was confusion and the mixing up of first-rate and third-rate material, with all the risks of leakage and mistaken inference that went with it. Indeed, the confusion in which vital intelligence was sometimes handled was revealed the following year by the Senate inquiry into the Pearl Harbor disaster.

This was not all about which Pott had to warn Godfrey. Military Intelligence (G2 as the Americans called it throughout the war) under Brigadier-General Sherman Miles, the Office of Naval Information under Captain Kirk and the Federal Bureau of Investigation under Edgar Hoover did not work well together. Godfrey was warned he would have to argue against American faith in competition. There was as yet no kind of joint intelligence machinery in Washington; indeed, nothing gave these three officers more pleasure than to scoop one another – which meant doing another department's job for it in order to show off. For example, the FBI, chiefly concerned with counter-espionage and security at home, had recently interested itself in offensive intelligence – that is to say, inquiries directed towards taking action against the enemy – in South America, where the Nazis had been very active among the large German colonies in Brazil and elsewhere. This upset the State Department. Again the Operations Division of the Navy Department insisted that the Intelligence Division should play no part in its deliberations or plans – the very situation which the OIC in London had been built up since 1937 to avoid.* It could happen, therefore, that the plots of enemy fleet locations kept in two separate divisions of the Navy Department would be seriously at variance. Senior officers and officials tended, through lack of experience, to be credulous and prone to sensationalism – which is not surprising in view of the extraordinary happenings they had witnessed in Europe since 1936. It was alarming to the British that the American estimate of German U-boat strength was a third higher than their own, in spite of the first-rate intelligence NID had passed on; also that the German Air Force was, in Washington, reckoned to be two and a half times as large as the Air Ministry judged it to be.

It became obvious to the visitors that the Office of Naval Information lacked prestige and was in worse shape than the NID had been back in the early Thirties. It was to put this right that Kirk had come back from London, and he needed Godfrey's help. ONI walked in fear of the State Department and even hesitated to ask that august body to put it into touch with the naval officers who had been attached to US consuls as intelligence observers.

Some of these facts Godfrey already knew from his long talks with Colonel Bill Donovan, known as 'Big Bill' to distinguish him from his great friend 'Little Bill' Stephenson in New York, the British Secret Service Chief Mr W. Stephenson. Donovan, a distinguished New York lawyer, then fifty years of age, had been turned by his active service in the First World War into one of the most lively and forward-looking amateur strategists of his time. Wherever there was a war or a civil war with modern weapons to be seen in action, or where the tactics of the future might be rehearsed, there Donovan would go, at his own expense and on his own initiative. He was in Abyssinia in 1936 and in Spain in 1937. No question of his having represented the American secret service on such inquiries arises – for there was no such thing. Nor did his association with our own SIS come until 1940. He said in 1939 that he was convinced that 'what we now call "unconventional" or psychological warfare would have a major place in the battles to come'.*

It had occurred to Donovan that the only administrative device by which unconventional warfare could be organized away from the hostile and conventional influence of the Army and Navy would be to associate it with Intelligence. That would provide secrecy, money, protection from political attack and press publicity, and possibly an opportunity to do the job himself. Certainly he showed no special gift for or interest in the plodding, meticulous methods of intelligence as practised, say, in the British OIC; although he had been excited by seeing facts and figures being put on to a plot and then being turned into orders which would move ships and perhaps save British lives and kill Germans. None the less, as Allen Dulles says in his *Secret Surrender*, 'while he often tangled with members of the Joint Chiefs of Staff about the role of intelligence and the conduct of unconventional operations, he held their respect and eventually gained their co-operation'.

The arrival of this dynamic American in London in the August of 1940 had been a godsend to Godfrey. Here was someone full of enthusiasm and optimism who was in the 'Blinker' Hall tradition of activity and initiative. (Indeed, one might describe the future founder and head of the Office of Strategic Services as America's version of Sir Reginald Hall.) He was known to be a close friend of the President, even though he was a southerner, a Catholic and a Republican; and the President's partiality for the Navy was well known. He came with the best authority. Having been called to Washington one day after the fall of France to testify on the Military Training Bill then before Congress, he was asked to join in a meeting with the President, Secretary of State Cordell Hull and Secretary of the Navy Frank Knox. All were deeply worried about the British situation, about which Ambassador Kennedy over in London could express nothing but doubts and fears. Would the Colonel therefore go to Britain and report back to the President personally as quickly as possible?

Donovan could have asked for nothing better. The visit he might anyhow have undertaken on his own behalf was now to be made with White House backing. His brief was to satisfy himself that Britain would continue to fight on alone as Churchill had promised. He was to find out whether the British had the means to carry out their promise and what

225

aid America could give to help them most effectively. That was the real purpose. The ostensible one, his cover, was to report on how Nazi fifth-column activities had helped the Wehrmacht overrun Europe so quickly, and what lessons the British could offer for counter-espionage work – a matter of grave importance to the Americans with their various large national groups not yet fully absorbed – Germans, Italians, Irish and so on.

Donovan took the opportunity to dig into everything that was secret and cloak-and-dagger, and he met Godfrey as one of the first in this field on the day of his arrival. After studying the organization and techniques of British Intelligence departments, he was convinced of what he already suspected: 'that America's military planning and its whole national strategy would depend on intelligence as never before, and that the American Intelligence set-up should be completely revamped'. (Again I quote Allen Dulles, who was one of Donovan's first assistants in the founding of the Office of Strategic Services.)

Despite the months spent talking with Stephenson in New York, who was encouraged to take the Colonel fully into his confidence, Donovan had been told that he would find the British difficult, secretive and patronizing. Whether these were normal characteristics of our representatives talking to Americans is open to doubt, but now they could not be afforded. The need to convince the President and his advisers that Britain was determined to fight on and win was desperate; because without American aid in weapons, goods and credit victory would be impossible. Donovan went back convinced and enthusiastic; he spent his last evening in England with Godfrey at his home, Braddocks, in Sevenoaks, where they sat up talking till the small hours.

That the evening was fruitful was shown in a private note sent to Vice-Admiral Tom Phillips, addressed from Braddocks and dated 2 August 1940: 'I have just had three hours with Donovan and attach a précis of what he told me regarding his intentions on returning to USA.' This was marked on 4 August to the First Sea Lord and First Lord, and on the same day Pound commented 'This is very satisfactory.' Churchill merely wrote three days later 'Seen.'

Later that month the DNI received from Donovan on the

notepaper of his law firm – no mark of secrecy or mystery here – a note of thanks: 'I shall always remember most gratefully your many courtesies and kindnesses to me. Certainly you aided me in getting a perspective that I could not have had otherwise.' Donovan saw the President and Knox and Hull and gave them a report very different from those sent by Kennedy, who reckoned the big German attack must come shortly and regarded his mission as over. Donovan urged the appointment of a 'sensible ambassador', who would go back and forth across the Atlantic and keep the two countries in touch; someone who could detect ways of making concessions without condescension, while insisting on and explaining prickly matters of sovereignty and protocol. Together with numerous requests for various weapons Donovan took back the suggestion of full collaboration in intelligence and access for the British to US consular officers' reports, especially from the French ports and North Africa. He recommended direct liaison between Godfrey and the American DNI, as well as the starting of direct and secret communications through special signal systems.

So Donovan was already converted in August 1940 to some of the ideas which Godfrey was to put forward eight months later. It is a sign of the resistance that Donovan had met in Washington that Godfrey should still want and need to go there a year later. In fact Donovan was not spending the interval in the kind of domestic lobbying which would be necessary to push his ideas through; he was making a 22,000-mile trip to the Mediterranean theatre of war for the President, at the end of which he reported on the strategic situation he found there, again favourable to the British. Only after this, in summer 1941, did he present to the White House his first plan for an intelligence organization bringing together political warfare, sabotage and guerrilla warfare with a special section inspired by what he had seen of the British Commandos.

Three months later the special cabinet committee set up to examine his plan, consisting of Knox, Stimson and Robert Jackson, the Attorney General, advised the President to authorize the Executive Order of 11 July 1941, setting up the office of Co-ordinator of Information:

227

To collect and analyse all information and data which bear on national security; to correlate such information and data and to make it available to the President and to such departments and officials of the Government as the President may determine.

Unconventional warfare, it will be noticed, is not in the brief, but there was an additional sentence which referred to 'such supplementary activities as may facilitate the securing of information important for national security'. Through that loophole Donovan was able to develop activities which led after Pearl Harbor to the creation of the Office of Strategic Services under the jurisdiction of the Chiefs of Staff. Then, for the first time, the United States had under one roof intelligence collection, counter-espionage, support of underground activities, sabotage and almost everything else that the armed forces, organized as they then were, could not do. No wonder that Donovan was sometimes suspected of wanting to be the Supreme Chief of Staff. Later, in 1947, when it became necessary to give the country a permanent intelligence organization for peacetime as well as war, there sprang from the experience and trained personnel of the OSS the now world-famous CIA.

The reader may feel by now that the narrative is straying far from the affairs of British Naval Intelligence. Yet this was all part of its business. Once the British Chiefs of Staff had authorized the DNI to cross the Atlantic on their behalf to arrange as much collaboration as possible,* it was inevitable that he should get involved in the earliest vicissitudes of American Intelligence, as it adjusted itself to new demands and ideas. It was also inevitable that he should try – as Donovan and others wanted him to try – to persuade men in Washington that they could be ready for war and better allies much faster if they learnt from the British through some of their failures and successes. William Stephenson, it has been pointed out, had already been working zealously and successfully to the same end, his appointment by 'C' having been inspired by memories of what Sir William Wiseman (like Admiral Hall, still alive and available for consultation) had achieved twenty years before. So what followed during the DNI's visit was a friendly, intelligent conspiracy to hurry on the process of change; and it was already clear in Stephenson's mind, as in Godfrey's, that the agent of change for them to back was

228

Donovan. But it must be done secretly and indirectly, otherwise Big Bill would be criticized as 'Little Bill's' stooge.

After a fortnight of talks in Washington during June, where Winant was doing all he could to help, Godfrey found himself up against a blank wall. His message to the American intelligence departments was not welcome. He could get nowhere with the FBI or the two service departments. Relations between them were so bad that it was his message of integration they disliked, not the support for Donovan which they did not yet know about.

Stephenson then advised Godfrey, after bringing in Sir William Wiseman (head of the British Secret Service in New York from 1914–18), that he must be allowed to state his thesis to the President. Wiseman spoke to Sulzberger of the *New York Times*, explaining why it was important that the British DNI should be heard; and Sulzberger rang up Mrs Roosevelt and asked her to arrange a dinner party which would allow an hour's talk between her husband and the British guest. This was done; it was at a friend's house on Long Island that he received the invitation to dinner at the White House – 7.30, dinner jackets – and he travelled back to Washington by the next morning's plane. He was received by Mrs Roosevelt and taken care of by two ADCs. The rest of the party arrived, eight in all, including two young relatives who had just returned from a photographing expedition to Upper Burma and Annam.

Then the President was wheeled in. Godfrey had been warned that he would almost certainly have his leg pulled by the President's making some provocative remark about the British or imperialism, and that he must on no account allow himself to get 'mad', as the Americans say. It was about the time when discussions were going on about the acquisition of American bases in British West Indies Islands in return for fifty old destroyers badly in need of a refit and not too seaworthy in many respects.

So there was the inevitable 'Hallo, Admiral, how did you come out?' and when Godfrey mentioned the Clipper via Bermuda, the President said, 'Oh yes, those West Indies Islands; we're going to show you how to look after them, and not only you but the Portuguese and the Dutch.' Rough stuff and rather brash, but Godfrey kept his eye firmly on the object of his visit and mustered up the semblance of a laugh. His host then turned on his incredible charm and conversation was resumed.

After dinner by some unobtrusive process FDR was got into his wheeled chair and a lift took them up to a drawing-room which seemed to be full of busts of former Presidents. For an hour they looked at a rather creepy-crawly film of snake-worship in what is now called Laos, and then, with a warning from Mrs Roosevelt not to keep her husband up too late, Godfrey was directed into the adjoining oval room – the President at his desk, and Godfrey sitting in the famous Lincoln chair.

Now, he thought, the moment had arrived for him to say his piece. But no: the President felt reminiscent and described to him in some detail his own visit to London in 1917, when he was Under-Secretary for the Navy, and his admiration for the then DNI, 'Blinker' Hall. Godfrey ignored the remark: 'Of course, Hall had a wonderful intelligence service but I don't suppose it's much good now', and then had to listen to a long description of how spies had crossed the German–Danish frontier every night, then went by boat to Sylt and flying-boat to Harwich. 'Blinker' Hall had clearly deployed some fantastic cover story to conceal his real cryptographic sources in Room 40 and the young Under-Secretary for the Navy not only swallowed and believed it, but even remembered to recount it to Hall's fifth generation successor twenty-four years later. At last Godfrey got a word in edgeways and said his piece. More reminiscences; then he said it a second time, and a third: one intelligence security boss, not three or four. He'd been in the oval room for an hour and a quarter; Mrs Roosevelt came in, and it was time for bed.

Driving home to his friends, Godfrey felt doubtful if he'd really made his point, but within three weeks Donovan had been nominated with $3,000,000 to play with as head of a new department, later to be called the Office of Strategic Services.

It is clear that Stephenson had made remarkable progress in finding and backing a man with whom the British could work as head of a proper secret organization. All that can be claimed for the DNI personally, and all he would wish to claim, is that he arrived with the latest information from London, as a practical sailor and with a set of ideas which had been proved by experience. That he may have done something very useful to the Americans was a by-product of a mission intended first and foremost to get better service for the British, then and in the future. He knew the danger to his other contacts of his being known to have visited the White House. He wrote:

I fear that for the time being I had, by meeting the President, made myself unpopular with the Secretary of the Navy, Forrestal, and with my old friend Kirk, who was cool and stony-eyed when I went to say goodbye ten days later. However, that wore off and our close collaboration was resumed when he returned to London as No. 2 in the US Naval Mission.

If the mission had run into difficulties over integration, it had been successful in interesting the Americans in other ideas. They accepted the idea and methods of the Joint Intelligence Committee and Joint Intelligence Staff as the master machine for processing the material required by the planners and commanders. They took British advice on techniques of interrogating prisoners of war. The OIC surprised them, because they regarded its work as part of operations and took some time to change that view. They were glad to have a specially prepared description of the organization and working of Godfrey's Division. What would the British now receive in return?

What they hoped for, and eventually got, was set out in a vigorous and urgent memorandum which Fleming prepared and presented personally to Donovan. To anyone who knew 17F's fluent and imperious drafting it was a good specimen of his style. Even if DNI's personal assistant had not become a world-famous writer of spy stories, the document would be of great interest, showing as it does the scope of wartime Intelligence and the ways in which it was thought that the Americans could help in this field even while still neutral; and it must be repeated, in the summer of 1940 there was no question of suggesting or admitting publicly or officially that the United States would actually fight the Germans.

The memorandum ran as follows:

231

In accordance with your request, the following suggestions concerned with the obtaining of intelligence through United States sources and the co-operation of US Intelligence Services with our own are submitted privately.

Admiral Godfrey, Director of Naval Intelligence, has seen these suggestions and concurs generally in them.

A copy of this memorandum will also be shown to Admiral Danckwerts.

It is requested that no action may be taken on any of these suggestions referring to the SIS without prior consultation with Mr Stephenson or without the full concurrence of his chief.

The State Department to send a circular telegram to all their diplomatic and consular posts in Axis or Axis-occupied territories, requesting information on the following subjects:

(a) State of morale (military, official and citizen).

(b) Bomb damage (especially locality, effect on production, percentage of unexploded bombs, value of new bombs).

(c) Suggested bombing targets with reasons.

(d) Health of the people and army (nutrition, hygiene, epidemics, efficiency of particular medicines, etc.).

(e) Rumours current.

(f) Efficiency of British propaganda (number of listeners, quality of reception, etc.).

(g) Military, naval and air, economic and industrial intelligence of a specific nature.

(h) Efficiency of civilian defence (fire-fighting, shelters, number of gas-masks, etc.).

(i) Prestige of the Party and popularity of individual party members.

(j) Prestige of the Services and popularity of individual officers.

(k) The main sentiments or emotions to be met with (e.g. war-weariness, fear of America, hatred of Russia, etc.).

(l) Any further remarks, including observations of an apparently trivial nature.

This section aimed at the quickest possible achievement of co-operation between existing American sources and ours. But there must also be improvements for the future. Fleming recommended that officers should be appointed for secret intelligence duties with important US diplomatic or consular posts, with the 'cover' of secretary, assistant attaché, cipher clerk or technical adviser. These men should be specially selected forthwith from the existing staff of the US intelligence services. They would then be put in touch with British agents in the field who had been instructed to co-operate with them and train them.

For disciplinary purposes these recruits would be under the command of the local SIS representatives during their period of training and would co-operate with services, funds and material when asked to do so. A section of, say, the State Department should supervise (without in the first place directing) their activities, and provide their requirements *without question or delay.* This would be the nucleus of an American SIS and after completion of training would become the United States SIS.

The headquarters of this would build itself up round their activities with the help of a senior officer from the British SIS who would be appointed to Washington for the purpose. 'These US officers must have trained powers of observation, analysis and evaluation; absolute discretion, sobriety, devotion to duty; languages and wide experience, and be aged about 40 to 50.' The absence of these qualities, Fleming pointed out, would reduce the value of the officers' reports and seriously endanger the security of our own SIS representatives. He even mentioned the names of one or two officers he had met in ONI.

Other ways in which the neutral position of the Americans might be turned to our advantage were put forward. Planning should begin on possibilities of obtaining intelligence by the 'oblique approach' method.

The principle of this was, for instance, that one of the best sources for Russian intelligence at that time was Turkey; one of the best sources of German naval intelligence was Sweden. If it was intended to withdraw American consular and diplomatic representatives from the Axis countries, preparations should be put in hand for the immediate infiltration into those countries of Intelligence Officers, holding passports of states unlikely to be affected by the breach in US–German relations.

Fleming went on to offer shrewd political advice. The American SIS, he said, 'should be under the protection of a strong government department and it should be insured by every means possible against political interference or control'. It should be constituted for the duration of the war only. It could be associated with, but in no way controlled by, the FBI

233

who, Fleming thought, had no conception of offensive intelligence and were incapable of adopting the entirely new
strategic mentality required. He concluded:

It is for consideration whether supreme power over the US SIS
should not be vested in the President, assisted by an executive
committee of three non-political persons, divorced from all other
duties. This committee might consist of one member from the Army
one from the Navy and one member from business or industry.

How far Ian Fleming was personally responsible for the
memoranda with which Donovan put his case to the President
is not clear. Certainly he worked very hard at drafting during
the three weeks he was in Washington. Godfrey's view now is
that he and Fleming overrated at the time their part in briefing
and boosting Big Bill, while underrating the skilful preparatory
work done by Little Bill Stephenson. At all events the document
in which Donovan finally presented his recommendations to the
President, reproduced below, is in a style quite unlike that encouraged in NID at the time, and one can imagine Godfrey's
reaction to any suggestion that a commander should be
promised 'complete' intelligence. However, the leading ideas
are recognizable to anyone who knew NID's thinking at that
time, particularly the recommendations on psychological warfare which the Admiralty was the first of the Service Departments in London to put forward and carry out!

Donovan Memorandum to the President
10 June 1961
Strategy without information upon which it can rely is helpless.
Likewise, information is useless unless it is intelligently directed to
the strategic purpose. Modern warfare depends upon the economic
base – upon the supply of raw materials, on the capacity and
performance of the industrial plant, on the scope of agricultural
production and upon the character and efficiency of communications. Strategic reserves will determine the strength of the attack
and the resistance of the defence. Steel and gasoline constitute
these reserves as much as do men and powder. The width and depth
of terrain occupied by the present-day army exacts an equally
wide and deep network of operation lines. The 'depth of strategy'
depends upon the 'depth of armament'.

The commitment of all the resources of a nation, moral as well as
material, constitutes what is called total war. To anticipate every

intention as to the mobilization and employment of these forces is a difficult task. General von Bernhardi says 'We must try, by correctly foreseeing what is coming, to anticipate developments and thereby to gain an advantage which our opponents cannot overcome on the field of battle. That is what the future expects us to do.'

Although we are facing imminent peril, we are lacking in effective service for analysing, comprehending and appraising such information as we might obtain (or in some cases have obtained) relative to the intention of potential enemies and the limit of the economic and military resources of those enemies. Our mechanism of collecting information is inadequate. It is true we have intelligence units in the Army and Navy. We can assume that through these units our fighting services can obtain technical information in time of peace, have available immediate operational information in time of war and, on certain occasions, obtain 'spot' news as to enemy movements. But these services cannot, out of the very nature of things, obtain that accurate, comprehensive, long-range information without which no strategic board can plan for the future. And we have arrived at the moment when there must be plans laid down for the spring of 1942.

We have, scattered through the various departments of our Government, documents and memoranda concerning military and naval and air and economic potentials of the Axis which, if gathered together and studied in detail by carefully selected trained minds, with a knowledge both of the related languages and techniques, would yield valuable and often decisive results.

Critical analysis of this information is as presently important for our supply programme as if we were actually engaged in armed conflict. It is unimaginable that Germany would engage in a 7-billion-dollar supply programme without first studying in detail the productive capacity of her actual and potential enemies. It is because she does exactly this that she displays such a mastery of the secrecy, timing and effectiveness of her attacks.

Even if we participate to no greater extent than we do now, it is essential that we set up a central enemy intelligence organization which would itself collect either directly or through existing departments of Government, at home and abroad, pertinent information concerning potential enemies, the character and strength of their armed forces, their internal economic organization, their principal channels of supply, the morale of their troops and their people and their relations with their neighbors or allies.

For example, in the economic field there are many weapons that can be used against the enemy. But in our Government these weapons are distributed through several different departments. How

235

and when to use them is of vital interest not only to the Commander-in-Chief, but to each of the departments concerned. All departments should have the same information upon which economic warfare could be determined.

But there is another element in modern warfare, and that is the psychological attack against the moral and spiritual defenses of a nation. In this attack the most powerful weapon is radio. The use of radio, as a weapon, though effectively employed by Germany, is still to be perfected. But this perfection can be realized only by planning, and planning is dependent on accurate information. From this information action can be carried out by the appropriate agencies.

The mechanism of this service to the various departments should be under the direction of a Co-ordinator of Strategic information, who would be responsible directly to the President. This Co-ordinator should be assisted by an advisory panel consisting of the Director of the FBI, the Directors of the Army and Navy Intelligence Services, with corresponding officials from other Governmental departments principally concerned.

The attached chart shows the allocation of and inter-relation between the general duties to be discharged under the appropriate directors. Much of the personnel would be drawn from the Army and Navy and other departments of the Government, and it will be seen from the chart that the proposed centralized unit will neither displace nor encroach upon the FBI, Army and Navy Intelligence, or any other department of the Government.

The basic purpose of this Service of Strategic Information is to constitute means by which the President as Commander-in-Chief and his Strategic Board would have available accurate and complete enemy intelligence reports upon which military operational decisions could be based.

(Sgd.) William J. Donovan

Washington, June 10, 1941

Once the Pearl Harbor attack had brought the United States into the war collaboration became not only easier but more urgent. One of the first reactions of the Germans to the new situation was to switch the weight of their U-boat campaign against the coastal waters of the United States, Doenitz calculating rightly that the Americans would be neither prepared nor equipped to deal with it. His success was frightening and it became obvious that diversion as practised by OIC in London was the only remedy to a disastrous state of affairs until air and naval escort organization were improved. It was decided to send Cdr Rodger Winn RNVR to Washington to see whether he could persuade the Americans to adopt the same methods and start a fruitful collaboration with their material and ours and that of the Canadians.

It is hardly surprising that the Americans were reluctant to grasp immediately the advantages of an organization for operational intelligence which the Admiralty had been learning over the last five years. The operations side of the Navy Department, COMINCH, were not in the most cordial relations with the Office of Naval Information, and it was quickly obvious to Winn after he arrived in Washington that if British methods of routing convoys and tracking U-boats were to be adopted, the section doing this work would have to be with the operational and not with the intelligence staff. For in the ONI's intelligence room as he saw it there was nothing of current operational importance; no one, he says, 'had grasped that U-boat intelligence had a strategic and tactical function'. Even with the able and forceful Commander Dyer in charge of the operational information room in COMINCH, it took three days of hard argument to create a good basis of co-operation. His 'initially sceptical and critical attitude' was overcome mainly by 'pitching the claims for British methods no higher than to be approximately right more often than sheer chance and the law of averages could explain'.

Then came the most difficult stage of the mission: to convert Rear-Admiral R. S. Edwards, the Chief of Staff. He was reputed to be overbearing and unreceptive, and junior officers stood in awe of him. When Winn first explained his methods, the Admiral commented that the Americans must learn by their own mistakes and had plenty of ships to spare. Winn replied that if the present rate of losses on the American side of the Atlantic was not soon checked, they would not have enough to spare. In any case, Winn said, 'we are deeply concerned about your reluctance to co-operate and we are not prepared to sacrifice our men and ships to your incompetence and obstinacy.'

Edwards then said that a lot of officers thought that spotting the U-boat was all a matter of chance and were against the policy of routing ships with any regard to U-boat positions.

237

Winn replied that he felt sure no one with Edward's experience would share such a view after he had heard the Admiralty's experience of the last two and a half years. He then hinted that London would be able to help with intelligence from special sources if they felt convinced that it would be properly handled. That made an impression.

Edwards then took Winn off to his club, where the latter's powers were tested by two long draughts of the Admiral's 'special'. After a meal that was something of an ordeal, they returned to Edwards's office mellow and friendly, and in Winn's presence Edwards sent for his chiefs of staff, told them he was convinced that a tracking-room must be set up and told them to get the accommodation right away.

Winn was then sent to see Admiral King who was interested, cordial and confirmed the arrangements. Much impressed by this success, Edwards then suggested to Winn that he should go to New York and explain to C-in-C East Coast, who was coping desperately with the U-boat offensive off the coast, that the anti-U-boat war must be controlled from Washington on an Atlantic scale, since it could no longer be treated as a kind of local difficulty. Winn, who had been strictly warned both in London and at the British Embassy in Washington against being drawn in to any American feuds or arguments, protested that he could not be expected to offer advice on a matter of such importance, which was an internal affair of the US Navy. Rear-Admiral Edwards, now the most dedicated of converts, insisted that unless Winn helped, nothing would happen.

So Winn went to New York with a non-committal letter of introduction explaining that he would outline to the East Coast Command the new methods of tracking U-boats. It was known that the Commander-in-Chief there was a close friend of Admiral Leahy, naval adviser to the President. If he were ordered by Admiral King to accept Washington control of U-boat tracking, then the decision would have been taken to the highest level.

It is worth recording that in the following year Admiral Edwards sent a personal request to the First Sea Lord that Winn should visit Washington again. Winn was summoned by Dudley Pound and Moore and asked why he was wanted. He said that his guess was that someone in charge of directing

238

merchant shipping was being obstructive to the tracking staff and that British advice would be needed to get rid of him. So off he went in the *Queen Mary* (the Americans had offered a plane) to test again the safety of the independently sailing ships which he had so often helped Godfrey to divert.

The end of the story of Anglo-American collaboration in intelligence work lies in the history of the Pacific War and in the later developments of the Battle of the Atlantic and in the great maritime assaults which have been dealt with elsewhere in this book. By the end of the war the ideal of complete integration which Godfrey had put forward in 1940 was almost attained, for example in Eisenhower's headquarters; but as the Americans gathered experience and developed their own techniques, their greater affluence and manpower enabled them to outstrip in some respects their tutors. None the less the period of learning – and particularly the middle years 1943-4 of learning together – is still remembered with gratitude by American intelligence workers.

11 Three heads are better . . .

It is convenient now to pass from the OIC to the Joint Intelligence Committee* from the point where the Admiralty brought Intelligence and Operations together to the point where intelligence from all three Services and other sources was applied to the strategic plans of the War Cabinet and Chiefs of Staff. It was only five minutes' walk or so from the Citadel in the Mall where the OIC served the Naval Staff to the Cabinet Offices in Great George Street, where the JIC served the Chiefs of Staff; but between the kinds of intelligence work being done in the two headquarters the contrast was enormous. If the men and women in the first were looking hours ahead, or only so many days as it would take a convoy to fight its way from Halifax to Liverpool or from Gibraltar to Malta, the men in the second (with a Foreign Office Counsellor in the chair)* were often looking weeks or months ahead, although they might sometimes be required to give a quick judgement on some sudden emergency or unexpected information. They were as inter-service as it was possible to be in those days and, as the Allies took the offensive, had to produce agreed views, acceptable to all intelligence departments, on the great strategic problems of the war. Would the Japanese attack Australia and New Zealand (paper of January 1942)? What would the Germans do to get more oil (January 1942)? Was the invasion of Ceylon by the Japanese likely (March 1942)? What would German strategy be in the next twelve months (July 1942)? – a very important paper pointing to an allied occupation of North Africa. When would the rocket and pilotless aircraft attack on southern England begin (autumn 1943)? And so on. On this kind of question three heads were better than one. The preliminary work of collecting intelligence about such a problem, discussing it and forming a view was done for the JIC, once it was fully developed, by its Joint Intelligence staff (or sub-committee). This consisted of senior staff officers (with junior assistants) representing the Directors of Intelligence from Admiralty, War Office and Air Ministry and representatives of Foreign Office and Economic Warfare. Day after day of patient and protracted argument on a single question, such as their masters had no time for, took place in the JIS; and when they had achieved agreement, it still remained to persuade each Director of Intelligence in an hour or two that the joint view was correct and that if he disagreed with it he was most probably wrong. As the Director might then have to eat words uttered publicly to the head of his own Service or recorded in a widely circulated paper, this process was not always either easy or gracious. As time went on, however, the Rear-Admirals and Major-Generals and Air Vice-Marshals learned to suspend judgement until their Captains, Colonels and Group Captains had produced collective common sense. There can be no doubt that this work of joint intelligence appreciation did a great deal to reduce inter-service rivalries and create a habit of objective study and discussion of common problems – something which the German service staffs seem never to have achieved.

One of the DNI's representatives on JIS recalls with amusement how one paper – in which the War Office was strongly interested – had to be completely re-written because of the absence from drafting meetings of the expert from the Ministry of Economic Warfare. The problem was to decide whether the Germans could in fact attack from southern Russia through the Caucasus and Turkey towards the Middle East. What had been agreed seemed to be reasonable and good until the men from MEW pointed out that all coal stocks for the Turkish railways were at the western end of the system and therefore not available for an enemy advancing from the east. All the assumptions about timing, wagons available, single-line working, and the need to bring up coal from central Europe were therefore wrong. It is perhaps unnecessary to add that the second paper pointed to a conclusion very different from that of the first.

In such a committee the Senior Service was, of course, only

primus inter pares. Seldom did a question that was exclusively maritime come before the JIC and its auxiliaries; but the Admiralty had a strong interest in watching for any disposition to ignore such maritime realities as Britain's absolute dependence on oil imports brought by sea, or the effect of an overseas assault on the number of escort vessels available to fight U-boats. An appreciation of enemy strength and intentions signed by the JIC that was taken seriously by the Chiefs of Staff in London and Washington was bound to affect the allocation of Allied resources. If, for example, they were assured that German morale, civilian and service, was being deeply affected by Bomber Command's attacks, then the Admiralty's effort to get more aircraft for Coastal Command or to have naval targets given a high priority by Bomber Command would be likely to suffer. Contrariwise some naval intelligence appreciations might be seen by the RAF representatives as overstating the range of Japanese carrier aircraft operating in South-East Asia. Sometimes virtually everyone, regardless of Service or Ministry, would disagree with the Committee, as when it forecast in early May 1941 on its own initiative a German attack on Russia between June 20 and 25. (It occurred on 21 June.) 'The Directors of Intelligence and the Chiefs of Staff', said the naval representative at that time, Captain Paton, 'thought we were all mad and we all nearly landed in the loony bin.'

Mr Cavendish-Bentinck, who was then Foreign Office chairman of the three Service Directors and their colleagues of the JIC (the masters of the JIS), writes:

Early in 1941, I think March or the end of February, I noticed reports from Poland that the Germans were increasing the length of the runways of the airfields in Poland and reinforcing these runways. It occurred to me that this was not being done for the benefit of Lufthansa! A little later we received reports that the Germans were beginning to subsidize again anti-Bolshevik organizations in the Caucasus. These two pointers led me to suggest to my colleagues on the JIC that the JIS (its advisory sub-committee) should be directed to prepare a report on the possibility of a German attack on the Soviet Union.

This report was prepared and was based on all sorts of information additional to the two items mentioned above. I well remember the officer who was then Secretary to the JIC telling me that he thought the JIS had gone mad in predicting that the Germans intended to attack the Russians in the near future; when I told him I had recommended that this report should be prepared, he gave me one of those looks of contempt to which I grew accustomed from 1939–1945. If I remember right, it took a little time to convince the Chiefs of Staff that the Germans intended to go for the Russians.

About June 10 or so, I spent half-an-hour with Anthony Eden in the latter's room at the Foreign Office trying to convince Maisky that the Germans were going to attack and that this attack would take place on either 21/22 June or 28/29 June. I added that I would put my money on 22 June. Maisky refused to believe this.

How did a body of such influence come into being? Today the Joint Intelligence Committee is virtual master of the British intelligence machine. Thirty years ago it was less than a year old. Nowadays it is difficult, even for those old enough to have worked with it in those earliest days, to understand how military planning was possible – let alone the discussion of government and foreign policy – without some meeting of minds, some filter through which all would pour their information, some process of systematization and presentation. Yet it was possible – so long as war did not break out. Somehow or other the unco-ordinated information from the Secret Service, from the Foreign Office, from the Services, from the serious newspapers, found its way through their Private Office into the minds of some senior Ministers.

But in such an informal system there were grave faults and gaps. Rumours planted by enemy agents on the 'old boy net' went up to the highest level with reports from trusted sources; information on Allies, for example, on the state of the French army, was scanty and sometimes grossly misleading. There was no constant check in 1938 on the credibility of information and deductions from it, or on the general defence situation, such as the JIC was to be making five years later as it reported to the Chiefs of Staff. Without such control, one can safely say, the military brain of Britain lacked a substantial part of memory and an important part of logic. Appeasement, whatever one may say for and against it as a policy, was rooted by present Intelligence standards in ignorance.

The idea (first mooted by the Churchill Committee of 1922

on defence cuts) that the intelligence departments needed some meeting place and joint authority originated in the Deputy Chiefs of Staff Committee during 1935–6, and their recommendation was considered by the Committee of Imperial Defence. What it proposed was simply that 'the co-ordination of Service intelligence should be carried out by an inter-services intelligence committee composed as under and meeting at the request of one of the members'. The members were to be the Deputy Director of Naval Intelligence, the head of MI 1 of the General Staff and the Deputy Director of Air Intelligence. This modest advance was approved and on 30 January 1936 the JIC came into being as a new sub-committee of the Committee of Imperial Defence. Six months later the Chiefs of Staff agreed to an enlargement of its functions which would ensure the co-operation with it of the Joint Planners. This decision in principle was excellent, even if it did not work in practice for some time to come; the idea that Intelligence should know what Plans had in their minds was unfamiliar.

Then came the 'cold war' of the late Thirties with its scares, threats, planting of rumours and false intelligence, causing alarm and bewilderment among Ministers. It was found necessary in April 1939, for reasons to be described below, to form a Situation Report Centre made up of the Foreign Office representative and three Service Directors to:

collate intelligence received from abroad and to issue daily secret situation reports in order that any emergency measures which may have to be taken should be based only on the most reliable and carefully co-ordinated information.

This need for a day-to-day alertness seems to have overcome both the original unwillingness of the Directors to meet daily and the wish to delegate inter-service co-operation to deputies, for in June 1939 the Directors recommended that the two bodies should be merged. Then came the final step towards the consolidation of the Joint Intelligence Committee in the Whitehall hierarchy when it was decided, after war began, that it should become responsible to the Chiefs of Staff Committee in permanent session. The men who pushed this idea through, among them certainly Godfrey and his predecessor Rear-Admiral Troup, deserve all credit for giving

Whitehall just in time this substantial advantage over the German and Italian intelligence staff organizations.

Typical of what had to be coped with in 1939 was the following incident. Just before Easter the Minister in Berlin telegraphed to the Foreign Office that he had received reports that he could not ignore stating that German bombers might make a surprise attack on the Home Fleet:

I am informed from a reliable source that the three quotations from the Wilhelmshaven speech given in my immediately following telegram and printed in this evening's *Angriff* fully represent Herr Hitler's frame of mind. Informant who is in contact with the War Ministry has stated that the first sign of German intentions, which will be kept secret until the last moment, will be a lightning attack on British fleet with the object of delivery of a knock-out blow. There will be neither an ultimatum nor a declaration of war. War Office officials declare that Herr Hitler alone will decide the time for action and personally issue the vital order without consulting the competent military advisers.

I realise that the above is very sensational and I have no evidence that such action will take place in the near future. But I feel that as we are dealing with a maniac who is violently roused against Great Britain you should be aware of this contingency.*

Because of this report it was thought prudent to order immediately that a portion of the Fleet's anti-aircraft guns should be manned, and it was agreed by Ministers in Cabinet that the First Lord should just mention the fact in a speech he was preparing. On Tuesday, 4 April, the day after this alarming telegram was received, Lord Stanhope was to be the guest of honour on board the aircraft carrier *Ark Royal* for the inauguration of the Royal Naval Film Corporation, intended to make available for the Fleet the best and newest modern films. What was said by the usually solemn and rather boring First Lord, in his Edwardian high collar and morning dress burst on Fleet Street that evening like a bomb:

Unfortunately there are others who are not with us tonight, because shortly before I left the Admiralty it became necessary to give orders to man the anti-aircraft guns of the Fleet so as to be ready for anything that might happen. Long before guests came aboard this ship sixteen anti-aircraft guns could have given a warm welcome to anyone who happened to come this way.

245

Such was the dramatic consequence of the Minister's warning from Berlin – a first-class newspaper sensation. Whoever planted the scare on the Cabinet (Admiral Canaris was suspected) notched a bull's eye. For one indiscretion led to another. Mr Chamberlain's Government, in what was described as 'the national interest', tried hard through the D Notice system to prevent the newspapers publishing what the First Lord had said in the presence of a score of reporters. *The Times* and *Daily Telegraph* did as they were asked, the *Daily Sketch* published it in all editions; the *News Chronicle* withdrew it from the first edition but published it later on the grounds that the BBC had broadcast it to the Empire at 9.30. According to the *Daily Telegraph*, this was the first time that a 'D' notice had been ignored.*

Mr Chamberlain, when questioned in the House on 5 April, said that 'no other orders had been given by the Admiralty than that this practice should not be relaxed even on so special an occasion, the normal practice being in time of tension to retain some of the men on board their ships in readiness to man their guns'. As for the use of the D notice to suppress something that hundreds had heard, the Prime Minister remarked pathetically: 'Apparently my efforts to spare the public unnecessary agitation were not altogether successful.'

The world-wide publicity given to this gaffe caused the Government much embarrassment, unable as they were to point to anything more than 'reports', unchecked and ungraded. Indeed, the First Lord had not thought of consulting the DNI before leaving for Portsmouth.

At about the same time Sir Robert Vansittart (then diplomatic adviser to the Government) informed the Foreign Secretary that he had reliable information of German submarines patrolling outside Plymouth, Portsmouth and the Thames Estuary. Inquiry later showed that both 'sibs' (as war of nerves rumours were called when we started to devise them ourselves for Hitler's benefit) had been planted, one by the head of the German Secret Service, Admiral Canaris, and the other by a German agent in Switzerland. Without machinery to turn to for verification and reassurance, it is not surprising that the Cabinet were gullible. Hitler already had a reputation for springing surprises and his war of nerves had been going

246

on for some time. Moreover, there was sometimes a grain of truth in such reports; indeed, similar warnings from Copenhagen in April 1940, accurately forecast the attack on Norway.

It was intolerable that the British Cabinet should be exposed to any kind of rumour that future enemies might plant either in its social circle or on individual Ministers. Thus it came about in April 1939, at DNI's suggestion, that the 'Situation Report Centre' already mentioned was set up. It was to study and collate urgent intelligence received from abroad and issue daily secret situation reports, on distinctive dark green paper. In other words, it was to be a first line of defence against scares.

This *ad hoc* deployment of intelligence forces could not last. To have the three Service pundits working together only for the scotching of rumour was manifestly absurd, and when the JIC was finally set up its scope had been expanded. From now on they were free to consider 'any further measures which might be thought necessary in order to improve the efficient working of the Intelligence organization of the country as a whole'. For example, they could – as they later did – criticize and make recommendations about the work of the Secret Service and about the organizing of topographical intelligence for future operations; they could advise on the expansion or shrinking of certain services, and set standards of quality for all Whitehall; they supervised, though they did not control, the cryptographical services referred to elsewhere as Station X. They could also co-opt anyone they wished to consult regularly – an innovation which was to bring in after May 1940 the Security Service (known in those days as MI 5); the Ministry of Economic Warfare with its industrial intelligence and expertise on the blockade; the Inter-Services Topographical Department at Oxford; and the Inter-Services Security Board (ISSB). The last, set up in the spring of 1940, controlled security in all the great offensive operations of the next six years, administered the mass of operational code-words, to the selection of which Churchill devoted loving care, and developed in a special committee the arts of deception and counter-propaganda by rumour.

Thus early were the British able to avoid the outstanding weaknesses of German Intelligence: the collection and judge-

247

ment of material by four or five organizations working independently, preyed on by the jealousies of rival Services and
watched suspiciously by the Party and its security machine.
The JIC became strong enough to stand up to the prejudices of
any Chief of Staff or Minister, whether expressed to it directly
or through one of the Directors. Its basic independence and
scepticism were well expressed in the last paper written in 1945
by its staff as a leaving present to its masters. It was called
'Why the Germans lost the War', a closely argued, well
documented account of Hitler's mistakes. No doubt the Chiefs
of Staff would have preferred to be told why *they* had *won* the
war; but that was not the Intelligence approach to such grave
matters.

The next development was naturally a growth of contact
with the planners, but before anything like integration was
achieved there were growing pains. For example, the Joint
Planning Staff strongly opposed the wish of the Intelligence
men that they should work next to one another; the planners
were in the Cabinet War Room and the JIS in the same building, but some distance away. Thanks mainly to the DNI's
support for the Secretariat's case, the opposition was worn
down and new accommodation was given to the JIS with the
Cabinet War Room in January 1943.

The JIC – and its JIS sub-committee – continued with
constitution unchanged throughout the war. The same
chairman presided throughout. The range and continuity of
his experience and his position as Adviser to the Director of
Plans, were of great value to his Service colleagues, even if they
were sometimes suspicious of his readiness to speak for all of
them at the weekly meetings with the Chiefs of Staff. His
patience and diplomatic scepticism helped the Directors to
weather some dangerous gusts of inter-service disagreement
and personal dislike.

On the whole the verdict has been that the joint intelligence
machinery worked well and for that its naval members take a
full share of credit. They were encouraged by their Director to
take an independent line and keep the highest critical standards;
they had ready access to him in need. Forecasts of enemy
strategy and intentions were mostly accurate, although at times
the language of their reports would have been firmer had they

not been obliged to reconcile the views of five departments. From 1943 onwards the intelligence labours of four years were bearing good fruit, as the enemy records show, and that made judgement surer.

None the less, individual Directors of Intelligence did not always loyally back the joint body. Certainly between 1943 and 1944 one Director (not the DNI) got cold feet about an appreciation which carried his signature and advised his Service Chief privately against the views of the JIC as a whole. Innate suspicion and dislike of intelligence among senior officers in operational departments still smouldered on, and they preferred at times their own 'hunches' to the evidence of a wealth of factual material in their intelligence divisions. One mistake would be long-remembered to discredit all that came after. Yet, although the JIC were collectively up against a strongly critical and sceptical body of men, they finished the war high in the esteem not only of the Chiefs of Staff, but also of their arch-critic Winston Churchill, and his Ministry of Defence Staff.

If the existence of the JIC ensured that intelligence would be organized and seen as a whole, it did little to provide a joint presentation or point of view about enemy intentions until its Staff (JIS) got into its stride. How that staff worked from the naval angle may first be illustrated from a familiar passage of history.

In the early summer of 1942 the American and British Chiefs of Staff were in London, engaged in urgent talks about what could be done that year to satisfy the insistent demand of Roosevelt, Churchill and Stalin that the strain must be taken off the Russians by offensive action in the West.

The Americans much favoured the establishment of a bridgehead in the Brittany or Cotentin peninsula, even though they admitted how hazardous it would be, and how unlikely it was that the available forces would be able to exploit a landing. The alternatives were either to reinforce the British forces in Egypt, which were not doing badly at that time, and drive the enemy from Tripolitania, or to make a landing on the north-west coast of Africa and exploit it quickly eastwards. Thus, the Allies would by a major pincer movement drive the Axis powers out of North Africa and use that area as a

249

springboard for an amphibious operation attacking southern Europe.

The JIS gave it as their opinion that if the suggested operation were to be more American than British, then the opposition by the French in Algeria and French Morocco would be slight in the area around Algiers, though probably quite stiff at Casablanca. However, they gave their view that organized opposition to the landing would last only for a short time.

This was a plan that the Americans were at first most reluctant to accept, because they wanted to launch the decisive offensive on the Germans in Europe as quicky as possible, and clear the way for settling accounts with Japan. There was also in London strong feeling for a return to France, whipped up for political reasons and stimulated by a genuine sympathy for the fearful ordeal of the Soviet armies. There was also Soviet propaganda nagging at the conscience of the western Allies by demanding the 'second front now' and Nazi propaganda trying to commit the British and Americans to an operation that the Germans knew could well be disastrous for their enemies.

From the first it was the naval arguments against an attack on Northern France that were the strongest. There were far too few landing craft to carry across the Channel the forces necessary to defeat the German troops in the West; even if a foothold were won and held, say, on the peninsula behind Cherbourg, the task of keeping up supplies and reinforcements by sea would be enormous. The mobility given by maritime power would be sacrificed and the capacity to threaten and surprise all round the vast coastline of occupied Europe foregone. For German intelligence could make a fairly accurate calculation of what shipping was available and would not accept the possibility that Anglo-American forces, once committed to a major assault in France, could make other major landings elsewhere. In other words, the Germans would be able to concentrate their forces for the counter-attack.

The positive naval argument, from the British point of view, was that the Mediterranean must be opened up for the safe passage of Allied fleets and supply convoys to the Middle East and for merchandise and war supplies to and from India and the Far East. It was only by doing so that the tremendously long and uneconomic hauls round the Cape could be eliminated and so save hundreds of thousands of tons of shipping each year. The British Chiefs of Staff, led by Sir Alan Brooke, had to contend with the strong opposition of the American Navy, led by Admiral King, in any consideration of this Mediterranean strategy.

The Intelligence estimates of German and French reactions to the landings were wholly justified and these proved remarkably accurate. Intelligence-wise, the DNI was able to argue in a paper of August 1942,* that invasion convoys coming from the US to North Africa on a route as far west as possible, would have a fair chance of avoiding the U-boats, which were not doing too well at the time; and that any reinforcement of U-boats inside the Mediterranean once the landing had been achieved would present to the enemy serious difficulties. Indeed it was easier to detect and destroy U-boats in that sea than in the Atlantic, and the Straits of Gibraltar, a difficult passage for submarines at any time, could be made into the neck of a jam-pot for the destruction of Doenitz's wasps.

This joint staff, in which officers of the rank of Captain, Colonel and Group Captain represented their Directors, each with a junior officer chosen for his intellectual record in civilian life, had one habit of mind which one would not expect to find either in the War Cabinet, or in the Chiefs of Staff, or indeed in any military headquarters actually fighting the enemy. It set out consistently and stubbornly to see the various problems put before it exclusively from the enemy's point of view. How would Hitler assess the possibilities? What advice would the German Navy give the High Command? How deeply obliged would the Germans feel to help the Italians? How much would Hitler be prepared to weaken his effort on the Russian front if he suddenly found the 'soft under-belly' of the 'European fortress' exposed to allied menace? What collaboration was there between Berlin and Tokyo? Was an Axis pincer movement against the British position in the Middle East, so spectacular and attractive in theory, really practical politics?

The value of this way of looking at the facts and prospects of war was considerable; not so much for its positive grasp of the enemy point of view – though this was the main business of intelligence – as for its critical influence on the concourse of facts, ideas, political and personal influences pressing on the conduct of the war in London and Washington. 'But this is how the enemy may, or must, see it; these are his resources, his positions, the distances he has to cover, the principles of strategy he has so far followed. He *is* probably capable of this but he is certainly not capable of that'; this kind of staunch reminder, from a small body of men who gradually achieved a collective intellectual integrity which no amount of ministerial cajolery could shake, was salutary.

Let it be admitted, however, that this was a difficult exercise. In the first place, it really required first-rate political intelligence, which the Foreign Office was neither equipped nor trained to provide. Secondly, it was almost impossible to make allowance for the peculiar quality of Hitler's mind or the extent of Japanese fanaticism; no amount of clear-headedness and objective argument could anticipate the intuitions of neurotic and vain creatures. Thirdly, it required an instinctive understanding of German and Japanese ways of thinking and of the Staff processes by which their military decisions were reached which was rare in Whitehall.

This special service to the Chiefs of Staff and their Planners had evolved slowly. First it was known in early 1941 as the Future Operations (Enemy) Section; then as the Advanced Planning Enemy Section and finally as the Joint Intelligence Staff. Neither FOES nor APES was a happy combination of initials for novel and untried committees, and JIS had the advantage of making clear the relationship to the JIC its master.

As already done for the JIC it is worth tracing the history of this idea of inter-service appreciation of enemy intentions. Admiral Godfrey recalls – and so does Admiral Sir Charles Daniel who was a planner with him – that in the years between the wars students at the Staff Colleges were encouraged to set down and examine *all* courses of action open to a potential enemy; but they were not encouraged to select any one of them as more likely than the rest. It was argued by instructors that such a choice would give a wishful slant to the student's thinking about the action to be taken by his own forces. He must not have a mind closed to all the various means that might be used against him; nor was he ever encouraged to think of his country as being in the state it actually was during 1939–42 – desperately on the defensive.*

Godfrey, who had been instructing at Greenwich between 1928 and 1930 recalls the first sign of change as coming from the Imperial Defence College about 1934. Major-General Dill, who was then directing Military Operations and Intelligence, and Rear-Admiral Dickens, who was then Director of Naval Intelligence, suggested that their two departments should work together on appreciations of what possible enemies might do in certain circumstances. The striking novelty was the suggestion 'that Intelligence should be responsible for those parts of the work which dealt with the enemy's possible course of action, factors which might influence his choice of course, and the course that was most probable in all the known circumstances'.

At that time Godfrey was deputy to Captain King, Director of Plans at the Admiralty, where it was considered the planners' job to produce the whole appreciation, including the aspects mentioned above. A danger was seen in two bodies drafting one document. So DNI was asked to give the Director of Plans all available information, leaving it to the Planners to draw all deductions. What the latter had not taken into account was the possibility that the DNI might have available in wartime information so detailed and conclusive about the enemy's intentions from all kinds of sources that to leave him out of the final assessment would be somewhat absurd. The matter was, anyhow, dropped and did not come back into Godfrey's mind until five years later, when he had become Director of Intelligence.*

In November 1939, after two months of 'phoney war' he circulated in the Admiralty a paper suggesting danger spots at which the Germans might strike. Nazi propaganda had been saying 'look out for unexpected actions in unexpected places' and it was clearly the duty of British intelligence so far as possible to exclude strategic surprise. Plans Division received the paper sympathetically, but the fiery little Vice-Chief of Naval Staff, Admiral Tom Phillips, remarked that it read to him like the *Daily Sketch*. For a few months DNI remained discouraged by this douche of scepticism, but a chance to try again occurred in April 1940. Pound, the Chief of Naval

Staff, had asked Rear-Admiral Bellairs (a good friend of Godfrey's) to turn his mind to 'appreciations of the German point of view', and Godfrey suggested that Bellairs should work with the Division and act as deputy on the Joint Intelligence Committee when appreciation of enemy intentions came up.

It happened that the JIC, after only six months of war, also felt that this was a legitimate activity of Intelligence, but argued that it should be done properly by a body on lines similar to those of the Joint Planning Committee, and as part of the structure of the Chiefs of Staff organization. For the time being, however, Godfrey proposed that 'one, or perhaps two officers should be closely associated with the Joint Planners in the Cabinet War Room, so that their day-to-day needs could be met and an intelligence appreciation rapidly woven into a planning appreciation'. This should join the two bodies together 'in a more intimate way than is now possible'. The idea was approved by Pound on 13 May 1940 and the necessary appointments were made. It was therefore Bellairs, with the help of a few officers still at the Imperial Defence College, who formed the nucleus of the future JIS; and from the first Godfrey saw to it that they had access to all the best sources of information and that crystal gazing should be discouraged as much as kow-towing to the hunches of senior officers.

It was, not surprisingly, Bellairs' old partner, Dill, who made the next move. He had become Chief of the Imperial General Staff during the disastrous 1940 summer and asked that an Enemy Planning Section should be formed. Godfrey, stating the qualifications as 'recent knowledge of Germany and Germany's high command, good judgement and good staff experience', asked for Captain Troubridge, recently Naval Attaché in Berlin, but now at sea, as his representative. After the Naval Secretary had suggested other names, one of them Captain Mountbatten, the First Sea Lord agreed that Troubridge's recent experience of Germany should be used in this way. So Troubridge took the chair in the new body and had as colleagues Major-General Mackesy, who had commanded forces in the Norway operations, and Air Commodore Vachell, as well as Mr Ivone Kirkpatrick of the Foreign Office.*

The first task of the FOES was to give a forecast (from

the German point of view and signed ADOLF HITLER) of enemy strategy for the spring of 1941. In preparing this the value of the 'five angles', from which all such appreciation should be viewed, soon became apparent. For example, although the Foreign Office, Air and Army members wished to include the invasion of England as a German high priority target for the spring of 1941, neither the Navy nor the Ministry of Economic Warfare was enthusiastic; the former because he knew Room 39 and the OIC greatly doubted the German Navy's capacity to undertake an operation of such magnitude, the MEW because it foresaw difficulty in arranging the build-up of a force large enough to carry out a successful invasion. In the end a compromise was reached; the Committee made the Germans state that although the invasion of England was all important, this could not be done without first defeating the RAF over southern England and Northern France.

The Committee was called before the COS Committee and cross-examined on its conclusions, which incidentally included a remarkably accurate forecast of the German attack on Greece. This placing of the invasion of England in a secondary role was by no means popular at high level, since the Prime Minister was still using the supposed threat as an incentive to production; the urge to train and equip the Home Army largely depended on the line of pep-talk at lower levels which found expression in the simple phrase: 'Hurry, boys, they may be landing any time.'

The first discussions were timid and inconclusive. It was hard to believe that what they might opine would matter. Back in the Ministries, where the members of FOES were supposed to get their facts and figures, there was a good deal of fun poked at this effort to think like Hitler. The average intelligence officer could not see, and it was very difficult to help him to see, how the kind of items he was collecting in his files might contribute to a picture of how the Germans or Japanese were thinking. The arduous process of twisting the mind to think like the enemy was new and anything set down on paper was liable to sound pretentious and cause derisive laughter. But Troubridge enjoyed the acting and after a week or two results began to show.

Troubridge recalled in a letter to Godfrey, written after the

255

war, how later FOES was directed to appreciate, again from the German point of view, the significance of Rommel's reinforcement in North Africa and how General Mackesy contributed to a Middle East appreciation the opinion that the Sirte desert was 'impassable' for any considerable force before the autumn of 1941. How right he was; but his differing with the 'experts' doomed the FOES and a short time later the order came out of the blue that it was to be abolished and another Committee 'on G 1 level' set up in its place. This was styled Advanced Planning Enemy Section ('APES'). Its terms of reference were to appreciate such situations as were referred to it by the Chiefs of Staff, but its advice was to be forwarded through the several intelligence departments or sections before presentation to the JIC for later presentation to the Chiefs of Staff. In other words, the 'crystal gazers' were firmly smacked down.

Although the new body did some valuable work, the actual value of the appreciations was much reduced by the time lag between their completion in the Committee and their arrival on the COS table. The 'experts' in the several intelligence sections of the departments nearly always found something with which to disagree, not realizing that any such appreciation involving the 'five angles' must be a compromise and that what appeared faulty from, for example, the purely military aspect was due to some cogent view advanced by the Navy, or perhaps MEW.

It did not take Troubridge long to realize that if these appreciations were to be of any use they must come in to the Chiefs piping hot; circulation round the departments was hopeless and unnecessary. He therefore (backed by DNI) wrote a paper suggesting the institution of a Joint Intelligence Staff on the same lines as the planning and operations staffs, working directly under the orders of the JIC. If a situation demanded an appreciation the Chiefs would call for it from the JIC, who in turn would pass it on to the new staff. The answer could be considered by the JIC and amended if necessary, being finally passed to the Chiefs of Staff under their (the JIC's) signatures.

The War Office demurred at this for some time but finally agreed and APES was formally replaced by the JIS as the junior body in the spring of 1942.

It has already been pointed out that during the later years, German *naval* intentions, albeit serious (e.g. the Schnorkel submarine), did not excite much inter-service enquiry, except perhaps from MEW. Problems of the Japanese Navy were handled primarily in Washington or Ceylon, of the Italians in Cairo. Attention in London was concentrated on German military reactions to Anglo-American and Russian offensives. Thus NID's representatives risked redundancy.

To avoid this, they assumed step by step the roles of cross-examiners of the Army, Air Force and Foreign Office representatives. It was a delicate and sometimes resented function, though easier within the junior team because they were all amateurs. (In civilian life the soldier was a history don and the airman an advertising agent; the naval representative was a barrister.) For example, the perennial sin of the soldier, as briefed by DMI, seemed to be to inflate the number of German divisions: there must have been some psychological need for the British Army to reinsure in this way after the traumas of Dunkirk and Crete. Certainly Hitler made full use of this predisposition; one of his deception plans was to multiply divisional numbers. Twice a year, the junior team prepared a reference list of Enemy Strengths and Dispositions, which was distributed pretty widely to Commanders-in-Chief and others. When preparations for this list first began the War Office would produce a statement showing the German Army growing at an alarming rate, with an impressive 'mass of manoeuvre' or reserve, whereas MEW believed that the German manpower position was rapidly deteriorating.

Then the negotiation in committee would begin. The airman could usually be persuaded to join a demand that the War Office should produce its evidence. If this was refused the Navy would suggest that its Director might not sign the report – always a potent threat. Then the military departmental 'expert' would attend and they would grill him, however exalted in rank, quite vigorously. Eventually, after allowing time and phrasing for face-saving, the War Office would usually agree to knock off the more flagrant of their German divisions, e.g. the SS Division 'Mussulman', to which they had become particularly attached.

The Air Ministry seemed to the Navy to suffer from the

257

opposite defect, namely a desire to depreciate the number of German fighters. Here the psychological motive may have lain in a desire to present a consistently buoyant view of the effects of RAF bombing on German industry. The naval representatives were less successful in probing this evidence and correcting this bias than in the case of the War Office, chiefly because the airmen presented their case in so technical a form and with such a wealth of formulae and other expertise that 'one hardly dared to question the conclusions'.

The Foreign Office – according to the Naval Members – took a rather lofty attitude towards the JIS. On the rare occasions when the latter disagreed with one of its drafts, the Foreign Office either ignored the JIS or adopted Jesuitical methods in order to get their way. There was a period during 1944 when the staff were discussing the Allied re-entry into Europe. The Foreign Office were very keen, probably rightly, to get British soldiers into Greece; but the Army felt itself very short of men and would not consider this additional sideshow, unless there was some assurance that the commitment would be negligible and temporary. So the junior team was asked to assess the 'Greek commitment'. Its first impressions were that if British troops went in with the King of Greece as he returned to his throne, conflict with the Communist guerrillas would tie us down for months, if not for years, and would suck in more and more reserves.

This draft appreciation did not suit the FO at all. They sent over their Greek expert, who was convinced – and said rather convincingly – that only a few hundred British soldiers need be landed, just to show the flag. Enthusiasm for Great Britain would do the rest. There would be no difficulty about withdrawing the troops after a month or two. Nothing the three young Services representatives could say would shake this expert. As his view was eventually accepted by the War Office, the Ministry chiefly affected by the problem, it was not reasonable for the committee to go on with the fight, especially as they believed that the FO policy of treating the freedom of Greece as a British interest would ultimately be justified at whatever cost.

It might seem as if the JIS were continually quarrelling. This was not at all the case. 'A tremendous corporate spirit

258

developed,' says a former naval member, 'spreading over the Joint Planning Staff and other bodies housed in Great George Street, for example, the Prime Minister's map room staff; the institution of a joint mess where we lunched and dined when under pressure was chiefly responsible.'

Indeed, their method of working would have been impossible without such a spirit. The staff functioned in two parts. The first team took the more urgent work; and the second took the longer term work and any reassessment of enemy strengths and dispositions required in previous papers. Each of the five members took the chair in rotation for two or three months. Each brought up his department's brief; and although MEW on oil, Foreign Office on German morale, Admiralty on future U-boat threats and Air Ministry on the decline of the Luftwaffe's fighter force would each in its turn command special authority, nothing was accepted without discussion and anyone could criticize anyone's draft. Every point of difference was thus brought out before the problem reached the hard-pressed Chiefs of Staff and War Cabinet. This was a time-saving as well as a head-clearing process. The Secretaries toiled over every sentence in the draft, which was then sent to Ministries' experts for approval. Then a re-draft was submitted to the Directors of Intelligence who, when the matter was important, would meet specially to pass it. Only too often they would not invite a member of the JIS to be present, because one or two Directors had objected to being shot down around the table by brilliant junior officers. Sometimes, to the dismay of the staff, they would see their clear and firm deductions watered down by their seniors to the sort of woolly compromise paper which says 'they may do this, on the other hand they might do that' – and brings intelligence appreciation into disrepute.

A good example occurred in 1942, all the more interesting because we now know – and indeed guessed at the time – that the Germans had not made up their own minds about the action which JIS was required to forecast. Those who were planning the Allied landings in North Africa asked for a firm opinion of what the Germans would do when they realized what the objective of 'Torch' was. Would they at once occupy the whole of France, move into Tunisia, and reinforce their armies in Tripolitania when the Allies landed in Algeria and

French Morocco? Firm intelligence about their intentions there could not be obtained, because the Germans and Italians had not planned against such an operation and were in the event to be taken completely by surprise. None the less, there was good intelligence about the demand on their resources, the dispositions of their U-boats and aircraft and the political and man-power limits within which they would have to work.

Sound military strategy would forbid the Axis to send further forces to North Africa at a time when they had still achieved no decision on the Russian front. To accept further commitments across the sea or along an even more extended coast line would be to play the Allies' game, which was precisely to extend and exhaust the enemy by the use of maritime power all around their flanks. But the JIS knew Hitler was completely unorthodox; repeatedly he had threatened to throw out the Allies wherever they landed, and, if necessary, to open a new theatre of war. So, after long and detailed arguments, it was decided that Hitler would do all these things and that it would be wrong to make a forecast based only on sound strategical arguments which might weigh with German staff officers but not with the Fuehrer.

What was the result? An unsatisfactory compromise, due to disagreement between staffs on such elementary questions as whether Germany would invade Spain – where NID was in no doubt that the Germans had neither the troops nor the aircraft nor the ships to complete the job.

Similar divisions of view held up decision on what the Italians might do when the Allies landed in Sicily and Southern Italy. Intelligence pointed to a quick collapse following the appearance of our troops; but this view ran against the conviction that men always fight best in defence of their own soil. (The same happened later over Japan.) The JIS was solidly for the Intelligence view; but thanks to the pressure of senior persons on their Directors (not on the DNI) both views were incorporated into a 'may and may not' formula. 'A dismal tale of orthodox logic being allowed to displace intelligence pointers' said Captain Baker-Cresswell, DNI's representative at the time.*

It would be absurd to leave the impression that the Joint Intelligence Staff were always right. Sometimes they went badly wrong, and their seniors went wrong. They had to decide, for example, whether the Germans would abandon Southern Italy after the Salerno landings or not, and said that the stand would be made only on the Apennines. In fact German forces held on for a long time south of Naples. On the other hand an RNVR officer, now a QC and MP, who was assistant to both Captains who represented the DNI on these bodies, reported two years after the war:

I think I may say that our forecasts were generally correct. We were particularly pleased with our assessment, in spite of the disagreement of the Americans, of the effect of the North African operations. The Americans were terrified that the Germans would march through Spain to cut our lines of communication. They also tended to overestimate the resistance of the French. Indeed, a great part of our functions lay in the necessity to soothe other commands, particularly commanders on the spot, who were always inclined to exaggerate the capabilities and successes of the enemy facing them.

Our failures lay really in our inability to appreciate the extreme obstinacy of Hitler. More than once we forecast that he would withdraw to shorter lines either in Italy or Russia or the Balkans in order to economize divisions. I still believe that he would have done better if he had followed our advice but it is undeniable that we gave the wrong impression on the general question of the disposition of his forces between the various fronts, partly for the reason given above and partly because the War Office were always determined to exaggerate the degree of opposition that the allies would be likely to meet in any landing in Western Europe.

The same officer, who twice went to Washington to assist the Americans in building up similar machinery, found that the Joint Staffs there never seemed to achieve the impact that their London counterparts could claim. Inter-service jealousies, far deeper than they were in Britain, were only part of the explanation:

There was always the impression seeping through that it was an entirely academic exercise, that the local commanders would take their decisions, or that the Chiefs of Staff would allocate their resouces irrespective of anything that was said by the intelligence organizations.

From Captain Charles Drake, Senior Member of Room 39 but also DNI's senior representative with the JIS from 1943 to the end of the war, I have this revealing anecdote about the Prime Minister and his view of how intelligence should be produced by his JIS:

Every now and then we got a direct 'prayer', as it was called, from the Prime Minister, which came to us generally through General Ismay, asking for our immediate and quick appreciation of some particular point. Then, of course, we had to get to work very quickly and always the result had to be produced on one half sheet of paper, because that was all that the PM would read. There's no doubt about it, he kept us very much on our toes.

I remember how – it must have been about June 1943, when General Alexander was pushing up Italy against pretty strong German and Italian opposition – a telegram addressed to the Chiefs of Staff arrived late one evening. I happened to be the duty officer and was sleeping with the telephone by my bedside. About half past one in the morning the telephone rang. I answered it and recognized the voice of Brigadier Hollis, who was the Chiefs of Staff's secretary, saying to me:

'Is that you, Drake? Have you seen the telegram that's just come in from Alexander, giving his views about the German reinforcement of Italy should the Italians collapse?'

It gave a lengthy view about what might happen within the next few months, which would need a good deal of work. So I said to Hollis:

'Yes, I've seen the telegram: we shall be dealing with it in the morning.'

'Well,' he replied, 'the Prime Minister wants an answer drafted so that he can send it to Alexander by 10.30 *this* morning.'

I then said: 'But this is absurd, Hollis, because I've first got to get my Committee together and then we've got to draft something. We then have to show it to the Directors of Intelligence because it's important. We've then got to get it through to our own Chiefs of Staff, which means they've got to meet on it, and we certainly can't do all that by 10.30.'

'That may be,' said Hollis, 'but the Prime Minister wants it by then.'

I ought to have taken the clue, I suppose, when he said 'the Prime Minister', that there was something up – because Hollis always referred to him as 'the Prime'. However, I thoughtlessly said:

'Hollis, why don't you tell the silly old man to go to bed, and we'll get on with it as quickly as we can and probably have it ready tomorrow afternoon.'

Just at that moment a voice came out of the telephone saying: 'Who are you calling a silly old man?'

It was Winston himself, who had been listening on the extension telephone in the next room to General Hollis. Completely taken aback and only half awake, I said: 'Oh, I'm sorry, sir, I didn't know you were there,' to which he replied: 'No, I should think *not* – and why is it impossible to get me the answer by 10.30 in the morning?' I said: 'It won't be impossible, sir, I'll get them together and we'll start right away, if it's necessary.' 'Of course it's necessary,' he said, and then added 'Perhaps it would help in your deliberations if the silly old man came down to help you. I will be there in fifteen minutes' time.'

On hearing this I leapt out of bed, collected the others – shook them out of their sleep – collected the secretaries and tried to persuade them of the urgency of it all, which was difficult. However, I got them into their places half-dressed in sweaters with mufflers round their necks. I pulled down a map of Italy and we tried to look important. Then the door opened and in came the Prime Minister, wearing his rompers, sat down next to us, smiled a bit at me, and then looked at the map and said:

'Take that map away: we must have bigger maps.'

So I said: 'Oh yes sir,' and flipped that map up and pulled down another one of about half the Mediterranean, and he said:

'Bigger maps still.'

So up it went again, and down came another map of pretty well the whole Mediterranean and most of Africa.

'Bigger maps still.'

So I pulled down another one of about half the world and he said:

'That's better – but the colours are too bright.'

I said: 'We can't do anything about that, sir,' and he replied: 'No, well, leave it as it is,' and he then started on a dissertation about striking at the 'underbelly of the Axis', and how he thought we ought to go through Yugoslavia and also attack through the Aegean; after this had been going on for some time, he said:

'Well, gentlemen, I think I will leave you now to your deliberations.'

'All right, sir,' I said – and he went out, slamming the door after himself.

We were just heaving a sigh of relief, wondering what we'd better do next, when the door opened again, his head popped in and he turned to me and said:

'Would 3 o'clock tomorrow afternoon be satisfactory to you, Captain?' and I said: 'Yes, sir, that'd be much more convenient.'

He said: 'Very well; make it so. Good night.' And off he went to bed.

This did not happen often but we always felt we had near us this tremendous presence, which was going to drop on us suddenly out of the blue.

Indeed, in quite another way, I remember his coming to me and saying: 'I think, Captain, we must be kin.'

I said: 'Yes, I think we are.' Immediately he said, 'Why do you say that?' and I replied:

'Well, sir, I've read your *Life of Marlborough*, and in that book you describe how your forebear, Sir Winston Churchill, was married to Lucy Drake and they were the father and mother of John Churchill, first Duke of Marlborough, who's your distinguished ancestor.'

Churchill said: 'Do you mean to say you've read my book?'

I said: 'Yes, I have – both volumes.'

'And you believe it?'

I said: 'Yes, I know it, because that's supported from other evidence as well.'

'Good, Captain, then we're kin.'

12 Divers operations

This chapter describes and interprets a number of operations at sea in which one section or another of NID played a part of special interest or significance. Had these been included in earlier chapters dealing with particular departments, they would have complicated the reader's understanding of what was done. Here will be found a detailed analysis of the intelligence aspect of the controversial decision about convoy PQ17; a brief account of the origins of the St Nazaire raid and of what it was like to be an intelligence officer with the Home Fleet; an analysis of the difficult and wearisome business of tracking down the German armed merchant raiders; a report of a 'pinch' of enemy ciphers and equipment initiated by NID; and a highly personal narrative of how the Germans were forestalled in Iceland. They should be read as short stories interrupting a longer story, like Mr Jingle's tales in the *Pickwick Papers*.

Iceland

From the first day of war the Admiralty had kept an anxious eye on Iceland. If the Germans could gain control of airfields there, to say nothing of the value to an enemy of its ports and anchorages for U-boats on passage to and from the Atlantic (France had not yet fallen), the threat to Home Fleet operations and the trade routes would be deadly. As it turned out, German strategists for most of the war fought shy of oversea commitments with which sea communications could not easily be controlled; and there seems never to have been any serious plan to molest either Iceland or Ireland. But that was not known at the time, in the spring of 1940, and the German's striking success in Norway made it seem likely that Iceland would be next on the list. To add to this anxiety it was learned in NID that spare U-boat crews were living on the island as not unwelcome paying guests of the population.

It was decided to forestall the Germans by a quick and small-scale descent on Reykjavik in the Buchan style. Presumably it was hoped that this would attract less attention and provoke less reaction than a strong military demonstration. There were no troops in Iceland, only a hundred or so police. The British Consul-General there, Francis Shepherd, who was ordered to meet the party organized by DNI on the quayside at Reykjavik, was confident that there would be no resistance.

On Saturday, 4 May 1940, a Major of Marines called Humphrey Quill, then working in the Japanese section of NID, was sent for by DNI's deputy and told he was to go to Iceland on the 6th to capture the German Consul there, round up the spare U-boat crews, and set up a coast-watching organization. 'You're a fisherman, aren't you?' said Captain Stephens, 'it ought to suit you down to the ground.' Quill was told that the whole proceeding was 'irregular' – that was why it was being done by NID – and that he would have to take with him a barrister colleague named Pen Slade, later a KC. Slade was to watch over the legal side of things and help avert the more flagrant infractions of international law. 'Slade', said the DDNI, 'will have to wear uniform, so get him fitted out.' Quill accomplished this in less than twenty-four hours with the help of Moss Bros. on a Sunday.

On 8 May, Quill and his legal adviser sailed in HMS *Berwick* as part of a mixed supporting force of Royal Marines under General Sturges. Another passenger was to join the British Consul-General and assume the title of Minister. The inter-preter was a middle-aged teacher from Eton, whose tenancy on a salmon river had given him a good knowledge of Iceland; he also represented the interests of 'C'. Quill received before he left a large bundle of notes, he thinks £500, to be used for bribes and to finance the linguist from Eton.

Two days later at five in the morning the party landed at Reykjavik and was duly met by Francis Shepherd. Stealthily they set about their task, secrecy being almost defeated by the noise of a reconnoitring Walrus amphibian flown off from HMS *Berwick*. Escorted by a platoon of Royal Marines, Quill walked to the house of the German Consul-General (Herr Gerlach) and knocked on the door. When the Consul saw from his bedroom the British uniforms and the quizzical face of the Marine Major below him, he opened the window and harangued them in German on diplomatic privilege and international law. Eventually, however, he opened the door and submitted to arrest.

While Quill was interrogating him, his escort noticed a smell of burning coming from the floor above. Luckily they had brought a ship's portable fire extinguisher with them and were just in time to prevent the German wife, aided by his children, from burning the diplomatic ciphers and other documents in the family bath.

The episode was enough to send shudders down the spine of any civil servant back in London; indeed, the Foreign Office had at first strongly opposed the whole project. As it happened, on the very day Quill was treading so warily through the streets of Reykjavik, Hitler marched into Holland, and whatever diplomatic fuss there might have been from Berlin ceased to count.

Quill found the Icelanders reluctant at first to disclose the whereabouts of the U-boat men scattered in various parts of the country. Good money was being paid by the Germans, intimate attachments had been formed with the wives and daughters of absent fishermen, the laws of hospitality were strict. Above all, the Icelanders did not really believe that the British had the strength to keep the Germans out of their country if Hitler was determined to seize it. 'Why aren't you helping Holland instead of worrying us?' Quill was asked through his interpreter. DNI's money did the trick. The purchase of silk stockings, scent and other small luxuries soon persuaded some of the Icelandic families to give information about the U-boat men, who were eventually rounded up and before long recovered from the scurvy they had contracted in the barren interior of Iceland, when fed on the rations of wartime Britain.

The second part of Quill's mission was to set up in Iceland, which is larger than Ireland, an organization to watch the most rugged of coasts. Volunteers recruited from the locals came forward more readily when the Army arrived in force on 16 May to relieve the Marines; this convinced the Icelanders at last that the British intended to stay. A successful network of watchers was built up and Quill found to take charge of it a distinguished ornithologist and yachtsman, Lieutenant Conyers Lang, RNVR, whose large Belgian pilot cutter specially provided by the Admiralty's Small Vessels Pool, was the envy of his less sophisticated colleagues.

The consequences of this amateur, skilful and most irregular operation – so different from the highly professional, ruthless raids of Combined Operations – were momentous. When the Americans eventually took over the garrison duty, Iceland had become a fuelling base for ships and aircraft fighting the Atlantic battle, an anchorage for the Home Fleet's cruisers and battle-cruisers, and the base from which long-range aircraft carried out their sweeps against U-boats and raiders. 'Too little and too late' was a fair taunt against some British enterprises of that summer, but not against this swift and gentlemanly capture of Iceland from her Nazi-occupied suzerain, Denmark.

St Nazaire

Much has been written about the splendid, morale-raising and very destructive raid on St Nazaire, the German-occupied base on the west coast of France, in March 1942. But there can still be added, for the historian and connoisseur of the subject, some facts which vividly illustrate two points; first, the importance of showmanship in the presentation of intelligence and, secondly, the curious way in which vital technical details were found in time to brief fully the Sappers who went on this operation.

It is possible, also, in giving this evidence to fix precisely when the idea of the raid was conceived. The historian may insist that this moment is the date on which the proposal appeared on paper; but in this case there is verbal, backed by documentary, evidence of when St Nazaire was first mentioned as a target. It comes from the head of the NID section dealing at the time with France and the Low Countries, Lt-Cdr George

Gonin, RN, already mentioned elsewhere for his part in the intelligence planning of the Normandy invasion.

It would be natural for Gonin to talk over with his colleagues in the German section and with the German fleet specialists in the OIC, any intelligence received about the bases at Brest, Lorient, La Pallice, and St Nazaire which enabled the U-boats and the surface raiders leaving the Baltic to feel confident that they could, in case of damage, make for a dockyard or shelter without running the gauntlet of the Atlantic exits to the North Sea. The *Bismarck* had been caught trying to reach France and already people were wondering how soon the *Tirpitz* would be seen making a similar sortie. If she did, only one dry dock could take her – the new one at St Nazaire; if that could be made unusable, her effectiveness would be halved.

At the end of June 1941 Gonin represented NID at a meeting with the Directorate of Combined Operations and the Executive Planning Staff at which targets for raids across the Channel were called for. Interest at the time was confined to small objectives across the narrow waters, but he used a lull in the discussion to mention St Nazaire to Captain French, who was in the chair. Shortly afterwards Plans Division proposed this attack which, on Gonin's advice, was strongly supported by the Intelligence staff. While his section began to collect the necessary information, C-in-C Plymouth was instructed by the Admiralty to prepare a raid on this defended base 400 miles away across the open sea.

In some notes written in the following October to assist Charles Morgan (whose sketches for a history of NID have already been mentioned) Gonin recalls the next steps. First he asked Air Intelligence to have a large model of the base made at Medmenham, where air photographs were being used with rapidly growing success. He then visited the station and discussed with the photographic experts the very detailed report which they had written. Photographs were enlarged to the size of a table and it was possible to show in memorable detail not only the gun positions and the buildings to be attacked but also the doors to them.

So it was that by 15 September a meeting at the Admiralty, at which the Chief of Staff from Plymouth and the Chief of Staff from Combined Operations were present, decided on a rough plan. One or two dates in October were suggested, one of them Trafalgar Day. However, C-in-C Plymouth, Admiral Forbes, had second thoughts: it would be necessary for the expedition to sail two or three hours before dark, and he judged it certain that it would be spotted by enemy air reconnaissance, which would make surprise impossible. Although the Admiralty were very enthusiastic for the scheme, it was judged that the man on the spot must not be forced into an enterprise against his better judgement. SOE were instructed to destroy the locks by sabotage – which was impossible in view of their size and the guards on them.

It was the impressive and fascinating detail of the pictures from Medmenham that encouraged Gonin to continue the campaign in favour of the target which eventually led to success. Gonin recalls:

Early in 1942 Admiral Mountbatten became Chief of Combined Operations and at once began a keen search for targets. I extracted the docket and took it to his Intelligence staff together with the big photographs. The new chief was keen at once and realizing the difficulties, got Admiral Forbes personally to attend a meeting. I was not present at this but I heard that Mountbatten very skilfully persuaded the C-in-C to change his mind and fired him with his own enthusiasm.

All the intelligence available was handed over to CCO's staff and Lt-Cdr Moorhouse, RNR, began preparation of the docket. The only real difficulty arose from the growing demands of the Sappers for detailed information:

It was possible to meet them because a colleague knew an official of the Institute of Civil Engineers in Great George Street (oddly enough, a stone's throw from the planners' office) who recalled that his Institute's Proceedings had published full details of the new dock when it was opened, with detailed technical drawings.

It was only after the raid, talking to survivors, that its planners realized how essential the tiniest technical detail had been to the Commandos on the quay, working under murderous fire, in the dark, with only a few minutes to do what they had to to the vast gate. Yet there had been moments, Gonin says, when he and his section had begun to feel exasperated; for the more they gave, the more was asked by the insatiable Sappers.

The special contribution of the OIC to this operation, apart from its normal guidance on swept channels and on German naval habits, was the secret of the identification signals with which the destroyer *Camperdown* (cut down to look like a German) answered the enemy searchlights and so gained a precious minute or two while the Germans hesitated whether to fire or not.

'Pinches'

Before the mind's eye of all officers in operational intelligence, whether they were serving the allied or the Axis navies, there hovered always the hope that somehow an enemy warship would be seized and boarded, her entire cipher equipment and confidential papers taken off, her crew captured intact and their ship sunk without trace. Then there would be some chance of getting into the enemy's secret wireless traffic, if only for a week or two, and thereby testing the accuracy of other intelligence sources against the unchallengeable A1 intercept. Evidently for such an intelligence operation to succeed, the Navy bringing it off must keep it secret from the Navy to which it is done; otherwise the latter will change its ciphers immediately on learning that its ship has been captured and its books possibly compromised.

This was precisely the requirement that NID, in the spring of 1941, had put to the Home Fleet. German trawlers, almost certainly unarmed, were sending home weather reports from the area around Iceland–the Faroes–Jan Mayen island which should assist the German Naval Staff in calculating just when surface raiders (like the *Bismarck* and the battle-cruisers) could make a dash from Norway to the Atlantic under cover of fog and general bad weather. The approximate position of these trawlers, which were equipped for patrols of eighty days, had been plotted from regular D/F fixes on their reporting transmissions. Though imprecise, this would give a force of cruisers and destroyers making a careful search a reasonable chance of detecting a tiny trawler even in those ice-bound and fog-veiled seas. It was made clear to all ships taking part that secrecy was vital, and that the sole object of using such force as might be necessary was to persuade the crew to abandon ship or surrender before the captain had time to destroy all his papers and equipment.

The first sweep was made on 7 May 1941, when three cruisers and four destroyers began to search in a line ten miles apart north-east of Iceland and roughly half-way between the Faroes and Jan Mayen. After two hours, smoke was sighted between the cruiser *Edinburgh* and the destroyer *Somali*, and the trawler, on sighting the British ships, made a dense screen of white smoke and dodged in and out of it. The destroyer opened fire at 6,000 yards and after a few salvoes the crew began to abandon ship. Captain Caslon 'having shown', in the words of Vice-Admiral Holland, 'just the right amount of force' placed the *Somali* alongside the trawler *Muenchen* and signalled for the prize crew from the *Manchester* to go aboard, accompanied by an OIC wireless specialist, Captain Haines, RN.

Although the wireless set had been broken up and the cipher apparatus thrown overboard, the ship was intact and valuable papers were found, which were sent back to Scapa post-haste in the *Nestor*. After the *Muenchen* had been sunk the rest of the force continued its search for two days further north but without success.

However, the turn of the more northerly ship, the *Lauenburg*, was yet to come. On 25 June a smaller force, one cruiser and three destroyers (from the 10th Cruiser Squadron) set out from Scapa to see if it could work a bit faster than its forerunner. There was thick fog as they hugged the ice-bank near Jan Mayen island but an HF/DF bearing from the *Bedouin*, supported by another from the Admiralty, brought the *Tartar* within sight of the enemy. The cruiser *Nigeria* opened fire with 6-inch practice projectiles and all the ships closed at full speed. It must have been a terrifying experience for the trawler's crew, who took to their boats after the second salvo, making no attempt to scuttle or damage their ship. Within twenty minutes a boarding party from the *Tartar* had taken charge and a thorough search was being made, again with the advice of an NID wireless expert, this time a Lieutenant RNVR trained at Station X. A valuable haul of documents and cipher material was made which was to have decisive and lasting effect on the conduct of the Battle of the Atlantic by the OIC. In due course their Lordships informed C-in-C Home Fleet that the operations had brought 'results of inestimable value'.

It may be wondered why the *Lauenburg* and the *Muenchen* were not brought back to base, as was the captured U110 later that summer. In each case the officer commanding the force considered the possibility but decided against it, because of the risk of the trawler being seen under escort by the regular German air reconnaissance over the area. It was important that the fate of the ships should remain a mystery, at least until the names of the captured crew reached Germany through the usual Red Cross channels. If the German naval staff suspected that their wireless security had been endangered by a capture, they would at once take steps to cancel its current value to British cryptanalysis. NID were delighted with the success of these carefully planned 'pinches' and were amused to see that the Vice-Admiral commanding the 18th Cruiser Squadron advised the Admiralty 'on an operation of this kind the presence of an expert is essential: information of some importance was found in quite undistinguished-looking documents'.*

A less important but comparable 'pinch' had been made on 23 February 1941, during 'Operation Claymore', the raid on the Lofoten Islands in north Norway. The German trawler, *Krebs*, several times hit during the first attack, was seen drifting and burning, with her crew taking to the boats. Then a white flag was waved, a British boarding party was sent which found the captain's cabin undamaged and recovered from his desk a locked box containing spare wheels from a cipher machine. Neither of the cipher machine nor of the signal books was there any trace. Leutnant zur See Hans Kupfinger had carried out promptly his orders to destroy everything that could help enemy intelligence, but was killed before he could finish the job.

An SOI at Sea

How a Staff Officer Intelligence with the Fleet, keeping in daily touch with the OIC, was able to suggest and advise on operations was described to the author by Commander Edward

Thomas, DSC, Staff Officer Intelligence to the Home Fleet for two years.

When Rear-Admiral McGrigor arrived at Scapa to command the 10th Cruiser Squadron towards the end of 1944, he found six weeks without action between each Arctic convoy to Russia too boring, and clamoured for something to do. As the Home Fleet planning staff was cautious and somewhat unimaginative, no suggestion was forthcoming from there. So McGrigor's own staff thought up something of their own without consulting Intelligence; but were promptly shot down at a morning staff meeting, on the grounds that there would be no enemy ships where they proposed to go. Thomas writes:

After this meeting, I was correcting my top secret charts in the inner staff office when I felt a dig in my ribs. It was the Admiral, who challenged me jokingly to produce an idea myself. So I mentioned that Commander Denning had advised me some time before to suggest a cruiser sweep down that part of the Norwegian coast where German convoys were now passing by night in order to avoid attack by the RAF's No. 18 Group, i.e. the coast roughly between Stavanger and Lindesnes. The idea had been greeted on C-in-C's Staff with the remark 'It stinks', but I thought it worth reviving. The shipping route was unprotected by islands and skerries on this stretch, but there were prohibited areas running parallel to the coast and to seaward of the shipping route which, in the opinion of OIC, masked lines of deep anti-submarine mines laid some years earlier. Cruisers and destroyers should be able to engage shipping targets with gunfire from positions to seaward of these minefields, and navigation was good there because of the numerous radio beacons, lighthouses and so on.

McGrigor at once saw the possibilities and said he would put the planners on to drafting an operation – which they did without a murmur. As a result the cruisers went down there twice and got good results on both occasions:

On the second sweep he took me with him. After a good deal of excitement, we found a convoy and started shooting. At the height of the mêlée there was a most tremendous bang to seaward. Everyone looked at me and asked: 'What was that, Bluebeard?' I suppose that is how Intelligence stood with the Home Fleet; but it did me no good. The play of the contingent and the unforeseen, as H. A. L. Fisher called it, never lets up. The cruisers took violent avoiding action and put the destroyers on to hunt. We learned later that the Germans, unknown to NID, had started sending a U-boat to cover the night-time convoys. We were lucky to get away with it.

Raiders

One day in the summer of 1940 a young RNVR sub-lieutenant in the French section of the Division was told that the collapse of France had left no work for him to do, and that he should report to Captain Clayton down in the basement of the Citadel. For some reason the Director thought that his deputy in charge of the OIC should have a personal assistant with a role similar to that of Fleming's in Room 39. Clayton, however, saw no reason for giving himself such assistance – this work was much more compactly organised and less wide-ranging than the Director's – and he pushed the officer, Patrick Beesly, on to Denning with orders to find a job. It was this casual decision, not untypical of the way the Services used to allocate their civilian reinforcements, that began the training of the man who later became Winn's deputy at tracking submarines.

But it was not on U-boats that Beesly sharpened his wits and learned about wireless intelligence, sea distances, German naval tactics, and routing problems. Denning set him to a relatively new task; to find out and file and plot whatever could be discovered about the enemy's armed merchant raiders now thought to be at sea. At that early time nothing was known about them beyond a few unexplained sinkings (for example, of the British *Scientist* on 3 May) which had been attributed to U-boats or to the normal hazards of the sea, and odds and ends of rumour from places far apart. Just lately on 18 July, survivors from two merchant ships sunk in the mid-Atlantic had arrived at a small West Indian island with stories of a raider that was not a warship. Ten days later, further to the south, the poorly armed British armed merchant cruiser *Alcantara*, to the dismay of the Admiralty, got the worst of a brief action with what might have been that raider or a second one. (In fact it was the same warship.) Search by cruisers of the South American Command was fruitless; they were too few for the vast area to be covered, with no hard intelligence clues to guide them. The enemy was still reaping all the rewards of surprise.

275

Not until much later was it learnt that the original war plans of the German Navy included the conversion of twenty-six merchant ships into armed raiders which should threaten and disorganize our merchant shipping movements all over the world, and distract and disperse the cruiser strength of our main fleet. The first of them was to start operating mostly in the Indian Ocean in February 1940. In fact a 'first wave' of three were at sea by the end of 1939 and three more were operating in the first half of 1940. Hitler had arranged with the Japanese to provide anchorages where no questions would be asked and there were supply ships known to NID, waiting in neutral ports to assist in fuelling and victualling the raiders. Beesly was therefore taking on what was on the way to becoming a complex operation. Every slightest clue must be plotted and listed, positions estimated and ships identified by specially devised titles or descriptions that could be used in signals to the Fleet. Whatever hard facts could be accumulated must be passed on in secure form to merchant ships likely to need them; this, as the Admiralty took a little time to grasp, meant every ship that was likely to sail independently out of convoy any-where in the world.

Whereas Denning's own main work on the battleships and cruisers, minesweepers and escort vessels, minelaying and air attacks was (once the *Graf Spee* had been dealt with) for the most part confined to the Baltic, North Sea, Channel and North Atlantic, Beesly soon found himself concerned with the oceans everywhere. There was one raider which, with grudging aid from Russian icebreakers, forced its way along the icebound northern coast of Siberia to the Bering Strait and so into the Pacific for a surprise incursion – a daring and quite unforeseen journey. There was another raider which gave herself a refit in the French-owned Kerguelen Islands in the Indian Ocean and another at Maug in the Marianas; another was lurking off the Freetown–Capetown convoy route. On the vast range of charts needed, the first attempts to pin down the positions or track the movements of ships like *Thor* or *Penguin* looked heartbreakingly inadequate.

The intelligence problem fell into three parts. First was the silence of these ships on their vast journeys. Though centrally controlled from Germany they kept immaculate wireless silence except when making rendezvous with supply ships or making for home. Then they used a special kind of ultra-brief signal (*Kurzsignal*) which could be picked up only by specially trained operators in their German Command headquarters. Nor did they ever go near any port or place where they might be identified or photographed. Thus both the British 'Y' stations and the neutrals' cameras were avoided. They were ordered to be content with small gains, to avoid risking their ships by action with warships or defended shore targets and to rely on the cumulative effect on us of losing two or three ships a month. Second, they had great skill in disguise. If one of them could be identified as the pre-war M/S so and so, of which pictures existed in London files, it was not much help; for their funnels and topmasts were telescopic, they could fit dummy funnels and topmasts, false bulwarks and deck houses; re-painting was carried out swiftly at sea by a crew of 300–400 strong so that a description sent out by the Admiralty one day could be out of date three days later. Lastly, the raiders used tactics designed to prevent their victims sending the emergency raider reports which the Navy's cruisers were everywhere waiting for. Either they would open fire without warning, or warn the cargo ship or tanker that any attempt to signal would mean instant destruction by their formidable 5.9 inch guns, or they would attack by night – one carried a motor torpedo boat capable of 37 knots. Most carried one or two aircraft with which they could keep out of the way of warships or spot victims before they were spotted themselves. Having made an attack, the raider would steam away from the area for twenty-four hours at 16 knots.

Intelligence hopes therefore rested almost entirely on the bravery of captains who defied these threats and signalled at once a sighting and a position which could be recorded on Beesly's plot. Other sources were detailed description by sur-vivors or escaped prisoners who might turn up as late as six months afterwards; chance encounter with ships fast enough to see but escape the raiders (which had only moderate speed) or whatever prisoners of war from other branches of the Kriegs-marine could tell their interrogators. There was no more pain-fully accumulated or more frequently revised mosaic in NID than the one concerned with raiders.

To add to the confusion, these ships at one time or another enjoyed no less than four names: for example the original name of Raider C before she was converted was *Goldenfels*: her warship name was *Atlantis*; her German number was 16; and her NID label was Raider C. Those alphabetical labels were simply the sign of a time when Beesly could identify raiders only by gradual elimination of scanty evidence: this incident reported at 'X' must be the work of a raider different from the one responsible for another sinking at 'Y' 900 miles away on the same day. So the latter having already been called 'A' the former was called 'B'. If there was then another raider report or mysterious sinking in a position which neither 'A' nor 'B' could have reached in the time available that would become provisionally Raider 'C'. From such slender beginnings tracks were built up of the raiders' journeys and knowledge formed of their tactics and habits from which intuition and deduction could provide clues for the Navy's sweeps. By the time the German raiding was at its maximum Beesly had reached 'K' and there the series stopped. At the end of 1941 there were no more at sea and by the end of 1942 the threat had been mastered.

The effort that these pests imposed on the Navy's surface ships when it was under strain simultaneously in northern waters and in the Mediterranean was considerable. The ideal weapons against them were the very long-range aircraft or the light aircraft carrier, both non-existent or in short supply until 1942. By the end of 1940 raiders had sunk fifty ships of 366,000 tons and in the first six months of the following year thirty-eight ships of 191,000 tons: compared with the achievement of the U-boats or with the volume of shipping at sea these losses were negligible. The raiders could not achieve decisive results but the Navy felt their challenge keenly.

Every issue of the Weekly Intelligence Review prepared for the Fleet by Beesly's colleagues in Section 19 contained the latest facts, silhouettes, possibilities; biographies of each raider were gradually built up, their captains identified, their tactics described. But it took the Admiralty over two years to build up a system by which one of our warships, having challenged a suspected raider, could find out quickly from the base whether the name under which she replied was genuine or not.

Thus when Raider 'F' (*Penguin*) was finally caught by the cruiser *Cornwall* in the Indian Ocean she at first identified herself as the Norwegian *Tamerlane* and sent out signals purporting to come from her which were immediately queried. To heave to within range of such a ship, with its powerful 5.9 inch armament, while a boarding party investigated was highly dangerous, as the Australian cruiser *Sidney* had discovered, in November 1941, when sunk while sinking the *Kormaran* (Raider G). Not until the whereabouts of every allied merchantman on the high seas were plotted daily in the Admiralty and made available to all commands wishing to check an identity, was it possible for a cargo ship or warship to beat this bluff. And the Admiralty never quite succeeded in getting the intelligence to the Merchant Navy skippers.

There was, however, in the skilfully planned German operation a weakness which was eventually detected, almost certainly because Beesly working under Denning in the OIC was in hourly touch with the men watching U-boats and every other kind of ship in the enemy Navy. It was clear that the Germans had an elaborate supply ship organization which could be used by any kind of commerce raider: the pocket-battleship out on a fortnight's hunting, the U-boats going beyond their usual patrol limits, the raiders staying at sea for a year or more. Such far-flung operations depended on successful and undisturbed rendezvous in secret positions on the high sea, during which not only fuel and food but also ammunition and other requirements could be passed on. Although OIC never identified the secret rendezvous points, other clues began to offer themselves by D/F fixes and wireless traffic. In the early summer of 1941, at the time of the *Bismarck* and *Prinz Eugen* foray, the OIC calculated that this break-out of warships was timed to coincide with other movements and that a whole covey of supply ships might therefore well be at sea in mid-Atlantic. So it proved; and in a sweep by the Home Fleet during June, which is discussed more fully in the Chapter on the sinking of the *Bismarck*, nine scattered and disguised supply ships were caught. It appears from the German archives that this was a deadly blow from which the raider strategy never recovered; it was the equivalent of losing two or three overseas bases.

Typical of the exploits of this efficient and cunningly handled naval guerrilla was the story of Raider C, already mentioned. Leaving German waters at the end of March 1940 disguised as a Russian merchant ship bound for Murmansk, she turned west on reaching the far north and slipped unobserved through Denmark Strait and into the North Atlantic. Then she was ordered southward disguised as a Japanese and sank the British ship *Scientist* on 3 May on the Capetown–Freetown route. This was the first clue about her mission to reach London. After laying mines off Cape Agulhas, she went into the Indian Ocean disguised as a Dutch cargo steamer. Having sunk a couple of important ships, capturing secret mails and invaluable merchant navy code books, she lay low during September in the Sunda Straits between Java and Sumatra, thousands of miles east of where she had first made her kill. There she captured and kept in company two Norwegian tankers, and in December reached the already mentioned remote Kerguelen Islands. Not until November 1941, while acting on orders as a supply ship to a U-boat on her way home to Germany was she caught and sunk at a rendezvous south of the Equator by the cruiser *Devonshire*.

It was both the strength and the weakness of the raiders that they kept clear of convoys, the escorts of which would have been too strong and too fast for them. By concentrating on independently sailing ships they achieved the important moral effect of challenging the Admiralty's claim to be able to choose safe routes for ships fast enough to avoid U-boats, and at the same time greatly reduced the chances of being detected. Having sunk a victim, the raider would make off in a direction chosen in the light of good intelligence about British routes and dispositions. While Beesly and his colleagues were trying to find some logic or pattern of behaviour in her traceable movements, her captain would be trying to make his course as unpredictable as possible. Nothing in the story of the maritime war illustrates more vividly the baffling central problem of naval intelligence: the vast distances to be watched and searched in the oceans of the world, east and west, and the huge scale of operations in which a section of the Atlantic a thousand miles wide would be described as 'the corridor'.*

Taken from the Weekly Intelligence Report of 12 December

1941 (Raider Supplement No. 2) is the following account of the tactics so far as they were known to NID some eighteen months after the hunt began. Secret at the time, this would have reached all naval officers for personal reading; but merchant skippers would hear about it only during the briefing at base when they received sailing instructions:

The tactics employed have varied with the individual captains. When raiders first began operating they appear to have approached their victims on a gradually converging course, relying mainly on their innocent appearance, and *on merchant captains' ignorance of the existence of disguised raiders.* Fire would then be opened without warning in an effort to destroy the W/T room before a distress message could be made, and also to prevent resistance being offered.

This method is still scoring successes, but owing to the increased vigilance of merchant ships and the more frequent transmitting of 'Q' distress signals, raiders have been forced to rely more on night attacks. The victim, having been located by aircraft reconnaissance or by masthead lookout, is shadowed throughout the day, and at nightfall a course is shaped in accordance with the merchant ship's last observed course and speed, to intercept during the night or at dawn. In several cases the positions of merchant ships have been betrayed during the day by excessive smoke and at night by sparks and even flames from their funnels.

Another method which has been employed when a raider approached a victim from ahead, has been for the raider to hold on to her course without at first approaching too close, but when abeam, suddenly to turn in and attack. A variation of this is for the raider to continue on her course until out of sight and then to turn and remain out of sight over the horizon, using her speed to close in after dark.

Whatever the method of approaching the victim, the attack is always sudden and severe, the primary targets being the bridge, W/T room and gun. No attempt is made to spare the crew until the destruction of these points has been achieved, and in some cases firing has continued for twenty minutes or more both with the main armament and with pom-poms, long after it was obvious that no attempt at resistance was being made. Torpedoes are apparently used only to 'finish off' a disabled vessel. Torpedoes have, however, been effectively used in engagements with HM ships.

281

If one intelligence lesson of the raider campaign is the amount of information that can be built up from small bits of apparently unrelated detail, the other is that letting one's own forces know what has been learned about the enemy is just as important. Promulgation – that is to say the passing on – of intelligence was quite often slow or incomplete, either because of excessive secrecy or because of the sheer administrative difficulty of reaching ships all over the world. There is no doubt that the casualties – for example, the loss of the cruiser *Sidney* – from raider action might have been substantially smaller if what was known about them had been circulated more fully and swiftly.

'*The Answer is in the Negative*'

There is no difficulty, on the face of it, in understanding the person who says 'Nothing has happened, therefore the situation is, so far as I know, as it was.' Despite the negative opening, it is obviously a positive statement of information. Yet the importance of such negative intelligence in war is sometimes misunderstood; and the person offering it may find himself ignored or disbelieved. A classic case – interesting and important because the consequences were so disastrous – occurred in the handling of the PQ17 convoy to Russia in July 1942.* The First Sea Lord, Dudley Pound, who personally ordered the ships to scatter because he believed that German heavy ships, among them the *Tirpitz*, might be on their way to attack the convoy, preferred his own judgement to the negative assurance given him by his intelligence experts. This he was fully entitled to do, but an analysis of the intelligence problem shows the error in a fresh light.

What was at stake in this operation had better be stated first. Owing to U-boat and torpedo-bomber attacks launched from Norway on the ships abandoned by their escorts, 23 ships out of 35 were lost, with 3,350 vehicles, 430 tanks, 210 aircraft and nearly 100,000 tons of other cargo. To the Russians, desperately pressed by the German army at that moment, it was an exasperating failure and Stalin's reproaches to London were bitter and even malicious. He had been pressing Roosevelt and Churchill over weeks to hurry on the delivery of cargoes held up in American and British ports; but the Admiralty and Commander-in-Chief Home Fleet had agreed only with the deepest misgivings to attempt the passage of a large convoy in summer conditions which, they argued, would suit the 200-odd German aircraft based on northern Norway. It was, moreover, a time when not only the *Tirpitz* – sister ship to the *Bismarck* which had taken so long to sink – was up in Trondheim ready to attack, but also the pocket-battleships *Scheer* and *Lützow*, the heavy cruiser *Hipper* and a large force of destroyers. Never, either before or after 4 July 1942, was the available German task force of heavy ships so strong – at a strength indeed, to take on the Home Fleet force which regularly covered the Arctic convoys. It had only one weakness – the lack of an aircraft-carrier to provide fighter cover far out to sea against the Home Fleet's carrier-borne torpedo bombers – and this was crucial.*

A further complication – of which Churchill in his history seems to make rather too much – was the presence of the American battleship *Washington* with the Home Fleet and two American cruisers *Tuscaloosa* and *Wichita*. That they should be there was a sign that the Admiralty's resources were stretched to breaking point in the Mediterranean, Atlantic and North Sea, as indeed was the Americans' strength in the Pacific. If Hitler and Raeder were afraid of losing big ships, because they had so few, so then were Churchill and Pound. They were not in the mood for a death or glory battle against the mighty *Tirpitz* and her squadron. But, on the Royal Navy's aggressive record to date, the German Naval Staff could not count on that; indeed, they seem to have assumed the opposite. Neither side on 4 July fully realized how strained and nervous was the other. It seems fair to say, in considering the narrative that follows, that Pound's worries about the general situation at sea made him incapable of understanding the caution of the Germans, of recalling, for example, how the *Tirpitz* had recently had a narrow escape in a surprise attack by the torpedo bombers of the *Victorious*.

If the fears were deep, so were the temptations strong. If the *Tirpitz* could be brought to battle by the Home Fleet's covering forces of *Duke of York*, *Washington*, and the aircraft-carrier *Victorious* with her capacity for wide-probing search and long range torpedo attacks; or even if the British destroyers could

283

once again demonstrate their training and skill in a night action, then a decisive blow at German naval strength – Hitler's fleet in being – might be struck. With the *Tirpitz* out of the way or seriously damaged, the Home Fleet could spare ships for the Mediterranean, the Atlantic escorts could be strengthened, the American ships could be released for the Pacific. Likewise on the German side: to destroy a major convoy to Russia at this moment, perhaps to strike a crippling blow at British naval strength (had not the *Bismarck* sunk the *Hood* in minutes?) would be a tremendous tonic to the morale of a German people which had expected but had been denied a quick victory against the Russians.

Thus there were complex and weighty political and strategic arguments in Dudley Pound's mind when he asked his intelligence men down in the Citadel a few direct questions. They gave to the best of their ability simple factual answers; but Pound wanted exact times, exact locations on which to base a most difficult and hazardous judgement. A spy on board the *Tirpitz*, communicating instantaneously with the OIC in an unbreakable cipher would have been the answer; but such perfect service exists only in novels. The best that could be offered was general wireless intelligence about the whole German naval and air disposition in Norway; the service of a group of reliable agents in Altenfjord where *Tirpitz* had her hiding place and refuelling base; a series of D/F fixes or an unaccustomed pattern of wireless traffic if the *Tirpitz* or her escorting destroyers broke silence. To this Commander Denning (whose work has been explained earlier) added four years' experience of daily, intensive study of German warship habits and intelligence obtained from a dozen different sources. It was his job to judge what the Germans *might* or might not in due course do; Dudley Pound's was to judge what the British and American warships and the convoy *should* do now. In the event Pound himself made the positive intelligence judgement and decided that the convoy should scatter, knowing that shore-based bombers could reach the unescorted merchant ships and that U-boats were around in numbers. How did this happen?

It was not unusual for the First Sea Lord to come down at any time to the Citadel and look at the plot in either the submarine tracking room or in Denning's room where he could study the plot of surface ship operations. There he could talk with the men on the job; keep them in touch with his thinking and bridge that gap which is always likely to open between Operations and Intelligence. It was to provide this meeting place that the OIC had been created.

In the early evening of 4 July, therefore, Denning was not surprised to see Pound, accompanied by the Assistant Chief of Naval Staff for Home Operations (Brind) and the Director of Anti-submarine Warfare (Creasy), come into his room. He knew what was brewing, as did Winn watching over his U-boats in the room down the corridor. Both realized this was one of the biggest convoy gambles of the war. The tracking-room faced the usual difficulties of getting accurate D/Fs from the Arctic region to give a picture of the U-boat concentration which was to be expected in the Barents Sea. Late on 3 July it had reported to C-in-C Home Fleet that the German aircraft shadowing the convoy were using beacon procedure with U-boats. And in the early morning of 4 July Home Fleet was told that the convoy had been shadowed and reported through the night. What the Admiralty knew the German Naval Staff would also know and pass on to the *Tirpitz*; the approximate position to be reached by the convoy at any given time on 5 July, together with the time needed by the battleship and its destroyers to reach it, could be calculated by both sides.

Denning knew that the *Tirpitz* and the heavy cruiser *Hipper* had sailed from Trondheim northward by the afternoon of 3 July and it would be normal for them to refuel at Altenfjord on 4 July if they intended to operate. At his suggestion a Coastal Command Catalina left Iceland and carried out a search of the Norwegian fjords, but without result. Thick weather over Narvik, where the *Lützow* and *Scheer* had been, prevented the taking of photographs. Likewise on 4 July there was no information from air search between nine o'clock and the late afternoon. Denning was therefore waiting anxiously either to hear from men on the spot that the *Tirpitz* and other ships had left Altenfjord, or to deduce from a successful photographic air reconnaissance (PRU) or other evidence that they were still there.

Upstairs in Pound's office senior officers were conferring on and off the whole of that 4 July. The Admiralty had become a complete operational headquarters, not merely advising and informing PQ17 and C-in-C Home Fleet in the *Duke of York* but giving them orders. Pound was in search of certainty; hence the nature of his questions as he stood for a few minutes in 8E. The dialogue, based on the recollections of two witnesses was of this order:

1 SL   Do you know if the *Tirpitz* has put to sea?

Denning If the *Tirpitz* had put to sea you can be sure that we would have known very shortly afterwards, within four to six hours.

1 SL   Can you assure me that the *Tirpitz* is still at anchor at Altenfjord?

Denning No. I shall have firm information only when the *Tirpitz* has left.

1 SL   Can you at least tell me whether the *Tirpitz* is ready to go to sea?

Denning I can at least say that she will not leave in the next few hours. If she were on the point of sailing, the destroyer escort would have preceded her and made an anti-submarine sweep. They have not been reported by our submarines patrolling off Altenfjord.

Without further comment, Dudley Pound's party then visited the tracking room to inform themselves of the U-boat situation. Winn told them that in the Barents Sea it was bad. Even if its strong force of escort vessels stayed with it, the convoy was in for a bad time.

When the First Sea Lord returned upstairs about 7 p.m. he had no firm and positive intelligence to show that the four German big ships, or the *Tirpitz* and destroyers alone, were already making for the convoy. If they were, the convoy escort of four light cruisers going as far on the way to Russia as it dared, would be in serious danger – and cruisers were precious. If they were not, and the *Tirpitz* were to leave now – or if it had left in the last hour or two – and if *the departure was promptly reported*, then the *Duke of York*, *Washington* and *Victorious*, in support 350 miles away to the west, might with the aid of carrier aircraft make contact and either bring the enemy to battle or scare him off.

286

While the pros and cons were being discussed at a staff meeting, called at 8.30 that evening, Rear-Admiral Clayton, the head of OIC and Denning's superior officer watched anxiously. Hitherto the advice of his experts had always been taken.* On this occasion it looked as if it might be ignored. The room was full of senior officers hot for certainty. Clayton was a much respected and shrewd retired officer, but not the man to take on battle with Pound and his Vice-Chief of Naval Staff, Vice-Admiral Sir Henry Moore. He might have summoned to his support the Director of Naval Intelligence, who was senior to everyone there except Pound and Moore; but Godfrey was on a tour of inspection in Scotland. Already, too, at eleven minutes past seven, Pound had ordered the cruiser force to withdraw westward at high speed. As Admiral Tovey, the C-in-C, later complained 'this [signal] is understood to have been due to U-boat information, but that fact was not known to the addressees'. It must have seemed to Tovey that the signal indicated knowledge not of U-boats but about the German big ships being at sea, a possibility about which they had been warned before sailing; for the cruisers had been originally ordered not to stay with the convoy east of a given point unless the Admiralty assured their commander that there was no risk from the *Tirpitz*. This clear expectation of *positive* intelligence had been stimulated by a still earlier signal from the Admiralty, sent off before Pound had consulted Denning, which said that cruisers should stay with the convoy 'pending further instructions' as 'further information' might be available shortly. This was timed 4.58 p.m. So the intelligence picture of those at sea was confused.

After a discussion of which no satisfactory record seems to exist, the view prevailed that the convoy should be dispersed immediately. It could not in fact scatter wherever and whenever it wished, if the German battleships should appear, because it was already close to the pack ice to the north and the enemy ships would be coming from the south. Although several officers appear to have opposed dispersal, the VCNS, Henry Moore, supported it. Pound then personally wrote out the signal to disperse 'owing to the threat from surface ships', timed 9.23 GMT – just two hours after his talk with Denning.*

287

When Clayton returned downstairs and told his officers of the decision, Denning was amazed and angry that his assurance that any move of the *Tirpitz* would be known had not been accepted. He begged Clayton to go back to Pound's room and stress the strongly-held intelligence view that the German big ships were not yet at sea. Clayton did so, but Pound seems to have insisted that there was no certainty and he could not now cancel the signals sent. What happened to the convoy in the next few days is well known. In the event the German ships – *Tirpitz* and destroyers – stayed until the morning of 5 July in Altenfjord, whence they made a brief sortie (duly reported to OIC) which was broken off when the German Command received intelligence showing that they had been observed by submarine and that a British aircraft carrier might be coming up.

From the intelligence point of view two features of the exchanges between Pound and Denning are especially interesting. First the latter's insistence on answering only the question as it was put: 'Do you know this has happened?' 'No, I do not, but if it had I would know very soon afterwards.' If Pound had gone on and asked 'Has your source ever let you down?' the answer would have been 'No, never so far; and if anything happened to him he has a partner.' This fact was very important in the situation – but a chief of naval staff does not ask detailed questions about sources. Denning knew, further, that the agent only reported at set times, working as he was at tremendous risk in a village on Altenfjord.

The second significant feature, already alluded to, is the reluctance to accept negative intelligence at its proper value, a weakness in human nature to which Sherlock Holmes more than once drew attention. Here was a very experienced intelligence officer with seagoing experience – who had been right in forecasting, against the views of the Board of Admiralty and Bomber Command, that the *Scharnhorst* and *Gneisenau* would make a dash for home through the Channel – saying that the *absence* of intelligence must be *positively* interpreted. Furthermore, Denning knew from his study of Hitler's navy that it was – the U-boats apart – the Cinderella of the Wehrmacht, starved of air support, denied an aircraft-carrier, under the personal orders of a Fuehrer who had been infuriated by the loss of the *Bismarck*. If PQ17 could be dealt with effectively by the U-boats and aircraft on the scene, the German command would certainly prefer not to risk their big ships. Denning could not know what we now know, that their commander was forbidden to carry out an offensive operation unless the carrier with the Home Fleet had been located by intelligence or reconnaissance beforehand.

Denning, looking back, now blames himself for not having stated his case at greater length and offered his hunch against that of the Chief of Naval Staff. But he had properly stuck to the principles laid down by Godfrey: that intelligence must be strictly separated from opinion if it is to retain its authority and reliability. He was, and still is, convinced that no intention of dispersing the convoy was in Pound's mind when he left the room; and Pound was the last man to shift responsibility on to the shoulders of a junior officer.*

One intelligence mystery has never been cleared up. At the Cabinet inquiry into the episode Pound is said to have stated that intelligence came in during the night of 3–4 July showing that the *Tirpitz* had evaded the British submarines lying in wait for her off North Cape and could be in position to attack the convoy on the morning of 5 July. Denning confirms that it was correct to say that NID knew she had evaded our submarines *on her journey up from Trondheim*; but the fact that she was known to have arrived in Altenjford on the night of 3–4 July does not justify the second half of the statement – that she could be in position to attack on the 5th. There was clearly confusion in the minds of both Pound and the First Lord on this point.

It is no part of this book's purpose to praise or blame Pound and the Naval Staff for what hindsight now shows to have been an unnecessary decision. But one point may be added to the criticism made in the Official History of Pound's liking for personal control of operations at sea. It was the quality of intelligence he was given that had made possible such a measure of direction from the Admiralty. That being so, should he not have relied on that intelligence when giving orders to C-in-C Home Fleet and Rear-Admiral Hamilton? Had he done so, he would have been proved right. For within an hour of his decision to scatter the convoy the expected positive intelligence, showing that the *Tirpitz* was not at sea, arrived – just, but only just too late.

Blockade-running

A good example of the kind of work required of the Denning team in the OIC was their coverage of the remarkable series of blockade-breaking operations between Gothenburg and Hull known as 'Rubble', 'Performance', 'Cabaret' and 'Bridford'. Beginning in January 1941, these achieved the removal from neutral Sweden to Britain across the North Sea first, of 25,000 tons of desperately needed ball-bearings and other special steel goods for aircraft and armoured vehicle building, carried in five Norwegian ships. Between October 1943 and the middle of March 1944, another 350 tons of steel specialities (and sixty-seven picked refugees) were brought over by converted motor-gunboats. This was not so much smuggling as blockade-running under the noses of the German Navy operating from its own ports and those of occupied Norway and Denmark, all the more irritating to the Nazi authorities because these were goods they badly needed themselves, and because the sight of the Red Ensign within hailing distance of German patrols was a sign to all Scandinavia that the war was *not* going as Hitler had planned.

For these steel-running operations to succeed it was necessary to have not only the best up-to-the-minute weather information, but also accurate and topical knowledge of the whereabouts of German destroyers, patrol boats, minesweepers and above all minefields. It was on the strength of NID's study of the intensive German mining of the Skagerrak, that Commander Sir George Binney, DSO, the Commodore of the operations, and the Admiralty Director of Operations, Captain J. A. S. Eccles, decided after losses and failures in 1942 to use gunboats with shallow draught instead of merchant ships in spite of the risks from the North Sea weather.

The intensity of the German effort to prevent this reopening in war of the peacetime Ellerman–Wilson service between Hull and Gothenburg (which is what it ostensibly was) can be judged from their keeping five or six of their scanty destroyer force frequently at Kristiansand for interception purposes.

Minesweeper patrols were maintained across the Skagerrak and a line of armed patrol boats at five-mile intervals kept watch near the Swedish coast. It was OIC's job, with the assistance of detailed and regular air reconnaissance and studies of signal traffic to watch these dispositions week in, week out, and advise the Nore Command as to when and how Binney and his 'merchant ships' might set out on their hazardous runs from the port of Immingham to Lysekil.

13 Handbooks for invasion

In no branch of Intelligence is its life-saving function more strikingly revealed than in the work which brings the seaman and his landing-craft on to the right beach and the soldier and his equipment safely on to, over and beyond it. If they are to have confidence in the map and chart references, the depths and directions, the distances and heights that they have learnt from their briefings for the assault, the material must have undergone expert research and scrupulous editing – which is what distinguishes good intelligence from mere information. So the fighting men who were landed by the hundred thousand in the face of the enemy in North Africa and Europe between the end of 1942 and the spring of 1945, and on the vast coast-lines of South-East Asia, needed behind them not only supply, communication, reinforcement, air support but also the resources of scholarship. No one who remembered, as the DNI did, the British ignorance and blindness at Gallipoli in 1915 (repeated in Norway in 1940)* could tolerate for one moment the average staff officer's casual disregard of what has come to be known as topographical intelligence. But to get its importance quickly understood it was necessary to tear the War Office away from its preoccupation with enemy order of battle, the Air Ministry from its obsession with German industrial bombing targets, and the Navy from its belief that rocks, shoals, shallow water and beaches are hazards to be avoided by ships, not overcome by them. The energy and outspokenness with which Godfrey and, after him, Rushbrooke, hammered home this need made DNI enemies in other Ministries and exposed NID to the charge of empire-building.

Before penetrating the relatively humdrum mysteries of this branch of Intelligence, it is helpful to consider how the planner sees and uses it. Assume that he occupies the position in which the three British Directors of Plans found themselves after the fall of France. The strength needed to go back into Europe against German and Italian resistance simply did not exist. Nor was it likely to come into being in less than two years. None the less there must be some idea of where to probe, where to strike and eventually where to concentrate; some type of operation to train troops for. The planner, unlike the intelligence officer, knows more about his own forces than about the enemy's; his thinking is influenced by what he knows of the endurance and capacity of his own ships (how much they can carry in how many trips over what distance) of the range of his fighter aircraft able to cover any attack, of the supplies needed by his troops and so on. To those considerations he adds the known dispositions of the enemy, where the defences in any one arm or all arms are weakest. Out of all this certain targets begin to show themselves, from tactical objectives like destroying a big radar station overlooking the Channel or anticipating a Japanese coup against French Madagascar, to strategic objectives like landing in the rear of the German expeditionary force in North Africa under Rommel and staying there. Hunches emerge, ideas are sketched out on paper, enthusiasts demand detail, sceptics demand even more detail.

It is here that the topographical or terrain experts come in. Sardinia has landing possibilities, so has Corsica; other things being equal how do the terrain conditions compare? A quick landing in the Andaman Islands, with the Japanese on the offensive still, might be possible and take some weight off the Americans in the Pacific. Is there a good, protected landing place? What would be the chances of leaving men there? What resources can the islands offer? Are there any personalities known to be loyal and friendly beyond doubt? Decision depends, though only partly, on what the topographical and political intelligence suggests.*

In theory, of course, the planners should start the other way round – with the intelligence that points to weaknesses in the enemy positions on which the terrain experts have provided a full brief; but with thousands of miles of coastline to work on, it was too much to expect that such briefs would ever catch up with all the possibilities. Less and less, however, after 1943 did the devoted topographers find themselves chopping and changing from one location to another as the planners changed their minds.

Every motorist and every mountaineer is using 'topographical' intelligence when he seeks not just to 'find the way' but to judge all the conditions with which his car or his legs will have to cope – the gradients, the bends, the bridges, the surfaces – and even the flora and fauna. But in war this dull, pretentious word took on wider meanings. For the task of the Allies was to introduce into areas about which their staffs were, more often than not, profoundly ignorant, huge mechanized forces and to keep them there. Would there be oil, water, railways, workshops, electricity supplies to maintain them? No one in peacetime had studied in detail the North Sea, Channel and Atlantic beaches of what was after 1940 to be occupied Europe; at least, no single group had collected and organized the figures and maps and pictures. 'Who would have thought,' said one rhetorical memorandum, 'when the Germans invaded Poland, that we should have to range our inquiries from the cryolite mines of Ivigtut to the Kamchatka peninsula, from the twilight settlements of Barentsberg and Longyear City to the one deepwater quay at Diego Suarez?'

Nor were matters much better in Asia and the Middle East. The British and the Dutch, the French and the Americans, did not realize until they were driven down to the South Pacific and out of south-east Asia how little detailed and accurate information they could take with them. When the time came to return by force of arms, the demand was for facts of every kind; about port capacity, geological structure of beaches, railway and roads systems, cover along river banks, local food and oil resources, power stations and hospital accommodation, possible airfield sites and vehicle parks. The ex-planters who offered their services to GHQ India were not good enough. The civil and railway engineer was needed; and with him the surveyor, the economist, the draughtsman, the linguist, the botanist and the geologist, the forester and above all the trained scholar. It was not just a question of defeating the enemy:

the population had to be won back and our own forces quickly made as dependent as possible on local resources.

Then everything that these men and women experts had to offer must be edited: the specialist superfluities pruned away, the presentation simplified and emphasized, if necessary like 'form-at-a-glance'.* The texts must be related to maps and charts and statistics; and the printer instructed and his proofs corrected; a perfectly produced, easily handled and readable job despatched to a fighting formation or a planning command which could rely absolutely on it. All this to be done in conditions of high security and discretion; for what could reveal more unmistakably the intention to invade Sicily than the sudden concentration of scores of highly intellectual people on the resources, ports, roads and general topography of that island? And to conceal the particular area to be invaded it was necessary to show an interest equally detailed and passionate in every part. It is an interesting point in intelligence work that the closest study of detail created a special security risk. For example, Norwegian pilots or skippers, closely questioned before a raid, were sometimes segregated and detained until the raid was over, much to their disgust.*

Thus, when all the technical specialists had finished answering the military planners' questionnaires, it fell to someone like 'the First in Greats' to bring it all under one pair of eyes and through one brain. So well thought of was this process by 1942 that Admiral Sir Andrew Cunningham asked the DNI that the operation orders for 'Torch' (the landings in North Africa) should be printed by the University Press at Oxford where all this work was being done. Little did ABC know of the inconsistencies and inaccuracies found by that distinguished classicist Freddie Wells and his woman assistant during a long night's editing of this most secret document – errors which, had they gone unnoticed, might well have cost lives or caused dangerous delays. I know no more striking instance of how the arts scholar can stand guard as effectively as the scientist over the fighting man.*

If this chapter describes in some detail how topographical intelligence was organized it is not only because the credit in the early stages goes virtually entire to the Naval Intelligence Division, but also because it produced perhaps the best example – outside the great combined headquarters of General Eisenhower and Lord Mountbatten – of the inter-service organization towards which the three Services have been struggling for the last twenty years. The story of its growth from tiny beginnings illustrates the radical effects on Whitehall conservatism of the impetus of war; so to tell it may be as interesting to the general reader as it should be valuable to historians. Much of it was fortunately recorded in detail just after the war.

First the particular sources drawn on for what I have called terrain intelligence must be recalled. Documentation from libraries, books and guides, business houses and individuals, newpaper offices and tourist agencies, learned societies and Lloyd's. Then people: specialists and ordinary individuals with special knowledge, refugees arriving from occupied Europe, and others – all to be contacted, interviewed, registered, accommodated, kept happy, their fares paid. Then photographs by the hundred thousand from every kind of source, together with drawings and picture postcards and personal snapshots; also the more sophisticated products of air photography. Then maps and charts and plans from all kinds of sources. If NID 6, as it was first called, seems to grow extravagantly, even bureaucratically, it is because the urgent and skilled handling of masses of material in reasonably secure conditions forced an early split into an Admiralty Photographic Library, a Contact Register, a Library Research Unit. Years of neglect were being made up for in months, and if empire-building began to show itself towards the end of the war, that was because there seemed to be no reason why a world conflict should not be the occasion for mapping and studying the whole world. *L'appétit vient en mangeant.* Or, as one of Rushbrooke's officers put it in a memorandum of June 1945 opposing the complete disbanding of topographical intelligence in peacetime, 'Total war demands total intelligence'.

To none of their projects of organization and experiment did DNI and his deputy directors give more enthusiastic attention. The scholar and navigator in Godfrey, fascinated by the very nature of topographical work and by the production of fine books, knew that the Navy would be called upon sooner or later to put the Army ashore in a score of places of which there were few accurate charts, no pictures, no scientifically assembled and up-to-date detail. As Navigation Officer of the *Euralyus* he had watched the landings at Cape Helles, V-Beach and Suvla Bay and remembered our deplorable lack of information about the topography of Gallipoli. That imperial defence planning in peace should have been so ill-informed seems now incredible; but it was so, and it required mighty administrative drive to ensure that British troops should not again be put ashore as hapless as Robinson Crusoe.*

The lack of topographical information in the Division files was worrying Godfrey as early as the autumn of 1939, when he discussed with Professor Mason and Mr Wordie, the Oxford and Cambridge geographers, how an organization might be set up comparable to NID 32 of the first war, which had produced handbooks and pamphlets. These, however, had been mostly educational and of little use to planners, the full extent of whose requirements was not grasped until the Services began to plan their first serious attempt at a combined assault of all arms. Scenting trouble ahead, in January 1940, he asked directors of operational divisions in the Admiralty – now beginning to dream of offensive raids on semi-occupied Europe – to give him as much notice as possible of their needs. He pointed out that 'intelligence planning and procurement must without question come before operational planning' – a point that took a little time to sink in. NID must know about the 'ideas' even before they became a plan, otherwise, they could not deliver in time what would be required.

Sure enough the moment came, within a few weeks, when the Vice-Chief of Naval Staff rebuked the DNI for not being able to provide immediately some information he wanted about Petsamo.* The Director's reply was that his staff was fully occupied with current intelligence tasks and there was no one to spare for the collection and long-term study of the mass of material that would be needed for the planners, who had, he pointed out, not yet indicated the priority of their requirements. Somewhere in the British Isles, he declared, there must be someone who knew all about anything if you could only find him; but to trace such people a staff and an organization must be provided. He requested authority from the irascible VCNS (Admiral Phillips) to build up a research staff – and got it. So the beginning of a vast enterprise was an unfair rebuke from on high which had been turned to good purpose.

By 28 March 1940, Mr A. F. Wells, Fellow and Praelector in Classics at University College, Oxford, was installed in the Admiralty as a civilian officer, strongly recommended by the Whyte's Professor of Moral Philosophy, Dr Paton. The terms of reference given to Wells were terrifyingly wide, betraying some ignorance of how much there was to find out. He was to tap such sources of topographical information (which was eventually to cover even hygiene, flora and suitable clothing) as shipping companies and business firms engaged in foreign trade, magazines and newspapers and technical journals, tourist and photographic agencies, travellers and explorers, and the learned departments of all the universities.

Wells – NID 6 – became at once the natural link between the NID and Oxford, where the Professor of Geography had already written reports for the Division and placed the School of Geography at DNI's disposal. This association was later to bring the whole of the NID topographical section out of blitzed London into Mason's Geography Building. Likewise, Mr Wordie, in the Scott Polar Research Institute in Cambridge, was able to help Wells with immediate material on Spitzbergen, Iceland, Greenland and Denmark Strait, where naval operations began on the first day of hostilities. Back in London a multitude of files were opened to Wells in the City before the severe bombing began: the Royal Mail Steamship Company, for example, handed over thousands of coastal photographs.

It can be imagined what surprise was felt in the great business and finance houses at the flood of requests for information about strategic areas which the layman assumed the Services to have built up long ago; also at the frequency with which representatives of the Admiralty, War Office and other departments would apply in quick succession for the same help, in complete ignorance of each other's activities.* When, as in the cases of Norway and Dakar, information was called for at short notice, there was a scramble for any scrap of information from any source. Scores of people learned quite unnecessarily that Whitehall was urgently interested in this or that corner of the world as each Ministry foraged independently. Indeed, it was already apparent that unless such intelligence work for future operations was put on an inter-service basis, absurdity and chaos would result.

Then, in April 1940, came the German invasion of Norway and the sudden demand for detailed information about her enormous and complicated coastline, landward approaches and communications system. Admiralty and War Office were caught napping. The lack of even the most elementary information was desperate; officers, like much-travelled Peter Fleming, who were with the British expeditionary force found themselves with no more information than could be found in a 1912 Baedeker. Everything was surprising; the depth of the snow, the size of the fjords, the scarcity of roads, the position and size of piers. This gap in British preparations had now become a scandal and in May 1940 on the prompting of DNI, a survey of topographical intelligence in the three Service Ministries was made. It was recommended that they should be authorized to increase their staffs for this work and employ experts 'either trained officers or technicians'.* Inside the Admiralty, this work needed the goodwill of the civilian branches; alerted by Markham, the Secretary of the Admiralty, the civil servants gave their unstinted help and accorded it an unofficial priority.

Godfrey urged during the discussion of the JIC report that each Director of Intelligence should appoint a deputy-director for Topography, which was bound to become in time a major activity. The deputies should then act as a sub-committee of the JIC, examine planners' requirements, prepare the question-naires for specialists and supervise the production of area reports. But these were early days for such root-and-branch innovations; and the Army and RAF complained it was not easy to find officers with sufficient knowledge to sit on such a committee. Nevertheless the DMI seconded J. R. M. Butler,* the Cambridge don, who subsequently became chief historian for the Official Military History of the war. DNI's proposal was rejected and it was agreed that the Services should continue to work independently, any co-operation between them taking place under the direction of the 'most interested party'. This, in the foreseeable circumstances of 1940, meant in most cases the Admiralty – the leading topographical question always being 'where can we land?' In view of later complaints that the

Admiralty was empire-building, this rejection of its proposal for an inter-service body is worth recording.

This incongruous, timid and, by the standards of 1944, utterly incomprehensible compromise ignored the fact that 'terrain intelligence', as I prefer to call it, is a single, coherent and indivisible subject. The geology of a coastal area, for example, is shown on the same maps as indicate the water supply for an inland area. Navy and Army arrive on a beach together. The pretence that the Navy, faced with the task of landing troops, should get its information independently of the RAF, which needs facts on which to base a plan for establishing an airfield or bombing enemy supply routes, is so absurd that to believe it one has to know the lengths to which inter-service rivalry and suspicion could then go.

Now comes a curious episode. In spite of the recommendation of the Directors of Intelligence assembled in committee (which is what the JIC was), neither the War Office nor the Air Ministry was inclined to create a special topographical section, but both agreed to use whatever the Admiralty could provide. This was, in effect, a small section housed in an ex-lavatory close at hand to Room 39 (the best the Admiralty could find) with three officers and a secretary. The head of it was Lieutenant-Colonel Sam Bassett, RM; his assistant was Wells, and they were joined by Captain Law, RN, a surveyor just returned from Singapore and lent by the Hydrographer of the Admiralty, who recognized the special importance of his department's experience in delineating a coastline. Into their little office poured a stream of calls and callers with both the most urgent and the most long-term inquiries. During June 1940, the section dealt – goodness knows how – with information about the Rhine–Main–Danube Canal, the Canary Islands and the Azores, the Zeiss works at Jena, the corn-growing areas of Italy, the width of the bridges in Iceland on the Reykjavik–Hvalfjord road, oil installations at Huelva and Lisbon, the hydrography and topography of Irish lochs (in case German seaplanes tried to land there) and the height of the breakwater protecting the French fleet at Mers-el-Kebir.

Most of such questions were answered by getting photographs and facts from persons in Britain with local knowledge; and that meant finding, following up and recording contacts in any part of the country. A Boer volunteered information for the Air Ministry about the Rhine–Main–Danube Canal, in the building of which he had helped; pictures of Tel-el-Kebir were borrowed from a Cardiff contact who had spent several years in Oran erecting oil tanks. A man with intimate knowledge of the marshes around Cherbourg was found keeping a café in Glasgow; and Peter de Bruyne, who knew every corner of the Antwerp docks (through which were to come the supplies for the final assault into Germany), was discovered acting as consul in Liverpool. So queries led to inquiries and inquiries to contacts and contacts to a register, which will be described later in this chapter.

As one talks to former members of this tiny section in its squalid room, one recalls with astonishment the improvisation and amateurism of that fearful summer of 1940. One hears again the tone of fussy self-importance, one sees again the secretive and even mysterious air with which officers scurried around London looking for what none of them had ever before thought of as 'military intelligence'. Projects and operations were being whispered about which had not the remotest relation to fact or possibility; impossible demands were made by staff officers who did not know what they were talking about.

Here is Colonel Bassett's diary note for Sunday 8 September, in the middle of the Battle of Britain:

Report on Casablanca was completed by Law and me in face of great difficulty. Lack of typists in central copying branch and delays through big air raid last night. Reached War Office for meeting 15 minutes late.

This report, with maps and photographs if possible, had been demanded at twenty-four hours' notice. Later on Tuesday 24 September, with the Battle of Britain barely won and the British Army less than one corps strong:

Asked by Future Operations Section (War Cabinet?) for reports on (i) north coast of Africa—Libya; (ii) Lisbon to Latitude 37° and as far as 5° West approx; (iii) Stavanger to Kristiansand with special attention to beaches near good ports. These reports to be ready Thursday p.m. Maps showing above were procured GSGS, Royal Geographical Society and RAF Stanmore.

Yet some of the jobs were in the most real sense operational. Three days after the new NID Section 6 first assembled, the evacuation at Dunkirk began (26 May) and Bassett took steps to bring together as quickly as possible every photograph and scrap of information he could find about the beaches and ports in France from which the rest of the British Army further westward might have to be shipped if French resistance collapsed.

Nothing of the kind existed in NID files, and it would have taken weeks to use ordinary research methods. Bassett therefore proposed that two reconnaissance parties should be organized for a quick on-the-spot survey of the beaches. As the War Office could spare none of its officers, the whole job was done by two parties of Naval and Royal Marine officers. Both were back by mid-June with photographs and notes collected just ahead of the advancing Germans. At the same time NID 6 was interviewing Royal Mail captains and others, with a good knowledge of the French coast. One of them was able to cover the whole stretch from Le Havre to Dieppe and another Cherbourg to Le Havre. Compared with the foot-by-foot description achieved in 1944 these interpretations were crude; but in 1940 they were remarkably better than nothing.*

In this same month of defeat and depression there was another important development: the first efforts of what was to become the Central Interpretation Unit (CIU) of the RAF. A firm called Aero Films at Wembley possessed the only VILT machine in the country which, from air photographs, could draw contoured maps with accuracy. Air photography of such quality quickly brought a revolution in every branch of intelligence and NID 6 was one of its first customers.

Although the section was kept busy with spot questions from such quarters as SOE and Vice-Admiral Submarines, it was not until August that they had direct contact with a successful and significant operation. In May they had obtained from the School of Geography in Oxford a fairly full illustrated report on the inland waterways of Germany, which they had passed to the Air Ministry. Then one day that department requested the presence of the 'chairman of the topographical section' at a meeting. Colonel Bassett, whom the title seemed to fit, armed with an empty brief-case for appearances' sake, attended and heard a high-level group of officers decide that the RAF should bomb the Dortmund–Ems canal. He was instructed to throw 'the whole of his section' (of three officers) into the search for further facts about the vulnerability of this strategic waterway. With the help of the Oxford report and a trip to South Wales to talk with a contact, NID 6 were able to produce a document giving cross-sections of the canal where it is elevated above the surrounding countryside. In due course the aqueducts of the canal were bombed.

Then, on 10 August, after DNI had warned the section that they would be expected to collect all naval information for future operations, there came a large and urgent questionnaire about Dakar. By the end of the week a full report on the French West African port had been prepared and to the assault force were supplied six master sets of photographs and maps, the text of the report and three thousand copies of individual photographs and charts. Fortunately, a few weeks before this, Combined Operations had asked for maps of Dakar and Senegal, which had alerted the section; and when DNI took its head to meet Admiral Sir John Cunningham, who was to command the expedition, they were not entirely unprepared except for his wish to take the section along with him.

What about security? Here were two or three people without military experience having secrets of future operations thrust at them, being obliged to comb London – indeed the country – for facts about named places. What precautions were to be taken? It now became obvious that officers working on topography for NID must devise their own methods of disguising and concealing operational targets. (It seems quite likely that the plan to seize Dakar was given away to the French and the Free French by, among other things, the careless competition of the three Service Ministries in the collection of information.) So Wells, when he went down to the 'Exclusive News Agency' in Roehampton made a point of buying photographs of *all* British possessions in Africa, selecting only incidentally views of French ports, including Dakar; while the London School of Hygiene and Tropical Medicine was asked to report on the very wide subject of probable casualty rates among troops moving across marshy ground anywhere in tropical latitudes, which happened to include the Dakar hinterland. Fiasco though it was, the Dakar episode put NID 6 on the map and requests for all kinds of information never stopped. By now air raids were making work so difficult in London that the section was moved in mid-September to an emergency office off the Edgware Road that had been prepared for the Admiralty. A fortnight later Bassett and his colleagues were told to pack up and prepare to move to Oxford on 10 October. There, Professor Mason had told DNI that they could have a number of rooms in the School of Geography, so that the section could work close to incomparable library resources and round the corner from the University Press, which was to undertake in topographical intelligence the greatest printing and publishing enterprise of its distinguished history. The basic conception was now beginning to form; bring all topographical work together in one place with all the apparatus of scholarship and a secure large, and up-to-date press; divide the work into country sections and give each its quota of specialists; have the editing under one authority; and add staff from all services and countries as required. This arrangement was as economical as it was logical. Oxford was considered safe, at least until Hitler began his Baedeker raids, and the secret operational work merged well with the normal activities of the University.

It is now necessary to go back a few months and examine the growth of the Contact Register. 'Why send a spy to get the facts we need if someone in this country has them already?' That, or something like it, was the question which led to the creation of a naval intelligence section merely to contact people, later to become an important joint services body working for almost every department in Whitehall. Godfrey had insisted to his Room 39 staff that there must be somewhere in the British Isles an expert on every conceivable subject; and that if he or she could be found, the clue would be found to other experts. For the upsurge of Nazism and Fascism in Europe, with its persecution of Jews and academics and non-conformist intellectuals and with its threat of war, had brought over, and was still bringing from abroad, through a score of different channels, experts in almost every field of topographical and technical and linguistic knowledge. 'Find out where these people are; have them vetted and questioned; then organize their knowledge and what it leads to' – that was the order that

304

went to NID 6 and led in January 1941 to the forming of a sub-section for contacts under Lieutenant Robert Harling, RNVR. Once the idea had been launched it grew like a snowball and by April there was a full-scale Register, directed by Mr F. M. Wonnacott, a palaeobotanist from the Natural History Department of the British Museum. This soon moved to Oxford to be near the topographical department, while the detective work in London continued under the roof of NID 21.*

Wonnacott's first objective was the immigration records of the Home Office's Aliens Department, then moved to Bournemouth. At first, with their bare and uninformative entries, they were of little value; but later they were to yield the names and whereabouts of four thousand persons ('contacts') whose topographical knowledge and the areas known to them, with dates of visits and residence, were recorded.

Once the Home Office understood how much was gained from these inquiries, it provided Wonnacott as a matter of routine with its arrival lists from airports and ports containing names and addresses of potential contacts from all over the world. Soon the inquiries spread far beyond local knowledge and terrain intelligence; people were discovered with all kinds of specialist qualifications and technical skills not yet harnessed to the war. The news of this quickly spread and helped to raise the status of the work in Whitehall, which had tended to look down its nose at NID's initiative. From the end of 1942, NID 21 as it was called, was working for everyone. A Whitehall department would inform the Register of its needs and interest; details of likely contacts were forwarded; and back would come requests for interviews. These would be mostly at Manchester College, in Oxford. There MI 5, at Blenheim close by, could arrange the security vetting and ten rooms were reserved every day up till 4 p.m. in the Wilberforce Hotel for individuals arriving from far and wide. The visitor, more often than not excited by meeting what he or she believed to be the famous 'Secret Service', would be questioned by geographers, hydrographers, economic experts and any appropriate specialists. Although every meeting of this kind was voluntary, inquiry always provoked much more information than was needed.*

By the end of the war, the Contact Register's entries in this country were 70,000 strong. There was another Register in the

Far East with a branch in Australia and an American parallel body had been started. One of its most notable products, believed to be still in existence, was a detailed geographical and personal index for Norway of 15,000 record cards which was invaluable in providing cadres for the reconstruction of the country after liberation. Indeed, it is arguable that the Register was as valuable after the war as before, for it provided large numbers of selected interpreters, civil administrators, nurses and doctors and liaison officers for the distressed and devastated areas left behind them by the Germans and the Japanese. The work was in a double sense life-saving.

Most contacts had something of value to offer. Detailed and up-to-date local knowledge which could be added to the products of existing topographical intelligence and air photography was most in demand. Photographs and maps and documents came next, with advice about local resources in power and water and oil. Through the elaborate network of the Register and its system of cross-references, an expert on Chinese junks was found in Iceland for the South-East Asia Command; a former Burma Road taxi-driver found in East Africa was flown out to do valuable work with Mountbatten's forces. When the planning of the American assault on the Mariana Islands began in early 1944, an artist was traced in England, who had spent much of his life there and was probably the only man in the world able and free to give the information required. Contacts included not only individuals but also numerous shipping companies, chambers of commerce, tourist agencies, banks and academic bodies, libraries and missionary societies, the British War Graves Commission, a sponge-importing firm which knew all about the Greek Islands, the oil and plantation companies of the Far East, crane manufacturers and dredging firms.*

Sometimes this contact work would start quite new intelligence trails, even new sectors in the intelligence empire. Lieutenant Patrick Reilly, RNVR, was originally sent by NID to collect names and information at the Royal Patriotic Schools, where all refugees from occupied Europe and other enemy countries were screened by the Security Service and then questioned for intelligence purposes. He found himself in a position with his military colleagues to produce such useful material about coastal defences, shipping movements and target intelligence generally, that the MI 19 section rapidly grew to eight Army, two Naval and three RAF officers. Likewise in the United States, where Harling had introduced the Americans to the arts of contact work, there was a rapid and at first disorderly growth of competing agencies. There were sometimes two or three American teams working on parallel lines. It was not until July 1944 that London was able to obtain from Washington topographical material on British theatres of operations, such was the Americans' suspicion and fear of British penetration of their commercial secrets. As there was precisely the same suspicion of American business aims at the London end, both sides were satisfied when it was agreed that American requests for intelligence of this kind should all be channelled through NID 21 and British requests would all be directed through its American counterpart.

This may not be the most thrilling of subjects for the historian; but to those who nourished the growth of the Register over four years it was exciting. To find the substitute for the spy, indeed someone informed in far greater detail than most spies could be, was in itself a satisfying experience; to know that each carefully questioned and recorded contact was leading to others, that the network was approaching completeness, gave at least the feeling of power and purpose organized by the counter-offensives after 1942. Order had been established where before there had been ill-mannered and confused muddle: three or four separate departments hunting round London for the same documents or photographs or information; losing or failing to return what they had borrowed; rubbing contacts up the wrong way by brusque treatment. Most remarkable of all was the way that secrecy, loyalty and trust were shown by thousands who felt they were doing their bit towards winning the war.

By the autumn of 1940 the birth-pangs of combined inter-service intelligence were growing sharper. Norway had shown up the deplorable gaps in knowledge; but it needed a fully-planned combined operation of some scale launched from Britain to convince some senior Staff Officers of the claims of terrain intelligence. The JIC and the Joint Planning Staff (see Chapter 11) were getting worried, and there was general agreement that a combined topographical organization was needed to act as a Central Clearing House for topographical information of all kinds. As a first gesture of inter-service co-operation it was agreed to form a special sub-committee of the Joint Intelligence Committee *ad hoc*, with officers representing all three services, and Colonel Bassett in the chair, to act as Central Clearing House. So it was called until February 1941 when it was renamed the Topographical Section of JIC. So the *de facto* position of NID 6 as the only organ was recognized and it received its mandate. It was to: act as a centre for collecting and collating the best available topographical information from the Service Departments and other sources; to produce reports and publications with everything of that nature that commanders planning and conducting operations might require; to supply the topographical information required by the Joint Planning Staff and Director of Combined Operations, either in the form of printed work or *ad hoc* reports for the more urgent jobs; to provide to all Service Departments topographical intelligence they might require and any information reaching it which might be usefully passed on. A tall order, for a veritable encyclopedia of world war.

Now the planners came into the picture. How were they to get facts and maps they wanted? Was the Joint Planning Staff, sitting at the right hand of the Prime Minister and the Chiefs of Staff, to make its requests to what was still virtually a minor NID section? Of course not. To cut a long story short, they were asked to tell their junior branches, the Strategical Planning Section, the Executive Planning Section and the Future Operational Planning Section to meet the new 'Clearing House' and revise their list of requirements, introducing into it clear priorities, instead of the existing jumble of immediate and contingency planning provoked by the Churchillian prayers. Out of this meeting came a list of urgently wanted areas from the Joint Planners to the JIC – Italian East Africa; Italian North Africa; the islands of Leros, Rhodes and Crete (in that order) – and the first full-scale standard questionnaire on which all future research was to be based. Previously questions had been asked higgledy-piggledy and often in unnecessary variety. The new pre-form, systemmatically laid out, intro-duced order. It was from this, in fact, that there sprang the famous series of ISIS reports (Inter-Service Information Series) which became known to all planners and operational commanders and their staffs.

The pace then began to hot up. On 11 October South Spain, in the vicinity of Gibraltar, East Tangier and Morocco, and South Norway (wanted by 27 October) were added to the list. And on 11 November Sardinia, Sicily and Tunisia – Sardinia by 16 November and the other two by the 24th. Historians of the future will marvel at the energy and optimism that these requests reflected.* They were not asking so much for detailed facts that would enable them to do something as for information that would help them to eliminate the impossible and concentrate on what could be done. Even so, the idea that Britain in late 1940 with no more than an Army Corps to spare, was capable of offensive operations in all those areas was fantastic; even the capacity to anticipate the enemy with defensive operations, e.g. near Gibraltar or in Greece, was strictly limited. Yet how else was the offensive spirit to be maintained in a country which felt certain it could not be defeated but had no idea how it was going to win? Indeed, this period of partly bogus activity was valuable in testing intelligence and eliminating futile targets.

In December 1940 at a meeting of the JIC a curious reversal of form took place. Godfrey's deputy reported that two reports on Tangier and Morocco would be ready for inspection shortly, emphasizing that they had been originally planned as covering areas of no great urgency. Now priorities had changed and they were being rushed out. The Director of Military Intelligence and his colleague of Air Intelligence thereupon expressed alarm lest these documents should be too naval in their content; the Clearing House at Oxford, they declared, must cover the requirements of all Services. They even went so far as to argue that Bassett's section (even now only seventeen strong) should be enlarged and extended on inter-service lines – which was precisely what DNI had been vainly advocating from the earliest stage of the topographical argument.

Still the battle was not properly won. A report by DNI to the JIC on 8 February 1941 went over the history of the Clearing House, described the work being done by the University Press, laid down that the priorities for the work should be directed by

JIC in accordance with the Planners' wishes. At last the co-ordinating committee of Deputy Directors – first proposed by Godfrey a year earlier – was set up, though not until the JIC paper of 24 October 1941 was it, at last, called a Department. By August the title of Inter-Services Topographical Section was beginning to appear, Army and Air Force officers were being appointed, thirty-three extra technical and clerical staff were taken on by the Admiralty and space had bcen offered by Mr Veale, the Registrar of the University, and accepted in Manchester College.*

What kind of men and women took part in preparing these handbooks for the offensive? To describe them is to highlight the outstanding qualities of the first-class intelligence officer as they were embodied, for example, in Wells, who became the department's Editor-in-Chief. A classic by training, his grasp of the military, economic and geographical material he had to supervise was only equalled by the clarity with which he handled it. Frederick Wells was a perfectionist and it was largely due to his example and insistence that no second best was good enough and that the ISTD achieved such a very high standard in its reports. It may be invidious to single out others, but the record should mention W. S. Watt, Fellow of Trinity and Tutor in Classics; Craven, Hertford and Ireland Scholar in the mid-Thirties and a double First, speaking French, German and Italian; W. S. Barrett (who produced the report for the operation against Madagascar in 1943), lecturer at Keble, Ireland, Craven and Paravacini Scholar, double First; and Charles Oldham, scholar of the same period; W. A. Sanderson, another good classic, who held a high position in an advertising agency and produced all the railway intelligence for the North African operation; W. A. Swinton of the British Museum. In each geographical section the editor and the surveyor lent by the Hydrographer collaborated as equals though the naval officer was usually in charge. Of these Captain Law was a founder member and in 1943 Commander Hughes was to create for Mountbatten in South-East Asia an organization for terrain intelligence on the Oxford model.

There were many regular officers, too, who provided an essential element of Service experience and guidance for the civilians in uniform and out of it. Colonel Sam Bassett, RM, the Director was a cheerful friendly officer with long experience of staff and intelligence work. His beach reconnaissances whilst serving as Staff Officer (Intelligence) at the Cape before the war had brought him to the notice of Godfrey. A good handler of men at all levels, not the least of his achievements at Oxford was welding the men and women of his department into a dedicated team. No one can have had a more mixed group from more diverse backgrounds, but at the club which he and his wife, Zoya, inaugurated in their own flat, all were made welcome. It was a relief to be able to relax here after the intense pressure of the day's work; ideas could be exchanged over drinks without security risks and newcomers including Norwegians, Americans and other nationalities all met one another.

Outstanding among the many women of the organization, by common consent, was Mrs Margaret Godfrey, the DNI's wife, who had assisted Bassett with the first organization of the office and then became the main contact with the University Press at Oxford, doing for Bassett to some extent what Ian Fleming did for DNI. It was she who would pass on once or twice a week the huge and costly orders for maps and reports and handbooks, acting also as direct liaison with her husband's personal staff in the Admiralty. In a family of scholars and specialists methodical in the treatment of nothing except facts, she was the greatest organizer of all.

From the first Norwegian officers and civilians were the most prominent of the Allies in the work on their own country, with which contact was kept through the small boat service called the Shetland Run (described on page 290). A steady trickle of skippers, port personnel, and agents kept the data at Oxford fresh and accurate; for example, the model prepared by the Marine Major Hicks for the X-craft attack on the battleship *Tirpitz* embodied the latest details from Altenfjord.* Later the American contingent grew in strength and experience, thanks largely to the interest Eisenhower had shown in contributing officers for the work on his own first big operation 'Torch'.

This is the place to digress briefly into the contribution made by the University Press. If the claims made for DNI's initiatives in this book are in some cases open to challenge by other departments, there is no disputing his part in bringing the

University Press at Oxford into the operational field. A minor point, perhaps, for the naval historian but an important one for the Press itself, which is very proud – but has not spoken publicly – of its part in printing first codes and ciphers for the Admiralty and then handbooks, operational orders and topographical reports for ISTD.

For the theory and practice of Intelligence the point of what follows is that the men in Room 39 had realized how the authority of the material prepared for the planners and fighting men was increased by a good, indeed a distinguished, appearance; far better a printed than a typed or run-off document. Moreover, if the work was done by a printer of repute, then it would be sure to be corrected both in manuscript and in proof with the utmost care. Once NID 6 had moved into Oxford it was natural that the immense printing orders from what was to become the inter-service centre for all terrain intelligence in Europe should go to the University Press.

Security was good. It was explained to the author by Mr Charles Batey (at that time Assistant Printer to the University) who was in charge of the operation, that military security had no novelty or terrors for an office that had long been printing four or five million examination papers a year. Mr Thompson of the Press would collect from Mrs Godfrey his material – beach reports for Norway or operational details about the Scheldt Estuary or material on South-East Asia that would be flown out to Colombo where good printing was unobtainable – and cycle a mile or so by the Parks to the Press.* There for a top-secret and urgent job a few hand-picked compositors would be put on the job at night with texts kept well away from charts and maps. The safe containing these precious documents was watched at night by one of the Home Guard company based on the Press and the finished work was then collected by the Stationery Office, who paid for it – incidentally furnishing the scarcest and best paper. Every one of thousands of copies had to be numbered and accounted for; and if there was any fear of leakage it was at the bindery stage where maps and orders came together to make sense even to a casual reader among the dozens of girls who were folding, cutting and binding.

Characteristically, Godfrey saw to it that this excellent service from Oxford was brought to the attention of the Board.

In a minute of 17 November 1942 he drew their attention to the ISIS report on Algeria produced for 'Torch': 'As a comprehensive piece of good craftsmanship and editing the work is probably unique and I doubt if a commander of an expedition has ever before been given his intelligence in such a complete, readable and legible form. General Eisenhower has written a very nice letter of thanks. Similar publications have also been produced recently for Burma, Sardinia and Thailand.' On which the First Sea Lord (Dudley Pound) commented the next day, 'This is a great achievement' and the First Lord (A. V. Alexander) added 'I agree.'

For the Printer to the University, Dr John Johnson, who had made all the arrangements for this great enterprise personally with the DNI, it had been an unusual and refreshing experience to work with a Service Ministry much more sympathetic and imaginative than he had believed possible. When the Godfreys were preparing to leave for India in the end of 1942, Dr Johnson asked them to accept one or two Oxford books to commemorate their work together. In a letter of 26 November he wrote this remarkable tribute:

The Press feels forlorn at the prospect of losing you both. Mrs Godfrey came in to say good-bye last night. The truth is, of course, that you, if I may say so without impertinence, have learned the great secret of giving a spiritual and human value to every side of life, including business life, and happily life (even business life) still responds to such treatment as this. And so it was easy for you, being you, to understand what few understand, that this printing business, as Batey and I envisage it, is here to give a selfless (not, I hope, characterless) service to those who come to it. We are all of us just one gang.

Back in London men from the typographical and newspaper world like Robert Harling, Patrick Reilly and Hippisley-Cox, all of them young RNVR officers who combined in singular measure persuasive charm and ruthless vigour, were building up the sources of intelligence from contacts, refugees and business houses. Dull-sounding work, perhaps, but in the atmosphere of the early days exciting and exacting because of the feeling that the tide must soon turn and information was being built up as ammunition for future offensives. There was the thrill of pursuit – of people, papers, books and secrets – and

313

also the satisfaction of seeing foundations laid for such vast enterprises as the Contact Register and the Photographic Library.

It is perhaps worth reminding Treasury officials that for men and women of the qualifications required at Oxford the salaries offered were of the grade paid to second-class commercial travellers. For an average working day of twelve hours in a seven-day week – which was normal in periods of pressure – the pay was £7 to £8 a week, out of which some of the married men had to maintain two homes. When Bassett, in March 1943, was pleading the case of his staff, he gave illustrations of the intensive work that was required. Three technical civilian assistant officers worked every day of the week until three or four in the morning, and on the last two days continuously for thirty-two hours (except for meal intervals). In producing the ISIS reports for the landing in North Africa, work went on at this rate of pressure for about two months; and the same is true of the period in 1944 before the Normandy Landings. Indeed, in Combined Operations Headquarters, on 1 May 1942, a memorandum was circulated advising its intelligence sections to suspend requests to Oxford for a while 'as the ISTD staff are working twenty-four hours a day and it is feared some may collapse'.

To return to the turning-point year of 1943, specialist sections distinct from the main producing section had begun to appear. Lieutenant Gerald Andrews, RM, had to himself an economic section reporting on resources; for the more resources a target area could offer the less shipping was needed to supply it. He also looked after the requirements of SOE. There came a railway unit from the War Office, a geological section and specialist in fire susceptibility, who could assess what kinds of roofs and what kind of building patterns presented the best targets for fire raids. There was also NID 11, the Photographic Library, which had originated with Wells's first sporadic collection of pictures in 1940 for impending operations. Thousands of photographs had been offered by the public to NID 6 and very soon there was a library in the making which needed only a staff and copying machinery. DNI pressed hard for action, and very soon the Admiralty Photographic Library was the largest single library of topographical photographs in the country, with a monthly output of copies to operational areas of more than 300,000. It led a semi-autonomous existence under Mr Rodney Slessor in the basement of the Bodleian Library. Its busiest hour was when the DNI appealed on the BBC for photographs to be sent in by the public about any foreign areas they knew. The response was enormous – people emptied their boxrooms – thirty thousand replied, instead of the ten thousand that had been expected. For a time, the sorting, captioning and filing staff of Wrens increased to hundreds. Some of the collections sent in were valuable ones which were housed in the Bodleian and returned after the War.

Maps of course needed similar special attention. A small unit at Oxford of draughtsmen and draughtswomen (twenty-one strong in July 1941) prepared, in collaboration with the Admiralty's own drawing office, the thousands of maps that went into the operation orders and plans for the next four years. As the basis of their work they used a large collection of *Times Atlases* contributed by the public after a wireless appeal. Printing was done by the helpful and efficient Geographical Section of the General Staff.

In Oxford the emphasis had always been on offensive operations into Europe either by forces based on Britain or by forces in the Mediterranean. For those areas ISTD could collect, print and deliver. Clearly they could not do the same for the operations developing in South-East Asia and the Pacific. In India, the base for all activity east of Suez, the Army was dominant and the NID could not expect to take the initiatives it had shown in London. The next best thing was to transplant as much of ISTD as would travel and see what happened. It would probably mean conflict with the Government of India and the Army, but Mountbatten personally supported the idea.

In August 1943 the South-East Asia Command was formed and it became clear that Mountbatten, its chief, would expect from his staff the same standard of terrain intelligence that he had been given from Oxford when he was chief of Combined Operations. In fact, as things were, he was unlikely to get it. For its best intelligence it had to rely on CHQ India, whence the Director of Military Intelligence had gone to London in June of that year to discuss with people at Oxford the forming of a topographical department on inter-service lines. The idea was that this should be an outpost of Oxford, which would produce the final and comprehensive work whilst India produced such interim and *ad hoc* reports as were needed for local planning and operational purposes. In the event, the outpost, which had only eleven officers for most of the time and seventeen in the last two months, was not up to the task.

Harling, who had been sent out by DNI on a mission to co-ordinate this work between the USA, Australia and India, reported unfavourably on India, and on 7 January 1944 DNI was asked to send out a small expert team from Oxford to reorganize everything. Not surprisingly, the request came from Major General Lamplough, an able and energetic Marine Officer, who had been DDNI under Godfrey and knew the complicated subject backwards. The Director of Military Intelligence in turn agreed that the reconstructed department should be under the control of Mountbatten's command and in March 1944 the party, headed by Cdr A. M. Hughes one of Oxford's naval surveyors, arrived on their very difficult mission.

Hughes's first report showed a mood of near-despair. The Indian ISTD had been badly organized and was under-staffed. There was too much stress on local knowledge, regardless of the incompetence of those who had it; security did not exist; photo reproduction was very poor; there was no Railways and Resources section to provide the information that would be desperately needed as SEAC moved into Malaya, Burma and Indo-China. What worried him especially was that he could not reproduce the Oxford system of having in each country section one specialist officer each on resources, geology, engineering and railways, because there were too few people. The American geologist he had been promised, for instance, could not be levered out of Karachi, where he was doing censorship duties. Tin miners and rubber planters, he emphasized, cannot do intelligence research or write clearly, and any reminder of the hard-learnt lessons of Oxford was resented by the authorities in the huge Delhi hierarchy. This was partly because Central Headquarters could not find the kind of Army officers that were needed and they had to be persuaded that 'globetrotters' were no good.

Despite lack of typewriters and duplicating machines, the

absence of good presses, compositors and proof-readers, they managed to keep just ahead of the demands of the troops in Burma. Hughes recalls one job which required the typing of some 400 wax stencils, running off on a Gestetner machine 300 copies of each, collation by hand of 120,000 duplicated pages, the folding and binding of 20,000 plans and the pasting-up of many thousands of photographs. In other words, India in 1944 was almost back where the Admiralty had been in June 1940.

At the end of 1944 a very worried and overworked Hughes returned to England to present in person the facts about the impossible staff situation. He had, for example, until the spring of 1945 only five draughtsmen who found themselves with sixty-one plans to deal with in a fortnight. It was an amazing effort but it was not the way to provide good intelligence. There was no worthy outside printer and Army printing barely existed. His long-term report on Central Burma had been at the printer for six months. On the other hand, the first full-scale operational report on ISIS lines had been specially written for General Stilwell in May 1944 dealing with the Mogaung-Myitkyina area – and had been highly praised.

Hughes went back to Ceylon,* to which his staff had been moved in April, feeling somewhat reassured by promises of help. But difficulties persisted, and the spring of 1945 brought a fresh spate of planning. Fourteen strategic areas in South-East Asia were selected for priority between March to August and Form-at-a-Glance reports, with text, photographs and plans, were coming once a fortnight, even after the Japanese surrender.

The experience in India and Ceylon had proved in the most painful and visible form the soundness of the Oxford experiment and the consequences of disregarding its lessons:

(a) There must be a staff of individual experts in the fields of geography, geology, hydrography, engineering (rail, road and water transport) and economics.

(b) They should be brought into combination, in close proximity, to work together on a given area, collecting, sharing and comparing all the available intelligence on that area.

(c) All their work should be collated through an editor, who checks and cross-checks in the process, so as to present a

317

co-ordinated and coherent picture of all the more or less permanent features of the area. For almost all the permanent and many of the man-made features will have operational significance.

That was the lesson and one can only hope that neither in the United States nor in this country has it been forgotten; for if there is one branch of intelligence in which a little money and a few persons used in peace will save lives, time and vast sums of money in war, it is this one.

14 Back into Europe

'This vast operation is undoubtedly the most complicated and difficult that has ever taken place. It involves tides, winds, waves, visibility, both from the air and the sea standpoint, and the combined employment of land, air and sea forces in the highest degree of intimacy and in contact with conditions that could not and cannot be fully foreseen.'

(Winston Churchill to the
House of Commons, 6 June 1944)

'My colleagues and I cannot but admit that the history of warfare knows no other like undertaking from the point of view of its scale, its vast conception and its masterly execution.'

(Stalin: message to
Churchill, 11 June 1944)

And, the great men might have added, an intelligence operation unparalleled in the depth of its detail, the scale and accuracy of the final picture, and the ingenuity of its deception measures.

As Admiral Sir Bertram Ramsay, Eisenhower's Naval Commander (ANCXF), wrote in his final Report: 'Intelligence for "Neptune" was the outcome of years of research with unequalled resources by large and specialized inter-service bodies. It was complete and detailed.'

It is difficult even now, when time has eliminated detail and brought perspective, to visualize how four years' plodding packaging of detail became the brilliant assault panorama of the Bay of the Seine, sixty-five miles wide as the crow flies from Barfleur to Cap d'Antifer, the distance from Portsmouth to Eastbourne.

It might be thought that 'Neptune', the operation of landing

319

in Normandy, must be primarily a naval intelligence concern. In fact, NID played most of the time second, or even third, fiddle to military and air intelligence. Yet what the Navy demanded of the OIC on D-day was, next to the Battle of the Atlantic, the most exacting assignment of the war. First, it required the most precise hour-to-hour facts about the enemy's movements and dispositions in the Channel, about E-boats and R-boats, submarines and special fighting craft, mine-sweeping and mine laying. Then for our own ships, whether on reconnaissance or on patrol prior to D-day itself, the enemy's swept channels and coastal shipping routes, all to be noted and fitted into the 'Neptune' plan. The Naval Staff also required appreciations of how the enemy would react at sea to the assault. Last, but in the long run most important, the closest watch had to be kept on attempts by Doenitz to cut the lines of supply and reinforcement to Normandy not only across the Channel from Sussex and Hampshire ports, but also from the Bristol Channel, from Liverpool and the Clyde, and from the United States and Canada.

This was all work for Clayton, Denning, Winn & Co. in the OIC, which found itself in the summer of 1944 more on top of the battle, more of an operational headquarters, than it had been since the days of Dunkirk. But for the study of the beaches and the cliffs, of the underwater obstacles and the coastal defences by gun and mine, of the sites for radar and the targets for naval bombardment, NID had first to work with and then largely depend on an inter-service Theatre Intelligence Section expanding from three to five hundred, in which leading personalities wore khaki. For the key to the enemy's defence system in France was his order-of-battle, and order-of-battle is to the soldier what ship movements are to the sailor: the evidence of the enemy's strength and intentions.

By spring 1944 Godfrey had been eighteen months away from the Division, but what was required under his successor Rushbrooke was precisely the close inter-service teamwork that was so hard to get in the early days. It meant the continuous exercise of firmness in a friendly spirit, a nice judgement of when the Director should support his officers working on 'Neptune' – or the naval point of view – and when not. The Division had to prepare and hand over all naval intelligence bearing however remotely on the coastal defences of occupied Europe across the Channel; then it had to take part, through its representatives among General Morgan's planners and intelligence staff, in digesting and shaping an inter-service product; finally it had to plan distribution of maps and charts, plans and photographic silhouettes to 4,000 ships and several thousand smaller craft. As if that were not enough, its officers were expected by the Fleet to provide any facts it might require for, say, German aircraft recognition, estimating the range and calibre of the enemy's coastal guns and dealing with the new pressure or oyster mine or the booby traps left in harbours abandoned by him.

Here an incident may be recalled which was unfortunately typical of the attitude taken by the Soviet Navy at the time. During March–April 1944 some small Black Sea ports were recaptured by Soviet forces and it was hoped in London that something might be found out about German booby traps, mines and demolition methods which would be useful in Normandy. For much depended on the speed with which Cherbourg, Le Havre and other ports could be brought into operation when captured. Moscow was asked that Lieutenant Shirley, RNVR, a bomb disposal expert, should immediately visit the Black Sea and make a rapid survey. Weeks passed in bargaining and obstruction by the Soviet naval authorities; when D-day came Shirley was still waiting in Sevastopol for permission. The denial of this important intelligence puzzled most people in NID except the new Deputy Director, Captain Clanchy, just back from a spell in Moscow as Naval Attaché, deeply disillusioned.

The parent of 'Neptune' was 'Operation Sea-lion', the German plan for landings in Kent and Sussex which Hitler first postponed and then abandoned. From June 1940, when France fell, to June 1944, when the Atlantic Wall was breached, there stretches an unbroken line of intelligence research and planning, which were first defensive, then offensive in motive. Indeed, in NID one man was chiefly responsible throughout the long vigil over the Channel: Lieutenant-Commander George Gonin, RN, a retired officer, who had spent many years in business in Antwerp and had made himself an expert on the barges, coasts, ports and inland waters of the Low

Countries and Northern France. Gonin's section began the study of the coasts across the Channel and the North sea at the time when it seemed that German landings must be attempted. That was before the Battle of Britain in September shattered for good German hopes of winning command of the air over Southern England and made it possible for Gonin and his opposite numbers in the War Office to set about switching from defensive to offensive thinking, which was to produce among other things his idea for the Commando raid on the lock gates of St Nazaire.

There was a certain exasperating irony in their labours. For the coasts about which they had to collect every tiny detail were in Allied countries. Such was the confidence in the strength of France that it had not occurred to British intelligence or planning departments that they might need detailed information about her beaches or those of Belgium, Holland and Norway or about the ports and the defences inland from these coasts. There was plenty of material to be had in Britain about the 'Neptune' area, once an effort was made to collect it; but it needed assessing and collating, and above all plotting on up-to-date maps. No one was to blame for this state of affairs; and the strenuous effort made to put it right was showing results by 1942. The Home Forces Command, set up to organize Britain's defence against invasion, remained in being after the threat had passed; and NID (1), War Office (MI 14) and the Photographic Intelligence units just beginning to emerge worked away on their recording and plotting. But until March 1943 there was no certainty of an assault across the Channel, and energies could not be concentrated on targets which the staff believed to be possible.

Not since the abortive Dardanelles landings of twenty-five years earlier had Navy and Army faced the possibility of combined operations against a defended coast on such a scale. There was no precedent for the demands that were to be made. For example, the Director of Military Intelligence wanted a set of 1 : 50,000 scale maps, covering to a depth of ten miles the whole coast from Ostend to Cherbourg, giving details of coast, beach and A/A defences, airfields, W/T and RD/F stations, dumps and installations. The Admiralty could furnish only up-to-date navigation charts with different scale and projection, without anything indicated inshore except the most obvious landmarks. Nor had it made any detailed study of the beaches and the water close inshore; for normally (as the Navy enjoys reminding the Army) sailors are concerned with avoiding rocks and shoals, not in getting over them and up the beaches. So landing craft needed both navigational guidance and beach intelligence. Which was military and which was naval? A nice point!

A further problem. No existing naval charts would be any use for precise and long-range naval bombardment of inshore targets; likewise the Army's maps, while providing distances and reference points for targets, would be useless for accurate positioning of bombarding ships. Moreover their maps were based on a sixty-year-old French survey, the accuracy of which was in doubt. Discrepancies of up to 800 yards were discovered, which might mean that ships would shell our own troops instead of the enemy. Obviously the military and naval requirements would have to be got somehow on to one kind of composite chart-map.

Working together, the Hydrographer's Department* of the Admiralty and the War Office Ordnance Survey Department could produce the 'chart-maps' on the required scale; but they would not be sufficiently large to make it possible to neglect the difference between the Mercator projection of the charts and the conical projection of the War Office maps. However, in spite of all the difficulties, chart-maps – asked for vainly in 1915 but now normal equipment for combined operations – were standardized in time for the landing of November 1942 in North Africa.

An example of the pangs that attended the birth of interservice planning is worth recording. The important committee meeting at which the Admiralty's Director of Navigation and the Hydrographer were persuaded that the Army grid system should be imposed on the naval charts was not without its hazards and comic moments. Those two officers, with representatives of Plans, Gunnery and Operations Divisions, met the NID representatives, with the head of the German section, Commander Tower, in the chair. The Hydrographer and the responsible civil servants argued that the cost of the change would be astronomical but they admitted that the job could be done – and fairly quickly. After two hours' argument in which the Director of Navigation was hardest to persuade, provisional agreement was reached, but the opposition insisted on the minutes being agreed after circulation. On leaving the meeting, Tower asked his officer from IL whether he had taken full notes; to which came the reply that he had been too busy arguing the case for the chart-maps to take any notes. However, the woman assistant to the German section had taken some notes and thought she could write up adequate minutes. Not surprisingly, the technicalities of the subject defeated her and it was clear that to present such minutes would wreck the agreement so laboriously reached. The NID man then explained the predicament to his Sapper colleagues in Home Forces (on whose behalf he had been arguing), and they kindly wrote out exactly what was wanted to achieve the planners' objects. The minutes were then readily accepted by all except their chief naval opponent; he protested, quite correctly, that they had been faked. Only by eating humble pie for an hour and protesting his ignorance of the subject was the NID officer concerned able to talk his angry senior officer into agreement.

Already in 1941 it had become obvious that it was not sufficient for the appropriate NID section just to pass on to the soldiers at Home Forces all the intelligence about enemy coasts opposite Britain that came its way. There would have to be a naval officer working side by side with the soldiers, plotting their results in the same way that he plotted his. The Navy must accept the role of second fiddle to the Army. The two kinds of intelligence were interdependent; for example, accurate noting of coastal defences for the Navy was not possible without an expert knowledge of the whereabouts of the Germany military units that would man these defences, and only the Army with its enemy order-of-battle could have that. Likewise they had a joint interest in and use for the results of air reconnaissance which over the years built up pictures of the coasts into one vast strip of amazing detail. To help him keep his plot the NID man, Lt-Cdr Rees-Millington, RN (Retired), engaged a well-known woman illustrator of books on birds' eggs, whose neat calligraphy and eye for detail were very appropriately employed.

All this time there was no particular section of the coast of occupied western Europe that interested the planners of the ultimate return. Intelligence was not adequate; experience of large-scale landing operations hardly existed until after 'Torch' in November 1942; not enough was known about the range of future fighter aircraft which would have to cover any major assault. None the less an Intelligence Staff for Home Forces had been formed in the War Cabinet Offices during that year and its main task was to keep track of the enemy's building of the Atlantic Wall (which began in winter of 1941).

As fast as the Germans and their forced labour constructed the large battery positions, the cunningly sited pillboxes, the communication trenches, the tank obstacles at beach exits, the fortified buildings on the fronts of seaside holiday resorts, intelligence was recording them. No. 140 Squadron (Army Co-operation) was taking endless pictures of beach gradients, and the material for coastal silhouettes at zero level from three miles to seaward was ready in the late summer of 1942. As soon as a new battery was spotted, photographs were taken and agents' reports laid on. Each battery had its own folder with the grid reference, latitude and longitude, siting and arc of fire, calibre and number of guns and so on. As time went on, the intelligence staff devised a rough formula for showing the strength of the coastal defences in each sector: the number of guns was multiplied by the calibre of guns in inches and divided by the length of the coastal strip in miles. By plotting the strengths on a coloured trace which could be laid over the great wall maps of the Normandy and Brittany coasts, it became obvious at a glance where the attack might have to be made. There stood out three soft – or less tough – spots: between the Somme and Le Havre; the bay between Le Havre and Cherbourg; the north coast of Brittany. The form could be seen at a glance.

In 1942 work on 'Round-up', the naval side of the projected invasion of Europe, formally began with Admiral Sir Bertram Ramsay as naval Commander-in-Chief designate and Captain V. Hughes-Hallett as commander of Force J, which was to train officers and men in the Isle of Wight and study landing problems there and in Scotland. Very soon this force had lost ships and men taken off to North Africa; but intelligence took a step forward with the forming of a Combined Intelligence

Section (CIS), in Norfolk House, St James's Square, London.

At this stage, in mid-1942, what was required first was 'intelligence, at short notice, which would enable a decision to be reached on the area or areas to be assaulted'. This meant keeping up to date a master chart of the whole Channel and North Sea area and four copies. Copies of all Admiralty charts of the area would also be kept corrected. When the actual area to be assaulted had been decided on, it was estimated that about ten different charts would be affected and that the planners would probably want twenty-five copies of each. Then in the spring of 1943 there was another change at Norfolk House. Lieutenant-General Morgan – who laid all the foundations for Eisenhower, Montgomery and Bradley – formed a staff to the Supreme Allied Commander (designate) of which he was chief, whence the title COSSAC. This was given a new naval planning staff for which Lt-Commander Rees-Millington did the liaison with the Admiralty, and in which Lt-Commander Richardson, RNVR, became Staff Officer (Intelligence) to the group.*

In May 1943, a storm blew up in this headquarters which were better ignored by history if it did not show the kind of difficulties into which large-scale intelligence work can run, and the kind of differences between Army and Navy methods that have had to be overcome in the long-drawn post-war struggle over integration of the Services. First the contrast between naval and military methods. When a military operation was planned abroad by the soldiers, a separate force was set up to train and prepare for it. Its Intelligence Chief would draw all his requirements from Military Intelligence, War Office; and until zero hour on D-day the Intelligence staff of the force did not operate. Intelligence in the Admiralty, on the other hand, because the Fleet is in constant operation was kept on a fluid day-to-day basis, with planning and intelligence in the early stages of any operation concentrated in the Naval Staff. What then was to happen in a great combined operation from our own shores?

At that date the invasion of Europe was, so far as the Army was concerned, still the business of C-in-C Home Forces, under General Sir Bernard Paget, who had succeeded Sir Alan Brooke. His headquarters were at Slough, three-quarters of an hour by car from London; but the military officers in the

Norfolk House allied intelligence staff, without a Supreme Allied Commander, were under his command. One of them had pointed out to him in a memorandum how material for the invasion of Europe was being studied by six different sections of MI, by the Admiralty, Norfolk House, Home Forces Combined Operations, the Combined Photographic Interpretation Unit at Medmenham, Economic Warfare and Foreign Office. There was wasteful overlapping and at no place was the total picture being studied, except perhaps at Norfolk House.

General Paget proposed that the right place for the Norfolk House staff was with him at Slough; when this idea was turned down, a block of buildings in South Kensington was suggested. This, too, was passionately opposed, notably by the NID representative who pleaded that a move would cut off the combined intelligence workers from the planners in Whitehall, with whom they were in constant contact, from their sources of intelligence in the Ministries and from Combined Operations HQ in Whitehall, who were conducting small operations against the coasts of Northern Europe, most of which had an incidental intelligence purpose. Then it was suggested that only the Army officers at Norfolk House might be withdrawn to Home Forces to concentrate on that Headquarters' role in the invasion plans. This, too, was opposed on the grounds that to break up a team of experts in this way would be criminal.

Home Forces for a time won the day and the team endured a painful period of exile at Ilchester House, cut off from its sources and increasingly out of touch.* But soon the drawbacks were admitted, and the combined Section, now known as the Theatre Intelligence Section (TIS) merged with the Supreme Allied Headquarters staff until it finally arrived in the spring of 1944 at Southwick, near Portsmouth.

The comment made to the DNI, Rushbrooke, on this episode by one of his officers is worth quoting:

It shows how the traditions, procedure and etiquette of the Services differ in ways that are not suspected in early stages and while work proceeds smoothly. There are often misconceptions and false assumptions which break surface in times of stress and crisis, revealing divergencies of aim and method, and causing confusion and suspicion of integrity and good faith.

When all had been said and done the fact remained that General Morgan, preparing the way for Eisenhower, inspired the utmost co-operation from his mixed staff. By the summer of 1943, he was able to say that they must be ready 'to assault the Normandy beaches about Bayeux by 1 May 1944'. 'I suggest,' he wrote in a document circulated on 15 July 1943 to a very few officers in the secret, 'it is necessary to adopt the outlook that "Operation Overlord" is even now in progress and to take all possible steps to see that all agencies that can be brought to bear are co-ordinated so as to bring about the state of affairs that would have to exist on the chosen day of the assault.'

How was it possible suddenly to be so specific? It had become apparent early on that the coastal defences of the Bay of the Seine were much weaker than any other landing area over which the RAF could give fighter protection from Britain. It also became evident, from close topographical study, that the landing beaches in this area, although not the best available, were quite reasonably good, and that various military features governing the choice – for example, sites for airfield construction, suitable ground for tank deployment, etc. – were good, even allowing for the Normandy bocage.* Every section of the coast from Brittany to Holland had been scrutinized with these requirements in mind, and the Bay of the Seine clearly offered the best compromise between all factors. But the very feature which explained the Germans' deliberate – if only relative – neglect of its defences was also the main difficulty to be solved by the planners; it was remote from good harbours. Le Havre was forty miles away from Arromanches at the bay's centre and Cherbourg fifty. It was during a discussion of this difficulty that Commodore Hughes-Hallet first suggested the building of artificial harbours.

With the date and the target area roughly known, the mood of the intelligence staff had become dynamic. Contact between Eisenhower's Naval Commander, Admiral Ramsay, and DNI became much closer, as Captain J. H. Lewes, RN, a leading member of the Room 39 group, joined Admiral Ramsay as Chief of Staff (Intelligence) in March 1944. Also there began, in November 1943, a series of 'low level' Wednesday meetings with Captain Clanchy, DDNI, in the chair, at which innumerable practical details and difficulties were thrashed out between the Naval men from Norfolk House and the NID sections concerned with 'Neptune'. In March, with the landings only three months off, another secret committee presided over by Ian Fleming, now Cdr RNVR, organized the flow of cryptographic and other Naval wireless intelligence available, or to be expected, from Station X during the vast operations ahead. It was easy to foresee that there would be a mass of important tactical and low-grade wireless traffic among the enemy naval and air forces operating in the Channel, which would be of vital importance to our own units at sea. How was material to get to the force commanders? In what form? With what delays? For a brief spell it was thought wise to channel all intelligence direct from Station X to Admiral Ramsay's staff, so cutting out the Admiralty's OIC. But they soon found that the handling of such material was far beyond their resources and experience, and the job was quickly returned to Admiral Clayton and his men in the Citadel, who had the vast signals and teleprinter machine of the Admiralty to draw on.

Yet another NID group, but with high-level representatives from Torpedoes and Mines, Scientific Research, Local Defences and Signals Division, invited all and sundry to raise any question or speculation about the enemy response to our assault. Talking was informal; wild ideas were not laughed at; laymen and experts stimulated one another's imaginations. What the amateur might suggest facetiously, the scientist did not automatically reject. At the first meeting, for example, they discussed possible methods of close defence that the Germans might use, including blinding and dazzling lights, high power electricity, blazing oil, spiked concrete mattresses on beaches, smoke screens, tear and other gases, flame-throwers. It was found that the use of high power electricity had not in fact been thought of, nor had the dangers of underwater hedgehogs to the Mulberry floating harbours been closely examined. Commander Denning pointed out to Admiral Ramsay's representative that the E-boats, which had been very active close to the south coast, might now be seeking intelligence rather than targets among coastal convoys. They might be using infra-red and bolometer ship-watching devices and it would be useful if E-boats could be captured rather than

329

sunk so as to check on their latest equipment. Later on, prisoners of war from these boats revealed that reconnaissance had indeed become their main task.

There was naturally deep anxiety about what the enemy might know. Confident though Whitehall was that very few, if any, agents were reporting back on our invasion preparations, it was worried about what might be discovered, despite Fighter Command's domination of the skies, by air reconnaissance, either visual or photographic. On 15 March Admiral Ramsay's chief intelligence officer reported that there had been no enemy reconnaissance over the south coast for a fortnight. In May, it was reported that the regular reconnaissances over our coasts had been increasing since 19 April. It is now known from the German records how unfruitful these were.*

The Director of Torpedoes and Mining was so insistent at this committee on the dangers to the Mulberry scheme of underwater explosive obstacles that a special concerted effort was made to collect every scrap of intelligence that might bear on mining. Clearly, as the Germans did not know where we were going to attack, they would be involved in an enormous outlay of material and labour if they tried to mine and place underwater obstacles along the whole French coast. Somewhere a sign of this would appear, somewhere on the line from the beaches to the factories where mines and explosives were known to be made. In March the German section received evidence that there had been some mining of shallow water and the erection in concrete beds of stakes tipped with explosives – but precise location was missing. In April there was reported from Germany and occupied Europe a demand for glass-blowers to assist in turning out mines; but nothing to suggest a really large-scale effort. In May Commander Tower of the German Section could report definitely: 'no *concentration* of beach obstacles in any one area'. Thus the danger which haunted DTM and other planners was kept in proportion, neither overlooked nor exaggerated.

When every speck and crumb of information that could be extracted from tourists' postcards, holiday guides, air photographs, agents' reports, prisoners of war and maps had been recorded, there remained unanswered queries which must be settled if armoured vehicles, guns and transport were ever to get across and away from those holiday beaches. Queries about depth and firmness of sand, the exact slope of the shingle, the natural anti-tank obstacles made by rocks and falls of cliff, the dead ground between coastal defences and the water's edge – above all the presence or absence of mines. Someone had to be sent; this was an example of how the eye and the knowledge of the spy can suddenly be indispensable. The men chosen must be experts; above all, they must not be caught or even seen: for that might give the enemy the hint he needed about the beaches chosen for landing.

Operation 'Postage Able' for the reconnaissance of the French beaches promised every conceivable hazard that an intelligence operation can offer. The story chosen for telling here is of midget craft X 20 with a crew of five under Lt-Cdr Willmott, RN, of whom the Commander-in-Chief Portsmouth was to write in February 1944: 'The cool and calculated bravery required to make this sustained and impudent recon- naissance under the very noses of the enemy and in the extremely unnatural conditions of life in X 20 is quite out- standing.' The reconnaissances were planned to take place during late December 1943 and January 1944; two east of Cotentin, two in the Channel Islands, and eight between Le Havre and Ostend. Willmott's assignment was to the Baie de la Seine where the landings were to be actually made. His orders were to ascertain where there were beach minefields and to bring back samples of mines if possible; to note types and dimensions of anti-tank walls and other obstacles; to study gradients of beaches; collect sand and shingle specimens, and find out the 'nature of inundations locally'.

OIC did the best it could for the expedition in the way of local intelligence based on its long and close study of German coastal traffic. Willmott was told that the bay was probably patrolled by armed trawlers in the dark hours only; for three recent inshore sweeps by our ships in daylight had failed to find any enemy. He was warned that there was frequent movement of small vessels and barges during darkness, but that the convoys from Le Havre to Cherbourg did not run regularly and dared not make the passage by day. The routes of these convoys were given in detail and a swept passage six to eight cables wide through the minefields was identified for him. He was particularly warned that German convoys would have escorts on a front as wide as two miles on either side and that the escort vessels would have hydrophones but no Asdic. Major Scott-Bowden, the sapper expert who went on the operation, was also shown 1:5,000 beach maps annotated in the light of photographic reconnaissance from the air.

The operation, thanks to the skill and patience of the party, was successful. On 18 January X 20 did a periscope examination of the beach at Les Moulins during the afternoon and at night the Major and Sgt Ogden Smith swam ashore (over 500 yards and back) and inspected the St Laurent beach. On the 19th the same programme was repeated further east and on the 20th Vierville was done by periscope only. Once or twice Willmott thought they had been detected, but satisfied himself that stray shots from sentries were not aimed at them. They returned with precious information. The bearing capacity of the beaches they had surveyed was 'adequate for all vehicles'. They found 'well compacted sand' but 'runnels existed at low water mark which might drown vehicles'. The shingle at the back of the beach on the average lay at a slope of 1 in 8 to an average height of six feet. They reported the stretches of beach where footprints showed there were no mines. High water mark was recorded as 25 yards from the back of the beach and low water 265 yards away. Depths of water approaching the beaches were checked against their charts, and the coastal silhouette was carefully compared with photographs. Such was the exacting standard of terrain intelligence set by the scholar-staff officers at their desks.

Penned up in their little craft for three days, cramped for movement and breathing, eating and performing their natural functions as best they could, in constant fear of detection, the crew of X 20 had a painful ordeal. Their Commander reported:

All personnel remained reasonably fit during the operation. Benzedrene and Hyoscine as prescribed helped in some cases although there were times when some members felt very bad. The effects, however, showed themselves forcibly during the days after return to base.

Lieut-Commander Richardson, RNVR, recalls for the edification of future intelligence officers his own experience

332

over underwater obstacles.* The Chief of Combined Operations (CCO) (Lord Mountbatten), was convinced from the earliest days that such obstacles in the most ingenious and grisly form would confront any operation. As papers came round once a fortnight, Richardson would write painstakingly that there were still no signs of such obstacles, that if the Germans *did* attempt to use them, we would at once from photographic reconnaissance locate their prepared dumps and that if they *did* decide to use them they would not know the place of our landing or the state of the tide to be expected and could not therefore place them effectively. Getting tired of repeating himself, Richardson wrote on a minute sheet:

> How doth the busy CCO
> Invest each empty shore
> With underwater obstacles
> That were not there before.

Ten days after this the dreaded obstacles began to appear all over European coasts like an infectious rash. They had not been revealed in dumps because there were no dumps; the Germans had simply removed tank and other obstacles from the roads and put them on to the beaches.

'Operation Torch' had revealed to NID and everyone else what neatness of organization and tenacity of security were needed when the moment came to distribute to the large forces taking part in such landings the intelligence collected for them. In 'Neptune' it was infinitely worse. Thousands – not hundreds – of ships and craft required it in clear and convenient form. It had to go out in time to reach everyone so that they could study it, but not too early to exclude late changes or to prejudice security. Every copy handed over had to be recorded and signed for. Planning memoranda, required for the lower formations had to include a long description of the whole of the enemy's defences.

One member of the intelligence staff at Southwick wrote down at the time what happened on the night before the great armada sailed. Admiral Creasy, chief of staff to Ramsay, told all those in the war room at 11.30 'It's time to turn in'; and so they all did, but they were up at the crack of dawn on that bright but unsettled June morning to read the first signals from the ships and craft they had set in motion and the first intercepted signals showing German reactions:

As they came in one by one, announcing accurate timely and undiscovered arrival, we knew that our long labours had not been in vain.* 'Neptune' – our plan – would be a success. The feat at which, as Admiral Creasy had once put it, the Spaniards failed and which in their turn Napoleon and Hitler had funked, had been accomplished. We felt a twinge of pride, a sharp elation, and then we returned to our desks. We who had planned this adventure now had to control it.

If 'Neptune's' success and 'Overlord's' subsequent triumph owed much to the work here described, a heart-warming example of inter-service teamwork which in 1939 would have seemed impossible, something is also due to the German failure on the other side of the Channel to achieve a comparable trust and co-ordination. One may doubt whether British deception measures would have been so successful had German intelligence work been more objective and less dominated by the soldiers' view of the facts. Because their agents' organization in Britain was by the summer of 1944 virtually useless as a source of tactical naval or military information, and because they had lost the power to make regular, detailed and deep air reconnaissance, the Germans seem to have been the more vulnerable to general judgements promising comfort rather than menace.

Their records show them, for example, appreciating that the Allies had an invariable technique or programme for assault from the sea. The *point of landing* would be (i) near at least one good port; (ii) not in the face of cliffs except on a wide shore; (iii) in deep water, where there was no surf and no reefs or strong currents. The *time* of landing would be (i) in fine calm weather; (ii) on a rising tide; (iii) and with a new moon. In the event the 'Neptune' landings took place at full moon, at low water, at several points before cliffs which were promptly scaled, and with considerable sea and wind. That such possibilities were not considered is all the more surprising because a landing exercise which was part of the deception plan (directed at a landing before Calais) was held shortly before D-day before dawn and at low water on the British side of the Channel.

It seems possible that the calculation of what Eisenhower's

armada could or would try to do in Normandy was influenced by memories of the advice given four years before to Hitler by his naval staff, when they were planning the invasion of Kent and Sussex. The sailors advised that for navigational reasons the best period for landing was two hours before high water. The soldiers demanded that for military reasons it must be before dawn; the actual crossing of the Channel must be during the hours of darkness with a certain amount of light for a very short period. These requirements (there were comparable requirements in the case of 'Neptune') limited the invasion dates to a few days in each month.

We now know that there was a violent scene between Admiral Schniewind and General Halder in August 1940, when the latter insisted that the attack must be on a broad front from East Kent to West Sussex, despite the 3½ to 5 hours difference between high water at Littlehampton and high water at Dover. It was not easy for the soldiers to grasp that either they must cope with an unfavourable tide or accept that the landings on the two flanks could not be simultaneous.

Eighteen days after 'Overlord' had begun, Group Command West of the German Navy sent to the Naval Staff in Berlin a report, signed by Admiral Krancke, on some aspects of the intelligence failure in the Bay of the Seine. What by the Allies must be regarded as partly good luck was for the Germans bad staff work, partly due to measures taken by the invasion force, partly to a difference of opinion between Rundstedt's anti-invasion Command (*Oberbefehlshaber West*) and the Naval Group Command about what the first reported invasion moves really meant or threatened. Beneath the starchy staff prose one can read bitter disappointment and an awareness that one or two fundamental errors of intelligence practice had been made. The report, dated 23 June 1944, began (the italics are the author's):

On the evening of 5 June the prevailing wind was NW force 6. *This weather did not seem favourable for an enemy landing.* The Commander, Naval Defences West, therefore decided not to send the flotilla into the Seine Bay, especially as the tide would have forced the boats to return to port about 02.00 (on the 6th). During the really critical hours before and at dawn patrolling could have been carried out only if it had been decided to leave the boats at sea in

M 335

daylight until the next high tide, which was at noon. *The situation on the night of 5–6 June did not warrant such a risk.*

News of the first parachute landings in Normandy reached the Group shortly after midnight. At first it was not thought that this was the beginning of the invasion. Air Fleet 3 and OB West, upon inquiry, judged the airborne landings at first as either unimportant nuisance raids or forced baling out from homeward-bound bomber formations. *Such an assumption was plausible,* since a report had been received from the Nice area a few days earlier of an air-borne invasion, which had later proved to be forced landings. OB West continued to view the parachute landings as of little importance, *even after incoming reports excluded any possibility of forced landings.*

Naval Group Command West had ordered full readiness for all forces under the Commander Naval Defences West immediately upon receipt of the very first report. As reports on airborne landings continued to come in, it was decided at 03.10 to order the western defence forces to put out for intensified coastal patrol, notwithstanding the evaluation of the situation by OB West. However, the tide had then made it too late for the boats of 6th motor gunboat flotilla to put to sea.

At 03.20, the Group received the first definite sign that the operation under way was not merely an airborne nuisance operation, but an invasion. At this hour, the Group received an Ozet (radar) message with the time-group 03.09, locating targets north of Port en Bessin on a southerly course. *This report and its proper evaluation were relayed immediately to OB West.* It was augmented by other Ozet reports, as they kept coming in. *OB West, however, did not take the same view as the Naval Group Command.* It continued to judge the enemy operation as of no particular importance. Only at about 06.30 did OB West gain the impression that a major landing operation was under way.*

Our locating stations were in such shape on the night of the invasion, despite preceding air attacks, that *early identification of an approaching enemy could be relied upon in all sectors of the Channel.* At about 23.00, on 5 June, instruments on either side of Cherbourg picked up eastbound shipping movements. There was nothing unusual in these movements, judging from the experience of the past few weeks and considering the fact that they appeared to take place along or close to the British convoy routes.

But when the landing fleet turned into the Seine Bay, it was not picked up. The decisive instrument for this registration would have been the radar station near La Pernelle; it must be pointed out that this station was out of order due to a preceding air raid. The radar stations on the Normandy coast did not record the approaching invasion fleet because the Arromanches equipment was jammed by the enemy. *This jamming alone did not indicate the landing, since similar interference had occurred on previous occasions.* In the Orne estuary the enemy fleet was registered only at dawn, when the ships could be recognized by visual means.

The first definite argument for the fact that the invasion had started was received by the Naval Command at 03.20 from the Ozet. Our locating system, however, was not capable of identifying the full scale of the invasion early enough to order the gunboats to put to sea; nor were the Ozet reports sufficiently detailed to form the basis for an action by the Army Command, such as a precautionary advance of armoured divisions.

Our torpedo boats, patrol boats and minesweepers put out immediately from Le Havre. Apart from disturbing the enemy, no results of consequence could be achieved.

It is fair to guess – but impossible to prove – that OB West were guilty of wishful thinking. Their defence planners had long ago decided that the Seine Bay was an unlikely landing place because of its distance from big ports; this conviction had been reinforced by a mass of intelligence, some of it of the highest grade, pointing unmistakably to Calais as the threatened area; in which case the expedition approaching the Seine Bay must be regarded as no more than a diversion to trick the armoured divisions into moving in the wrong direction. Against this conviction, simple factual hour-to-hour intelligence was not allowed to prevail. In other words, deception worked so well that the enemy thought the real thing was the deception. Can one ask for more?

15 The sin and the cure

'The art is to make the right deductions and present them to the Commander in clear and logical form. From my own experience I could not have been better served in this respect, with the result that the so-called fog of war was seldom more than a mist.'

(Field-Marshal Earl Alexander of Tunis*)

The patience of a rock climber; the scholar's application to dull detail; the cold objectivity of a research scientist; the intuition of the archaeologist handling fragmentary fact; the discretion of a doctor; the showmanship of a journalist and the forensic talent of the barrister . . . There is no point in prolonging the catalogue of what is ideally required in the highest grade of Intelligence work. Indeed, there would be no point at all in listing these qualities if the part that it plays in war had not been so generally ignored by commanders and historians, or if confidence could be felt that the lessons which emerge from this study are generally present to the minds of politicians and those who work for them. Such qualities make up the kind of capability – to use military jargon – that any good staff or cabinet should have available to offset the well-known weaknesses shown by men and women in the pursuit and exercise of power: impatience, vanity, readiness to generalize far ahead of the evidence, inability to see wood for trees, attention to gossip and rumour, reluctance to take pains with persuasion whether in speech or in writing.

Nor is there anything here peculiar to the Navy's experience. We have seen in this narrative instances of impatience in the absurd 'second front in Europe' agitation of 1942; of rash generalization in the appreciation of German military intentions; of wishful thinking in the appraisal of bomb damage. Countless other examples could be cited from the military, air, scientific and diplomatic history of the war on both sides. But the lesson should not be forgotten, as it had been by 1939. 'At that time', Godfrey writes:

338

none of the Assistant Chiefs of Staff or Directors of operational divisions knew anything about Intelligence. I myself knew precious little. There is no particular reason why we should have done, because the subject was swept out of sight during the twenty years of peace. A half-hearted attempt was made to establish an intelligence course at Greenwich alongside the Staff College, but it petered out.*

The so-called Intelligence Officer in a British battleship between the wars was often the Navigating Officer, presumably because he was a watchful type, sometimes with the Schoolmaster Lieutenant as his assistant in this vague activity. The actual terms of reference were contained in a little volume entitled 'Manual of Intelligence' – a work of singular dullness with a number of well-worn principles outlined. In practice the work consisted in the main of trying to preserve the security of the various ciphers and codes, and little else beside that. One had no briefing or instruction of any sort, but as a navigator one reported to the Hydrographer any navigational changes in ports visited.

When, before his departure at the end of 1942, Godfrey drew attention on paper to some general truths about the art, lessons most painfully learnt in three years of war, the memorandum came back from the First Sea Lord and his Deputy with no more than a tick and a date. To expect more was asking too much: only the greatest commanders indulge in self-criticism in the heat of war. Now there may be some value and no little interest in trying to distil from the successful activity of an able group of men and women a number of observations which would provide prolegomena – they could be no more – to a doctrine of intelligence. The attempt may at least start discussion of a subject which is barely mentioned in this country but which, in the United States, is usefully discussed both in and outside the academic circles.*

Let it first be established that the ablest commanders of the maritime war quickly realized the power of intelligence. When Fraser of North Cape was Commander-in-Chief Home Fleet, he made an official visit 'in full rig' to the OIC in 1945 to thank its officers for what they had done to help him. Tovey included a tribute to intelligence efficiency in his report on the sinking of the *Bismarck*. Even the irascible Ramsay, after the landings in Normandy, expressed admiration for the way intelligence had been collected and distributed and for the astonishing security maintained by scores of thousands of men and women. Cunningham, although he would sometimes treat intelligence officers to a kind of mischievous bullying, praised the meticulous scholarship and fine printing of his intelligence and operation orders for 'Torch'. Dudley Pound once said jokingly to Godfrey, as they talked in the First Sea Lord's room, 'If you give me such good intelligence I shall get the reputation of being one of the world's greatest strategists.'

There were of course failures, serious and numerous failures, mostly in the early days. The long time taken to detect the fact that the Germans were reading so much of our signal traffic; the farce of the Norwegian landings; the inability to intercept in the first year of the war the forays of the German pocket battleships and battle cruisers (even though *Graf Spee* was hunted down and killed); the underrating of air attack on surface ships and of Italian frogmen; the acceptance of Churchill's view that the *Repulse* and *Prince of Wales* might in some way deter by their presence at Singapore the Japanese southward aggression. Above all, perhaps, the refusal to believe that U-boats would attack on the surface and at night – an assumption that sprang from failure to analyse adequately the U-boat operations of 1917–18 and to study the trends in German naval thinking between 1936 and 1939.*

It was another sign of backwardness that the signals of those early days were badly drafted, ungraded, based on dubious sources. For example, on 7 April 1940 C-in-C Home Fleet received from Admiralty the following woolly signal:

Recent reports suggest a German expedition is being prepared. Hitler is reported from Copenhagen to have ordered unostentatious movement by one division in ten ships to land at Narvik with simultaneous occupation of Jutland. Sweden to be left alone. Moderates said to be opposing the plan. Date given for arrival Narvik is 8 April. All these reports are of doubtful value and may well be only a further move in the war of nerves.

'So what?' Admiral Forbes may well have exclaimed. 'Does the Fleet raise steam or not?' If the reports were dubious why send them? Why this hopeful note about the 'moderates'? And yet the very next day, 8 April, the invasion of Norway was in fact under way and a group of German warships was sighted by a flying-boat waiting to enter Trondheim Fjord. As Roskill remarks, it is strange that NID should not have made more of the warning received from Consul-General Copenhagen on 4 April; of the fact that the ice had cleared from the Belts on the 5th; and of indications of enemy activity northward that had been received. (It seems likely that the increased German naval signal traffic, drawn attention to by Station X, was thought in OIC to show no more than a reaction to our own mining operations off the coast of Norway.) Compare this episode with the sinking of the *Scharnhorst* at Christmas 1943 after Admiral Fraser had received the simple 'Admiralty appreciates *Scharnhorst* at sea.'

So there were grounds for a diffident, more sceptical attitude; and it is perhaps the obvious first moral to point in this 'terminal essay'.* Men of action, the commanders in operations, tend at first to be suspicious or even contemptuous of intelligence unless they have experience of its methods. The same may be said of politicians, who are less easily given training or guidance. During a staff meeting in Colombo in 1944 one of the DNI's most experienced officers, specially sent out to reorganize intelligence in South-East Asia, was told by his Admiral: 'I don't like all this empire-building of yours; I believe in going to sea, finding the enemy and sinking him.' To which the Captain RN thus addressed was brave enough to reply: 'It is your empire, Sir, that I am building up, not mine. You won't find the enemy without intelligence and he may well sink you if I don't tell you how strong he is.' Strange that such remarks should still be made after five years of war; but it has to be remembered that many officers in sea commands had not seen what intelligence in its full wartime vigour could produce. Ian Campbell, probably the best deputy director that the wartime Division enjoyed, admits that when, after three years in NID, he went to sea again to command destroyers with Arctic convoys he knew virtually nothing of what his old colleagues were doing to help him. Yet, when taking part later in 'Torch', he was struck by the 'extreme accuracy of the intelligence material given to every commanding officer on arrival for fuelling at Gibraltar'.

341

How quickly, too, memories fade. After the war, when the Berlin crisis of 1948–9 burst on the Admiralty, the historic submarine tracking room had to be rescued from civil servants who had turned it into a table-tennis centre. At the peak of that crisis a very senior officer leaving for the Far East was taken there, much against his will, to study the dispositions of the Soviet Navy. He had called as instructed on the DDNI, in the course of the visits to Admiralty departments customary on taking up a new appointment, and had said that he did not expect there was much to learn and did not want to waste time chatting. He was firmly told that he would be unwise to rest on his ignorance. His attitude was basically that of a Director of Signals who stated before the war began that a much expanded direction-finding network for Britain was unnecessary because the enemy would maintain wireless silence in all operations.

Let this, then, be the first axiom; *fighting commanders, technical experts and politicians are liable to ignore, despise or underrate Intelligence.** The reason for this must lie partly in their training; it seems to follow, therefore, that the activity is best entrusted to those who have enjoyed a special, or at least a more suitable, training. In other words, there is a strong case for laying down as a second axiom that *Intelligence should so far as possible be directed by civilians.* To say this is to fly in the face of British, as well as German, Russian and other practice, although the Americans since the war have given more and more power in their vast organizations to civilians. The post of C in London, for example, was occupied until 1939 by a naval officer, and Mr Asquith (who created it in 1911) is credited with the intention that it always should be. Each fighting service has regarded the directorate of its intelligence as a senior and dignified staff job – but not one for the 'fliers'. For the belief still prevails that it is more important to give orders and make plans than to get them right; and the best men in the fighting forces still shun a position in which their careers are likely to come to a premature close, with the rank of Commodore or Brigadier. (An outstanding exception is Field-Marshal Templer who was in Intelligence at the outbreak of war and became DMI 194–68.) It is also true, so far as the author can judge, that the most promising men in the Services have rarely been appointed to intelligence duties at any stage, and that in the Foreign Office the subject has been held in low regard. 'Our job', said one diplomatist to the author 'is not to spy but to maintain relations', the kind of attitude which has been discussed in the chapter on Naval Attachés.

But the case for civilian predominance in this work is based not merely on the Services' low regard for it. It has to do also with the war-time lesson that it is the lawyer, the scholar, the traveller, the banker, even the journalist, who shows the ability to resist where the career men tend to bend. Career officers and politicians have a strong interest in cooking raw intelligence to make their masters' favourite dishes. The image is crude and probably a little unfair; but it fixes the eye on the way information is used and twisted to justify views advanced or positions taken up. It may be to stake claims on the defence budget; to refute a rival service; to justify appeasement or bellicosity; to advance political purposes. The best illustration in this study is to be found in Churchill's handling of the U-boat sinking figures (Chapter 6). It is, as it were, the original sin of men of affairs who are used to shaping ends to means, of men with careers to make in the public eye, varying in strength according to background and upbringing. (Godfrey used to argue that sailors, because of the dangers and unpredictability of the sea even in peace, are rather more realistic and less sinful in this respect than soldiers!)*

Be that as it may, no one will deny that Intelligence can and should be the voice of conscience in a staff or cabinet (let this be axiom number three), and that the upright and outspoken intelligence officer is crucially important in that role. But most commanders are no more likely to admit what they owe to such a person than a man of good repute is likely to admit any debt to his psychiatrist. No regular officer who knew the Naval Intelligence Division well would deny that many of its major achievements were by civilian brains, allied, it is true, to naval tradition and resources, but none the less civilian habits, standards and training. Nor can it be denied that some women – only a few had the chance – showed great capacity for the most exacting intelligence work. One of them has been mentioned as finishing the war as the OIC expert on German coastal forces from Heligoland to Biarritz; she had been trained for the laborious piecing together of boring fragments of fact by her work as an archaeologist.

There, really, is the secret. Certain professions, certain kinds of university study, develop just those mental skills that intelligence work requires; what is more important, they encourage the kind of confidence in the making of judgements that may be undermined in the naval officer's career by the necessity to obey for most of the time a senior officer. It is not a coincidence that of the five outstanding intelligence officers seen in action during the war by the author, one was a barrister just half-way in his career, one a stockbroker, one a philosophy don (in the Army) at the beginning of his; another was an art historian and the last was a naval officer who wanted to be – and could have become had war allowed it – a lawyer. And it was notorious in the large and talented community of the Inter-Service Topographical Department at Oxford that the leading personalities were the classics don, Freddie Wells, and the Hydrographer's surveyor, Commander Hughes. That they should find it easy to work together on mapping the assault beaches seemed perfectly natural to both men. They had common standards of exact scholarship.

What, if anything, can be added on the subject of intuition?* The strict intelligence expert will reply 'Nothing': the word implies that understanding can take place without the reason intervening. That may be true in the arts and in religious experience, but in military matters it is nothing more than 'hunch'. What, then, are we to think of Hitler's uncanny intuitions about the weakness of the French and the readiness of Stalin to bargain with him? If he had listened to his intelligence advisers he would never have undertaken the attack on France and the Low Countries when he did. But these were political rather than military judgements: hunches about morale not about divisions and air squadrons. Their success encouraged Hitler to apply his intuitions to the battlefield as well, without having first analysed – or allowed anyone else to analyse – why his political hunches had turned out right. His success made it impossible for others to argue with him; the intelligence system serving him lost conviction because it was not listened to. As Sherman Kent, the American expert puts it in his book on Strategic Intelligence: 'When intelligence

344

producers realize that there is no sense in forwarding to a consumer knowledge that does not correspond to his preconceptions, then Intelligence is through.'

It stands to reason that the Navy, requiring the combination of outstanding executive and physical qualities that it demands in its officers, cannot hope to draw on intellectual prowess to the degree that the learned professions do; but the civilian also commends himself by a reasonable independence of service loyalties, even though he will temporarily share them enthusiastically. If put into uniform he is proud to be a naval officer, but nothing can make him first and foremost a naval officer. This feeling affects his independence of speech and judgement, his attitude to senior officers both in his own and other services; and there is no doubt that intelligent senior naval officers were mostly quick to recognize the unique authority of superior intellect and the scholar's integrity when they encountered it. They recognized it all the more readily when it was not allied to political office and personal ambition. Even specialists – in particular experts in torpedoes and mines, in navigation and signals, in gunnery and aviation – valued the questions asked by the well-trained RNVR, that is to say, civilian mind.

Of course in a staff of over 2,000 there were exceptions. Some civilians got swollen heads; some became pedantic and secretive; a few became submerged in the facts of which they were meant to be masters; some could not stand the pace. Yet the conclusion must be, as Godfrey and Rushbrooke would both agree, that the civilian contribution to Naval Intelligence was decisive and that dilution with regular officers worked.* Not only did it spare trained naval officers for service at sea, it also secured better work than could be got out of a comparable number of RN and RM officers. Admittedly, it was necessary to have in every key section a naval officer with a rank of Commander or higher to see that the civilians did not err through lack of sea experience or discipline or to maintain liaison with an ally or another Service. It was also necessary to have here and there a junior Admiral or Captain to maintain the right relations with the operational and specialists divisions of the Admiralty that NID was serving.

The lesson is clear: in peace as in war intelligence should be largely in the hands of civilians,* not of serving or retired

345

officers. They should be trained for and offered a career in what is essentially a new learned profession – the intelligence service. Their skill should be transferable from one fighting service or Ministry to another. The highest posts should be open to them. There is no conclusive reason why the head of intelligence in any service should be an officer in uniform, however able and experienced he may be.

The case for the civilian has so far been made without considering what forces he or she has to deal with besides those mentioned. They are inherent in the exercise of power, and the next general statement might well be that obsession and bias often start at the top.

In his unpublished memoirs Godfrey wrote the following:

> I think that we in the NID all fully realized that one of our principal functions was to protect our chief from the impact of false and wishful information: but what was only dimly realized during the Hitler War was the need to protect commands, staffs and information services from the effect of wishful intelligence emanating from the very top.
>
> The subordinate who, in the middle of a great war, conceives it his duty to correct an obsession or a misconception from on high, may be in for a rough time. He may have sometimes to bend so that he may not break. Regular officers with their built-in sense of loyalty and deference towards their seniors are temperamentally handicapped for such a task. They may fail completely and in the process of trying, suffer grievous harm.

Some commanders did not understand the difference between an executive decision ('we will do this') and an intelligence decision ('we must believe that'). In order to justify doing what they wished to do, they would persuade themselves that the evidence for action was other than it was. Others did not fully understand that they could not command intelligence and therefore should not try to do so. There was a significant little scene in the submarine tracking room at the Admiralty in 1943 when a new Assistant Chief of Naval Staff, who was taking over, came to acquaint himself with its work. He was a highly intelligent and reasonable Admiral who quickly reached with the members of the room a relationship of confidence and trust; but this was his first day and it seemed to him normal and natural to say at the end of the conference;

'Well, gentlemen, my policy will be to do this and that.' On which the RNVR Commander in charge firmly and quietly commented; 'Here, sir, we ascertain the facts first and do not let the policy influence the intelligence' – a courageous remark which a regular officer of the same rank might have found impossible to make. In different circumstances the right and duty of the junior officer or civilian to take such a stand could be exasperating and intolerable.*

An interesting example of the intelligence judgement being arrogated by the executive command occurred in the summer of 1944, when there was natural anxiety about what the U-boats could achieve against the coastal and cross-Channel traffic to Normandy. The OIC had sent out warnings that Walter boats* were being built, together with details of planned performance as they became known but it was virtually certain right up to D-day that no boat had left the Baltic for British waters. However, the staff at Portsmouth took seriously the sighting reports that came in from Channel units, despite Admiralty assurances that they were false, and ordered the removal of torpedo tubes from our motor torpedo boats so that they could carry depth charges against the new U-boats. The only effect was to weaken our units in their encounters with German E-boats operating in the Command.

Godfrey himself had in October 1940 a puzzling experience with Dudley Pound, whom he knew well and who was always accessible to his DNI and in no way 'anti-highbrow' in his attitudes. He informed Pound personally that the invasion of England was off, at any rate until the following spring. This was not a matter of opinion but of concrete fact, based on photographic reconnaissance of barge movements and military concentrations across the Channel, on knowledge of probable sea and weather conditions and on the special knowledge – passed only to a select few – that German agents captured on landing in Britain and now working for us, had been ordered from Berlin to lie low for six months.* The failure of the Luftwaffe to win the Battle of Britain had been decisive. Yet the War Office was telling the Admiralty in the same month that 'they thought the time would never come, except on account of weather conditions, when it would be safe to say invasion was off'.

347

On the strength of this advice the Admiralty might have wished to change the dispositions of the Fleet made to break up an invasion and reinforce the Mediterranean. But Pound knew there were good political reasons for wishing the public, and all concerned with the running of affairs, to go on believing as long as possible in the invasion threat – the greatest stimulus to effort the nation had ever had. Indeed, the Prime Minister was then doing everything in his power to sharpen anxiety in the United States about the fate of Britain and the possibility that its fleet might fall into Hitler's hands. Later, in March 1941, Godfrey realized that the First Sea Lord, for all these reasons, had either forgotten what he had been told or had not properly taken it in.

It would be an exaggeration to say that our strategy was therefore resting on falsehood, but the incident points to the kind of political self-deception against which it is one of the functions of intelligence to guard. It is on record that Harry Hopkins was telling Roosevelt in December 1940 from London that 'most of the Cabinet and all the military leaders here believe that invasion is imminent . . . I therefore cannot urge too strongly that any action you may take to meet the immediate needs here must be based on the assumption that invasion will come before 1 May 1941.' What worried Godfrey and others was that the pretence, with others which grew out of it, was kept alive well into 1942. It was used to justify the retention of large forces in Britain itself and had attached to it in some mysterious way the secondary myth that Germany had a hidden army of twenty or thirty divisions not involved in the Russian campaign as reserves, which could be switched at short notice to the attack on these islands. According to men who served on the Joint Intelligence Staff, this idea persisted for some time after General Sir Alan Brooke, whose task it was to prepare against invasion, moved from commanding Home Forces to become Chief of the Imperial General Staff. It was supported by the War Office, but was regularly opposed by the Foreign Office and NID and MEW.

As a further example of myth affecting strategy, the author is enabled to quote the experience of Godfrey who, on reaching India in February 1943, to command the Royal Indian Navy, found that the Government there had been told to prepare against a vast continental pincer movement on two fronts, from Japan and from Germany. This was in spite of a unanimous decision by the JIC in London, to which the Navy had been a party, that the ultimate aim of any German breakthrough past Stalingrad must be Baku and its oilfields, *not* Abadan, the Persian Gulf and eventually India to link up with the Japanese. The Directors from Admiralty, Air Ministry and Economic Warfare had had difficulty in persuading their War Office colleagues during six weeks' argument to drop the theory of an effective German–Japanese link-up; but dropped it had been. For there was no evidence then – neither is there now – that Japanese and German war plans were closely co-ordinated. Yet here was the RAF in India:

establishing layback aerodromes 200 miles inside India with bombproof overhead protection, the entire wooden ship-building resources of the west coast turned on to making barges for the Tigris and Euphrates, the Khyber Pass being fortified to the extent that hardly a mouse could get through, while a naval base was prepared in the Gulf of Kutch in case Ceylon was captured by the Japanese and the south-east coast of India invaded.*

Godfrey recorded at the time that the Finance Department in Delhi had not believed a word of this great strategy and had opposed the expenditure, but without success. The fact that events proved them right and the military wrong made them chary of responding to later and genuine demands. 'If the wishful intelligence which produced all these formidable results was aimed at stirring India up and inducing her to raise an army of two millions, it certainly succeeded and it may be regarded as the most ambitious and successful deception plan ever aimed at the British Empire.'

Occasionally the Naval Staff would try to 'cheat' with intelligence in the game of planning and forecasting. For example, in the autumn of 1944, deeply relieved and exalted by the summer successes against the U-boats, they were tempted to release some hundred escort vessels from the Atlantic to the Far East, where the limited size of the British naval force was harmful to our prestige and ability to influence the American conduct of operations. One Assistant Chief of Staff, with a closer knowledge of Doenitz's determination and resources than his colleagues, leaked the information to the OIC – who were aghast – and Winn was encouraged to present at the next anti-U-boat meeting a paper forecasting renewed and even increased U-boat activity the following spring, offering a most dangerous threat to allied sea communications to liberate Europe. Such was Winn's prestige that the plan was dropped, to the understandable irritation of Admiral Fraser, commanding the British fleet in the Pacific, who had been promised this reinforcement.*

A final illustration of this great and complex theme comes from a letter that Godfrey wrote in May 1954, to Admiral Thursfield, naval correspondent of *The Times*, who had asked for material to be included in his article for the *Dictionary of National Biography* on Sir Tom Phillips, who was Pound's deputy:

My recollection is quite clear that early in 1941 he told me he *had* been in the PM's good books and had spent many weekends at Chequers. Now that was all over and he sorrowfully confessed that he had lost the PM's confidence, was held at arm's length and had not seen him for two months.

He was never afraid to express an unpopular opinion: he had opposed the Greek expedition, in the success of which he had no faith, and felt that the reinforcement of Malta and the control of the central Mediterranean were all-important.

I remember his telling me that the PM had got angry and called him defeatist, which provoked the rejoinder that it was his job to give his sincere opinion on naval strategy, which he had done.

The politician and the commander and the civil servant are, however, entitled to retort to this warning against obsession in high places and reluctance to believe the facts, that the intelligence officer himself is prone to such weaknesses. Having formed and presented an appreciation of the enemy's intentions or strength, pride may prevent him admitting to himself and to his commander that new evidence has made it doubtful or even wrong. Likewise a person or a group of persons in a section can become interested in a particular place or ship to an extent that distorts their judgement and that of the operational people working with them. For example, the battleship *Tirpitz* was so closely watched day by day, so much reported on, made so much the object of inquiry and discussion that she mesmerized the Naval Staff by her mere presence,* long after the time she was in fact likely – as we now know – to threaten our trade routes either alone or in company with other ships.

In April 1940 NID were so engrossed in watching for attempts by German commerce raiders to break into the Atlantic that they missed the significance of the movements that led up to the attack on Norway. Bomber Command Intelligence had an entirely false impression of the accuracy of their bombing until night photographs filed at Medmenham were properly examined and interpreted. Eisenhower's intelligence staff – or most of them – believed so strongly in the autumn of 1944 that a counter-offensive by Hitler in the West could make no *military* sense that they overlooked his *political* calculation that it might induce the Americans, by causing heavy losses, to favour peace negotiations separate from the Russians, and underrated the intelligence indications that attracted the attention of the JIC back in London.*

This, the fourth proposition – *that intelligence judgements must be under continuous review and revision* – bears on a point that has been made to the author by several planners and operational officers. A commander and his staff who are closely and accurately informed about the enemy's weaknesses are tempted to make them the fixed starting point of their thinking. If the commander allows this to happen, he is allowing the integrity of his judgement to be unbalanced. His purpose should be to carry out the agreed strategy and secure the political objectives laid down by his government; but he is liable to substitute for them the purely tactical purpose of exploiting an enemy weakness he knows about – it may be lack of fuel, or the failure of reinforcements to arrive, or even the absence of the enemy commander on leave.

Brigadier Williams, chief intelligence officer to Field-Marshal Montgomery during the Normandy campaign and before that in North Africa, has emphasized that the Field-Marshal, who was very well served by his intelligence staff at Alamein and after, wished to know nothing more than the general 'shape' of the enemy's dispositions until his broad intentions for attack had been discussed and fixed. Then he was ready to listen to the detailed information that Intelligence could give him. (This was in accordance with what the Staff Colleges had taught.)

351

In 21st Army Group Headquarters the thoughtful and ready acceptance of such advice resulted partly from the lessons of success in the field and partly from General de Guingand's having been himself an intelligence officer before becoming the commander's Chief of Staff. (It may be noted in passing that a comparable wartime promotion was most unlikely in the Navy, for the author knows of no naval officer with serious experience of intelligence work who went on to high command at sea and contact with the enemy.)

A not dissimilar point is made by Lord Mountbatten. He has explained that in his combined headquarters in Burma he would instruct his operational planning staff not to inform the intelligence staff of what operation they had in mind until the broad pattern had been got on to paper. Then the intelligence could be applied to their ideas, producing what modification of detail or changes of mind it required. If the planners started with the detailed intelligence picture in mind, he argued, they were liable to be guided by the enemy dispositions; likewise the intelligence staff might be tempted to give their contribution a bias one way or inspired by their own view of what should be done. In theory, too, an intelligence officer should never press an operational idea, although we have seen this done successfully in the case of the St Nazaire raid and in mining and submarine operations proposed by the OIC.

Nothing said above affects, however, the validity of the very important principle that Intelligence must be able to ask not only what the planners are thinking but also about the problems of other divisions involved in operations. The story is told by an eminent civil servant of the reply given in the early days of the war to an inquiry (sent from Churchill's statistical office under Professor Lindemann) about the fuel consumption of the German Navy. The Admiralty's estimate seemed so high that the statisticians compared it with the fuel consumption of the much larger Royal Navy and found it higher. The department concerned then admitted that it had worked out its estimate of German consumption without knowledge of the British. A similar and more important lack of co-operation was recorded in January 1941 by Mr Justice Singleton, when asked by Churchill (who believed the Luftwaffe's numbers to have been exaggerated) to investigate the probable front-line strength of the German Air Force during the next six months. He found that the German section of Air Ministry Intelligence, when estimating enemy strength at the outbreak of war, had not been informed of comparable British figures and had therefore underrated the miscellaneous losses to which an air force is subject. Thus, as Lindemann pointed out to the Prime Minister, the difficulty involved in assuming the GAF strength to be nearly $2\frac{1}{2}$ times as great as our own, while their production was only $1\frac{1}{2}$ times as great, had escaped their notice.*

By August 1942 this lesson, at least, had been learnt. For example the German section of NID warned the First Sea Lord that the Navy's experience in Malta had been that bombing of protected submarine bases would not be effective unless it was kept up day and night and the submarines themselves were hit. Over Malta in the spring of 1942 the German effort had risen to between 200 and 300 sorties a day, but the 10th submarine flotilla was not withdrawn until 3 May. So the number of sorties needed to render Brest, Lorient and St Nazaire untenable must be of the order of 500–600 a day. Fighter cover, which the Germans operating from Sicily had over Malta, would be possible only over Brest and it was not to be expected that British heavy bombers would achieve the same accuracy as the dive bombers used by the enemy over Malta. Indeed, agents' reports and air photographs had shown that there was not the slightest possibility of U-boats being hit in the massive concrete shelters protecting them. Despite this warning, their Lordships pressed hard for all-out bombing assault on the bases nine months later, to the understandable exasperation of Bomber Command.

From these considerations there emerges a fifth axiom; *that intelligence must be the servant and not the master of operational policy.* It seems to clash with the view of Sun Tzu the Chinese philosopher of war: 'Now an army may be likened to water, for just as flowing water avoids the heights and hastens to the lowlands, so an army avoids strength and strikes at weaknesses. And as water shapes its flow in accordance with ground, so an army manages its victory in accordance with the situation of the enemy.' Fortunately for the sailor, and for the argument here advanced, the Chinese sage adds: 'And

353

as water has no constant form, there are in war no constant conditions.'

Here it is convenient to consider briefly two further related propositions. First, number six, that *just as absolute power is said to corrupt absolutely, so can complete knowledge corrupt completely*. Admiral Doenitz, having relied so much on the work of his cryptanalysts for the U-boat war, felt helpless when they went blind in spring 1943.* Other sources of intelligence, notably long-range air reconnaissance, had been neglected; the service of agents from Britain and the United States was poor. Likewise the American Admiral King sent a memorandum to the US Chiefs of Staff in May 1942, in which he warned them that he was holding his own in the Pacific only because of 'timely information' of Japanese movements. 'If the timely information should become unavailable in future and the present disparity of force is allowed to continue, disaster in the Pacific area is probable.' During the periods when our own cryptanalysts were most successful, the temptation was constantly to ignore and neglect other sources, instead of using the AI source to check the quality of the B and C sources.

Second, number seven, there is the obvious rule – so often broken – that *intelligence must keep its own communications under continuous review*. The enemy is always listening in, even if he cannot understand. He must be prevented from knowing what you know about him as well as what you intend against him. Sources must be guarded as well as plans. There must be constant alertness against deception, for those who practised it with the ruthless and methodical ingenuity developed by the British (civilians, of course, in the van) found their best targets in the obsessions of the enemy. Useless in June 1944 to be simulating an attack on Norway, to distract attention from Normandy, had not Hitler's obsession with this threat been visible for years in his wasteful diversion of German U-boats to the North Sea. Futile, likewise, to suggest in the autumn of 1942 Allied landings in Greece (instead of North Africa) if the Germans had not feared since 1940 an Anglo–American–Turkish–Soviet link-up in the Balkans.*

There must be, too, continuous attention to the enemy's lucky strokes, his anticipation of one's surprises, the coincidence

354

of unexpected meetings on land or sea – all of which may be signs that the enemy is eavesdropping on one's most secret communications. It is a vital task of Intelligence, or the security side of it, to see that these things do not happen; and if relatively little attention has been given to security in this study it is because the spirit of the NID was predominantly offensive.*

Intelligence by now may seem rather a prig; peering over people's shoulders, curbing the impetuous, contradicting the confused, reminding the forgetful, instructing the ignorant, humbling the proud, warning the careless and alerting the lazy. Has it no other face than that of the officer-don? Are the fiction authors, the memoir writers, the film scripts entirely false? Mason, Compton Mackenzie and Fleming, Le Carré and Deighton were after all, in the game. To these questions Naval Intelligence can give only a limited answer from its own experience. Yes; two requirements have so far not been mentioned. First, that *the intelligence worker must be prepared to be a villain, to be ruthless and dishonest in one role while being honest and tolerant in another.* Second, *he must be, or try to be, a good showman.*

Let us look first at this other face as this study has shown it: secretive, adventurous, stranger than fiction, sometimes heroic and tragic. Collecting sand from the Arromanches beaches under the enemy's nose; seizing ciphers from an enemy ship at sea; capturing and then using enemy agents against their masters; the secret 'bus service' from the Shetlands to Norway and back across the North Sea in all weathers; briefing the assault party for the St Nazaire raid; preventing the Spaniards from allowing the Germans to cover the Straits of Gibraltar with location equipment and infra-red cameras; finding the mesh and dimensions of the torpedo net around the *Tirpitz*; helping the Americans to form the OSS, later to become the CIA; breaking codes, bugging cabins, forging papers, busting safes, planting corpses. It is, indeed, a Janus-like creature and if this face is better known than the other it is not surprising. Even quite experienced naval officers could not – and cannot – shake off the habit of regarding intelligence as a sort of Pandora's box; they expected marvels.* Godfrey had to remind the Naval Staff of this when he reported in July 1941 on the preparations being made in Washington for a wartime organization:

Like all young intelligence services, the urge will be towards the production of spectacular and dramatic results . . . Donovan and his party of enthusiasts will have to go through a period of disillusionment before they settle down, and it is while going through this period that I think Fleming and I will be able to help them most.

Just as there is in the minds of most men and women some half-forgotten residue of the fairy stories that once thrilled them or of the words that momentarily gripped them from the stage, so there was in Whitehall – and in Washington – a half-remembered legend of fabulous intelligence feats of the First World War. 'Blinker' Hall was still alive; because he was never allowed to publish the truth about his work, fact about his work had never been properly sifted from legend. Buchan's novels, in particular, had strengthened the legend; and there is no doubt that any DNI was credited by his friends (as was C) with uncanny powers and by his critics with empire-building appetites.

This narrative should have shown in how many cases the initiative for new methods or fresh efforts did indeed come from Room 39, more often than not to be regarded with a suspicion not normally shown towards the Senior Service. Examples are the development of what has been called terrain intelligence, the Fleming scheme for an assault unit, and the bold and imaginative co-operation of NID sections with subversive propaganda. The author had personal experience of the resentment that could be aroused against the Division by the authority, and the freedom of decision and suggestion, that it gave to officers representing it on inter-service bodies for just such purposes.

So, it has to be repeated, Intelligence does involve subtlety and skulduggery. However extensive the development of wireless and other forms of machine-gathered intelligence, the individual traitor or victim of blackmail, the Quisling or the turncoat, the ambitious politician or discontented official, the underpaid railwayman or the impoverished Spanish fisherman, may often be a precious source of intelligence. He or she may provide information in bulk or essential brief clues; but the service is indispensable in a world of hostile rival states. So the intelligence officer may be handling the products of bribery, violence, cheating, treachery, lying and gross personal betrayal.* Or he may be handling merely the results of cunning intrusion into privacy, into the secrecy of confidential communications, or of the brilliant prying of the cryptanalyst. If he has no touch of the rascal in him when he starts, he will certainly have acquired it before he finishes; work in those strange branches of intelligence called deception and subversion leaves a lasting mark on the mind.

Salesmanship or showmanship – both words much disliked by naval officers – is a quality less usually associated with Intelligence but everyone who has had to negotiate seriously will know what is meant. Officers in NID found that there was a public and personal relations side to their work which had to be learnt by experience. Appreciations had to be presented firmly and authoritatively, but also in a form which was attractive, whether face to face, on paper, by signal or on the telephone. Brigadier Williams, a scholar by training, wrote Intelligence appreciations for his Commander in 'Monty language'. It was not always certain what might be the prejudices of the chief recipient: he might be one who rejected on principle any argument more than five hundred words in length, or one who enjoyed a piece of good prose provided the main point was reached quickly. It was never easy to decide between the virtues of conciseness and those of attractive chat. Indeed, it was wise to be ready with both. The officer also had to have sufficient personality to persist in presenting his case, however unwelcome it might be; he might even have to lobby or lay ground-bait, especially in operations in which another service was taking part.*

Denning used to warn his colleagues in the OIC that when an operational authority, whether a commander or a command headquarters, is committed to a course of action, it is very reluctant to change its mind. The Intelligence branch may be given the job of convincing it, in which case care must be taken not to be drawn into strategic or tactical argument but to stick to the positive, and especially the negative, information available. In the case of the PQ17 convoy, discussed in

357

chapter 12, the fact that enemy movements had *not* been reported from a trusted source should have been presented to Dudley Pound more emphatically as of *positive* value.

Denning used also to insist that the only guarantee of being listened to is to have a reputation for reliability over a long period of time, to refuse ever to titillate with what is merely 'interesting', to understand and allow for the immense uncertainties of weather and endurance that will attend any judgement of what a ship will or will not do. 'Elegant trimmings have no place in the intelligence officer's vocabulary; but the man who cannot tell a story is a dull dog.' He recalls the story of how in 1941 he warned Admiral Max Horton, then Flag Officer Submarines, that the OIC expected the *Scharnhorst* and *Gneisenau* to make their dash back to Germany up Channel. It was proposed to station the submarine *Sealion* off Brest to catch them in Douarnenez Bay, and Denning had assured the Admiral that her Commander would be given such precise intelligence about enemy minefields and swept channels that from this risk, at any rate, she would be safe. 'All right, I'll send her,' Denning remembers Horton saying; 'if anything happens to her, God help you.'

Winn in the tracking room had the same experience. It was necessary, he wrote:

to gain the confidence of the staff officers of the Home Fleet, Western Approaches, Portsmouth, Plymouth and Coastal Command. We found that the way to do it was to tell them outstanding, simple and interesting facts. It was not necessary to give details and reasoning and exact probabilities. *Once confidence had been established by results, we found that they would act on the intelligence we gave and not ask too many questions.*

Allowance had always to be made for boredom in the recipient. He would treat at first with great attention the product of some new source or details of some new subjects; but unless the subsequent material was spectacular – which is rarely the case – there was a tendency to pay less attention and to take the products for granted. This jaded and faded appetite has to be stimulated against the day of emergency when one wants to be believed. On the other hand, any kind of sensationalism leads straight to misunderstanding and exaggeration.*

Perhaps a comment may be allowed on a human weakness which very few are entitled to condemn outright in others. It is the impulse to say 'I know better', 'I've got my own views and information about this'; it is perhaps most common among older men, of great experience, whose statecraft or strategy are deeply influenced by analogies from the past. Take the Minute regarding the handling of intelligence sent by Winston Churchill in August 1940 to General Ismay:

> I do not wish such reports as are received to be sifted and digested by the various intelligence authorities. For the present Major Morton will inspect them for me and submit what he considers of major importance. He is to be shown everything and submit authentic documents to me in their original form.
>
> (*Second World War*, vol. 3, p. 319.)

Before very long the Prime Minister was to realize that he had undertaken a hopeless task; not only was the volume of intelligence vast but a lot of the best of it was incomprehensible without editing, collating and cross-reference. But he had this desire to see the original, to judge for himself, which can spell doom for the intelligence officer's authority and confidence. A reasonable residual right for a Prime Minister; but not justifiable as a regular practice. The tenth axiom might therefore be: '*The boss does not always know best.*'*

What the Prime Minister had ordered was a diet of raw intelligence selected by his own taster. One consequence was a judgement which provides one of the oddest passages in that great but not infrequently inaccurate book *The Second World War*. He describes (vol. 3, pp. 318–19) how there was some reluctance in London to believe that the Germans would attack the Russians in the summer of 1941 rather than come to some agreement to carve up Europe and the Middle East between them. The previous winter's intelligence could be read as showing a German concentration of forces in the east to bully and threaten rather than attack. Reluctantly, according to Churchill, the Joint Intelligence Committee came to the view that a second front might be opened up by Hitler and gave their first firm warning on 5 June 1941. 'Our Chiefs of Staff,' writes Churchill, 'were ahead of their advisers and more definite' and he quotes a message from the Chiefs of Staff to the

359

Middle East Command saying that large forces were being concentrated by the Germans against Russia and that they would march if the Russians refused the concession that would be demanded of them. He then justifies this claim by describing how he came across an item of intelligence which showed that Hitler wanted to have as much armour as possible available at the Polish–Russian frontier for an attack on Russia in May.

This item was capable of more than one interpretation, and it is fair to say that if the Chiefs of Staff did have access to intelligence denied to the JIC, then they were to be blamed, not praised; and if they were disregarding the JIC on such a vital matter they should have changed its personnel or told it to change its methods. 'In a lesser mortal,' one Director of Intelligence remarked when he read the anecdote, 'this episode would have betrayed a whole catalogue of intelligence sins: keeping something to oneself, scooping one's colleagues, making far-ranging deductions from one report.'

'I know best' also crept into the arguments of those who had been present at negotiations which others had only read about. When he was Director of Plans in 1936, Captain (later Vice-Admiral) Tom Phillips took part in the negotiation of the Anglo–German Agreement. Shortly afterwards he expressed the view that 'the present design of German capital ships appears to show that Germany is looking towards the Baltic more than in the past'. Even at that time this was a surprising remark. Later, when a member of the Board, Phillips was inclined to underrate the size of the *Bismarck* and *Tirpitz* and the capacity of the pocket-battleships because he had negotiated the tonnage limits which they had infringed.

One lesson of the Second World War has clearly been learnt – that *Intelligence is indivisible*. It is, indeed, significant that the first success in the integration policy pursued in the Ministry of Defence when Lord Mountbatten was Chief of the Defence Staff (1959–65), was in intelligence work. Perhaps this study will help to explain why the last of the Directors of Naval Intelligence, Admiral Denning, should have been the first of the Directors of integrated Intelligence.*

But the axiom that Intelligence is indivisible has more in it than the obvious truth that modern warfare makes impossible any rigid separation of sailors', soldiers' and airmen's sources – to say nothing of those of the diplomats, economists, scientists, and so on. It has also to do with the inter-service suspicions and jealousies already referred to. A striking case can be quoted from the experience of NID with Bomber Command, one in which the faults and the tendency to wishful thinking and prejudices on both sides are clear.

In March 1944 the Commander-in-Chief Bomber Command complained to the DNI, then Rear-Admiral Rushbrooke, that an intelligence summary circulated by the Admiralty had given a seriously misleading impression of the effect on U-boat construction of British and American bombing. This summary had expressed the view that the fall in U-boat numbers coming from the yards was so general that bombing alone could not be the direct cause. It seemed probable that the Germans had decided to cut down their building programme. The airmen's view was that the Germans might well have decided that their own overstrained resources could not cope with large-scale building of U-boats but that the RAF bombing and mining were largely responsible. They also argued that the supply to the yards of engines, accumulators and other equipment had been seriously affected. Asking for a more careful investigation, they suggested that the authors of this report had been trying deliberately to minimize the effects of the bombing offensive.

As it was the belief of some people in Whitehall – especially in the Admiralty – that the effects of bombing in Germany had been overrated for two, or even three, years before in order to maintain the priority in new aircraft and other resources given to Bomber Command, this complaint of bias and exaggeration from that source had an ironic interest.* There may well have been such a bias in the minds of some of those who approved the report; on the other hand, there were others present to guard against it. But it was the method of working of the Committee, not only its integrity, that was being questioned.

The DNI's reply, in which Ian Fleming had taken a hand, was as conclusive in content as it was conciliatory in tone. The last thing his Division wished to do was to belittle the efforts of Bomber Command. He himself had been surprised by the conclusions of the report and he described to Harris how it had been produced, not inside the Admiralty, but by an inter-departmental committee on which airmen were represented.

The Chairman, he pointed out, was from the Ministry of Economic Warfare; four representatives came from the Admiralty, four from the Air Ministry (one of them from Bomber Command), one from the United States Air Force, three from the Ministry of Economic Warfare and one from the research establishment called RE8. These had been unanimous that the reduction was due to the effect of the blockade; a sub-committee had drawn up a report on agreed lines, the Joint Intelligence Staff had accepted the conclusions after examining the evidence, and the Admiralty report was no more than the incidental result.

One must sympathize with 'Bomber' Harris who, having been nagged day in and day out in earlier times to turn his bombers on heavily protected naval targets, must often have had the feeling in the eyes of the Navy he could do nothing right.*

Yet, at the operational level, that is to say in the day-to-day work of the OIC on reconnaissance, mining, damage assessment, appreciation of enemy intentions in combined operations, the naval-air relationship was excellent. A barrister in RAF uniform would call daily to hammer out with the OIC the real state of the *Scharnhorst* and *Gneisenau* lying in dock in Brest; a senior RN captain acting as liaison officer at Bomber Command enjoyed the friendship and confidence of its Chief – indeed, Harris was rightly proud of the great success of his mining operations against German shipping in the Baltic, which owed much to OIC's meticulous daily study of swept channels deduced from shipping routes and other sources. The Navy's debt to Coastal Command's arduous and often dangerous reconnaissance work over German bases and against the U-boats was tremendous.

On the dangers of excessive secrecy among intelligence workers and between departments there is half a book to be written. The demand of the planners and operations staff – to say nothing of the politicians – that they should be told everything needs no explanation; the American intelligence expert, Mr Sherman Kent of the CIA, makes this point well:

It is interesting to speculate how far Lord Keynes would have got if libraries had withheld large blocks of economic data on the ground that they were operational, or how Dr Freud might have progressed if mental clinics had sealed their records against him on the ground that they were too confidential. Yet intelligence people are constantly confronted with this very sort of argument.*

'Security', he concludes, 'comes at a great cost in terms of results, and it should be allowed to interfere only so far as is absolutely necessary.'

But let us look at the difficulty from the view of the keeper of the secrets. He is constantly in fear lest the enemy discover through treachery and carelessness on the one side or by ingenuity on the other how much is known about himself. The layman may think it desirable that the enemy should respect and fear – if possible, overrate – that knowledge, so that he may be more cautious and less self-confident than he might otherwise be. There is something in this view of a reputation for intelligence on the one side being a deterrent to mischief by the other; but it is one of which the intelligence officer pure and simple is rightly suspicious. He must not risk having his sources compromised or used against him. He does not know how much the enemy knows of his methods and information already; he cannot guess accurately what pieces are missing from his opposite number's mosaic. It may be ninety per cent; it may be only five per cent. Better, therefore, to maintain complete silence and minimize the possible damage.

Obviously an intelligence department dedicated to this attitude would quickly become useless to the operational agencies it was designed to serve. The human tendency to hoard jealously is only too common; and the intelligence expert is seldom the best judge of the use to which his material can be put. The difficulty is acute when questions of publicity and propaganda arise, both in wartime branches of the defence operation.

An interesting solution to this difficulty was found by NID two years after the war began. At first press and publicity (as well as security) had been under the DNI, who found himself in the impossible position of withholding information with one hand while passing it out with the other. (See Chapter 3.) Having given up press and publicity, he then found himself pressed by the secret Political Warfare Executive to provide ideas and information beyond that given to the Press for use in propaganda and subversive operations against the enemy. That clearly could not be done by Press Division, for they would then be giving one lot of material and orders to their newspaper contacts for open use while giving another lot to covert organizations for limited use.

The alternative found was to create a sub-section of the DNI's personal staff called 17Z whose duty was to be in touch with all current propaganda and subversive operations of interest to the Admiralty and collect from all NID sections material required for them. This involved explaining to officers of the OIC like Denning and Winn what the current propaganda objective was (in most cases it had been chosen at their request or suggestion) and then obtaining from them current information about U-boats and surface ships which could be turned against the enemy through various radio, press and personal channels. Likewise, 17Z worked very closely with the prisoners-of-war section, getting from them material to be used either in BBC broadcasts to the German Navy or in the 'black' and 'grey' operations conducted by Mr Sefton Delmar under PWE direction.*

Because this work had as much to do with politics and planning as with intelligence, it was watched over by a special committee of the Parliamentary Secretary, the Director of Plans and the Director of Naval Intelligence, which met only when the operation ran into difficulties. The week to week planning was done under the Deputy-Director of Plans and Press Division were kept fully informed about and even contributed to the ideas and directives produced.

This ingenious organization is described at some length as a means – adopted by other Service Ministries – of providing someone to bridge the gap between the preference of the intelligence officer to release as little as possible for use and the hope of the political agencies that as much as possible would be published for operational use. A somewhat similar role was played by Ewen Montagu and his section 17M who brought together into one group of minds the purposes of a planned operation, the intelligence available about it, and the measures needed to deceive the enemy about location, timing and

THE SIN AND THE CURE

strength. There is no doubt that this is one way – there may be others – of overcoming the natural secretiveness of the expert in pure intelligence: to have an experienced intelligence officer planning the public or operational use of secret material with proper safeguards.*

Is there now anything useful to be added? Perhaps this – so obvious when it is pointed out but so generally forgotten. The basis of intelligence is the file; but the file depends on the man using it. Intelligence is the product of a team, and that team thrives on tradition and good morale as a regiment or a ship does. The essence of healthy tradition is continuity* and a condition of high morale is recognition. In neither respect was intelligence encouraged between the wars. It was this failure that led Godfrey, with Rushbrooke's support, to found after the war the 1936 Club, consisting of former officers of NID who would invite to dinners and parties – and later co-opt – successive Directors and selected RNVR or civilian recruits. After twenty-two years the club still meets, though at longer intervals and in dwindling numbers. So the spirit of the war years was kept alive and with it many of the facts and some of the judgements contained in this book.

It may assist discussion of a complicated subject to set out in the briefest simplicity what the author and those who have helped him consider to be the principal lessons of NID's experience:

1 Fighting commanders, technical experts and political leaders are liable to ignore, under-rate or even despise intelligence. Obsession and bias often begin at the top.
2 Intelligence for the fighting services should be directed as far as possible by civilians.
3 Intelligence is the voice of conscience to a staff. Wishful thinking is the original sin of men of power.
4 Intelligence judgements must be kept constantly under review and revision. Nothing must be taken for granted either in premises or deduction.
5 Intelligence departments must be fully informed about operations and plans, but operations and plans must not be dominated by the facts and views of intelligence. Intelligence is the servant and not the master.

365

6 Reliance on one source is dangerous; the more reliable and comprehensive the source, the greater the dangers.

7 One's communications are always in danger; the enemy is always listening in, even if he cannot understand. Intelligence has a high responsibility for security.

8 The intelligence worker must be prepared for villainy; integrity in the handling of facts has to be reconciled with the unethical way they have been collected.

9 Intelligence is ineffective without showmanship in presentation and argument.

10 The boss, whoever he is, cannot know best and should not claim that he does.

11 Intelligence is indivisible. In its wartime practice the divisions imposed by separate services and departments broke down.

12 Excessive secrecy can make intelligence ineffective.

13 Intelligence is produced from files but by people. They require recognition, continuity and tradition, like a ship or a regiment.*

Epilogue:
the end and the beginning of NID

The end . . .

Twenty years of peace and cold war were needed to prepare the fundamental changes in the Intelligence structure of the Navy and other Services to which the lessons of the war pointed – at any rate for a few forward-looking officials and officers. The natural wish in Whitehall – indeed, the urgent necessity – was to disband or cut down enormous departments, to discover as soon as possible the minimum accommodation and staff with which NID could work effectively. The Germans, Italians and Japanese had been decisively defeated; it was not clear to most people – nor did many of them care in 1945 – where the next threat of war might come from. The Russians, it is true, had been difficult in the last hours of victory, in some situations hostile and threatening; but it seemed unlikely, after the losses and damage they had suffered, that they would risk a major war for years to come.

Yet it was the behaviour of the Russians and their collaborators – first in Berlin, then in Austria, then in North Korea – that ensured only a short life for the British Government's plans to disarm, relax and concentrate on the reconstruction of economic and social life. Stalin achieved the notable feat of forcing a Labour Government to start vigorous rearmament. Thereby NID was saved from the steep decline into which it had fallen between 1918 and 1938 and was given a new, major task: the study of the threat to Commonwealth sea communications, first of the Soviet Union's submarines and aircraft, in the use of which former German officers were giving advice,

N

and then of the new nuclear weapons. It had also to consider the naval implications of Soviet political interest in areas like Indonesia, the Persian Gulf, the Arctic Ocean and the Red Sea.

Increasingly after 1948 this work was shared with allies. Either directly and bilaterally with the Navy Department in Washington, which had shown itself ready to continue close co-operation with NID in London; or less directly and multi-laterally with a dozen or more North Atlantic Treaty allies in Paris. Although the actual collection of intelligence remained mainly a national responsibility, NATO's Standing Group in Washington was responsible for supplying integrated intelligence to the supreme and subordinate commanders. From Norfolk, Virginia, the Supreme Allied Commander North Atlantic (SACLANT) promulgated purely naval intelligence to lower naval formations in the Atlantic Command, and in Paris the Supreme Headquarters was responsible for informing the European commands, some of which were naval. This kind of joint, integrated staff work, coming so soon after the great combined headquarters of wartime, must have encouraged in Whitehall the movement towards integration which was eventually to bring about the abolition of the post of Director of Naval Intelligence.

Between 1939 and 1945 changes had taken place in the priorities of Naval Intelligence which excluded any return to the limited pre-war organization. First, there was the rapidly growing demand for all kinds of technical and industrial information which NDI was not organized to supply from purely Admiralty sources; about electronics, under-water communications, new weapons and fuels, air missile developments and so on. Likewise, experience had shown the need for specialized financial and economic knowledge in assessing, for example, an enemy's capacity to resist blockade, to build ships, to subsidize allied navies. Such work had been done in wartime for the Service Departments by the Ministry of Economic Warfare, whose spokesmen had quickly become indispensable as civilian members of Joint Service intelligence and planning bodies. It had also been learned that political and press information was better organized from a single civilian source and that the efforts of NID and its military and air force counterparts to produce separate assessments of enemy economic capabilities and political intentions was pretentious and superfluous.

Such conclusions and theories had been much discussed in the last year of the war among Service officers, both regular and temporary, who had worked successfully together. By the summer of 1944 Rear-Admiral Rushbrooke, the DNI, was already receiving from members of his staff through Room 39 papers which advocated a post-war organization which would concentrate economic, scientific and much non-secret intelligence in a department which would be, so to speak, supra-service – meeting the needs of Admiralty, War Office and Air Ministry without coming under their direction. It was from discussions like these all over Whitehall that sprang in 1945 the decision of the Chiefs of Staff to establish a Joint Intelligence Bureau outside the Service Ministries under Major-General Kenneth Strong, who had been chief of staff intelligence to General Eisenhower in the Supreme Allied Headquarters during the North African, Sicilian and Normandy operations. This decision was to prove the thin end of the wedge of integration, the first move towards the changes in organization which are specially associated for the Navy with the period that Lord Mountbatten was First Sea Lord (1955–9) and then as Chief of the Defence Staff (1959–65) – that is to say as chairman of the committee of the heads of the three Services and their spokesman with the Defence Committee of the Cabinet.

Mountbatten, whose ideas were only slowly accepted in the Admiralty, had the advantage of an experience which was almost unique among his contemporaries; for he had been British Director of Combined Operations in Europe and later Supreme Allied Commander in South-East Asia where he was served by an integrated naval, military and air staff, the Intelligence part of which was under Major-General Lamplough, RM, a product of Godfrey's days in NID. Mountbatten had been convinced that the Services in peacetime must not go back to the old methods of running their affairs in three exclusive departments. Indeed, other officers and a few politicians realized then that the case for a single Ministry of Defence in peacetime was unanswerable. Those who could look into the seeds of time were already discussing a department which might absorb Admiralty, War Office and Air Ministry

369

(cutting it was hoped the long administrative tails of those departments) and would reduce the status of their political heads, the First Lord and the Secretaries of State for War and for Air.

Throughout his time as First Sea Lord (1954–9) Mountbatten was preparing the way for the Navy's eventual acceptance of such changes; and it was no coincidence that the officer appointed in 1960 to be Director of Naval Intelligence was Rear-Admiral Norman Denning, whose work from 1938 onwards in creating the Operational Intelligence Centre and later during the war advising on the movements of the German Fleet has been described in an early chapter of this book.*

Denning had been one of the earliest supporters of the idea of a Joint Intelligence Bureau and what would flow from its creation. As it turned out he was to be the last really independent DNI of all, for in 1965 the post was abolished after Rear-Admiral Graham had succeeded him with the old title but subordinated to the new post of Deputy Chief of Defence Staff (Intelligence). This was filled by the promotion of Denning, who with this title of DCDS(I) became adviser to the Chief of Defence Staff on behalf of all three Services.

Little of all this was known to the general public until in 1963 Mr Peter Thorneycroft's White Paper on the Central Organization of Defence (Cmd 2097) announced this decision:

Service Intelligence staffs and the Joint Intelligence Bureau will be pooled to form a Joint Intelligence Staff. Senior officers of each Service will still be responsible for presenting their professional views on subjects which primarily concern their own Service. But the staff as a whole will be integrated. It will be responsible . . . for producing a *defence intelligence point of view* on matters which are of interest to the Ministry of Defence. (Author's italics.)

In other words, the information and appreciations which were to form British strategy in future would be in the shape of an agreed joint Service document. Henceforth a single officer of high rank, the DCDS(I), whose post would rotate between the Services, would attend Chief of Staff meetings and speak from a single brief. An earlier recommendation of the Chiefs of Staff in 1963 that this post might go to a civilian – presumably immune from Service loyalties and rivalries – was ignored. Readers who have followed the account of the work of the

Joint Intelligence Committee in wartime (Chapter 11) may recognize here the full blossoming of ideas then only in the bud.

To carry out such drastic changes time was needed. For the Navy the departure from the Admiralty was a painful business and a majority of officers with staff experience were probably suspicious of the new régime for some time. At first, after the move into the single Ministry of Defence (the stage called 'co-location' preceded the final stage of integration) the Director-General of Intelligence (Major-General Sir Kenneth Strong) found that he could not yet decide priorities between Service requests for intelligence, could not deploy their staffs where they were most urgently needed or control selection and movement of persons. That integration implied such giving up of authority by naval, military and air departmental chiefs was not at first readily conceded. However, on 21 July 1965 Mr Denis Healey, Minister of Defence, announced the appointment of a Director of Service Intelligence and a Director of Management and Support Intelligence. (In that year the first was a Rear-Admiral and the latter a Major-General.) This made it possible to assert control over the whole administrative side of intelligence work (registries, overseas travel, briefing of attachés abroad) by one officer while another devoted himself to the collection and study of facts and views.

Thus, at the time of writing, the process of integrating Intelligence is well under way after some eighty years of independent – or almost independent – naval activity in this field. It must immediately occur to any naval officer who knew the old structure that a Chief of Staff under these new arrangements loses his right of access to independent advice. It can be argued that a First Sea Lord who cannot call for his own estimate of enemy strength and intentions can no longer offer independent advice to the Minister or argue effectively for the Navy's share of the defence budget. He, like his army and air colleagues, is entitled only to express 'professional views on subjects which primarily concern their own Service'. That the role and stature of the First Sea Lord has been reduced is undeniable; but it became obvious over ten years ago that the role of a Chief of Staff and his Minister was declining as soon as the Minister of Defence took all decisions on allocating money within the Services.

However, the intention behind recent defence policy has been deliberately to produce single-service attitudes (the 'defence-intelligence point of view' is only one example), to remove inter-service rivalries and to recognize the inter-dependence of Navy, Army and Air Force. So this falling away of the Chief of Naval Staff and his colleagues was envisaged – and indeed recognized by Mountbatten's critics – when Mr Harold Macmillan was persuaded in 1962 by his Chief of Defence Staff that the policy of integration – though it would be in the short run unpopular – must be in the long run right and cheaper.

There the topic must be left, for this epilogue is concerned only with the disappearance of the Naval Intelligence Division after eighty-three years of life. It will not be possible until 1995, under present regulations, for historians to tell the full story of these interesting and momentous changes. But it is clear, from the evidence of those who have taken part in the fierce controversies provoked by the policy, that a few naval officers (rather than the Admiralty) took the lead in promoting it, so bringing to an end the glamorous title of Director of Naval Intelligence.

The beginning . . .

Now it is interesting to consider how the Division first emerged. Improbable though it may now seem, the Royal Navy had no planners for war, no machinery of mobilization, no adequate intelligence organization through most of its period of supremacy in the last century. It needed the challenge of Russia in the Seventies, pressing down to the Mediterranean through the Balkans, and later the new fact of German ships steaming all over the world to frighten the Admiralty into the creation of a naval staff. Yet it was clear by the late Sixties to most people with inside knowledge that the Sea Lords, without skilled assistance, were being swamped by administrative detail in the new age of wireless telegraphy, steamships, railways and high explosives. It was not easy for them to foresee challenge from foreign navies and to plan in advance how to meet them. Once a decade there came an emergency which found the Admiralty unprepared and disorganized.

It was the Balkan crisis of 1878, during which Britain narrowly escaped war with Russia in defence of the Turks, that persuaded the Admiralty that it must improve its handling of intelligence. Indeed, that episode, which saw the Mediterranean Fleet entering the Straits in defiance of a Russian threat to occupy Constantinople, did much more: it enabled a few far-seeing minds to gain a point of principle. Once it was conceded by Ministers and Civil Servants that their Lordships should have the professional assistance of naval officers for intelligence purposes, there was no good reason why they should not be similarly assisted in preparing for war against the enemies about whom intelligence was warning them. Thus it came about that the emergence of the first naval staff and the growth of a naval intelligence department are inseparable in the twenty-five years before the First World War. The Director of Naval Intelligence was the first, and was to remain thereafter the senior, member of the Naval Staff directly responsible to the First Sea Lord. That fact probably gave him greater prestige with most naval officers than the activity of which he was in charge.

The alarm about the state of naval intelligence seems first to have been sounded in the last months of 1878 by the Naval Attachés in Paris and Rome, who separately urged that there should be in the Admiralty a small department under a combatant officer. Cdr Hubert Grenfell from Rome wrote that 'consular agents would not forward information of the most valuable nature while there is no well-known head of department on whose discretion they can rely'. Apart from studying the 'general organization and distribution of the naval forces of foreign powers' and 'acquiring an intimate knowledge of their fortification and of their naval ports and arsenals', this department should 'make suggestions for attack in case of hostilities'. In other words an intelligence department could also undertake planning. More bluntly Grenfell's colleague in Paris wrote that 'during the last two years it has been patent to all who had to do with the recent eastern difficulties that the intelligence in the Admiralty regarding the strength and distribution of foreign navies was very imperfect and that in some cases the information asked for could not be furnished'. This was not surprising when a solitary clerk in Military

Branch, digesting material in the intervals of other duties, represented the total strength for such work.

To these and other proddings Mr W. H. Smith, Disraeli's First Lord, reacted swiftly. In May 1879 a committee of admirals and captains recommended the creation of 'an Admiralty Intelligence Branch' under the immediate control of the senior Naval Lord; but the Civil Lord treated with scant courtesy the idea that naval officers should be used for such duties and insisted that an extra clerk would suffice. However, a year later a new First Lord – Lord Northbrook, a man of wide horizons who had been Viceroy in India and heard all about the problems of the Near East from his cousin Baring in Egypt – received a letter from Colonel Gordon, then in Mauritius, which gave the cause of naval intelligence a useful push.

Writing from 'this Patmos of idleness', Gordon asked why warships should not carry précis of information about the colonies and other countries, which could be kept up to date by the Intelligence Department of the War Office. 'Looking at the past events,' he concludes, 'it has certainly been owing to a want of knowledge that we have come to grief in many places; we have a great inclination to drift along till things come to a crisis.' Then, in a postcript: 'Next to having no information is the having information and keeping it shut up.' This was what was happening: information sent in from ships and from Consuls was not being properly recorded, collated and then redistributed to the Fleet.

All that happened for the next two years was that a certain Captain Ernest Rice who had been Naval Attaché in Europe, with a senior clerk to help him, started recording and collecting in one place information which was scattered among departments with their own special interests: the Hydrographer with his charts, the Controller with his details of foreign construction plans, Naval Ordnance and Transport studying foreign torpedoes and guns, none of which thought of their material as being useful to future naval operations. This was an improvement, but only slight, as was shown in 1882. After the Fleet had bombarded the forts of Alexandria, the Permanent Secretary of the Admiralty reported that 'in July we really knew very little that was useful and had not sufficient knowledge of the

Egyptian defences to enable a judgement to be formed whether six or eight ironclads were required to destroy them'. 'Who' he asked, 'is to undertake the task of compiling a gazetteer filled with information, with plans and sketches, relating to matters bearing on naval operations?'

At last, in December 1882 the Foreign Intelligence Committee was formed under Captain William H. Hall (father of Jellicoe's famous DNI, Captain – later Admiral Sir Reginald – Hall), with a Mr Hoste of Military Branch as Secretary. Their instructions were exacting enough: 'to collect, classify and record, with a complete index, all information which bears a naval character, or which may be of value during naval operations, to keep up our knowledge of progress made by foreign countries in naval matters and to preserve the information in a form readily available for reference.' It was to be expected that Hall, if there should be an overseas emergency, would be overworked. Sure enough, there were several major alarms in the next three years: the French naval operations in Tonkin, the troubles with the Mahdi in the Sudan, and the expedition to relieve and rescue General Gordon (who must have wished the Admiralty had taken his advice and given more attention to the navigation of the Nile), and the problem of transporting troops from India to the Red Sea during the south-west monsoon. On top of such immediate demands, Hall was making a comparative study of British and French gun manufacture and drafting plans for the protection of British commerce in war. One lesson was quickly learned: that where there is no planning section the intelligence section will be called upon to plan, and while it does plan all intelligence work will stop.

Two years later when the new Foreign Intelligence Committee seemed established and was doing useful work it came under official and public attack. The new Junior Lord of the Admiralty, Captain Lord Charles Beresford (involved twenty years later in the celebrated dispute with Admiral Fisher) denounced in a report 'a wicked state of things, there was no staff to prepare for war', he wrote; 'there should be a bigger intelligence department and it should have two sections, one of which should deal with war preparation and the other with intelligence – all under a Flag Officer'. The immediate cause of the agitation was the Pendjeh crisis on the Afghan border

375

with Russia, during which the Fleet had been ordered to shadow all Russian ships in the Pacific. The controversy in the Admiralty eventually reached the Press and Beresford's report was published in the *Pall Mall Gazette* of 13 October 1886. Although much of the information about Britain's unreadiness for war must have come from Hall's department, Hall himself was attacked by the Editor as a 'mere compiler of information, a contemporary gazetteer in breeches'.

Very quickly there was set up a further committee on which Beresford himself sat, which recommended that there should now be a Department of Naval Intelligence with a much bigger staff and under a Rear-Admiral. Quite revolutionary, and for the future of the Naval Staff decisive, was the recommendation that the new NID should prepare and keep up to date 'a complete plan for mobilisation' and 'prepare when directed to do so, plans of naval campaign'. With the advantage of hindsight it is not difficult to understand why, if war became more likely, the work of war planning and mobilisation would be split off from intelligence into separate divisions of a naval staff; but for the next twenty years NID exercised these functions and enjoyed a unique power and position in the Admiralty. It was in fact the Naval Staff in embryo.

As the possible challenges to Britain's naval position became more numerous and formidable – to Russia and France were added Germany and the United States on the oceans of the world and in the Mediterranean Austria and Italy – the Navy's response accelerated. The Staff College and the War Course at Greenwich, for example, were proposed by the DNI, Rear-Admiral Reginald Custance, and approved in 1900: for the first time the Navy was to acquire and discuss a strategic doctrine. Two years after that a trade division was added to NID and the first papers were written about the routing of merchant ships in war. NID had become the centre of much of the thinking and argument set going by the publication in 1889 of Mahan's book on the influence of sea power.

The period of NID supremacy was not to last long. In 1909 a committee of Ministers, deeply concerned to find that the two senior Admirals afloat disagreed between themselves and with the War Office about war plans for assisting the French against a German attack, decided that a proper staff of trained officers

376

must be set up: the trade division of NID was abolished, and the war and mobilization divisions were turned into a new Naval Mobilization Department. This sensible reform left NID, which had become a virtual naval staff, shorn of half its strength and functions, back where it had been in 1887, collecting and collating intelligence. It also left the First Sea Lord without anyone to discuss and collate plans for war, as the DNI had done. However, when Churchill as First Lord insisted in 1912 on creating a staff structure which made a clear distinction between War Information, War Plans and War Arrangements, under a chief of war staff, the Naval Intelligence Division retained its senior position and the Director retained direct access to the First Sea Lord.*

It has been already described in this Epilogue how in the Sixties NID was merged with other Service intelligence divisions into a department of Service Intelligence in an integrated Ministry of Defence. That change was brought about largely by the personal efforts of Admiral of the Fleet Lord Mountbatten, who was Chief of Defence Staff 1959–65 and Chief of Naval Staff 1955–9. It is therefore interesting to record that his father Prince Louis of Battenburg who was Director of Naval Intelligence in 1902–5 was one of the most energetic advocates of a specially trained staff of naval officers to run the intelligence, planning and mobilization work of the Navy. He did not hesitate to point to Moltke's organization of the German General Staff as a model for the Admiralty to study. 'The NID as now constituted,' he pointed out to Sir John Fisher in 1902, 'is modelled exactly on Moltke's great creation. Its three main divisions have their exact counterpart in Berlin. We thus have the skeleton ready to hand – it only wants clothing and placing on a higher pedestal'.* By this he meant that the DNI should be given such a position that his views, or rather the 'well-digested and focused opinion of the many and versatile brains at work in his "shop" cannot be lightly brushed aside or ignored'. The Director, urged Prince Louis, should be a member of the Board, second only to the First Sea Lord and that officer's first assistant. 'Preparation for War, in every particular, should be in his charge, but it must be applied in a comprehensive manner.'

Fortunately, perhaps, for Intelligence as such, this claim

was not conceded; but the insistence that preparation for war should be intellectually as well as administratively thorough made its mark. Of the work of Custance his predecessor in this 'misnamed department' he wrote: 'with irresistible but hardly perceptible force, it has backed up the Naval Lords, invaded every department of the Admiralty, and it is no exaggeration to say now that no question of importance greater than, say, a change of an article of uniform, is decided upon without the NID having its say'.

How the Division met the challenge of the First World War is a theme which has still to find its historian.

Appendix

DIRECTORS OF NAVAL INTELLIGENCE 1882–1964

Hall (father)	1882	Hotham	1924
Bridge	1887	Domvile	1927
Beaumont	1894	Usborne	1930
Custance	1899	Dickens	1932
Battenberg	1902	Scott	1935
Ottley	1905	Troup	1935
King-Hall	1907	Godfrey	1939
Slade	1907	Rushbrooke	1943
Bethell	1909	Parry	1946
Jackson	1912	Longley-Cook	1948
Oliver	1913	Buzzard	1951
Hall (son)	1914	Inglis	1954
Sinclair	1919	Denning	1959–1964
Fitzmaurice	1921		

Notes

Chapter 1 The room and the man

PAGE 2

Godfrey was described by one of his junior officers as a tall tapering man, with a head of imposing size and authority balanced upon a heroic torso and the legs of a dancing master. He looked like one of those Western Chinese that the French and Americans reckon Englishmen to be. This impression doubtless derived from the Admiral's unwavering pale blue-grey eyes, set beneath a domed cranium, which could be by turn merry and amused or cold and steely. He talked very clearly and fast in a misleadingly soft voice.

PAGE 3

The kind of talents and personalities that are gathered together in an intelligence staff may need the special attention of someone who combines the knowledge of a solicitor with the emollient skills of a *maître d'hôtel*. These qualities were combined in Merrett who could pass on his chief's warnings about their wives' insecurity to resentful senior officers as well as he could advise on the troubles of a member of the Division whose family burdens had been underestimated by a cruel Admiralty and succeed.

PAGE 4

At one time it consisted of two stockbrokers, a school-master, a KC, a journalist, a collector of books on original thought, an Oxford classics don, two RN officers, a barrister's clerk, an artist, an insurance agent and several women assistants.

PAGE 5

Line 22. The committees at which NID had to be represented included in May 1943 the Axis Oil Committee of the War Cabinet, Joint Intelligence, Ships' Names, Beach Survey, Enemy Shipping Losses Assessment, U-boat Assessment, Radio Counter-Measures, Cipher Security, Inter-Service W/T Security, Joint Planning Staff of the Political Warfare Executive, German Service and Civilian Morale, Inter-Service Security Board.

Line 29. The real father of Room 39 and by far the most experienced officer there was Paymaster Captain S. Woodhouse who in addition to being head of the NID Secretariat shared with the Civil Assistants Mr Miller and later Mr Johns the arduous task of instructing newly-joined reserve officers, and civilian assistants in the ways of the Admiralty and the internal Admiralty procedure for converting ideas into 'action'.

PAGE 6

People came to Room 39 with all kinds of schemes of skulduggery and divination. An apparently promising idea was to charter a fishing trawler and poke around the western ports of Ireland to report enemy activities. This was before it became clear early in the war that the Germans would probably respect Irish neutrality. The skipper was as credulous as he was adventurous and went ashore after an alleged spy, only to be arrested by the police who courteously released him through the British representative in Dublin.

A middle-aged couple in Woking so besieged the Division with letters and telephone messages that an officer was instructed to test in the Director's waiting room their method of divining the whereabouts of U-boats by poising a pendulum over charts of the North Atlantic. If it swung clockwise there was a German submarine present, if anticlockwise it was one of our own.

PAGE 14

In October 1941 Pound told him he could not keep this promise. His policy was to employ at sea those who had done well there, and to keep on land those who had done well there. Godfrey would, therefore, have to continue indefinitely as DNI.

PAGE 15

A grave international crisis was touched off by the arrival at Agadir on 1 July 1911 of a German gunboat, sent as a warning to the French against the annexation of Morocco. The episode and the unreadiness of the nation to deal with it gave a tremendous impulse to reforms in Whitehall, among them the creation of an active secret intelligence service (MI 6) and of a defensive one (MI 5). The respective heads were Cdr Mansfield Smith-Cummings RN and Colonel Kell, both of whom Godfrey visited. There was always a naval officer in charge of MI 6 until Admiral 'Quex' Sinclair died in December 1939.

PAGE 16

Line 9. When the *Repulse* evacuated British and other men, women and the children from Palma, Majorca, in 1937 a British artist and his wife were 'charmed and surprised to find anything beautiful aboard a warship, including Roy de Maistre's "Blue Tower" picture'. The Captain's day cabin was indeed unusual by the austere standards of those days: comfortable, in excellent taste, well designed for the hearing of music, bearing the stamp of expert advice from an architect friend, Brian O'Rorke. When teased about it, Godfrey would recall that the post-captains of Nelson's time took pride in the elegance of their furnishings and the quality of their hospitality.

Line 19. In 1942 Godfrey was to see exactly how difficult it was to get a first-class officer moved from an operational to an intelligence job. He proposed in January to appoint Captain J. A. S. Eccles, then Director of Operations (Home), as head of Intelligence Centre Far East. Eccles had had long training as a Japanese interpreter and specialist and was the only cryptographer who had had a successful naval career. At the urgent request of the Chiefs of Staff it was agreed in January that Eccles should leave in April, but in May he had still not left and Godfrey returned to the charge. The situation in the Indian Ocean, he emphasized, was most dangerous; C-in-C Eastern Fleet would never get the intelligence machine it needed without Eccles. However, Eccles was at the time directing Coastal Command operations, organizing some of the biggest troop movements of the war and helping Combined Operations with their future plans. After a hard paper tussle, Pound intervened with the words 'There is too much going on in home waters for Captain Eccles to be spared.'

NOTES

Line 10. In the early summer of 1939 the head of the section of German Military Intelligence Staff concerned with Britain was sent to London to find out whether Mr Chamberlain's Government seriously intended war if Poland were attacked. The visit was open and above board but not given publicity. DNI was one of those who entertained Count von Schwerin so that he might talk with people like the Chief Whip, Mr R. A. B. Butler and others. Schwerin said that it was most difficult to get unwelcome intelligence past his immediate chiefs to the heads of Army and State. His British section had only three or four officers, he said, against thirty or forty in the French section. He realized the British were in earnest and he would say so in Berlin. He promised to let Godfrey know what success he had. Two months after war began, there came an anonymous communication from an unmistakable source, saying that the 'message had been delivered but not believed'.

Line 29. See Chapter 4.

PAGE 18

There is an excellent description of how these contacts were used for the recruitment of such personalities as Ian Fleming in John Pearson's *The Life of Ian Fleming* (Jonathan Cape, London, 1966. Chapter 9).

Chapter 2 Sources

PAGE 19

It is a principle of sound intelligence work—as opposed to journalism—that factual information is promulgated only if action is required. To circulate items to headquarters and commanders because they are 'interesting' is to waste the time of busy men and on occasion to risk extraordinary consequences. None the less, commanders and Ministers liked—as they still like—interesting tit-bits; and Heaven help the director of intelligence who denies to his chief of staff a morsel that has been presented to the chief of staff of another Service.

PAGE 20

Vice-Admiral Sir Ian Campbell, who was a Commander in charge of the German section when the Wehrmacht moved into Norway in

1940, gives an amusing example of AI intelligence by sighting. 'Very early one morning in the first crisis days, Admiral Godfrey came to the night desk with the First Sea Lord and other senior officers, to ask what was the latest news. Had the Germans got to Trondheim? It seemed so petty to say I don't know so I picked up the telephone, asked for Continental Trunks and got through in a few minutes to the Vice-Consul there in Trondheim, a naval officer. "Any sign of the Germans", I said breezily. "Yes", was the reply, "I can see the Huns coming up the hill and I've just burned my books".'

PAGE 23

In 1943, experience had shown the need to expand the grading system to make allowance for the inference which is part of the intelligence officer's job. It was therefore agreed by all Services that where inference was included without giving reasons for it, a figure should be used as a prefix followed by A, B, or C. Thus: 2A meant the facts allow one reasonable interpretation; 2B that they allowed more than one interpretation but the one suggested is the most likely; 2C indicated a case where there are various possibilities but attention is drawn to one of them.

PAGE 26

During the Six Day Middle East war of 1967, early in the morning of 6 June, Israeli intelligence monitors claimed to have intercepted a radio-telephone conversation between President Nasser in Cairo and King Hussein of Jordan in Amman. In this talk they were said to have agreed to accuse American and British aircraft of assisting Israel. The Israelis made public this fact on 9 June and on the 10th the *Daily Telegraph* was able to publish the tests made by Professor Kersta in New Jersey proving the authenticity of the Israeli tape recording. From the point of view of Intelligence the story is remarkable not only for the carelessness of the Arabs but also for the readiness of the Israelis to reveal their successful eavesdropping.

PAGE 27

Line 15. See the account of the capture of the weather ships *Muenchen* and *Lauenburg* on page 272.

Line 26. This is fully discussed in Chapter 4.

385

PAGE 29

The most remarkable instance of harm done and opportunities lost by not passing on this kind of intelligence from fear of compromising the source is described on pages 150-4 of Marder (*From Dreadnought to Scapa Flow* by Arthur J. Marder, [Oxford University Press, London, 1966]). It could be argued that the failure of the Admiralty to pass vital A1 information to Jellicoe lost him a decisive victory at Jutland in May 1916 and affected the whole course of the war.

PAGE 32

The use of overseas bases for this and other intelligence purposes is an aspect of their value which is often overlooked by those who regard bases as no longer necessary for the exercise of sea power.

PAGE 33

By October, 1942 there were sixteen naval 'Y' stations covering the world's oceans. The working of the system is fully described in Chapter 5.

PAGE 35

Early in 1940 the Chief of Air Staff asked in the Defence Committee for permission to bomb Emden where a concentration of U-boats had been observed from air photographs. Dudley Pound, who had heard nothing of this, asked that NID should be consulted first. The query went to the OIC and Admiral Clayton rang up Commander Denning at his home to check. Denning pointed out that Emden had never been a U-boat base and there must be some mistake. Clayton ordered him to get into the Admiralty car that was being sent down to him and visit Wembley where he could see for himself the photographs. Denning did so and ascertained that the concentration was of barges which had been mistaken by inexperienced interpreters for U-boats. Consultation between the intelligence departments of Whitehall was still in its infancy.

PAGE 36

After the *Scharnhorst* had been unsuccessfully attacked by Home Fleet torpedo bombers in mid June 1940, reports on the operation pointed out the importance of placing a ship accurately first and attacking her afterwards. Sightings by the attacking a/c were ten in number.

One was corrected from the a/c eighteen minutes after the original transmission; in two the position group was corrupt; in another the course originally reported as 900 was on investigation amended to 010, and in the fifth the position reported had one degree of longitude error. 'It is impossible to exaggerate the importance of accuracy when reporting the enemy', was the comment made on the Report of Proceedings. This shows some of the difficulties of accurate sighting and reporting, although it must be remembered that this was early in the war.

PAGE 37

These U-boats, with turbines driven by gases produced from the combustion of diesel fuel and hydrogen peroxide, were designed to reach very high under-water speeds for short periods.

PAGE 43

See Chapter 6 where the DNI's argument with the First Lord on U-boat sinkings is described.

PAGE 45

A remarkable example of how intelligence can be provided by unconscious indiscretion in the press is to be found in David Irving's *The Mare's Nest*, (Kimber, London, 1964) – page 255. During the V1 attacks on London, in 1944 one of Lord Cherwell's statisticians plotted seventy obituary notices from *The Times* and eighty from the *Daily Telegraph* which – making allowance for the preponderance in those newspapers of Kensington and Chelsea obituaries – would place the mean point of flying-bomb impact at Streatham Hill (from *The Times*) and at Clapham Junction (from the *Daily Telegraph*). The results were dangerously near the truth at a time when the Germans, misled by our deception methods, were trying to achieve sufficient accuracy to blot out the area from Tower Hill to West-minster.

PAGE 46

Line 14. In *The Times* of 19 August 1967 Mr Lambert, Conservative MP for Edmonton West in the Canadian House of Commons, told a reporter that the Dieppe Raid of 1942 'made D-day easier when it came'. But it was 'simply worked out on paper by staff officers and there were factors that they had not taken into account'. He himself, for example, 'landed with Churchill tanks on a shale beach quite unlike the ones on which he had been training in England, and the shale simply broke up the tracks of the tanks'.

Line 33. The contact register mentioned in Chapter 13 was lucky enough to find the man who had laid the mine defences for Madagascar's main port, which was the target of Operation 'Ironclad' in May 1942. He was able to trace them with fair detail on a map.

PAGE 49

On this episode, almost the first occasion on which NID was seriously tested (and the last in which the First Sea Lord undertook personal interrogation), the official history points out that the German pocket-battleships, battle-cruisers and (though not yet in service) the *Bismarck* and *Tirpitz*, could easily be confused at sea. 'It is now known,' writes Roskill, 'that, although without any intention to confuse identification, the Chief Constructor of the German Navy adhered deliberately to certain broad features in all the heavy ships designed by his department, and this produced a strong similarity in their silhouettes.' Fortunately each ship in each class had some special characteristic which high level vertical photography could pick up.

Chapter 3 From cold to hot war

PAGE 53

Outstanding among them was Gerald Dickens, then a Rear-Admiral, who was DNI from 1931–4. A friend and collaborator of Richmond, the Navy's leading thinker on strategic matters, Dickens vainly warned his superiors about the menace from Japan and the significance of her carrier building.

PAGE 54

Line 2. Likewise on the outbreak of war the Inter-service Training and Development Centre, the only body that had been working on landing against enemy resistance, was disbanded and members told that 'there would be no combined operations in this war'.

Line 19. In January 1936, the DNI reported his drawing office as 'snowed under'. He asked for two shorthand-typists to be appointed 'in order to keep the more secret work within the Division as far as possible, and encourage officers to dictate instead of drafting by hand'.

Line 25. Sinclair, Fitzmaurice, Hotham, Domvile, Usborne, Dickens, Scott, Troup.

PAGE 55

It seems likely that Norman Denning, like his brother Tom, Lord Denning, Master of the Rolls, who wrote the famous Report on the Ward-Profumo-Keeler case, had a natural talent for the law. Indeed, his appointment to the Admiralty in 1937 was designed to develop it. At a course on accountancy that he had attended as a Paymaster he had done so well in his law papers that the deputy Judge-Advocate of the Fleet told him he should eat his dinners and read for the Bar against the possible early retirement which threatened so many Lieutenant-Commanders in those days. To that end Denning was appointed to NID where he quickly realized that his work would leave no time to read for an alternative profession.

PAGE 57

Denning defined operational intelligence as 'that part of naval intelligence organization which concerns itself solely with obtaining, deducing, coordinating and promulgating intelligence which immediately affects any naval operation being, or about to be, undertaken by British or Allied, or any part of the British or Allied, fleets.'

PAGE 58

From Dreadnought to Scapa Flow, by Arthur J. Marder (Oxford University Press, London, 1966. Vol. 3, pp. 150 ff).

PAGE 59

On a smaller scale the Admiralty OIC was reproduced in Alexandria, Colombo, Hong Kong and Liverpool.

PAGE 61

Line 13. Troup spent a busy three days in February 1939 handing over to his successor. Godfrey was taken to meet Admiral Sinclair, then head of the Secret Intelligence Service. They talked over the gaps in our preparations, grumbled together about the information supplied by the Foreign Office and the rumour planting by the Germans. 'Whatever happens', Troup said to Godfrey, 'someone will say "I told you so." ' The only British strategy he could detect was to stick by the French, enforce the blockade tightly and bomb Germany.

Less than a year later one of the very bright young men working in Professor Lindemann's statistical section serving Churchill (then First Lord) was surprised to find a belief in the highest quarters that a German collapse was possible within six months. The occasion of his discovery was a dispute between the Ministry of Food, which wanted to bring into force its excellent scheme for rationing sugar and so save shipping space, and those in the Government who maintained that such a step would depress morale at home and give the Germans tremendous encouragement. This, indeed, was the view supported for a while by the First Lord himself, according to Sir Donald MacDougall who told the author the story.

Line 28. The lunchtime meeting at the Carlton Grill at which Godfrey met Ian Fleming for the first time is vividly and accurately told in John Pearson's *Life of Ian Fleming*, op. cit.

PAGE 63

The relations of the Admiralty with Ministers and Parliament, whether in peace or war, are sown with mines on which senior officers can blow themselves up. In 1940 one of the DNI's staff provided Lord Chatfield (a retired Admiral of the Fleet and *the* naval elder statesman) with information about welfare in the merchant service. This was used in a debate in the House of Lords and aroused the indignation of the Minister of Transport. For not obeying an Admiralty order forbidding members of the staff to provide 'a member of the Legislature with information' Godfrey received minutes of displeasure not only in the green ink of the First Sea Lord but also in the red ink of the First Lord. Considering the lobbying that goes on nowadays by Service departments with Members of Parliament and the briefing of Opposition front-benchers, which is tolerated if not allowed, the incident seems curiously archaic.

PAGE 72

The decision about who should receive straight information and secret intelligence was one of the most difficult that fell to the Division. In 1942 the DNI faced a demand from a Minister to see material from a very exclusive source. The person in question was reputed to be garrulous in political company. Godfrey decided to consult Sir John Anderson, then the overlord for home affairs, who had an unrivalled knowledge of the workings of government. Having heard the delicate problem stated, he asked Godfrey to come back in three days' time for a considered answer. 'Looking rather like a judge without his wig', Sir John pointed out that the Minister's job was, in essence, 'to defend the vote of his department in the House. The acquisition of the information he was asking for was not paid for out of his vote and he had therefore no valid claim to receive it.'

PAGE 73

One curious incident in DNI's experience of the Press is worth recording. In November 1939, he asked Rear-Admiral Thursfield, the Naval Correspondent of *The Times*, to work out a scheme for a body of naval correspondents at sea and to discuss it with C-in-C Home Fleet, whom he was visiting. Somehow this came to the notice of Churchill, who expressed grave displeasure at this sign of preference for *The Times*. Was it – people wondered – because Lord Beaverbrook had been offended?

Chapter 4 The wireless war

PAGE 77

The results of cryptanalysis are useful to intelligence for operational purposes only if they are 'current'; that is to say a signal must be read shortly after it is made.

PAGE 80

Line 3. In January 1940, the submarines *Seahorse, Undine* and *Starfish* were lost in the Heligoland Bight. After this disaster ciphers carried by submarines were cut drastically and separated from those of the Fleet.

Line 40. One of DNI's security tasks was to ensure that the literal text of a signal, for example of congratulations from Admiralty to ship, was never reproduced in the Press without skilful scrambling. However, it is now known that the Germans were not interested in this form of intelligence.

Completely secure arrangements were also made for the thousands of messages transmitted to Churchill on his way to and from conferences – for example the meeting with Roosevelt aboard the *Prince of Wales* in August 1941. There, signals covered not only day-to-day Government business but all information needed to reproduce the plot in the Cabinet War Room wherever he might be.

Line 4. On 15 June, 1940, Admiral Forbes, C-in-C Home Fleet, protested to the Admiralty about the 'quite unexpected appearance of enemy forces, in the far North on June 8 which led to the sinking of the *Glorious*, two destroyers and a liner'. He demanded an overhaul of the air reconnaissance methods being used. 'The enemy reconnoitre Scapa daily if they consider it necessary. Our reconnaissances of the enemy's main bases are few and far between. It is most galling that the enemy should know just where our ships always are, whereas we generally learn where his major forces are when they sink one or more of our ships.' Inadequate British air reconnaissance, we now know, was only part of the story. (Roskill, *The War at Sea*, HMSO, London, 1954–61, vol. 1, p. 198).

Line 6. Roskill, op. cit., vol. 1 p. 267 says: 'A great set-back for German naval strategy at this time was the change by the Admiralty of naval codes and ciphers. The insight into British operations, which had lasted so long, then came to an end. Knowledge of British movements had spared German vessels many a surprise encounter with superior forces and this had become an element in operational planning.'

The intelligence aspect of the sinking of the *Scharnhorst* is discussed on p. 36–7.

For Doenitz's account of this action, see *Memoirs* of Admiral Doenitz (English translation. Weidenfeld & Nicolson, London, 1959).

Ibid, p. 328.

PAGE 89

Line 21. Doenitz writes plaintively: 'As we ourselves had no organized air reconnaissance at our disposal my opposite number Admiral Horton was able to take a look at my cards without my being able to look at his.'

Line 34. Great care was taken by both Naval staffs never to reveal that a warship had been boarded and that its cipher material possibly taken. See the account of the weather-ship capture in Chapter 12.

PAGE 91

The majority of signals when deciphered contain much jargon and many blanks. To translate and interpret them quickly and fully the cryptographer needs a constant supply of technical information, dictionaries, handbooks, telephone directories from enemy sources, as well as full information about his forces' current operations.

PAGE 100

The way it was planned to use the civilians shows the scope of this intelligence activity. There were to be twenty-nine charge hands and 152 operators. Posts were vacant in 1938 for only seven and thirty-five respectively.

Chapter 5 The tracking room

PAGE 104

End to end escort by surface ships between the USA and the UK was achieved in June 1941, but end to end escort with aircraft did not exist until May 1943.

PAGE 105

Normally every ship capable of more than fifteen knots would be routed independently and at any moment there might be 200,000 tons of shipping crossing the North Atlantic with no protection except its speed and the Admiralty's intelligence. After the trade and operational plots had been combined early in 1942, not only all the convoys but also all troop convoys, independent troopers and sometimes warships on passage were controlled by Hall's team.

Having captured the French Navy's signal school at Brest in 1940 and studied records of British convoy diversion orders based on fixes of U-boat positions, German intelligence was able to judge the accuracy of British methods early on.

Also useful was the German Navy List and reports in periodicals received through Switzerland with reports of births of U-boat Commanders' children, from which deductions about leave could be made.

Line 13. It is worth emphasizing at this point that had the tracking room been adequately staffed for complex and protracted research work, the insecurity of our own signals (described in Chapter 4) would almost certainly have been detected earlier than it was. The cunning with which U-boats appeared in the course of convoys which had certainly not been reported by German air reconnaissance, and the way in which convoy diversions were countered, might have been detected as unmistakable evidence of Doenitz's access to some of our signals. The discovery was not in fact made until early 1943.

Line 39. Once a month – at critical periods once a fortnight – these same interests confronted one another in the Anti-Submarine meeting at which the ACNS (UT) would take the chair, and to which Admiral Sir Percy Noble and later Admiral Sir Max Horton would come from Liverpool. Here would be also C-in-C Coastal Command, the commanders of 15 and 19 Groups, DOD(H), DDIC and 8(S) himself. Here, witnesses testify, the formidable barrister, Rodger Winn, with his three (later four) stripes was sometimes roughly handled by the professionals; but Patrick Beesly, his RNVR deputy (with only two stripes but no less stern independence) admits to having been given a smoother ride.

It needed many months of experience to ascertain which of the D/F stations were the most reliable.

It is a technical question of some interest whether individual estimates of positions should have been standardized in form. One might say the transmitter was within 30 miles radius of 45°N and 25°W where the cords came together; or it might be described by drawing a rectangle and saying that it was within 25 miles north or south of a line from 46°N 24°30'W to 45°N 27°30'W.

PAGE 113

One of the most remarkable feats of routing in the whole war was the bringing together of four hundred ships off Gibraltar for the 'Torch' landings in 1942. Hall and Winn were given thirty-six hours' notice to plan the movement of the slow convoy from the Bristol Channel and the fast one from the Clyde on a course far west of Biscay to avoid the U-boats coming and going from their French bases.

PAGE 114

A group of escort vessels not attached to one convoy but free to act as reinforcement where needed.

PAGE 119

Line 18. The techniques of U-boat tracking were imparted to the Americans even before they came into the war. Commander Knowles of the US Navy, who became Winn's distinguished opposite number in 10th Fleet, wrote: 'Owing to sightings and contacts not available to the Germans, while the U-boat keeps wireless silence our tracking room often knows more of particular U-boats' positions than does Admiral Doenitz himself.'

Line 23. One of Winn's assistants, sent to the United States to advise his opposite number, Commander Knowles, on U-boat matters, returned to England in the *Queen Elizabeth*, then running unescorted as a fast troopship with the better part of an American infantry division on board. He was allowed to study the course and diversions laid down for the captain, which included at one point a sharp northern turn. He confesses that his confidence in the judgement of the tracking room was less, but only a very little less, than complete.

PAGE 120

Line 12. Even the celebrated visit to the Citadel of Stafford Cripps in 1942 did not cover such matters. As a proof to the Commons of his readiness to accept criticism and advice on the conduct of the war, Churchill chose Cripps to make a special inquiry into the fight against the U-boats. Their Lordships, rather alarmed by this

Socialist and civilian intrusion, drew some comfort in the fact that in the OIC they had one brilliant barrister with whom to confront another. So when Cripps entered the tracking room, the gold braid which escorted him faded away after a few minutes and the two legal men touched blades and fenced happily for a useful half-hour.

Line 37. Described in *Max Horton and the Western Approaches* by Rear-Admiral W. D. Chalmers (Hodder & Stoughton, London, 1954).

Chapter 6 Churchill and Godfrey

PAGE 126

In 1948, before any war diaries of politicians or commanders had been published, Godfrey wrote: 'Did Churchill's long years in opposition to all government leave him with a feeling that we all shared the delinquencies of those politicians that he so consistently bastinadoed in public? Certainly his written words gave the impression that he thought we all needed a good shake-up and comb-out . . .'

PAGE 127

In a speech to the House of Commons on 8 November 1939 he said: 'It is very difficult to give assured figures, because many a marauder who is sunk in deep water leaves no trace behind. There must be a doubt and dispute about every case in which we have not had a survivor, or a corpse, or a wreck to show. But I think it would be a fairly sound conservative estimate that the losses of the U-boats lie between two and four in every week according to the activity which prevails.' – *War Speeches*, 1939–45, vol. 1 (Cassell, London, 1951).

PAGE 129

Line 26. A parallel war of nerves was waged against the French by German demonstrations of their great strength in the air and rumours of how it was to be used.

Line 34. To nip such rumours in the bud, Godfrey arranged with Sir Horace Wilson in the early summer of 1939 to have a private line laid on from his office in Downing Street to the Admiralty, so that the kind of information being planted on members of the Cabinet through diplomatic sources might be checked and refuted.

Line 40. See page 135.

PAGE 130

Actually nine known sunk was correct, and sixteen probables got back to base.

PAGE 133

The economist, Sir Roy Harrod, throws light on these matters in his book on Lord Cherwell (then Professor Lindemann). His statistical section, set up in the Admiralty in September 1939 and moved into the Prime Minister's office when Churchill, six months later, took over No. 10 Downing Street, gave special attention to the figures and facts about the enemy produced by the Service Departments. It questioned the pessimism, for example, of Air Ministry estimates of German bomber strength and of the Ministry of Shipping's accounts of the net tonnage situation. 'If Churchill wanted to keep the people in good heart, the Prof wanted to keep Churchill in good heart.' – *The Prof. A Personal Memoir* by R. F. Harrod (Macmillan, London, 1959).

That there was good reason for this scepticism is recalled by Sir Donald MacDougall, then a young economist in the section. When the Admiralty was asked for an estimate of the fuel consumption of the German Navy, it was found that the amount calculated was greater than that used by the British Fleet with its world-wide activity. At this early stage statistical methods in the Service departments were crude – a weakness which Godfrey had foreseen and made provision against. Hence his resentment at the Lindemann take-over.

PAGE 134

In December 1940 Churchill was to say that 'we must recognize the recrudescence of a threat which a year ago we seemed to have mastered'.

PAGE 137

Even after the *Gorizia* disclosure the Admiralty adhered strictly to the treaties, even to the extent of cutting down the *Suffolk*'s quarterdeck when she was given an armoured deck, thereby depriving her of the reserve of buoyancy that nearly led to her being lost after the abortive bombardment of Stavanger airfield in 1940. But the *Suffolk* survived to help shadow the *Bismarck* to her doom.

Line 21. The source for these statements is correspondence between Troubridge and Godfrey after the War.

Line 34. In a Minute of 29 August 1941 Churchill wrote to the First Sea Lord *inter alia*:
'The fact that the Admiralty consider that three K.G.V.'s must be used to contain the *Tirpitz* is a serious reflection upon the design of our latest ships, which through being under-gunned and weakened by hangars in the middle of their citadels, are evidently judged unfit to fight their opposite number in a single-ship action. . . . How foolish they (the Germans) would be to send her out, when by staying where she is she contains the three strongest and newest battleships we have, and rules the Baltic as well.'

It may be observed that the same Minute contains one of the earliest references to the idea of sending a K.G.V. battleship to the Far East as a deterrent to Japan.

Similar deception was achieved with the 8″ cruisers like the *Prinz Eugen*, which were supposed to be like our own cruisers of 10,000 tons. They were in fact 14,475 tons standard displacement and 18,500 tons at deep load – nearly half as big again as our ships of the same class. Likewise, the *Scharnhorst* and *Gneisenau*, purporting to be smaller than the British battle cruisers, exceeded their published displacement by 6,000 tons.

Roskill, op. cit., vol. 1, p. 398, mentions that in March 1939 the Board decided to reconstruct *Hood*, whose armour would not withstand German 15-inch shells, with more horizontal and vertical armour. Before work could be started, war broke out.

Chapter 7 Who betrayed the *Bismarck*?

See Roskill, op. cit., vol. 1, p. 374. Denning recalls seeing early in May an agent's report stating that the *Bismarck* had ordered two sets of charts, which were wrongly delivered to Swinemuende. He thought this worth mentioning on the telephone informally to the Intelligence Staff Officer at Scapa, although the head of the OIC thought it of little value. Denning knew that the battleship had been doing exercises in the Baltic and that any request for charts could probably have something to do with operations in other waters.

PAGE 146

About a week later Denham was pleased to receive a signal from the First Sea Lord 'Personal – your message started a series of operations which ended yesterday in the sinking of the *Bismarck*. Congratulations.'

After the war Denham found in the German archives a signal from the Chief of the Abwehr, Canaris, to German Naval High Command, dated the morning following his report: 'Have positive proof that British Admiralty has received report of outward passage of *Bismarck* and *Prinz Eugen*.'

PAGE 148

In a speech at Weimar to naval officers on 17 December 1943, when the Atlantic battle had turned decisively against him, Doenitz said: 'In all circumstances we must conduct the naval war, now and in the future, with the navy's own air reconnaissance. As quickly as possible we must remedy this deficiency in the war at sea.'

PAGE 151

Admiral Wake-Walker, who was in command of the shadowing ships, was surprised and chagrined on visiting the Admiralty later, to receive from the First Sea Lord not a congratulation on his success but a severe rebuke for having lost contact.

PAGE 154

Line 5. The author found out by chance from an officer in the destroyer *Lance* that his was one of two destroyers with the Home Fleet assigned to the *Bismarck* operation which had D/F. The ship unfortunately lost all power in the Pentland Firth and took no part in the operation.

Line 12. By plotting on an ordinary chart great circle bearings were distorted.

PAGE 156

It should be said at this point that the *Prinz Eugen*, as she went off on her own to contact the tankers waiting for her, had excellent intelligence to guide her. She knew the routes of the HX convoys, the extreme limit of the American aircraft patrols and other secrets in her 'cruiser warfare' or commerce raiding.

PAGE 157

Curiously enough Admiral Tovey had a similar thought of intervening from a distance – to advise Admiral Holland in the *Hood* 'that the *Prince of Wales* should lead the line so that the better-protected ship would draw the enemy's fire'. He did not do so because he did not consider 'such interference with so senior an officer justifiable'. (Roskill, op. cit., vol. 1, p. 399.)

PAGE 158

Spichern was missed in the great round-up of June and was scuttled in Brest in August 1944 when the Germans evacuated the port.

PAGE 159

See Roskill, op. cit., vol. 1, p. 544, and *Prinz Eugen* log.

PAGE 160

Line 11. The sinking of the *Lauenburg* is described on page 272.

Line 16. The *Breme* was in fact sunk by the heavy cruiser *Sheffield* and the *Gonzenheim* was scuttled as already stated.

Line 28. She was sunk off West Africa on 15 June, having surrendered after interception by the *Dunedin* and aircraft from the *Eagle*.

Line 32. *Babitonga* had been scuttled on interception by the *London* off the W. African coast on 21 June and the *Alstertor* was caught off the west coast of Spain by the *Marsdale* and the 8th destroyer flotilla on 23 June.

PAGE 161

The captured German archives show, broadly speaking, that the Nazis feared their own traitors more than their enemy's cryptographers. They had, in other words, more confidence in their own efficiency than in the loyalty commanded by their political system. The relationship between efficiency in intelligence and freedom in society is an attractive theme for speculation, perhaps even for research.

Chapter 8 Prisoners of war

PAGE 165

There were about ten RNVR, one RM Captain and WRNS officers at the Combined Services Direct Interrogation Centre (CSDIC) with the necessary clerical staff. There was also a liaison officer from Coastal Command, and an American officer from Op. 16Z who joined the section in civilian clothes well before Pearl Harbor, and was followed by others.

When war began this work was under NID 1, the German Section. As work increased NID 11 was set up to handle both the German and the Italian work. Then in 1941 control reverted to the country sections for Germany and Italy through sub-sections 1/PW and 3/PW.

PAGE 166

Sir David Hunt in his book *A Don at War* (Kimber, London, 1966) p. 64 says of prisoner-of-war interrogation when dealing with German soldiers in North Africa:

'The best approach was to put your questions in an easy authoritative way as though you had not the least doubt that an answer would be forthcoming. Instincts of discipline were usually strong enough to ensure that the answer was given. The comradely approach was no good; the interrogator had to be rigidly regimental. I well remember many occasions when senior German NCO's would rack their brains in the most conscientious manner to drag up every detail about something which might interest us – the performance of a new anti-tank gun, for example or an order for a future operation.'

PAGE 169

Line 2. See Roskill, op. cit., vol. 3, Pt. 1, pp. 40–1.

Line 34. The Schnorkel was an air intake and diesel exhaust mast which enabled a U-boat to operate just below the surface and recharge batteries while at periscope depth. It was fitted in boats after attacks by aircraft carrying 10cm radar had made life impossible for Doenitz's men on the surface. By mid-1944 thirty boats had been fitted. See Roskill, op. cit., vol. 3, Pt. 1, p. 18.

Diving depths. On page 21 of vol. 3, Part 1 of *The War at Sea* (op. cit.) Roskill describes how U449 was sunk after five hours attack by depth charges set to explode between 500 and 750 feet.

See page 169.

The stool pigeon's technique would be to enter into casual conversation with the prisoner, encourage him to let down his hair on some grievance or strongly-held view, and then lead the talk round – on this or a subsequent occasion – to technical or operational questions. Pretending to be an airman he might say: 'We're not getting the kind of radar we ought to be having. How are things in the Navy?' Or being a U-boat man, he would ask whether the promised new search receiver had arrived yet, or whether the milch-cows (tanker submarines for refuelling at sea) were a success or whether anything had been heard of the new Walter boats. There was always a risk that a prisoner would recognize a stool pigeon and so make him useless. So it was normally arranged that the stool pigeon should see the prisoners unobserved before being allowed to meet an individual. He would never be allowed to mix with a number of men. In spite of all precautions the stool pigeon was sometimes rumbled and then had to leave the centre for good. Some went to a special camp for anti-Nazi prisoners where no questions were asked about a man's past.

The nerve centre of an interrogation camp was the 'M' room, from which all listening and transcribing was done and which was wired to the prisoners' cells or cubicles. Not more than eight could be covered at the same time, even with a staff of over 100, taking leave, working in shifts and experiencing normal sickness.

Line 19. The extent of the reverse may be judged by using Doenitz's own criterion of the price in U-boats for tonnage sunk:

   1943 March 477,000 tons—cost – 12 U-boats
           April   245,000 tons—cost – 15 U-boats

May   165,000 tons—cost – 40 U-boats
June   17,000 tons—cost – 17 U-boats
July   123,000 tons—cost – 37 U-boats

In October 1943 for the first time British and American combined merchant fleets were larger than they had been in 1939.

Line 25. See Churchill, *Second World War* (Cassell, London, 1948–54, vol. 4, pp. 615–30).

Line 33. The Minute appears on page 163 of vol. 5 of the *Second World War*: 'Let me have a short report on the character and quality of the U-boat prisoners now being taken, compared with any other significant period of the war.'

PAGE 177

Each new officer appointed to CSDIC spent a period listening to the work of experienced interrogators.

PAGE 180

Staendiger Kriegsbefehl des BdU Nr. 512 10 November 1943.

Chapter 9   The Attaché's art

PAGE 184

Line 19. Sometimes the NA's appointment may be purely social in purpose and none the less useful for that. In Budapest, for example, the reason for appointing a Senior Captain was that the Regent, Admiral Horthy, delighted in talking naval shop and could be approached confidentially on that basis to discuss other matters.

Line 31. One problem that was never far from the front of a DNI's mind was the possibility that a friendly foreign Naval Attaché, to whom he had given important information, might pass it to his government in a cipher or code which would be read by unfriendly governments. There were cases in which the DNI knew that the communications of the government in question were insecure. He would then have to find ways of either delicately drawing his attention to the fact or of suggesting that a cable or a letter would be safer, or even that British communications might be used.

PAGE 186

Hillgarth had been 'spotted' by Godfrey during one of the many calls made by the *Repulse* in the course of the Mediterranean Fleet's rescue work, mentioned in Chapter 1. He was also in regular contact with Admiral Pound when he was C-in-C Mediterranean.

PAGE 187

When the ore ships were successfully run from Gothenburg to Britain, the Swedes were upset because the Admiralty allowed the BBC to boast about the operation.

PAGE 188

Line 9. NA Madrid had to keep in touch with C-in-C Mediterranean and the Flag Officer Gibraltar, about whose knowledge nothing could be taken for granted. 'In Gib', wrote Hillgarth, 'people think that Algeciras and Cadiz represent the whole of Spain. When they talk about Ferrol or Cartagena it is as if it were part of a far country.'

Line 31. One regrets having to record that NAs thought little of journalists as sources. In countries where the press was not free, editors and reporters were of low quality and ill-informed. In other countries they were sometimes useful, but generally inaccurate. On the other hand, the resident correspondents from quality newspapers in Britain and the United States, and of the BBC and CBS, could be useful, because they were often allowed to travel wherever they wished without restriction or observation.

PAGE 194

See Rt Hon. Sir Samuel Hoare, Viscount Templewood, *Ambassador on Special Mission* (Collins, London, 1946, pp. 15–16).

PAGE 195

Goldeneye was the code word given to these measures, and later adopted as the name of the house that Commander Ian Fleming built himself in Jamaica.

PAGE 196

Hoare, op. cit., p. 183, tells how the Germans were in error about the destination of the convoys they had watched assembling off Gibraltar, thanks to ingenious deception plans which also took in the French authorities in N. Africa: 'Stohrer had given a dinner party two days before the landings. An officer of the Spanish Naval Staff, who was present, insisted that the Allied expedition was destined for Africa. The Ambassador scouted the suggestion and declared that he had the best possible information that the objectives were Italy and the E. Mediterranean. The naval officer . . . was so persistent that Stohrer eventually reported it to Berlin, but with a note that stated that it was a Spanish opinion and that all the German intelligence organisations in Spain were unanimous against the idea of an African invasion.'

PAGE 199

See Churchill, op. cit., vol. 2, p. 425, and Roskill, op. cit., vol. 1, p. 311 ff. Roskill makes it clear that Consul-General Tangier sent warning of the French movement a day before Hillgarth, but it was not even deciphered in the Foreign Office for several days.

PAGE 200

The Man that Never Was, by Ewen Montagu (Evans Brothers, London, 1953).

PAGE 202

The 12,000 ton German supply ship *Altmark*, which had accompanied the *Graf Spee* on her last raid, escaped from the British search of the South Atlantic and reached Norway. There, in Jossing Fjord, she was boarded from the destroyer *Cossack* and 299 British merchant seamen were rescued. This determined and justified breach of neutrality made a deep impression all over the world.

PAGE 205

At one time this was known as the Foreign and Political Department; but Foreign Office objections to the implications of this title led to the adoption of the meaningless 'Military' to describe the department dealing with the international implications of Admiralty policy.

PAGE 206

In October 1942 a fresh protest had to be made against the reporting of Malta convoys from an observation post outside Ceuta and another overlooking the harbour of Algeciras.

NOTES

PAGE 208

Line 12. Examples of intelligence sources in Sweden have been given already in Chapter 2.

Line 40. The destroyers had been bought from Italy and were homeward bound in company with a depot ship on an itinerary agreed with the Admiralty. On arrival at the Faroes, a British destroyer division under Captain Caslon appeared and ordered the ships to be handed over, the crews being moved to the depot ship. It took days for the British Ambassador in Stockholm to get any information from the Foreign Office which might lead to remedial action. The C-in-C Admiral Tamm, according to Denham, showed great patience while awaiting the release of his ships. Eventually the crews were re-embarked and the destroyers left for Sweden.

Denham went to meet the ships at Gothenburg: 'though I got some black looks here and there, none could have been more disarming than the divisional commander, Captain Hagman.' What particularly rankled was the damage done by indiscriminate British looting. Denham assisted the board which assessed the damage, amounting to 1,000,000 kroner.

PAGE 209

Outstandingly useful were the Norwegians in Stockholm who invariably shared intelligence both with their Swedish neighbours – who reciprocated – and their British Allies.

PAGE 213

Denham learnt to his dismay after the war that certain of his signals had been intercepted and read by the Germans, thanks to their capture of secret books in Bergen in 1940. As pointed out in Chapter 4 the Germans were reading the interdepartmental cipher from that time until June 1945.

Chapter 10 Showing the Americans

PAGE 216

Line 14. See Barbara W. Tuchman, *The Zimmermann Telegram* (Constable, London, 1958).

NOTES

Line 27. Admiral Kirk commanded the US Naval assault group in the Normandy landings of 1944, and after the war was for a time US Ambassador in Brussels and Moscow.

PAGE 217

Also very helpful was Mr John G. Winant, who succeeded the pessimistic and defeatist Joe Kennedy as Ambassador to London in March 1941 and who became a frequent visitor to 36 Curzon Street.

PAGE 218

By the winter of 1941 the Admiralty was receiving the detailed dispositions of the US Fleet, air locations all over the Pacific, details of aircraft types carried in aircraft carriers, and plans for the Navy's expansion.

PAGE 219

Three years later, when C-in-C Royal Indian Navy, Godfrey was to note how commercial and political penetration and espionage were thinly camouflaged in American practice. High-grade businessmen dressed as officers appeared in India, evidently with plenty of money, and entertained lavishly.

PAGE 221

'C', that is to say the head of the Secret Intelligence Service, had already in New York a representative who had made huge strides towards persuading the Americans to follow our example and, among other things, to set up a secret service, if only for wartime. Mr Stephenson in New York had full authority to speak for Colonel Stewart Menzies in London just as Major-General Beaumont-Nesbitt, former DMI, could speak as Military Attaché for the War Office. But neither was in a position to put forward a scheme as bold and comprehensive as was conceived for the Godfrey mission. The task was further complicated by the fact that there was no separate head of air staff in Washington.

PAGE 224

Line 3. A Fleet exercise directed from the Admiralty in 1937 had convinced their Lordships that the co-operation then existing between the Intelligence and Ops. staffs was not sufficiently close to work well in the increasing speed of naval war. They accepted the

407

argument that an intelligence staff as organized in peace aims at long-term results and cannot cope with the rush demands and decisions required by operational staffs in wartime.

Line 39. Donovan used to quote Churchill: 'There are many kinds of manoeuvres in war, some only of which take place on the battle-field. There are manoeuvres in time, in diplomacy, in mechanics, in psychology; all of which are removed from the battlefield, but react often decisively upon it, and the object of all is to find easier ways other than sheer slaughter of achieving the main purpose.'

PAGE 228

Post-war research into the growth of JIC recorded this visit to co-ordinate the arrangements for the exchange with the USA of all forms of intelligence and Godfrey's report on it. DNI was to include SIS, SOE and Security but not the Air interest, Chief of Air Staff having demurred because there was no separate American Air Force. DMI considered himself represented in Washington by the Military Attaché.

Chapter 11 Three heads are better . . .

PAGE 240

Line 2. Consisting of the Director of Naval Intelligence, the Director of Military Intelligence, the Chief of Air Staff (I), the representative of the Ministry of Economic Warfare and a Foreign Office Chairman.

Line 14. Mr Victor Cavendish-Bentinck was promoted from Coun-sellor to Assistant Under-Scretary of State while Chairman of the JIC. The representative of Economic Warfare had the rank of a Director.

PAGE 245

In his *Sailor's Odyssey* (Hutchinson, London, 1951), Cunningham comments on this telegram: 'At the Admiralty we were most sceptical about its authenticity; but after consultation with the Foreign Office it was decided to order Commander-in-Chief to take precautions.'

PAGE 246

Under a long-standing voluntary arrangement between the Newspaper Proprietors' Association and the Government, the newspapers undertake in the national interest to withhold publication of matter which is made the subject of a 'D' notice drawn up by a committee in which officials and press representatives sit together.

PAGE 253

Line 3. American staff workers in General Eisenhower's headquarters as late as 1944 were still observing this principle of *not* selecting for the operational division the enemy course of action that intelligence showed to be most likely. British staff officers had given it up three years earlier.

Line 29. Wohlstetter's work on Pearl Harbor points out that the US Director of War Plans refused to let the Director of Naval Intelligence have any hand in estimating enemy intentions.

PAGE 254

The author, who was the first secretary of this new body, learnt much from his chairman – a shrewd, cordial and Falstaffian character – including one invaluable stratagem. 'Never', he said, 'tackle the difficult matter on the agenda first. Bring it up about an hour before lunch and it will be settled quickly.' The joint at the 'Senior' (United Service Club in Pall Mall) in those days was off at an early hour, and I did my best to get Troubridge there in time for his cut.

PAGE 260

One of DNI's Captains writes: 'It was difficult to get the Directors to trust the JIS common sense. They had often made up their minds from their own ministerial brief and were loth to depart from it. We *all* felt on several occasions like calling on the Director and saying "either trust me or get rid of me". '

Chapter 12 Divers operations

PAGE 273

One reason for carrying an expert on such expeditions was that German cipher keys were often tabulated in soluble ink on flaming pink paper whose use might be misunderstood by a boarding party.

NOTES

PAGE 280

Lieutenant Arthur Hutchinson RNVR, who succeeded Beesly as Denning's assistant, recalls the mixture of despair and amusement with which he watched Admiral Harwood (victor of the River Plate battle but at the time Assistant Chief of Naval Staff) describing with a sweep of his arm how the *Richelieu* and a couple of cruisers from Dakar could be sent to 'close the corridor'.

PAGE 282

Since March, on Hitler's orders, a force of U-boats, long range recce aircraft and bombers had been assembled for attack on the Arctic convoys in the improving weather conditions; and in April Pound had warned the Defence Committee that losses might become so great as to render the running of these convoys too costly. (See Roskill, op. cit., vol. 2, p. 127.)

PAGE 287

Line 5. Mr A. L. Hutchinson, then Lieut RNVR and assistant to Denning, writes of this meeting: 'My most vivid recollection is of a very tired-looking Dudley Pound sitting gazing in a mesmerized fashion at a small scale chart of the Barents Sea area, calculating with a pair of dividers where the *Tirpitz* could be at that time. These calculations were, of course, based on nothing more solid than the "farthest position" at the ship's operating speed, based on the assumption that she had left harbour immediately after the last sighting of the ship.'

Line. 40. It seems probable that Pound, having taken his decision, would have immediately informed Churchill of it. If he did so, then it is hardly surprising that he should have refused to change his mind. But this is conjecture.

PAGE 289

Admiral Sir Henry Moore, who supported Pound's proposal to disperse the convoy, clearly recalls his belief that the *Tirpitz* was already at sea when the evening meeting assembled. He has given the

410

author these comments on the chapter: 'I expect Denning is right in thinking that Pound had not decided to disperse the convoy when he left Denning's room, but had he made up his mind from the answers he had received that the *Tirpitz* could be at sea? I cannot remember now whether I had a talk with Pound between that visit downstairs and the final meeting at which the decision to disperse was taken. If Pound had got that impression from Denning's answers and had told me, that is, maybe, how I got my impression that the *Tirpitz* was already at sea. If not, where did I get it from?'

Chapter 13 Handbooks for invasion

PAGE 292

In his *Gallipoli* (Batsford, London, 1965) Mr Rhodes James describes how Rear-Admiral Wemyss was sent in February 1915 to the island of Lemnos to establish a base at Mudros for the Fleet and 50,000 men. 'He found that there were no facilities for loading and unloading ships, that there was only one tiny pier, no depot ship or supplies of any kind, no accommodation on shore for the Army . . . and wholly insufficient water resources.'

PAGE 293

Mrs Hughes of the Inter-Services Topographical Department recalls driving up to London from Oxford in the early hours of one morning in 1943 carrying in her car a model of a location in the Andaman Islands which had been urgently called for from Cabinet Offices via Room 39. There the plasticine mock-up was handed over to General Hollis to show to Churchill personally.

PAGE 295

Line 6. FAGS, or form-at-a-glance reports, condensed from longer and more formally presented documents, offered information on an operational area in the handiest form that could be devised, with the minimum of formal prose – almost in the style of the later Baedekers. The DNI was told in December 1942 by the head of the topographical staff at Oxford how Mountbatten had taken the 'Form-at-a-glance' on Sardinia to Chequers, and how the Prime Minister had 'expressed

411

great enthusiasm over it and had carried it away with him to a Cabinet meeting'.

Line 21. Not, it must be emphasized, for fear of treachery, but merely to guard against the kind of indiscretion committed by a Canadian sergeant who, when arrested for being drunk shortly before the Dieppe raid, said, 'You can't do this to me; I am booked to go on the Dieppe raid.'

Line 36. Cunningham is quoted in Oliver Warner's memoir of him as writing 'I think Power was responsible for most of the co-ordination, and I believe he dictated for about four days without stopping, with four Wren stenographers on duty and another four standing off and waiting to come on. All this preliminary work was done at Norfolk House, in St James's Square, where we worked in closest contact with the Americans, as well as the Admiralty.' – *Cunningham of Hyndhope* (John Murray, London, 1967, p. 183).

PAGE 297

Line 9. It is a striking coincidence in the history of NID 6, that the stretch of French coast about which they made in June 1940, their first primitive beach report, was the same that they later studied and described down to the finest detail for the Normandy landings of June 1944. The skimpy collection of photographs pasted on to brown paper of folio size, linked with text, was to become the elaborate and beautifully produced work, in thousands of copies, of a University Press. What started as a tiny NID section had become, by December 1944, an inter-service department 541 strong.

Line 31. The files on Finland contained only two brief newspaper cuttings.

PAGE 298

The pressure on NID 6 and its rapid growth can be directly traced to Churchill's unceasing flow of offensive ideas, which continued when he moved from the First Lord's Office to No. 10 in May 1940. Each had to be studied if only to be rejected.

PAGE 299

Line 18. The story goes that the Prime Minister had already asked Mr Attlee to make a quick investigation into the reasons for the lack of intelligence about Norway. Attlee asked for the Service Department files containing the relevant facts to be sent over to him immediately. The War Office folder made available in some panic had written on it 'SFA'. When Attlee showed this to the Prime Minister the latter said: 'And what may this mean?' 'I suppose it means Sweet Fanny Adams,' replied the Deputy Prime Minister. 'I sincerely hope,' remarked the Prime Minister, 'that there is no other interpretation to be put on these letters.'

Line 32. Now Sir James R. M. Butler, MVO, CBE, MA.

PAGE 302

Before all the British were out of France, the preparations to go back to Europe had begun: for on 12 June 1940 the Combined Operations Headquarters was set up in Whitehall to plan and organize – first under Keyes and then under Mountbatten – such raids as could be afforded until major offensives became possible. Combined Operations and NID 6 were in touch on the 13th, starting on a servicing job which began with the first small reconnaissance raid between Boulogne and Berck on 23 June 1940, and culminated in the major assault on Dieppe in August 1942.

PAGE 305

Line 8. How the direction of labour sometimes worked is revealed by the experience of this skilled research worker. Having volunteered for war-work, he was sent to the Admiralty and there allocated to the War Registry where signals are handled and distributed. After some disagreeable days delivering papers to irate naval officers, each with his own in-tray system, he was luckily recognized in Room 39 by the DNI's secretary, Ted Merrett, to whom he was known. It happened that the need for someone to run a contact register was then occupying Merrett and he at once suggested that this specialist from the BM should be relieved of his menial duties and given the job. This incident, like the appointment of a marine biologist to a signals department, mentioned in an earlier chapter, suggests that the Ministry of Labour's methods were not as lunatic as sometimes appeared.

Line 38. Much care was taken over the proper use of contacts; when several departments were interested in one person, joint interrogations were arranged to spare time and expense. A close watch was kept for enemy agents and collaborators posing as refugees. A few 'lunatics', who believed they were dealing in NID 21 with the Secret Service and had their own idea for winning the war, had to be kept at bay by patient letter-writing.

PAGE 306

What I have called the Hall touch showed itself towards the end of 1942 when Godfrey, assisted by Fleming, entertained to dinner at the Savoy Chairmen and representatives of Hambros Bank, ICI, Lloyds Bank, Shell, Rhokana Corp., John Brown, Unilever, Samuels and Glyn Mills and Southern Railways, with the object of creating a distinguished panel of patrons for the contact campaign. It worked!

PAGE 309

Mr Peter Bryan of the Norwegian section, remembers being asked in the middle of the night for snap reports on one sheet of paper about ports and coastal areas, some for CCO brainwaves, others just to provide cover for other questions.

PAGE 310

There were strong protests from this distinguished Unitarian seat of learning that Government occupation would cripple its work; but inquiry showed that war had reduced the number of its students to a single figure.

PAGE 311

For this attack pin-point information was provided about the small islands in the approaches to the fjord so that the craft could re-charge their batteries by surfacing on the way in and shelter on the way back. The section also planned the crews' escape route to Sweden.

PAGE 312

At first nothing less than a personal courier would do for the delivery of proofs; and a member of the staff known as 'Milky' Smith would travel up to Paddington on those packed war-time trains, looking important in a first-class carriage reserved all to himself. Later the security precautions were less conspicuous.

PAGE 317

Cdr Hughes had already made his mark assisting the Americans in their creation of terrain intelligence. Although he had been unable to persuade the Navy and the Army to build up an inter-services department around the new office of Strategic Services unless they controlled it themselves, he had at any rate left behind him a clear idea of the doctrine. Capt. E. M. Zacharias, Head of the Foreign Intelligence Branch in the Navy Department wrote to the British Embassy: 'He has done a splendid job and his efforts will be extremely useful to us in crystallizing opinion regarding the best methods to pursue in effecting co-ordination of activities engaged in this work.'

Chapter 14 Back into Europe

PAGE 323

The immense and skilled labours of the Admiralty's Hydrographer for 'Neptune' can hardly be over-praised.

PAGE 326

Richardson found, as was often the case with Admiralty representatives on joint staffs, that his opposite number was a Major-General with a staff four times larger than his own.

PAGE 327

General Paget may have believed he was a candidate for the Supreme Command. Be that as it may, some officers felt so strongly about the move that they organized a protest in Whitehall through Mr Duncan Sandys – and not long afterwards they were back in London occupying two top floors of Peter Robinson's store in Oxford Street.

PAGE 328

That the outstanding intelligence officer in this work was Major John Austin, the Oxford don, was the agreed opinion of his naval colleagues. He had the quick, clear, unemotional judgement of a future Professor of Metaphysics. The whole German order of battle was in his mind's eye and any significance it might have in connection with submarine pens, dumps, marshalling yards, and later V1 and V2 sites. His memory was photographic, but he never trusted to it alone and felt he could consult anyone on any point without loss of dignity. His method was to 'let the donkey workers work' but to keep an eye constantly on the results. 'Austin Friars', as he was known to his naval colleagues because of his evident austerity, was invincible in argument.

PAGE 330
Throughout these months discussion was also going on, in the closest secrecy, about the enemy's V1 and V2 preparations against Southern England.

PAGE 333
It was in the early winter of 1943 that Rommel took over command of the invasion defence in France and ordered the utmost effort to stop the Allies *on the beaches*. Previously the plan had been to attack them as they concentrated inland. A tremendous effort to multiply miles of obstacles above and below low-tide mark then began and continued until 'D-day' itself.

PAGE 334
The only serious complaint about the accuracy of beach intelligence that the author has been able to trace was that photography did not reveal that enemy pillboxes were sited only for enfilading fire and were therefore blind on the seaward side. This made them less vulnerable to bombardment from the sea.

PAGE 336
Failure of weather intelligence played its part in deceiving the Germans. They had no U-boats in a suitable position to report from the Atlantic the comparatively small area of high pressure moving in to give the brief favourable break which made landing possible.

Chapter 15 The sin and the cure

PAGE 338
In a foreword to the war memoirs of Sir David Hunt, *A Don at War* (Kimber, London, 1966).

PAGE 339
Line 12. In the pre-war Navy it was normal to give about half a day's instruction on methods and sources of intelligence to those selected officers who attended the Greenwich Staff Courses. But even this cursory initiation seems sometimes to have borne fruit. The

NOTES

capture with all her secret documents of U110 on 9 May 1941 certainly owed something to the fact that Commander Baker-Cresswell, who was commanding the escort of convoy OB318, had been at Greenwich three years before and had been told the story of how British naval intelligence had thrived in the previous war on the signal books taken from the German cruiser *Magdeburg* by Russian divers. He has told me that when Lemp's U-boat surfaced, after a number of depth-charge attacks, his instinct was to ram her and avenge the two ships she had just torpedoed. Having seen red for a few seconds, his trained judgement reasserted itself when he saw the German crew abandoning ship and he realized that here might be a golden chance of capture.

The full story of this remarkable episode in the Atlantic battle is told in *The Secret Capture* by Captain S. W. Roskill RN (Collins, London, 1959).

Line 38. The outstanding exception is Mrs Wohlstetter's book on Pearl Harbor. Its great qualities may lend point to Godfrey's view that there should be no sex bar in intelligence: 'a clever and knowledgeable woman will do every bit as well as a clever and knowledgeable man, and will probably be more discreet and security-conscious.'

PAGE 340

Commander Malcolm Saunders RN, the chief authority on the German naval archives, points out that this failure to study past and contemporary developments had an exact parallel in the failure of the War Office (and its French equivalent) to grasp how Germany would use her armour in the campaign of 1940. Published books and articles by Captain Doenitz and Colonel Guderian, readily available before the war, seem to have been ignored or simply escaped notice.

PAGE 341

I borrow the expression from Harold Nicolson's *Curzon: the last Phase* (Constable, London, 1934) where he offers some brilliant contributions towards a doctrine of diplomacy which, to judge by the performance of recent British Foreign Secretaries, have been overlooked or forgotten.

PAGE 342

An unconscious assumption can sometimes be as dangerous as a hunch. Godfrey and his contemporaries declare that the quality of

417

the French Army was taken completely for granted in the late Thirties. No arrangements had been made to ensure that the French Navy, if the Army failed, could communicate by secret cipher with the Admiralty. It was Fleming's view that had such communications existed the tragedy of the Oran bombardment could have been avoided.

PAGE 343

Systematic training in the collection and presentation of factual political intelligence was not given to Foreign Office staff. The best political intelligence, in NID's experience, came during the war from special staffs recruited for the Political Warfare Executive, most of whom were journalists, scholars and persons of non-diplomatic experience.

PAGE 344

I owe to Captain Stephen Roskill the knowledge of what must be one of the most far-seeing appreciations ever made by a British naval officer. Lord Jellicoe, after a tour of the Empire to study the principles of a future imperial strategy, reported early in 1920 that the ultimate aim of Japan (in case of war) would be to invade Australia but that her initial move would be to seize advance bases in New Guinea and the islands to the east or in the Dutch East Indies; that Japan would attack our own bases, notably Hongkong and Singapore, either prior to or concurrently with the acquisition of the advanced bases. He saw no reason why Japan should not be able secretly to concentrate enough shipping to transport a fully equipped army of 100,000 men against Singapore. Once they had captured that base they would 'paralyse to a very great extent the operations of the British Navy'.

PAGE 345

Admiral Godfrey comments here: 'The word "dilution" should not be read as meaning any weakening. My predecessor began recruiting civilians because the Navy was short of first-class brains and could not spare any for intelligence work. I used the word "dilution" only when the Second Sea Lord would no longer give the Division RNVR officers and we had to recruit civilians who would remain civilians. The next stage was to put women in men's places, but I was almost too late, for so many able women had been recruited elsewhere. "Dilution" became a catchword which I used because it worked.'

PAGE 346

Rodney G. Minott, *The Fortress that Never Was* (Holt, Rinehart and Winston, New York, 1964), writes that in SHAEF 'The British had learned to rely upon a tremendous number of civilians who eventually held senior appointments in their military intelligence. Many were academicians and their attitude was that of scholars in uniform even though the majority were required to have extensive combat-experience before assuming staff duties.'

PAGE 347

Line 8. Denning, then a Paymaster Commander of high standing, recalls being turned out of the First Sea Lord's room in 1944 (it was Cunningham) when he insisted that two of our cruisers had over-estimated their success in action against German destroyers in the Bay of Biscay. He said he preferred 'the judgement of his captains' to what OIC might produce with their 'black magic'.

Line 14. The Walter boat, driven by the combination of diesel fuel with hydrogen peroxide, was planned to reach very high speed under water for short periods. The technical troubles that arose were so serious that no Walter boat was sent on active service during the war. See Roskill, op. cit., vol. 3, Pt. 1, p. 17.

Line 35. On 3 September 1940, four German agents landed in open boats between Hythe and Dungeness, having been towed from Boulogne to a point south of Dungeness and then cast off. They were captured by coastguards. They had food for fourteen days, £30 in banknotes, transmitters and codes. They were convinced that invasion was coming by mid-September and had been sent to report on Army reserves and defence measures. Three days later another agent landed by parachute near Nottingham, carrying a W/T set. Sent from Brussels, he had been told that £200 would keep him going until invasion began and that his batteries would last for sixty days.

PAGE 349

Quotation from Admiral Godfrey's personal diary.

PAGE 350

The most recent and most remarkable example of this tendency that the author has found is reported in the Stennis Report on the Cuban Military Build-up (Select Committee of the Armed Services 1963). It suggests that the failure in Washington to foresee the Soviet attempt to instal offensive missiles in Cuba was due partly to a tendency to 'discredit and downgrade reports of refugees and exiles', because they were untrained observers; but even more to 'the predisposition of the intelligence community' to the philosophical conviction that it would be incompatible with Soviet policy to introduce strategic missiles into Cuba. In other words, intelligence had agreed on a pattern of Soviet behaviour as it had showed itself in Eisenhower's day as President and failed to make allowance for the change brought about by Kennedy's methods, just as the British Joint Intelligence Staff sometimes failed in 1943 in trying to anticipate Hitler.

PAGE 351

Line 1. The only time that this ship used her main armament against an enemy was in a raid on Spitzbergen on 7 September 1943, when she bombarded shore installations. In a Minute to the First Sea Lord of 29 August 1941, Churchill wrote '*Tirpitz* is doing to us exactly what a *King George V* in the Indian Ocean would do to the Japanese Navy. It exercises a vague general fear and menaces all points at once. It appears and disappears, causing immediate reactions and perturbations on the other side.'

Line 17. The Nazis, misinformed about American determination to end the war, played on Allied fears of a prolonged last-ditch resistance in southern Germany which would bring them into conflict with the Russians. To this end they spread the idea of an 'Alpine fortress', known as the 'redoubt', which had been prepared for the last stand. This rumour campaign was comically reinforced by Allied propaganda playing back to the Germans the idea that the Party was preparing a snug retreat while the ordinary soldier fought and died in the front line. There is no doubt that the American decision to drive southward across Germany was influenced by this myth. – See Minott, op. cit.

Vice-Admiral Campbell recalls attending a meeting of the Chiefs of Staff as DDNI, which discussed German intentions:

'It was just before the Germans' Ardennes effort which we had discussed in JIC earlier. We had certain movement and signal traffic indications but RAF rather played it down. The Chiefs of Staff rather took the same view and told JIC to watch it. While we "watched" it happened! JIC failed I think and everyone was loath to sound an alarm and so upset current plans and operations. (Wishful thinking?)'

PAGE 353

See Churchill, *Second World War*, op. cit., vol. 3, p. 35.

PAGE 354

Line 8. None the less a high standard of intelligence work was demanded from U-boat commanders on their war patrols. 'The representation of facts,' said the standing order, 'is to be separated from your personal reflections, reasonings and conclusions . . . The text must be comprehensive, intelligible and self-sufficient without having to refer to other sources.' On returning from patrol a U-boat could have ready, six fair copies of its log admirably typed and with track charts ready for distribution. The original was taken by the CO to his Flotilla Commander, who commented at the end of the log. While the boat was refitting or the crew resting, the CO would call on Doenitz for a thorough discussion of his patrol and review of his log. The best current available operational intelligence was thus ready for boats starting on patrol.

Line 38. A splendid example of deception playing on enemy obsession during the campaign in Italy is given in *A Don at War* by David Hunt pp. 253–6 (Kimber, London, 1966).

PAGE 355

Line 7. Sometimes it does not matter if the enemy can read intentions from signals. If action is taken so quickly that he cannot react, his interception may not matter; and the time saved by *not* enciphering and deciphering can amount to several hours in, say, an army or army group.

Line 39. One may recall the rhapsodical letter of Ambassador Walter H. Page to President Wilson dated 17 March 1918: 'I do study these men here most diligently who have this vast and appalling war job. There are most uncommon creatures among them – men about whom our great-grandchildren will read in their school histories; but of them all the most extraordinary is this naval officer – of whom, probably, they'll never hear.' He meant 'Blinker' Hall.

PAGE 357

Line 5. For an amusing account of corrupt and useless agents see Hunt, op. cit., pp. 240–2.

Line 32. See on page 273 the account of an intelligence officer's experience with the Home Fleet. The green stripe inside the wavy rings of the RNVR uniform could be as great a handicap as the General Service badge was to intelligence officers working with cavalry regiments in an armoured division.

PAGE 358

Line 40. While writing this book the author was asked to talk to an audience of senior intelligence officers about the parallels between intelligence and newspaper work. When he mentioned the disastrous effects of feeding isolated tit-bits of striking intelligence to high-up officers during the last war, there was a modest wave of laughter which made it clear that the practice still goes on in Whitehall.

PAGE 359

The tendency of independent headquarters and private armies to try to collect their own intelligence is noted in the book by Sir David Hunt already mentioned. He points out (p. 134) that those who organized the famous raid on Rommel's headquarters at Apollonia in November 1941 would have been warned, had they taken Intelligence into their confidence, that the German General would not be there on the day chosen for the operation. Similarly Combined Operations Headquarters in its early days showed a disposition to collect its own intelligence staff, including scarce and valuable surveyors from the Hydrographer's department. It was only when the DNI assured Sir Roger Keyes of personal attention to his needs for topographical intelligence by the growing organization at Oxford that the trend was checked.

PAGE 360

In the integrated machinery of planning, operations and intelligence under the Chiefs of Staff, what was formerly the staff division of the DNI is now known as DDSI (N) Deputy-Director of Service Intelligence (Naval). But one suspects that if NID's body lies a-mouldering in the grave its soul goes marching on.

PAGE 361

It was the painful duty of NID to assess the results of bombing in terms of damage known to have been done to ships, U-boat pens, building yards, etc. Sometimes not always, they were disappointing. The sincerity with which claims were pressed and the heavy casualties among bomber crews created a tense atmosphere in which the truth could easily be obscured.

PAGE 362

This story may be contrasted with another, contributed by the NID officer who studied the effects of bombing on the German U-boat bases in France. In January 1943, just before the tide turned in the Battle of the Atlantic, Bomber Command with its new radar and location techniques made a series of devastating raids on Lorient and St Nazaire. Intelligence from those places was by now excellent, and it quickly became clear from secret sources as well as from air photographs that the U-boats' shelters were unharmed and that their sailing programmes had been little affected. Area bombing had hurt only the French civilians.

The NID officer and his opposite number in the Air Ministry found little difficulty in submitting almost identical reports, and the Naval Staff had to recognize that the use of heavy bombers for which they had fought since summer 1940, when the shelters were being started, had proved futile. Yet no one seems to have recognized at the time, as the RAF returned to its offensive against Germany, that if the results of bombing were shown by good intelligence to be indifferent, there was no reason to suppose with worse intelligence that better results could be achieved by bombing in Germany. Just after the Normandy landings, however, a saturation RAF raid on the E-boat base at Le Havre (on 14 June 1944) did paralyse the German coastal forces which should have been harassing the 'Overlord' convoys. (Roskill, op. cit., vol. 2, pp. 351–2.)

PAGE 363

Sherman Kent, *Strategic Intelligence for American World Policy* (Archon Books, Hamden, Connecticut, 1965).

PAGE 364

See his *Black Boomerang* (Secker and Warburg, London, 1959).

PAGE 365

Line 5. This section was started by the author in 1941. From 1943 to the end of the war it was conducted by Christopher Serpell, now diplomatic correspondent of the BBC.

Line 11. In a civilian ministry continuity is represented by the office and person of the Permanent Under-Secretary and his staff. An intelligence department too, needs a permanent, high-ranking civilian official, who will ensure that knowledge gained in the past is not forgotten and lessons once learned not ignored. The effect of the present system of 2–3 year appointments to directorships of Service Intelligence is as described to the author by one officer: 'I spent a year learning my job, eighteen months doing it and six months getting ready to hand over to the next man.'

PAGE 366

In a letter to the author following a discussion of this chapter, Admiral Godfrey wrote: 'More study is needed of the effect on Intelligence, including communications of: Anonymity, Genius, Irritability, Intolerance, Memory, Patronage, Popularity, Promotion, Vanity, War Fatigue—and Churchill and his Senior Officers.'

The Epilogue: the end and the beginning of NID

PAGE 370

See Chapter 2. The appointment was made by Admiral Sir Charles Lambe who succeeded Mountbatten as First Sea Lord. As Director of Plans during the War, Lambe had worked closely with NID and he supported the appointment of a trained intelligence officer against those who wanted to see the post go, as it traditionally had gone, to an executive officer of mainly operational experience.

PAGE 375

Line 13. In 1917, under the threat of the unrestricted U-boat war, the purely advisory war staff became the naval staff proper and the posts of Chief Naval Staff and First Sea Lord were merged in the person of Lord Jellicoe.

Line 31. Admiral Mark Kerr, *Life of Prince Louis of Battenburg* (Longmans Green, London, 1934, p. 165).

Abbreviations used in text

The key initials which constantly recur, are the following:

Director of Naval Intelligence	DNI
Naval Intelligence Division	NID
Operational Intelligence Centre	OIC

Less common and generally explained in the text are these:

Assistant Chief of Naval Staff	ACNS
Allied Naval Commander Expeditionary Force	ANCXF
Anti-submarine	A/S
Commander-in-Chief	C-in-C
Chief of Combined Operations	CCO
Confidential Book	CB
Deputy Chief of Naval Staff	DCNS
Deputy Director Naval Intelligence	DDNI
Director Operations Division	DOD
High Frequency/Direction Finding	HF/DF
Director of Signals Division	DSD
Inter-Services Topographical Department	ISTD
Inter-Services Security Board	ISSB
Joint Intelligence Committee	JIC
Joint Intelligence Staff	JIS
Ministry of Economic Warfare	MEW
Naval Attaché	NA
Office of Naval Intelligence (American)	ONI
Office of Strategic Services	OSS
Personal Assistant	PA
Political Warfare Executive	PWE

Royal Naval Volunteer Reserve   RNVR
Secret Intelligence Service   SIS
Special Operations Executive   SOE
Vice-Chief of Naval Staff   VCNS
Interception and monitoring of signals   Y Service
Weekly Intelligence Report   WIR

General index

427

Gneisenau, 35, 45, 149, 156, 157, 161,
  288, 358, 362, 398
Goldenfels. See *Atlantis*
Gonzenheim, 158, 159, 160, 400
Gorizia, 137, 397
Gothenburg, 209, 290, 404, 406
Gotland, 145, 209
Graf Spee, 95, 276, 340, 405
Great Britain and the German Navy,
  Woodward's, 140
Greenland, 298
Greece, 309

Hälsingborg, 209
Hardy, HMS, 79
Hipper, 283, 285
His Majesty's Stationery Office, 312
Hood, HMS, 13, 144, 145, 148, 149,
  150, 151, 152, 154, 156, 284, 398,
  400
Hull, 290
Huelva, 300

Iceland, 196, 265, 270, 298
  bribing the Icelanders, 267
  British occupation of, 266–8
  coast-watching in, 268
  U-boat crews in, 266, 267
  value as a base, 268
Immingham, 291
India, Axis strategy against, 349
Information, Ministry of, 125
Intelligence,
  Admiralty requirements for Nor-
    mandy landings, 320
  axioms, 342–65
  effect of fall of France on, 322
  failure of German near D-day,
    334–7
  grading of, 22–5, 223, 385
  importance of civilian talents in,
    343–6
  lack of co-operation between depts.
    in, 352–3
  political distortion of, 127, 128, 129,
    133, 135
  pre-war neglect of, 53–4, 416–17
  successes through interrogation,
    168–71
  uses of topographical, 293–5
Intelligence Sources, 19–21, 356–7
  agents, 38–41
  air photography, 19, 24, 34–5, 57
  captured documents, 31, 272, 417

censorship, 45
double agents, 51
friendly observers and refugees,
  47–8
high frequency direction finding,
  31–4
interception of messages, 25–30
naval attachés, 51–2, 183–4
other services, 49–50
press and radio, 42–5
prisoners-of-war, 19, 24, 41–2,
  164–5, 166–8, 171, 172–5, 176,
  401
sightings, 35–8, 48
survivors, 48–9
sympathetic foreign civilians, 188
technical and tactical (our ships),
  48
topographical records, 45–6
wireless traffic study, 42
Inter-Service Information Series reports, 309, 313, 314
Inter-Service Security Board, 5, 247
Inter-Service Theatre Intelligence
  Section, 320, 327
Inter-Service Topographical Department, 45–6, 247, 308, 310–11,
  314, 315, 344, 412, 422
  the Indian, 316
Israeli intelligence in 1967 war, 385
Istanbul, as intelligence centre, 52,
  187, 188
Itchen, HMS, 169

Jan Mayen island, 271, 272
Joint Intelligence Bureau, 369, 370
Joint Intelligence Committee, 300,
  307, 349, 351, 359, 360, 371,
  420
  development of, 243–5, 247–8
  forecasts German attack on Russia,
    242, 243
  inception of, 240
  naval concern with, 242
  work of, 240, 241, 249–51
Joint Intelligence Staff, 241, 242, 248,
  249, 250, 251, 252, 348, 409
  appreciations by, 259–60
  development of, 252–6
  failures and successes of, 261, 420
  naval probing of other services on,
    257–8
Joint Planning Staff, 248, 307, 308
Jutland, Battle of, 58, 215, 386

Kent, HMS, 3
King George V, HMS, 70, 135, 149,
    151, 153, 155, 157, 158, 420
Kormaran, German raider, 279
Kota Penang, 158
Krebs, 273
Kristiansand, 301
Kupfinger, Leutnant zur See, 273

La Pallice, 269
La Pernelle, 336
Lance, HMS, 399
Landro, 203
Lauenburg, German weather ship, 3,
    109, 160, 272, 273, 400
Le Havre, 328, 331, 423
Leander, HMS, 96
Leros, island of, 308
Life of Ian Fleming, John Pearson's,
    384, 390
Life of Prince Louis of Battenburg,
    Admiral Mark Kerr's, 424
Lisbon, 301
    as intelligence centre, 183
    oil installations at, 300
London, HMS, 159, 400
London School of Hygiene and
    Tropical Medicine, 303
Lorient, 47, 269, 353, 423
Lothringen, 159, 160
Luftwaffe, the,
    failure in Battle of Britain, 347
    fails the Bismarck, 148–9, 150, 151
Lützow, 283, 285
Lysekil, 291

Madagascar, 218, 310, 388
Madrid, as intelligence centre, 52,
    183, 186, 188, 194
Magdeburg, signal books of the, 28,
    417
Malta, 353
Malvernian, 159
Man that Never Was, The, Ewen
    Montagu's, 405
Manchester, HMS, 149, 272
'Manual of Intelligence', 339
Maori, HMS, 172
Mare's Nest, The, David Irving's, 387
Mariana Islands, the, 306
Marsdale, 159, 400
Max Horton and the Western Approaches,
    Rear-Admiral W. D. Chalmers',
    396

Medmenham, RAF photographic
    HQ at, 34, 269, 270, 351
Merchant Ships' Code, 84
Mers-el-Kebir, 300, 301
Midway, Battle of, 29
Midway Island, 21, 28, 29
Mining, collection of intelligence on,
    330
Ministry of Economic Warfare, 247,
    255, 257, 368
Morocco, 309
Moscow, limited naval intelligence
    from, 52
Muenchen, German weather ship, 3,
    160, 272, 273
Mulberry harbours, 214, 215, 329

Narvik, 46
Naval Attachés, 373, 403, 404
    activities of German, 189, 202
    duties of, 51–2, 183, 184, 189–90, 194
    in Washington, 52
    loyalties of, 182–3
    surveillance on, 185, 187, 189, 209,
        213
Naval Intelligence, Director of,
    functions of, 2, 5
Naval Intelligence Division, 68–9
    axioms of, 365–6
    before World War I, 373–7
    committees represented on, 382
    Contact Register, 296, 304–7, 314,
        388, 413, 414
    delays in recruitment for, 99–101
    D/F plotters, 111
    early information received by
        Room 39, 10
    failures of, 340–41
    French section, 322
    geographical section, 5, 19, 184,
        315
    German section, 37, 163–4, 168,
        330, 353
    headquarters, 1, 2
    in conflict with the executive, 346–7
    incorporated in Defence Intelli-
        gence, 370–1
    information section, 65–7, 70, 71
    Italian section, 61, 164
    Japanese section, 61, 164
    map unit, 315
    naval intelligence required for
        D-day from, 320–1
    1936 club, 365

General index of names

434

Index of NID personnel

Donald McLachlan

Donald McLachlan, born in London in 1908, was
graduated from Magdalen College, Oxford, with
first-class honors in philosophy, politics and economics.
Before World War II he was a foreign correspondent for
the London *Times*, taught at Winchester College, and
edited the *Times'* education supplement. After his
wartime service (for which he was awarded the O.B.E.
and the Legion of Merit) he was, successively, foreign
editor of *The Economist*, deputy editor of the London
Daily Telegraph and first editor of the *Sunday Telegraph*.
Mr. McLachlan now contributes regularly to the London
Evening Standard and *The Spectator*. His previous books
include *Defense in the Cold War* (1949) and *Atlantic
Alliance* (1951).